BLACK F CAUSE...

NOT JUST BECAUSE...

The case of the 'Oval 4'
and the story it tells of
Black Power in
1970s Britain

WINSTON N TREW

WNT
TREW BOOKS
LONDON

Black for a Cause ... Not Just Because...
by
Winston N Trew

3rd Editon

SYMBOLISM OF THE SANKOFA BIRD USED AS A DECORATIVE ELEMENT IN THIS BOOK:

The concept of SANKOFA is derived from King Adinkera of the Akan people of West Afrika. SANKOFA is expressed in the Akan language as "*se wo were fi na wosan kofa a yenki.*" Literally translated it means "it is not taboo to go back and fetch what you forgot." SANKOFA teaches us that we must go back to our roots in order to move forward. That is, we should reach back and gather the best of what our past has to teach us, so that we can achieve our full potential as we move forward. Whatever we have lost, forgotten, forgone or been stripped of, can be reclaimed, revived, preserved and perpetuated. Visually and symbolically the concept of Sankofa is expressed as a mythic bird that flies forward while looking backward with an egg (symbolizing the future) in its mouth.

Book design, cover and Sankofa bird symbol designed by:
Pamela Marin-Kingsley, www.pammarin-kingsley.com

TREW BOOKS LONDON

For more information contact:
winstontrew@msn.com

Website:
www.blackforacause.co.uk

Those who profess to favour freedom yet deprecate agitation are those who want crops without ploughing up the ground. They want rain without thunder and lightening. They want the ocean without the awful roar of its mighty waters. *This struggle may be a moral one; or it may be a physical one; or it may be both moral and physical; but it must be a struggle.* Power concedes nothing without a demand. It never did, and it never will. Find just what people will submit to, and you will have found the exact measure of injustice and wrong which will be imposed upon them; and these will continue until they are resisted with words or blows, or with both. The limits of tyrants are proscribed by the endurance of those whom they oppress.
—Frederick Douglass (1857) quoted by Stokely Carmichael in *Black Power: The Dialectics of Liberation Conference*, (1967: 171), Pelican, edited by David Cooper. (*The* fuller version quoted here is taken from *Frantz Fanon and the Psychology of Oppression* by HA Bulhan, (1985:278), Plenum Press.)

Men make their own history, but they do not make it as they please: do not make it under self-selected circumstances, but under circumstances existing already, given and transmitted from the past. The tradition of all dead generations weighs like a nightmare on the brain on the living. And just when they seem to be occupied with revolutionising themselves and things, in creating something that did not exist before, precisely in such epochs of revolutionary crisis they anxiously conjure up the spirits of the past to their service, borrowing from their names, battle slogans, and costumes in order to present this new scene in world history in this time honoured disguise and this borrowed language.
—Karl Marx (1852) 'The Eighteenth Brumaire of Louis Bonaparte'
Die Revolution, 1852, New York

We can ask primal questions but we can never stand near the beginning. Our questions and answers are in part determined by the historical traditions in which we find ourselves. We apprehend truth from our own source within the historical foundation. The content of our truth depends on our appropriating the historical foundation. Our power of regeneration lies in the rebirth of what has been handed down to us.
—Karl Jaspers, *From Dostoevsky to Sartre: The Existential Philosophers* (ed) Walter Kaufman 1977: 127

OVAL FOUR

THEY TALK OF LAW AND ORDER BUT NEVER JUSTICE FOR OUR PEOPLE THEY LET US ROT BEHIND BARS BUT THAT WILL NOT STIFLE THE EDUCATION OF OUR CHILDREN

FASIMBA 1972

To my mother and father, my ancestors

To my children, to whom I will become
one of their ancestors

To Hyacinth who has never doubted me

CONTENTS

Chapters	Page

FOREWORD

Winston Trew and three African-Caribbean friends were getting off the escalator at the Oval London Underground Station, south London, late on a March 1972 evening when they were physically pounced on by a squad of Transport Police officers. The aggressors—motivated by racism and led by a Sergeant Ridgewell, a man with policing service in Southern Rhodesia (now Zimbabwe)—were bent on making criminals of these and other black people. The community struggle for their political and legal defence made them into the celebrated 'Oval 4'. Black Britain was familiar with others such system-challenging 'victims'— the Brockwell 3, the Cricklewood 12, those arrested at the Leeds Bonfire Night, to name a few. Ironically Winston and his associates were heading home from a committee meeting in north London to plan the defence of activist, Tony Soares, of the Black Liberation Front (BLF) against false and incendiary charges. Winston Trew's book is his account of the background to, the details and the related effects of this incident.

Far too few genuinely moving, informative and politically engaged books of autobiographical narrative analysis have emerged from the post-Windrush communities in Britain; this narrative stands as one of the first, moving our story on from struggling for civic representation to struggling now against over-representation. Ours has been an experience framed by long-denied 'institutional racism'. Its belated official admission (in the Stephen Lawrence Inquiry) has simply provided cover for its more oppressive operation. What else can be the meaning of our massive over-representation in those stop and search figures, on that dubiously legal DNA database, in penal and mental institutions? How else do we explain the exclusion of our children from schools, the general educational under performance of our children, our disproportionately high unemployment, and the targeting of our young people through such dangerous legislative measures as the bogus doctrine of 'joint enterprise?' The Britain we face is not the one of self-regarding liberal myth, but one actually more akin to W. B. Yates' "dark insensitive pig of a" place.

Winston Trew migrated to Britain as a child in the 1950s: a member of a family with early Caribbean migratory experience. The story he tells is multi-layered. He recounts and analyses his own schooling in south London where he learnt survival skills against pupil and teacher racism; his coming to political and cultural consciousness there in the early 1970s 'black power' era—which he insists had its own dynamic rather than being a copy/echo of the African-American situation; his informative and skilful weaving of contemporary African-Diaspora musics (Jamaican and Black American) into his account; his involvement in the political formation the South East London Parents Organisation (SELPO) and its offshoot the FASIMBAS in which he learnt some useful martial arts—organisations about which he offers the first substantive and insider-based narrative. Winston Trew tells of his above-mentioned false arrest, the violent police interrogation; his clever and effective thinking-on-his-feet decision to drop provably impossible admissions into his forced confession. He reports his conviction, imprisonment and release as one of the 'Oval 4'; of the exposure and disbandment of the British Transport Police squad responsible for his fate and that of several other African-Caribbean youths. The book recounts too his relentless archival, legal, moral and philosophical pursuit of the agents and agencies of decades-long British state criminalisation (which his own exemplified). His experience is at one end of a spectrum of oppressive State policing; at the other is the not infrequent murder of African youth and others in Britain. Winston speaks with tragic-dramatic effect of the case of Nigerian David Oluwale—whose murder by drowning in Leeds was another illustration of the "from Bobby to Babylon" progression

Winston triumphed over not merely that illegal attack by the British state but from the effects of a brain haemorrhage in November 2003 from which he woke "two weeks later in Kings College Hospital not knowing who I was, where I was, or why I was there... I did not understand what I was being told nor could I remember where I lived, walk straight or keep my balance without the aid of a Zimmer frame." It is from this that he recovered to write this book.

Winston Trew's **BLACK for a CAUSE**... is a good and informative book. It is, accordingly, very welcome, should be bought and widely read.

Professor Cecil Gutzmore
August, 2010, London

ACKNOWLEDGEMENTS

I am most grateful for the discussions and exchanges of ideas I had with the following people: **Menelik Shabazz, Film Director,** formerly of the Black Liberation Front and the *British Film Institute;* **Tony Soares,** former member of *Black Liberation Front;* **Dudley Arthurs,** member of SELPO's central committee, for the photographs and documents he provided; **Sterling Christie** (*Chris*), Fasimba and member of the 'Oval 4;' **Jah Shaka,** former Fasimba and International Black music ambassador. I am indebted to **Jessica and Eric Huntley** for their reminiscences and exchanges of views on the 'Oval 4' episode. I am also grateful to **Jonathan Sims** in the **Social Science Section of the British Library,** St Pancras, for tracking down a document vital to the writing of Chapters 2 and 3. A warm thank you to **A. Sivanandan,** Director of the Institute of Race Relations, whose advice and comments were invaluable; my appreciations to **Professor Cecil Gutzmore,** political activist and academic and **Colin Prescod,** Chair of the Institute of Race Relations, film maker, and activist for their very helpful suggestions for improving the text 'Black for a Cause.' I am further indebted to **Professor Emeritus Geoff Palmer** of Heriot Watt University, Scotland, for his much valued comments on my use of a 'trickster strategy' to illuminate the acts of resistance I describe in the book. My thanks go also to **Professor Paul Gilroy** of Kings College, London, in whose book, *The Black Atlantic,* I found the necessary angle of vision to tell my story.

Winston Trew
July, 2010

INTRODUCTION

What about the Half?

> What about the half that's never been told?
> What about the half that's never been told?
> Look how long it's been kept a big secret
> Look how long it been hide'ed away
> The half, the half, the half that's never been told
> what was hidden from the wise and prudent
> Now reveal to babe and suckling
> The half, the half, the half that's never been told
> **(Dennis Brown, 1971, Sunshot Records)**

> I will open my mouth in parables.
> I will utter things which have been kept secret
> from the foundation of the world.
> **(Matthew, Chap.13: 35)**

What the book is about

The book, as the title indicates, tells of the case of the 'Oval 4' and the story that case reveals of the hidden history of Black Power organisations, their social, cultural and political activities in 1970s Britain, rallying against the force of Western history that stood in opposition to the struggle for Black emancipation. '**Black for a Cause**' is published in an attempt to put on record the work undertaken by one such organisation, the Fasimba, that operated from a base in the south-east London area between 1969 and 1974.

This account is given through the story of my membership of the Fasimba, my arrest, trial, imprisonment, and release on Appeal in July 1973 as one of the 'Oval 4' from a 2 year prison sentence after being found guilty in November, 1972, on charges arising from a physical confrontation with undercover officers from the British Transport police at the Oval underground station in London, March 1972. The 'Oval 4' case, it is suggested, stands at the *intersection* between the attempts by the British police force to criminalise young black males in London and the efforts by Black organisations, Black activists and black people generally to resist and fight police corruption and judicial collusion.

The story to be told has *never been told before* and is therefore part of the *hidden history* of modern and *independent* Black political struggle, the development of the idea of a black community, of social and cultural development and social change in modern Britain. At the same time it addresses our arrest and membership of the Fasimba as an example of attempts by the British police to criminalise black males in London and an example of one the ways in which the Special Branch attempted to counter and disrupt the work of black political organisations. Their political aim we envisioned was to undermine the legitimacy of black settlement, black community and black protest in modern Britain. At that time, we understood that there were several tactics used by the Special Branch to discredit and undermine Black Power politics and Black organisations. One tactic was to associate Black Power politics with 'terrorism' by arresting its members on 'terrorism' offences. The second was to discredit its members by accusing them of 'criminal' offences, often resulting in their jailing. We understood Tony Soares' arrest as an example of the first type and our arrest as an example of the second type.

In particular, what the book reveals is the work done by the Fasimba in not only waging a community-based campaign to take on the judicial establishment to secure the freedom of the 'Oval Four' but to also discredit the activities of the 'anti-mugging' squad and its leader, Detective Sergeant Ridgewell, as a former Rhodesian policeman intent on framing innocent black people. It was he who made a controversial claim as his reason for fleeing from Ian Smith's Rhodesia in 1965, and is the same undercover officer who admitted in Court in 1973 to be the look-out for mainly 'coloured' youths travelling at night on the Northern line: people whom he regarded as 'suspicious persons' because they were "coloured."

Though imprisoned on *criminal charges*, the 'Oval 4' case was, at the time, considered a *political 'Cause Celebre'* (*Time Out*, Nov, 1972; April 1973; July 1973), raising as it did many questions not just about police conduct on the night but also about police conduct towards black people generally. In August 1973, the *West Indian World* (3/8/73) accused the police of being in a "state of war" with black youth in London, a "war" in which the 'mugging scare' emerged as their weapon of choice. Such activities by the police and press only served to reinforce the already tattered relations between them and black communities (*'Police Against Black People', Race & Class*, 1979).

An article in *Grassroots*, the Black Community newspaper, entitled

"*We Are Not Afraid*" (1976), quotes Commander Marshall's evidence to the 1976 Select Committee on Race Relations and Immigration, where he admitted that:

> Recently, there has been a growth in the tendency for members of London's West Indian Community to combine against the police by interfering with police officers who are affecting an arrest of a black person. In the last 12 months, 40 such incidents have been recorded. Each carry the potential for large scale disorder (see also Gutzmore, *Race & Class,* 1983: 20).

The reaction of the police had been to, firstly, outlaw this form of resistance by equating it with 'lawlessness' and to a breakdown in 'law and order' in black communities. This led in particular to the increase in police attempts to arrest young people and an increase in 'rescue' attempts by young people from those communities in response to this arrest strategy. The second strategy was to launch a so-called 'war on mugging' campaign against black young people from the very urban areas in which resistance to the police had occurred. In other words, the 'war on mugging' represented a *criminalisation* of black resistance to police aggression because since the introduction of the 'mugging' label in August 1972 by the *Daily Mirror* and the redefinition of 'robbery' by the police, not one person, black or white, female or male, has been charged with or convicted of a 'mugging.' In fact, no such crime is recognised by or exists in English law and yet the term is still commonly used as *shorthand* for violent robberies committed largely by black youths in inner city areas (Gutzmore, *Race & Class*, 1983; Smith, 1984).

In an influential study of policing in the 1970s, '*Policing the Crisis: Mugging, the State and Law and Order,*' the authors (Hall and others, 1978:43) observed:

> It cannot escape our notice where this institutional police mobilisation first reveals itself—the South London area and tube stations: or who is being picked up in the anti-mugging 'sweep'—above all, groups of black youth. So the specific targeting against 'mugging' has the closest links with another, more exclusive, though equally powerfully charged context: the seriously deteriorating relations between the police and the black community, a feature of community relations during the 1970s. It

must seriously be asked whether the sensitisation of the police to 'mugging' was altogether unrelated to that other troubling saga of 'police power and black people' (see '*Police Against Black People,' Race & Class*, 1979; Gutzmore, *Race & Class*, 1983).

Given that the 1970s was a period of Black activism with organisational support for black communities against police brutality, the idea that the 'mugging scare' was being promoted by the police and press as a counter to the general resistance in black communities and by black young people to police tactics is not too far-fetched. Moreover, the *criminalisation* of black youth by the 'mugging scare' should be seen also as a cruel *distortion* of the investment made by Caribbean parents in their young, who were seen by Black organisations as representing the hopes and future of black settlement and development in Britain. It is suggested therefore that while the ESN issue sought to blight their *educational* futures, it was the 'mugging scare' that would saddle many with a false *criminal record* to blight their future *employment* prospects.

SECTION 1
'IS IT BECAUSE I'M BLACK'?

The story is told over two Sections. The first Section, '**Is it because I'm Black?**' adopts the title of a Soul song by Syl Johnson released in 1971 and was as popular and well known among many black people as was *James Brown's* hit, '*Say it Loud, I'm Black and I'm Proud,*' released in 1968 at the height of Black Power organising and protest in the USA. The basis of the song's popularity was that it spoke of and made public a question, and a possible answer, that must have been in the hearts and minds of many black people in Britain, the Caribbean and the United States for years but was not often voiced. While Black Power ideology provided a political and cultural window for many expressions of Blackness, the release of this song added another dimension as it spoke openly about the *emotional* and *social* frustrations caused by racial discrimination, economic hardship and the thwarted dreams and ambitions that resulted from this discrimination and hardship.

It was one of many songs that gave voice to what was often 'felt' but 'never spoken,' gave a 'form of words' to unspoken thoughts and feelings. It therefore seems fitting that it should be the title of the section which tells the story of case of the 'Oval 4,' not just as an example of a great injustice we experienced from the police and judicial system because we were black, but also to illustrate the background to the historical consciousness of the time.

The early 1970s was punctuated by protests, songs of protest and the search for blackness, such as in the reggae version of the soul hit '(To be) *Young, Gifted and Black*" (1970) by *Bob (Andy) & Marcia (Griffiths)*—written and sung originally by *Nina Simone* (1970), and a more 'rootsy' version by *Rupee Edwards* called '*Herbert Spliffington.*' *Prince Buster* also did a version of '*Young, Gifted and Black.*' There was the reggae version of the *Temptation's* (1969) Soul song '*Message from a Blackman*' by *Derrick Harriott* and the *Chosen Few* and a version on the same rhythm by *Prince Buster* called '*Ganja Plant.*' There was '*Tell it Black*' by *Big Youth*, a version of '*Black Magic Woman*' by *Dennis Brown*, which itself is a version of the original by *Santana*. There was also '*Black Cinderella*' by *Errol Dunkley* and its many versions, especially one the Jamaican DJ *I Roy*, called '*Sound Education.*' They are just a *few* of the many soul and reggae songs consumed by young people in Britain that raised important questions about being black.

'The half that's never been told'

What the Chapters in Section 1 reveal about the mechanics of our arrest and the 'tactics of resistance' used in the police station will come as a surprise many—not least to those who were in the British Transport Police and the Director of Public Prosecution (now Crown Prosecution Services) at that time. The '*half which is now to be told*' was known to only a few in the Fasimba. Its *fullness* was certainly hidden from our legal team and from our supporters in the Black (Power) community. The song by *Dennis Brown* '*What about the half?*' released in 1971 is a fitting way to code the sentiments I am expressing in telling this part of the story. These matters are revealed and discussed fully across **Chapters 1, 2 and 3** when I focus on the "*half that's never been told.*" What actually happened in the police station is fully discussed in **Chapter 1**, the trial in **Chapter 2**, and **Chapter 3** discusses my experience of prison life, the community campaign to free the 'Oval 4,' the Appeal and an analysis of the 'anti-mugging' campaign and Ridgewell's arrests.

Chapter 4 concludes Section 1 with another *untold story*; that of Det. Sgt. Derek Ridgewell's ignoble past as further evidence is revealed of his dishonesty and corruption—ideas that the Transport Police, Trial and Appeal Court Judges refused to even contemplate. On this issue, the words of the song by *Culture*, the Ras Tafari group, are most relevant, warning that: "*When you're going to dig a pit, my brother, don't dig one always dig two,*" and is a fitting way to phrase the sentiments expressed on Det. Sgt. Ridgewell. As readers will conclude, in his efforts to 'dig a pit' for the four of us and other black young people, he was also digging a pit for himself.

SECTION 2
BLACK FOR A CAUSE

The work of the Fasimba as a Black organisation is another *untold story*, hitherto unrecorded and up until now hidden from public view. The Fasimba were among a number of Black organisations operating in London during the early 1970s that attempted to intervene and shape the course of the social, cultural and political development **in** and **of** black communities. **Chapter 5** opens Section 2 with the story of my entry into the Black Cause as a member of the Fasimba and introduces the nature of debates and differences of opinion in black families and communities about the importance young people 'taking up' Black Power. At that time, the British Black identity was still being shaped and Black Power made an important contribution to the content and context of this development and shaping. Indeed, one of the greatest achievements of Black Power political culture has been the *erasure* and *discrediting* of the title 'coloured' as a description of a 'West Indian' or 'immigrant' identity and its replacing with the individual, collective and militantly oppositional identity, '**Black.**'

Chapter 6 goes on to explore the social, cultural and political activities of the Fasimba as a *youthful Black organisation*, tracing its origins and emergence in south-east London as the Youth or Political wing of SELPO, the *South East London Parents' Organisation.* Founded by four Garveyites from Jamaica, it began with a Supplementary School run on Saturdays to combat the channelling of black children into schools for the educationally sub-normal, outside of 'mainstream' schooling. SELPO and the Fasimba went on to establish a wide range of services to the local black community, such as self-defence training, education and drama classes; was the inspiration behind the youthful Sound System *Shaka Downbeat,* now nationally and internationally known as *Jah Shaka (and the Fasimbas)*; forged political links with the *Black Liberation Front* based in north and west London, and with a youthful Caribbean Marxist organisation, the *Youth Forces for National Liberation (YFNL)* in Jamaica, with a base in north London.

Adopting the phrase '**Black for a Cause ...Not just Because**' is intended also to make a conceptual link between Sections 1 & 2 and to provide an answer to the question posed by Syl Johnson's 1971 song, '**Is it because I'm Black?**' Here we have a transmutation **in** and **of** the concept of Blackness, moving from *object* to *subject* status and this movement is explained by discussing the case of David Oluwale, a 1950s Nigerian migrant who has the dubious 'honour' of being the first in the line of over 1000 black people, mainly men, to have died in Britain in police custody or as the result of their involvement with the police since 1969 (see '*Deadly Silence: Black Deaths in Custody*,' Institute of Race Relations, 1991).

In the final **Chapter, 7**, entitled '*The 'Oval 4' Episode and the Ethics of Black Resistance*,' I bring together my experiences and thinking as one of the 'Oval 4' and as a Fasimba Black activist, and discuss in some detail the *ethics behind the tactic* I used in the police station to try to resist *and* undermine the police case against us. This leads on to a discussion of the dynamics of my personal and political struggle to construct and articulate an *ethical basis* for this act of resistance, which itself was linked to the wider aims of the Fasimba and of Black Power. In such a situation, it was my understanding that the *ethics* guiding one's actions should be based on a consideration of what was the 'right,' 'proper' and 'honourable' thing to do, and acting on those considerations.

SECTION 1

'Is It Because I'm Black'?

CHAPTER 1

The Arrest of the 'Oval 4'

The dark brown shades of my skin,
only add colour to my tears.
Oh, that splash against my hollow bones,
that rocks my soul.
Looking back over my false dreams that I once knew,
wondering why my dreams never came true.
Is it because I'm black? Somebody tell me what can I do.
Something is holding me back,
Is it because I'm black?
(**Is it because I'm Black**?
Syl Johnson, Twinight Records, 1971)

What have I got?
Why am I alive anyway?
What have I got?
They just can't take away
(**Ain't got no..... I got life**,
Nina Simone, RCA, 1968)

"Sitting here in Limbo"

There I was sitting alone in the cell of a police station trying to piece together the events that led me to be there in the first place when I heard voices outside the door and a key in the lock. My heart jumped and blood thumped through my chest and temples. My body became tense. My head and throat was hurting from having had a 'taste of police hospitality' earlier that evening; they must have come back to give me another 'helping.' The door opened and there stood two policemen, one in uniform the other in civilian clothes. The one in civilian clothes was huge and wore a blue Navy-type jacket. The uniformed officer stood by the door, as if to keep 'watch' while the one in civilian clothes walked toward me. I will call him the 'Behemoth.' I was sitting on the bed/bench and stared at him as he lumbered in my direction.

"Shit," I thought, *"I know what he's come to do."*

"Is your name Trew?" he demanded.

"Yes," I replied, cautiously.

"Stand up when I'm talking to you. Get over there against the wall. Take your hat off. You've been attacking my officers, haven't you?"

He spoke rapidly, giving me orders, making demanding statements with no time for me to think.

"No."

"Don't lie to me. So my officers are lying are they?" he shouted.

I didn't answer this time as I knew it was a trick question: to say 'no' was to agree with the police version of events and invite a punch to my face or stomach for 'attacking' the police, to which their injuries were testimony. To say 'yes' was to also invite a punch to my face or stomach, or even worse, for denying his accusation. But he did neither. He must have had worse in his mind for me. By this time he was standing very close to me, 'staring me out' and 'closing me down.' He was physically bigger and taller than I and my back was against the wall. There was nowhere for me to retreat. His voice was gruff, rasping and demanding. He reminded me of a regimental sergeant major type, an army drill sergeant. He was trying his best to intimidate me. I wasn't intimidated just apprehensive. I just stared into his eyes, trying to predict what he would do next. I had taken off my tam (my woolly hat) which I held in both hands and both hands were crossed at my groin for protection. *I had thought about refusing to do so but then realised the last thing I wanted was to have this 'Brute' grab or hold onto me*; he had already come too close to me which was neither comfortable nor safe. "Put your hands by your side," he ordered. With that command, I knew exactly what he was going to do: crush my testicles with his knee. I couldn't even move away from him to dodge his 'knee blow' as he had closed in on me.

As I knew what **he** was going to do I knew also what **I** was going to do. This was it; he was ready for me but what he didn't know was that I was ready for him. Whilst slowly moving my hands from protecting my groin I stared into his eyes. When my groin was exposed, he flashed a quick look at my groin area and bought his knee up, suddenly, towards my groin. Instantly, I lifted my right leg up across my groin to block his move. His knee thudded into my thigh. *"You bastard!"* he exclaimed in shock and disappointment, realising he'd missed his target and lost the element of surprise. In 'consolation' for that miss, he grabbed my face and slammed my head against the cell wall behind. With no hat on the sound of my head hitting the wall behind me echoed in the cell. He stormed out, slamming the door behind him. I sat down holding my throbbing head. I felt for blood. Thankfully there was none; my skull didn't crack open, as he'd probably intended. Instead, there was just one big bump; a 'coco.' Well, if this was a sample of what I was going to get then there was little chance of me surviving the night without a serious injury, or even two. As I felt my throbbing head, I wondered what was happening to the others I'd been arrested with.

The 'Behemoth' had expected to leave me doubled-over on the floor and paralysed by serious pain in the police cell. I had managed to outsmart this man, but for how long? He'd soon be back, perhaps with others. I stole a moment of self-congratulations and a smile. I was one of the Fasimba who practiced a Japanese style of Martial Arts called *Wado Ryu*, and part of this training involved anticipating offensive moves from your opponent, either to defend yourself or to counter-attack. In this we learned two 'rules.' One was that when faced by any opponent you should always look into their eyes as they will momentarily 'look' at their target and this 'looking' tells you where they intend to strike. We were taught this rule two years before Bruce Lee explained it to his young apprentice in the opening scene of 'Enter the Dragon.' We were taught also that when your opponent is about to move, there is a sharp intake of breath. In *Wado Ryu* we are taught to breathe through our nostrils not our mouths. We would 'Kai' though our mouths to emphasise a strike, but always regulated our breathing through our nostrils. While the 'Behemoth' was setting me up for his strike, I saw him momentarily look at my groin area - to 'position' his knee. He was that close to me that as he lifted his knee to crush my testicles I heard him gasp, inhale. In an instant I brought my leg right leg up and across my groin to block his move. It was a technique we practiced a lot in *Wado Ryu* training. *It worked! I was faster than him. Bastard!!* But almost immediately my thoughts returned to what was going to happen to me that night. More of the same I expect, so I couldn't afford to indulge myself any further in self-congratulations about outsmarting the 'Brute.' I had to remain alert and focused. Again I wondered what was happening to the others. They were probably getting the same treatment was my guess.

Fighting for our lives at the Oval Underground

My thoughts returned to the question of **how** and **why** I ended up in a police station cell with yet another policeman trying to injure me. Simply, it was because we had a fight with a group of them at the Oval underground after they accused us of "nicking handbags."

BLACK FOR A CAUSE ...

It all began on the morning of Thursday 16th March, 1972. It started off as any ordinary Thursday and as usual on that day I left my home at about 10am to sign-on at the Peckham labour exchange in Bellenden Road at 10.30 that morning. It was a short distance from where I lived. I had to sign-on every Thursday and was a date I had to make each week; and I couldn't be late. As I shuffled in the queue to sign-on that I had been unemployed for the past week, the headlines on the front page of the *Daily Mirror* I had in my hand was on the war in Northern Ireland: *"MPs Rage at Ulster Peace Go-Slow."* This reported on the worsening political situation in the British colony. On the previous day, 15th March, the Northern Ireland PM, Brian Faulkner, had been invited to have a 'crisis' meeting with Edward Heath, the British PM, on the following Wednesday. The question asked in the report was why next week, why not now? As the government's 'peace initiative' was about to 'stall' a week was seen as far too long to wait for that meeting. The inside pages carried more stories on the conflict in Northern Ireland with the headline: *"Two Soldiers killed by Ulster Car Blast,"* reporting that *"two bomb experts died in Belfast last night after they had blown-off the boot of a bomb-laden car."* The *Provisional IRA* had booby-trapped a car.

The other story was about the *"Big Swoop in Hunt for Aldershot Bombers in London,"* and reported on the dawn raids by the Special Branch in search of 'Republican sympathisers' after a tip-off to the police. The Special Branch had been searching for the *Provisional IRA* after they had set off a car-bomb outside Aldershot Barracks on 22nd February, killing 7 people, as a reprisal for the 'Bloody Sunday' killings in Northern Ireland on 30th January, 1972 when 13 Catholic Civil Rights protesters were shot dead by the Parachute Regiment—which was based at Aldershot Barracks. Eric Heffer, the Labour MP, asked for an urgent Commons debate on the raids as four of the homes raided belonged to members of the *International Socialists* which, he said, *"gets to the fundamental political liberties of the British people."* The *Evening Standard* (p.6) quoted the contents of a letter from Paul Foot to the *Times:*

> Since no one in their right mind would consider that the IS (International Socialists) is responsible for that explosion, what was the purpose of these extraordinary visits? Could it be that the main intention was to seize

as much information as possible about the Socialist organisation for the general background information of the Special Branch?

Thinking about those police raids reminded me that Black activist, Tony Soares, had also been arrested over a week ago by Special Branch as he too signed-on as unemployed. I along with other Fasimba were going to a meeting at *Black Liberation Front (BLF)* headquarters later in the evening to discuss his case and wondered if the police knew about that meeting. Although we weren't known as 'Republican sympathisers' we did support the call by Irish Nationalists for political self-determination and for a united Ireland as it mirrored the Black Cause for political and cultural self-determination and the goal of Pan-African unity. I glanced around the room to see if anyone was watching me; but why would they be watching **me,** I asked myself? I dismissed the thought as fantasy. Although on paper I was unemployed, my *real job*, my 'righteous' work was doing voluntary community work as a member of a Black Power organisation called the Fasimba. It was based in Brockley, near Hilly Fields Park. On the previous Saturday, 11th March, there was a meeting between members of the *sub committee*, of which I was a member, with the *central committee* to discuss Tony's case.

Tony was a prominent and active member of the *BLF* and had been arrested the previous week by Special Branch detectives and charged with 'incitement to murder' and 'incitement to cause explosions.' When we heard the news we concluded that he'd surely been 'set-up' by Special Branch. It was decided at the meeting that the *propaganda committee* should attend to represent the Fasimba at the meeting and report back to the *central committee* the following Saturday with what we should do as an organisation to publicise his arrest and campaign for his release. *Bunny, Chris, Omar, Sister Andrea* and myself were members of the *propaganda committee* and it was decided that we five should attend the meeting the coming Thursday to work out what to do to publicise his case. The Fasimba had formed an alliance with the *Black Liberation Front (BLF)* at the end of the 1971 to work together on issues of common concern. Tony's arrest **was** an *issue of common concern* and the meeting was planned to pool the political and cultural creativity of both organisations to confront this new development in the 'war of position' between Black Power and the British State. We had all agreed to make our own way to the meeting in north London. When evening came and despite me having all day to get ready, I found myself rushing out my home at about 7.45 to leave for north London to arrive by 8.30pm. I was going to be late. Damn it! 'Top of the Pops' had already started with that DJ Ed Stewart so I should have left the house already. I dashed out, said "see you later" to my wife and ran to the bus stop to catch a 36 to the Oval. One came as soon as I got there. Looking back there was no way I could not have been at that meeting. *Shit! I thought I must have been hurrying to meet the damn police!*

Secret police or transport police?

My mind returned to the police cell. I was sitting on the bed/bench with my thoughts running wild and my worst fears and fantasies racing through my mind. My head still throbbed. I knew it wouldn't be long before I'd get another visit from some policemen bent on more revenge for the fight at the Oval. I was in for a beating and I knew it, but beyond that were these policemen really after us because of the meeting we had with the *BLF*? Was this something to do with Tony Soares' arrest? Did they actually know we were Fasimba members and were waiting for us at the Oval? The one on the platform that seemed to be waiting for us was among the group we ended up fighting. What did they *really* want from us, I wondered? These were the first questions that came to mind. But, I thought, we couldn't have been followed from the meeting with the *BLF* because we raced down the escalator at Manor House station and had caught the wrong train. We would have 'lost' whoever was tailing us. Why were they so adamant on searching us? What did they expect to find? All that rubbish about us "nicking handbags" was probably a tactic to delay and detain us.

In my mind I rehearsed the events that led to the 'big fight' at the Oval that night. I recalled at the meeting that an idea for a poster was put forward by *Omar* to illustrate Tony's case: it was of a huge white man's hand (the state/police) reaching into a large bag (the 'black community') to seize someone they had identified as a 'threat' (Black radicals). The caption would read something like *"Today, its Tony, tomorrow it might be **you**!"* On the sleeve of the white man's hand would be written the names of other black people who had been killed, injured or framed as a result of police action, such as David Oluwale, Aseta Sims, and Joshua Francis. Tony was an active and well-known member of BLF and like most members contributed to the production and distribution of *Grassroots*, a Black Community newspaper. His 'offence' according to the Special Branch was that as Editor he was also known as 'Jamal' and in that guise had allowed to be reprinted in *Grassroots* (Vol.1, no. 4) an article on making a Molotov cocktail from the American *Black*

Panther Community Newspaper (vol. 4, no.2), which had been freely available in Britain (*Police Against Black People, Race & Class* 1979:8). I had even bought copies the *Black Panther* newspaper at *Collets* bookshop in Charing Cross Road in 1970 and 1971 and copies of the banned book '*Guerrilla Warfare*' by Carlos Mariguela from there and from *Compendium* bookshop in Camden Town to sell on our Saturday bookstalls.

We had taken Tony's arrest and the charges against him quite seriously, not only because the Fasimba sold and distributed *Grassroots*, but his arrest took place a week before the Special Branch raids in search of *IRA* 'sympathisers' and in the wake of a bombing campaign against politicians and the police said to be by a group calling themselves the '*Angry Brigade*.' Most of all we took the view that by Tony's arrest the Special Branch was attempting to associate the *BLF* in particular and Black Power in general with the 'urban guerrilla warfare' tactics attributed to the '*Angry Brigade*' and with the 'armed nationalism' of the *Provisional IRA*. The consensus was that Tony Soares' case was politically motivated, both in terms of the specific charges made against him and in terms of the political context within which was arrested. Their purpose, we envisaged, was to destabilise and undermine Black politics in Britain.

Rushing to meet Ridgewell?

The meeting ended about 10.15pm and as *BLF* members were conscious that we had a long way to travel, after a quick exchange of "good-byes" we left the building and walked outside. *Ossie, Chris's* brother, had arrived earlier with a van to give us a lift home but the van was too small to take all of us so after some discussion we agreed that *Chris* and *Andrea* would take the van home with *Ossie,* and the three of us—*Bunny, Omar* and *I*—would take the underground. We set off towards Manor House station. We hadn't got far when *Chris* ran and caught up with us, saying he would take the underground to the Oval with us, making the three four. On the way to the station *Chris* told us why he had arrived late to the meeting; that while he was heading for the Oval on a no. 36 bus, he ended up taking on a white man who was harassing a Black sister on the bus. After going to her defence and 'landing a few blows' on the man he chased him off the bus somewhere in New Cross Gate and had to wait for another bus. He was not too pleased as the incident caused him to be late for the meeting he was looking forward to attending. We agreed that he had done the right thing and then filled him in on what was said before he arrived. We were to have a *sub-committee* meeting on the coming Saturday evening to brief other committee members and to discuss what other things could be done to highlight Tony's case. At the Sunday meeting the *propaganda committee* would report to members what was discussed and announce what we were planning to do assist the 'Free Tony Soares' campaign.

I remembered that we were descending the escalator at Manor House station when we heard a train coming. Thinking it was our train we ran down the escalator and boarded it. It was when it arrived at Turnpike Lane that we realised we were going the wrong way. Rushing to board a southbound train, we settled down to the journey south, towards the Oval, to our meeting with Ridgewell and our destiny. I didn't remember anyone following us at that point. Even if we were being followed we would have lost them when we ran for the wrong train; they must have been waiting (for us) at the Oval. The journey to north London and the meeting had us all exhausted and we wanted to get home. Going south seemed quicker even though we had to change at Leicester Square station to get a southbound Northern Line train to the Oval. There were very few people in the carriage we got into so we were able to relax and talk freely. *Omar* settled down to read a copy of *Soul Illustrated*, a black American newspaper, and the rest of us talked about *Chris'* fight and reflected on the meeting and Tony's circumstances.

Getting off the train at the Oval, I realised that we were in the last carriage and had to walk some way towards the exit. Ahead of us at the exit at the end of the platform we noticed a stocky and podgy white man waiting there and looking in our direction. To us he was easily recognisable as a policeman in 'plain clothes' not only by his 'suspicious behaviour' but also by his give-away blue Anorak—policemen in *disguise* all wore blue Anoraks in those days! He was 'acting suspiciously' as he was making no attempt to exit the platform and tried his best to appear as if he was waiting for someone—looking in our direction while pretending not to. But there were no other passengers behind or immediately in front us. As we got closer we passed him but kept an eye on him. This time of night the presence police either in uniform or in "plain clothes" was not altogether unexpected, unusual or 'overtly' suspicious. The fact was that white men hanging about and posing as 'policemen', 'drunks' or 'thugs' was a matter of routine late at night in south London, either around pubs or clubs. The underground would be no exception, so the policeman in civilian clothes could have been hanging about there for any number of reasons. *Chris* said that we needed to stay alert.

We nodded in agreement as we could do little else. Even if we had suspected mischief there was no other exit from the platform. At the bottom of the escalator quite a crowd of people were there as a northbound train had also arrived.

It was crowded so I suggested we walk up. *Bunny* and *Chris* agreed saying we should keep together. *Omar* kissed his teeth, telling us to leave him alone. He said he was tired and wasn't going to walk up, and continued to read the black newspaper while riding the escalator. We couldn't see the person we suspected was a 'plain clothes' policeman any longer who, by then, must have disappeared into the crowd. The three of us walked up, *Chris, Bunny,* followed by myself. *Omar* was far behind us. *Chris* suddenly stopped walking saying that he couldn't pass as two white men were blocking the way. They were just standing there and not walking at all. We just rode the escalator to the top (Unbeknown to us these two were also undercover policemen).

No sooner had I skipped-off at the top of the escalator and turned left towards the exit than two white men suddenly appeared, each one grabbed me, holding my arms and dragging and pushing me against a wall over to the right. I swore, asking one what they thought they were doing. There were other white men pushing, shouting and swearing at the others. I could hear them saying: "*Get over there! Move! Get over there! Get the fuck over there!*" There was a lot of shouting. They shouted at us, we shouted at them. They pushed us, we pushed them back. I shouted, "*What the hell do you think you're doing? Who the hell do you think you are, pushing us like that?*"

We're police!

The man standing in front of me (Ridgewell) answered '*We're police.*"

I replied "*So! What do you want?*" "*Where's your ID?*"

Ridgewell replied: "*Never you bloody mind! Some of you blokes have been nicking handbags, and we're gonna search you lot.*"

We replied, variously:

"*You must be joking or just fuckin' mad*"

"*Which bags?*

Who from? Where? When? Where are they?"

"*We've not been stealing any handbags.*"

"*Search who? You're not searching anyone.*"

"*Anyway, how do we know you're police?*"

"*Show us your ID.*"

What they were saying was so ridiculous that we tried to move away from them but they blocked our way, pushing us back. An argument started. There was more pushing and shoving. I was trying to move away from the wall and the men before me were shoving me back against it. To make things worse they began standing quite close to me, trying to 'crowd me' and then began to 'push-up' against me. I said "*Look, don't fuck, just get away from me.*" There was more pushing, shoving and grabbing as we tried to move from against the wall.

Where's your ID!?!?

I thought it quite odd that as 'policemen in civilian guise' they were refusing to show their ID and became suspicious that they *might not be regular policemen*. Because we suspected they **were** some sort of undercover police, probably Special Branch, we decided to call their bluff and followed one another's lead with the ID request. "Where's your ID? Just show us some ID." The argument soon shifted away from them wanting to search us to us wanting them to identify themselves, as we continued to refuse to accept that they were police.

Omar suggested that they might be just "drunks or even thugs."

Chris said "You lot are out for a laugh after a good drink; the pub's just closed, hasn't it?"

I heard *Bunny* insist: "Just show us some ID."

I nodded in agreement, looking at Ridgewell who was becoming quite frustrated at our defiance. After all we were political activists and knew our rights so there was no way this lot could out-argue us. But an argument started between me and Ridgewell about him wanting to search us, when I heard *Omar* tell one of the men standing in front of him, angrily: "*Look, just stop pushing me, just stop it.*"

I could see from the corner of my left eye the man pushing him against the wall. I was a bit surprised as this man was smaller in stature than *Omar* and was acting so aggressively. He must have been drinking some 'Courage' beer, I thought. *Omar* was standing the other side of *Chris*. I was standing nearest to the ticket barrier, *Chris* was next to me on my left and on his left was *Omar*, then *Bunny* furthest away from me. There was a lot of shouting and I could see a crowd gathering.

Then one of the men in front of me whispered something to Ridgewell and in apparent frustration and annoyance at our defiance began to insist: "*turn out your bloody pockets.*"

I looked at him, laughed and said mockingly, "*You lot must be jokers.*" Ridgewell lost his cool and rushed forward, trying to put his hand into my left hand coat pocket; I pushed his hand away; he then tried to hold me and I pushed him away; in another act of frustration he said something like *"Fuck's sake"* and suddenly grabbed a brown paper carrier bag I had out of my left hand, ripping it open and spilling its contents on the ground. Out fell a child's colouring book, a Nunchaku (a martial arts 'rice flail') and a knife.

"Look, stop pushing me ... just do that again and see!!"

"What's this?" he demanded to know, looking puzzled, as he picked up the Nunchaku (ignoring the knife) and held it towards me.

"An exercise stick ...." was my answer and before I could go on I heard *Omar* shout *"I said stop fuckin' pushing me."*

Chris, who was next to him, coaxed him saying *"Omar, take it easy."*

Omar was vexed and replied, angrily: *"Well tell him to stop fuckin' pushing me. Just mek him do it again an' see."* He looked at the man and dared him by saying: *"You jus' fuckin' do that again an' see."*

It was becoming clear to me that these men were acting as most white males do in confrontations with black males: they try to close-down the distance between you and them by standing very close to you. This was a favourite tactic of white boys in school where standing quite close to you, staring you down, was often a tactic to set you up for a 'Scottish kiss'—a sudden head-butt to the nose, eye or forehead or the usual knee to your balls. As young black men, we would not choose stand that close to any opponent, black or white, but keep as much distance as possible between you and that person. As someone who went to school in Peckham with white boys in the 1960s I had learnt two rules from routine confrontations with them in the playground and on the streets: first, keep your distance and; second, if you get hit do not go down, do not fall; run, flee, escape, or your safety was at risk. If you did fall then that was it: your head, face, ribs, testicles would be met with a barrage of vicious kicks by steel-toe capped boots, sometimes alternating with bone-breaking heel-stamps, while calling you all the *black bastards, dirty niggers, fucking wogs, black cunts* they could utter.

Policemen or not these white men had crossed important *interpersonal boundaries* and, for me, that sort of behaviour just wasn't on. I didn't even want any of them standing so close me to as I knew what this could mean, much more grabbing me up, as Ridgewell did. 'Draping us up,' pushing and shouting at us was one thing, which immediately prepared us for a fight, but when they started to 'push up' themselves in our faces, as they did, trying to 'close us down' and corner us, then it would be only a matter of moments before a fight broke out.

From what I could make out the little man in front of *Omar* was doing just that and he was already on a 'short fuse.' I turned my attention back to Ridgewell in front of me when I heard a sound as like a loud 'crack'/'slap.' I looked to my left to see the man who had been antagonising *Omar* lying on the ground. (I found out later that he was floored by a *Gyakuzuki,* a reverse punch). That was it. All hell broke loose. "Oh Shit," I said to myself.

The Big Fight

The tense stand-off broke into a sudden flurry of movement, Ridgewell dropped the Nunchaku and rushed to the aid of the man on the ground, and the man who had whispered to Ridgewell appeared before me. I put my glasses into my right-hand coat pocket and tried to move from against the wall, looking for space. The man named 'North' lunged towards me so I landed a left 'front kick' (a Maegeri) into his stomach. I felt my foot go his belly. He went down. I remember asking myself: "*Is this supposed to be a policeman I'm kicking? Why is his stomach so soft?*" I heard someone behind me, who grabbed me partly around the neck and shoulder. I shook him off, and he fell on the floor to my right. It was a man called 'Mooney.' From the ground he grabbed my legs and I toppled over. I was struggling to free my legs from him when 'North' grabbed me from behind in a 'headlock' type grip around my throat. 'Mooney' continued to hold my legs while 'North' tightened his arm-lock around my neck. I found myself being dragged to the side of the escalator. 'Mooney' let go of my legs and as I struggled to stand up, 'North' increased the pressure on my throat. I could hardly breathe. I felt weak.

I could see a crowd of people looking at me and were shouting at him as he tried to choke me and he, in turn, shouted to me to "*Keep still, stop struggling.*" I had to stop for him to ease his grip on my throat and he quickly changed this to an armlock, which I could have undone but I was weakened.

I should have been faster on my feet, I told myself. He and 'Mooney' hustled me into a side room.

Once in the room, Ridgewell pushed me against the wall, shouting "*you've bloody had it, you've bloody had it*" while pointing his finger in my face. I could see *Omar* and *Bunny* being restrained by uniformed officers who seemed to have appeared suddenly, but not *Chris*. *"One's got away,"* I heard someone say. *"Great" I thought, "He'll get help."* But it was all over for us. I sighed and resigned myself to capture. More uniformed police appeared and seemed to be everywhere and crowded into the small room. Handcuffed to a uniformed office and escorted by 'Mooney', I was hustled out of the small room, across the Booking Hall area towards the exit to the street. As I was walking out of the station I saw people standing and looking at me, well all of us. I passed a white woman lying on the ground to my right, apparently semi-conscious.

In the van I was put to sit on the left hand side handcuffed to the uniformed policeman. 'Mooney' sat on the other side of me, warning me in a whisper: *"Just you wait 'till we get to the station, just you fuckin' wait."* He was warning me of the beating I was going to get at the station for throwing him to the ground. At that point I regretted not immediately stepping in his face while he was on the ground. I could only think of all the 'street fighting' techniques that I could have used to get away. But I had not come mentally prepared for a fight, despite the Nunchaku in the carrier bag Ridgewell ripped open.

They dumped someone onto the floor of van and to my surprise it was the very woman I had seen lying on the ground at the Oval station. An undercover policewoman got in and sat on the side seat opposite me. I'd not seen her before. On our way to the police station the police woman began to slap the middle-aged woman about the face calling her: *"Bitch! Nigger-lover! Bitch!"* with each slap and the woman on the floor just moaned. The journey to the police station wasn't long, as the man with an Irish accent continued to whisper his warning into my ear. He was ignoring the policewoman's assault on the semi-conscious woman. *What a situation!* Here was this man of Irish descent warning me of the beating he was going to give me once in the police station, and in front of me was a woman slapping-up another woman (whom I later realised was also of Irish descent). I then wondered if the van was taking us to Brixton police station. I'd been there before, when I was 16, and got a few slaps to my face and boxes around by head from the policemen who took me there. They had hit me because they and I were in the darkness of the 'Black Maria' van. This time my plain-clothed escort just wanted to hit me for revenge, or so I thought at the time.

As soon as the van pulled into a police station, the three of us were bundled out and hustled through a darkened corridor into the Charge Room and it was in this dark corridor that the man carried out his whispered-warning, punching me twice in the back of my head: "You fuckin' bastard," he said with each punch. The force of the blows caused me to topple forward but he and the officer to whom I was handcuffed prevented me from falling by hauling me back upright. I became disoriented and my head throbbed with each rapid heartbeat.

Once in the light of the Charge Room I was un-shackled from my escort and the others from theirs and ordered towards a bench to sit. We checked on one another that we were each alright and on any injuries we had and speculated on what had happened to *Chris*. "No bloody talking," Ridgewell shouted. The undercover policemen from the Oval seemed quite jumpy, talking fast and loud. Ridgewell, who was also quite hyped-up and edgy, was asking, "Where's the Sarge? Where's the Sarge?"

The white woman in the van was carried in by two policemen and dumped on the floor of the Charge Room. She was murmuring.

"Is she drunk?" someone asked.

"Have that lot been searched?"

"No."

"Well search 'em!"

Before this could happen, the 'Sarge' Ridgewell had been asking for appeared. They all surrounded him and Ridgewell began to talk fast, telling him how they had seen us acting suspiciously and stopped us to question us and we attacked them, pointing at us as he spoke. "One of 'ems got away" he reported. The 'Sarge' came over to us and asked us if it was true that we attacked the officers while doing their duty. We said "no" we hadn't but that they had set on us at the Escalator and started pushing, shouting and provoking us into a fight. We didn't even know they were policemen, we said. Ridgewell showed him the injured officer, who by now was able to stand unaided. He still seemed disoriented. The 'Sarge' didn't look pleased. He asked what the charges would be and Ridgewell and his crew began suggesting what these might be: assaults, loitering with intent, obstruction, insulting behaviour, were all mentioned, but nothing about us trying to steal.

"You got no bloody rights!"

In the midst of this verbal melee, uniformed police bought *Chris* into the Charge Room. We all stared at him. *He didn't get away,* I thought. My heart sank. *"God, we're in for it tonight."* I was glad to see him and not glad to see him. He was cut and scratched about the face, there was blood on his hands and clothes, and his clothing was torn, rumpled and dirty. With his capture, all hope of us getting a message out faded. We were now at the mercy of the policemen whom we had just fought and injured. In a last attempt to get word out I claimed our right to a telephone call. Ridgewell shook his head, indicating a 'no' and when we stressed that we knew that each of us had a legal right to make one telephone call, he raced over towards the bench we were all sitting on and shouted into my face: *"You got no bloody rights!"* After being searched and property taken away and signed for I was finger-printed. The one with the Irish accent tried to 'friend me up' asking: "You OK?" I just 'cut my eye' at him. We were put into separate cells and I would not see any of the others until Court the next morning.

The 'confession' statement: Ridgewell's first attempt

That's the **how** and **why** I came to be in this damn police station! After what seemed a long time I heard voices outside the door again. Don't tell me he's come back to try again. *Shit!* The door opened and two other policemen in uniform came towards me; I tensed my body and wondered what they were going to do. I had expected more 'activity' from them in the cells, but this time they took me up a narrow staircase and into a room to be 'interrogated' supposedly after being 'softened up' by the 'Behemoth.' The room was full of policemen, some in plain clothes, others were in uniform. News of the fight must have got around the station. I was put to sit at a table. Several of the men moved to the table and sat around it staring at me, trying to intimidate me, I guess. I was expecting to be hit at any moment by anyone from any direction. My body was tense. I was on 'standby' and was prepared to block/absorb as many punches as I could while I worked out what to do.

Ridgewell showed me a statement already written saying that I had tried to pick someone's pocket on the escalator, and had assaulted them and I wanted to make a statement. I told him it was rubbish.

"None of it had happened," I told them. *"I'm not going to make any statement about anything and I'm not signing anything. I've got nothing more to say."* On my refusal he punched me in my face. It was a signal to others to also punch and slap me about the face and punch me in my ribs and on my arms several times. I covered up my face with my arms in defence. *"Bloody sign it"* he demanded. A punched thudded into the side of my head. I covered my head with my arms and all I could hear were more threats of violence. I said nothing. Ridgewell swore, telling me: *"You ain't goin' nowhere till' you sign that bloody statement."* Again I said nothing. He leaned forward over the desk and shoved a pen in front of me to sign the statement. It flashed through my mind that what he wanted me to admit to wasn't what he originally told us at the

underground station—that we had been 'nicking' handbags. Now we were trying to pick pockets. *"You must be joking,"* I said. "I'm *not signing that. It's not true."* The group of 'intimidators' moved closer, staring at me intensely. One feigned a punch at me. I shifted in the chair. Someone else punched me in my back. The atmosphere in the room was tense. There was a long period of silence, probably only a minute or so but it seemed like ages. Ridgewell nodded his head at two men and told me to get up as they each held onto one of my arms *"Oh shit"* I thought, wondering what was going to happen next. I was hustled out of the room, down the narrow stairs and back to my cell.

The cell door slammed shut. I was alone in the silence. My face was throbbing and felt swollen; my body also ached. I sat on the bench/bed wondering what was happening to the others, what the police might do next and what I should do. A strategy seemed to be unfolding where they would threaten and then beat me to try and get me to sign a self-incriminating statement. How much more was I going to take? Should I retaliate? Looking back at what happened at the Oval station I realised that the police did not to give us a chance to think or to collect our thoughts. Even when we tried to calm the situation down, they would raise the stakes with a bout of pushing and shouting—as when *Chris* urged *Omar* to "take it easy." To all intents and purposes we'd been 'set up' and were caught in a trap. In the midst of it all I remembered that Malcolm X said once that we should 'preserve' our lives as it's the 'best thing' we've got. "But if you have to give it up, let it be even-steven." The stakes were not that high ... yet. I also wondered if preserving one's *life* was always equal to preserving one's *freedom and dignity*. How was this all going to end? What the hell should I do?

The 'confession': Ridgewell's second attempt

I heard voices outside the cell again. My heart began to thump. The door opened and in stepped the 'Behemoth' and Ridgewell. I expected another beating so I tensed by body in expectation. Ridgewell was looking pleased as he rushed over. "Look," he said, thrusting a sheet of paper before my face.

"Your mate's admitted it."

"Admitted what?"

I looked at the paper and there at the bottom was a scrawl that looked like *Omar's* writing. But what was written above was basically the same rubbish I was asked to sign before; that we'd crowded a man on the platform and that we crowded another man on the escalator, and that we fought with them after they introduced themselves as police-men. But what stood out was that it was I who was named as the one that tried to pick these pockets. "Rubbish" I said, giving it back to him.

Is this what they're coming with, I asked myself?

"He's put you in it," was Ridgewell's reply. "What you got to say then, eh?"

I said nothing. I was wondering what this meant. Is this how they planned to stop us?

"You're not going anywhere 'till you make a bloody statement?"

I didn't answer him. *They must have beaten him to sign it,* I thought. I was taken upstairs again but his time it was Ridgewell, the 'Behemoth' and the usual group intimidators. Ridgewell pushed the original statement before me with a pen to sign. I ignored it, wondering what to do. Ridgewell was telling me how bad it was going to be for me that night. He stressed that my mate had "put me in it" so I needed to say my bit. I knew he didn't say any of that or sign it voluntarily so what did it mean? "You must have made him to sign this" I said. "It's rubbish." But knowing the statement was rubbish was not enough. What was he trying to tell me by him signing it? How could I counter what the police were trying to do? I read the statement again and didn't find any clues to anything. This was getting complicated and the pressure was taking place in the same room in which I had been beaten-up earlier on.

But this time the 'Behemoth' was present and was standing by a table with a big book before him. The room didn't have as many 'intimidators' as before but as I knew I could be hit by anyone from any direction at any time the situation was just as perilous for me. Again they sat there staring at me.

I sat at the same table as before. The 'Behemoth' was telling that there was no way out for me. He was thumbing through that big book and began to read from it, asking me about various crimes committed in Brixton and Stockwell. He wanted to know which among us had committed them.

Are they serious? I asked myself.

"Who was with you on this job" he demanded?

"Was it Christie?"

"No. It wasn't any of us. You've got this all wrong. We were just coming home from a meeting."

He ignored me and then read out incidents of various robberies and bag snatches and mentioned an off-license robbery.

"Was it you who hit the old man in the shop?" I heard him ask.

"Course not."

"Was it Christie?"

I didn't answer. I was wondering what to do next.

"It *was* Christie."

"It wasn't any of us ... we weren't there…what is it with you?" I exclaimed, realizing that I was getting weary and tired.

How was I going to subvert their case?

I wondered how much longer they were going to keep this up. I had no idea what time it was or if any help was on its way. Were they trying to wear me down? They'd asked nothing about Black Power, Tony Soares, the BLF meeting or the Fasimba, or where we had been and why. They just kept on about handbag snatches and robberies. Was this some elaborate game? By now they would have run checks on who we were, visited our homes and reported back to those who wanted us detained. Were these men asked to intercept us at the Oval, to detain and search us and held for further questioning if anything 'incriminating' was found? What was behind this? They'd searched us and found nothing to do with bag snatches or pick-pocketing, nor any Manuals on urban guerrilla warfare or recipes for making explosives. What was their game? Or had we just walked into a 'stop and search' operation? We had rejected their 'stop and search' tactics and had to use 'righteous force' to resist their aggression, causing a 'big fight' in the Booking Hall. But they'd given us no other option as we certainly weren't prepared to be manhandled by them. This would have been an *unexpected* turn in events for those undercover policemen who appeared to have 'lost control' of the situation.

The threats, beatings and forced statements were some of the tactics I felt they were using by which they thought they could exercise some control over us and the situation. *If this failed then I imagined their next move would be to plant us with something really incriminating, like empty purses and wallets.* The 'war of position' now took the form of a battle of 'wits' between me and my 'interrogators' as well as one of physical endurance by me. What was at the back of my mind was an **expectation** of more violence. I was apprehensive and I was angry. I was vexed! It wasn't just avoiding that crippling knee-blow aimed at my groin or having my head banged against the wall, or the many punches to the head and body and slaps about the face, or even the shouting and the threats, but an expectation of more of the same as a consequence of 'surviving' the first wave of beatings and threats. My 'fearful self' felt that after some time they might find ways I hadn't thought of to wear me down by violence and force me to sign a self-incriminating statement. If that attempt by the 'Behemoth' to knee in my balls had been successful I would have been in serious pain and probably would have given in by now. I had to think my way out of that becoming a possibility and try to exercise some influence over the inevitability of events that night. The angry part of me could not, would not accept defeat.

Then it came to me. What the police did not know was that I had taken with me into the police station a 'concealed weapon' and I decided it was time to use it against my interrogators. It was an 'instrument' they did not know I had in my possession and one that no search could or would find, no matter how thorough. In fact it was a 'weapon' they didn't even know existed in the form it did, least of all possessed by me. Because I was trapped in another situation with my back against the wall and with no place to turn, I drew this 'weapon' and targeted it on the police case. And they didn't even know it was being used against them. They wanted me to make a statement under their conditions and the threats and beatings were being applied to force me to agree to make a statement under those conditions. What I did was to sidetrack this by deciding to agree to make a statement but under my conditions; under conditions chosen by myself; conditions I had designed and defined as subversive. I believed that if I didn't try to outwit them their plan might succeed.

'Making it all up' to fool the police: 'the half that's never been told'

After weighing up the situation I made a conscious decision to subvert and undermine the police case by *contaminating* the whole statement by admitting to crimes I could later prove were impossible for me to have committed. *My appearance of compliance and surrender was really a manoeuvre, a tactic of resistance, an act of defiance.* I was seeking to out-manoeuvre them and resorted to what is known in Jamaican folk culture as a 'higher science,' to a tactic *greater* than the 'science of deception' they had at their disposal. It was what I go on to describe in Chapter 7 as a *tactic in a strategy of counter-deception.* This would be a 'righteous deception' over 'unrighteous people' and an 'unrighteous situation.' I wanted to establish my innocence by some means but the police seemed to have closed down all avenues and all possibilities. My use of this 'weapon' was bolstered by the fact that I knew something they did not know, and I knew they didn't know it. For the next hour or so following the 'formula' set out by the 'Behemoth' in his reading aloud from the 'unsolved crimes' book and the promptings from Ridgewell,

I *admitted* to crimes that I knew nothing about, producing made-up stories about crimes I knew could be proved in Court as impossible for me to have committed. The 'Behemoth' read out the details of a number of 'crimes' that they hadn't arrested anyone for, mainly robberies and bag snatches—in Brixton and Stockwell, areas I didn't really know.

He seemed very keen for me to admit to crimes in that vicinity, perhaps to improve the 'clear up' rate for that area and mark them as 'solved.' Initially I went along with them and agreed that I was committing a couple of crimes in the Brixton/ Stockwell area, but always on a Thursday morning when I could prove later I was elsewhere. I had actually signed on at the Peckham labour exchange at 10.30 that very morning and I knew this would be a 'cast iron' alibi that they could not discredit and could not smear. *This was what I knew that they did not know*. Ridgewell was keen for me to admit to some incidents in Kennington. *Again I agreed to one or two but always on a Thursday morning around 10.30am.* I was not too keen on continuing to admit to the 'crimes' suggested by the 'Behemoth' and Ridgewell as *I did not know* the area, so when asked what other 'jobs' I had done, I decided to 'make up' some of my own as I was determined to exercise some control over what I would admit to. Having learnt the 'formula' from Ridgewell and the 'Behemoth,' I admitted to committing crimes in Rye Lane indoor market on Thursdays, always in the morning when I was signing on in the labour exchange just down Peckham High Street. The only variance from a *Thursday morning* was 'doing jobs' in the market on a *Thursday afternoon* when the market was closed and no one was there at all.

Brixton indoor market is closed on a *Wednesday afternoon* so I admitted to committing crimes in there on a *Wednesday afternoon* and on a *Thursday morning* at the time I was at the labour exchange in Peckham. As I spoke this nonsense Ridgewell eagerly wrote it all down. I admitted to committing crimes in Kennington and Oxford Circus on the day and time I was signing-on at the labour exchange in Peckham. So as they wouldn't think I only stole only from white people, I admitted to stealing from fictitious black people as well. I even dared to admit to stealing a handbag from a fictitious black woman outside Peckham bus garage knowing it was a few hundred yards from Peckham police station, where it would have been reported if it had happened.

I tried my best not to include any of the other three in these scenarios. Ridgewell continued writing hastily, at times asking me to slow down so he wouldn't miss a word. I looked at him; he seemed particularly pleased and relaxed. I daren't show any sort of satisfaction.

I even wondered for a moment if this tactic was going to work. It was too late anyway. I was already caught in a trap. The only way out for me and the others seemed to tamper with the trap that had been set in such a way that it would also trap my tormentors. I knew that the others knew the Peckham area pretty well and would see that the bus garage robbery as a 'made-up event' and would, hopefully, follow suite. It was the only way I could think of sending a message to them about a possible way out for us.

Ridgewell spotted a pattern in my *admissions* and asked why I always chose Thursdays for my 'crime sprees.' "*That's the day when women go out shopping*" I told him falsely, but convincingly. He wrote it down, adding some 'verbal' of his own my about wife and children. The 'success' of this deception was confirmed in its use by the prosecutor, John Rodgers, in his opening address to the jury and by their appearance in Press headlines: '*Thursday: Day for Muggings.*' In the same vein, the *Daily Telegraph*, (9/11/72) reported that:

> "Trew is alleged to have told the police that Thursday was their best day for going out stealing as "that's the day when the women go out shopping." He was alleged to have said that he had done "lots of jobs" not only at the Underground stations but at bus stops and street markets. He worked the Oval Underground station on Thursdays. "It was my idea because I was out of work and have a wife and three children."

I knew that Friday and Saturday were really the main shopping days for both black and white working class women in Brixton and Peckham. Their swallowing of this deception confirmed to me that they didn't even know that shops and markets in the Peckham area of south London closed for half-a-day on Thursday afternoons. I smiled on the *inside* but maintained a deflated composure on the *outside*. After what seemed like a long time, I became mentally exhausted and couldn't think clearly anymore. I didn't want to confuse or contradict myself so I told them those events were all I could remember. (My imagination had actually dried up and I could not make-up any more scenarios). Ridgewell looked 'well pleased and satisfied' He read the 'confession' back to me, made some 'corrections' and eventually I signed it, trying my best to spoil my signature as I did so. This ought to 'sheg-up' their case, I told myself. I knew they would eagerly show this to *Chris* and *Bunny* and them seeing how ridiculous it was would follow my lead and 'invent fiction' themselves. *Chris* knew that I signed-on on a Thursday morning. It was the only way I could think of getting on top of the situation and disrupting the chain of inevitable violence.

I knew I could prove in Court that the crimes confessed to were not only ridiculous but impossible for me to have committed, and hoped this revelation would taint the whole document. It would call into question how these 'confessions' were obtained in the first place and raise questions about the honesty of the whole police account of what they claimed they saw us doing that night, and how we came to make these admissions. In this way the showing of our innocence would be the discrediting of the police. As it stood, it would be their words against ours and I knew that our own testimony as black men without independent witnesses would carry little weight, if any, with a jury against the testimony of the white policemen and their version of events. I hoped that the inclusion of the made-up thefts in the 'confessions' and their exposure as fiction would poison the police evidence against us. I didn't know what the police actually wanted so it was one way of sending them off-track and away from what I felt they might well be after from us: information about our precise relationship with Tony Soares and the BLF. I was still convinced that this was the work of the 'secret police' and began to believe that there might be an *informer* in the Fasimba.

Camberwell Magistrates Court

When I was taken to be formally charged early that Friday morning, I was shocked at the amount of charges they read out and put to me. This seemed to last about 20 minutes. *"Good God"*, I thought, *"I've condemned myself."* As the made-up robberies, attempted theft and assault charges were read I counted at least separate 15 charges that seemed mostly to be built out of the false 'confession' I made. I sank into despair and immediately regretted the fake 'confession' as a tactical move against the police. I wondered if *Chris* and *Bunny* had done the same thing. Sometime later in the morning I was taken from the police station, with the others to Camberwell Magistrates Court and put into separate cells before facing our accusers. It was while peeping through the opening in the cell door that I saw *Bunny's* grotesquely swollen eye as he was passing. His right eye was swollen, cut and partially closed. Tears stung my eyes as I looked at him. Was this what I was trying to avoid, I asked myself? I cried inside and sank into deeper despair.

Not long after that I was taken out to a room to meet our barrister, George Davis, and there I saw the others for the first time since our arrest. Was I pleased? We all stared at *Bunny's* eye and at one another and asked if we were all okay. George Davis asked if we were all okay. We all nodded a 'yes', adding that it had been a rough night for all of us. He had our charge sheets before him and took our personal details. We were each asked about the circumstances of our arrests at the Oval underground and of the conflict with the undercover policeman. He asked about the charges and the statements and how we got to sign them and told that we were threatened and beaten. *Bunny* told that he received his eye injury because he was not prepared to sign any statement. Hearing this for the first time we asked him which policeman injured his eye, but before he could answer our legal representative put his forefinger to his lips, bidding us to be silent. He told us to only speak when answering his questions. *Chris,* we were told, had also been charged with assaulting and stealing the police woman's handbag during his escape-bid from the Tube station. We were all shocked and realised the extent to which the police were prepared to go to convict us. Barrister, George Davis assured us that we will all be okay in the Court and not to worry unduly. He told us that he was going to apply for bail and that the police would oppose bail and would want us remanded in custody. I was anxious. I didn't even want to think of that as an option.

In the dock

On entering the dock in Courtroom, it was like passing from one world into another, like emerging from a dream-like state into the abrupt light of awakening. I looked around the courtroom and into the Gallery. I saw the familiar faces of Fasimba members. I saw Marie, my wife; she stared at me intently with both worry and joy on her face. I smiled to tell her I was okay. The hearing was called to Order and the proceedings began. Again as all our charges were read out collectively they sounded more damning and terrifying, even bizarre. I didn't even remember some of the things I'd made up. The barrister, George Davis, spoke on our behalf saying that we would deny all the charges vigorously.

When it came to the question of bail, the police immediately opposed bail, citing the quantity and type of offences, including attempted theft, theft and violence against the police, all admitted by us in signed statements. Our barrister intervened to emphasise that these were only allegations and that both the 'confessions' and the allegations would be refuted at trial. After some submissions from our barrister, citing the lack of convictions against three of the defendants and the charitable community work of the four of us, we were eventually granted bail—on condition that we report to a local police station weekly. This was a small inconvenience compared to our previous night. At least we would be out of police custody. Outside the entrance to Camberwell Magistrates Court we posed for the famous picture that graphically showed Bunny's grotesquely swollen eye and our swollen faces and lips. Our pose of *relaxed defiance* went on to act as an icon for the 'Oval 4' Defence Campaign.

'Self defence is no offence'

With the exhausting Court appearance over, we melted into our respective homes to bathe our wounds, get back in touch with our families and friends, and come to terms with what had happened to each of us and what might happen. Marie kept asking if I was going to prison. I would have liked to have said an emphatic "no" but all I could say was "I don't know." I went over and over that fateful evening in my mind, wondering if I, well all of us, could have avoided what took place the previous evening. Looking back, the whole event seemed to have taken place in a different reality, in one that operated by different rules.

Once the fight was over at the Oval and I had been 'captured' my prime objective had been to survive the night as best I could and with as little injury as possible. But this objective relied on me dissuading the police from inflicting injuries over and above the beating I knew I would get for fighting with them. They had applied violence and threats for me to sign a *prepared statement*. To prevent further violence concocting all those fictitious 'crimes' seemed to me to the only logical thing to do under those conditions and for those reasons. But sitting in the comfort of my home and listening to the echoes of those 'crimes' in my head as they were read out in Court, but this time part of a wider narrative over which I had no control, made that decision to make a false 'confession' seem a suicidal act. I had concocted them all as fractured, disjointed and hollow scenarios, acts that I could get a jury to view as 'see-through' scenarios—as meaningless fiction; but the police had put them together in a way that was frightening. It became what Claude McKay had referred to in his poem *"Outcast"* as *'the white man's menace'* and was a *'menace'* that persisted beyond the confines of the police station, followed me home and rested in my head. They began to torment me.

The beating *Bunny* got told me that the police had been quite determined to incriminate us however they could. I thought again how the 'Behemoth' tried to injure me. Suppose I wasn't a practitioner of Karate and hadn't managed to block his attempt knee me in my balls it would have finished me, I told myself? My face was swollen and my neck, back of my head and body ached. *Omar* ended up with a swollen and burst lip; *Bunny* came away with a grotesquely swollen eye and face; and Chris took home with him bites from the police dog and a broken tooth from the 'Behemoth' for his attempted escape.

Together we determined to fight this case on two fronts. In Court we would mount our *legal defence* against the criminal charges and outside Court wage a *political campaign* against Ridgewell himself and the work of his 'gang.' We were still unsure if we had been stopped by the 'secret police' or if the Transport police were part of the plan to stop us, so the issue of covert Special Branch involvement was still outstanding. Maybe the Transport police had been 'set on us' very much like the hunting dogs were sent out by plantation owners to track-down and catch 'runaway slaves'—as what seemed to have happened to *Chris*.

Building our defence, out-manoeuvring the police

In the months following our release on bail we met several times and decided on our defence strategy and tactics.One tactic was already set in place; the false 'confession- statement' by *Chris* and me. I explained the reasoning behind this to the others: that it was the only option left available to me. Our strategy was not just to secure our freedom but, at the same time, to undermine and destroy the police case against us. Thus, in the public account of our confrontation with Ridgewell and his 'gang' we would say that we *did not know* they were plain clothes police when they accosted us, and even though they said they were police they did not identify themselves. When we asked for their ID we were told "*Never you bloody mind* ..." It is certainly true that at no time did they formally identify themselves as undercover policemen but we would keep out of the public domain the fact that we actually suspected that they *were* undercover policemen, mainly by the suspicious behaviour of the one we spotted on the platform (in his give-away blue Anorak) and by the arrogance and deception of the others who 'rushed us' at the top of the escalator. We became very suspicious as to who they really were or might *be* when they tried to detain us, presumably as they called for reinforcements when they realised we were not falling for any of their ploys. More importantly they could not tell to us who we had tried to rob, where this took place or the identity of those who had complained about being accosted by us. All Ridgewell could tell us was we'd been "nicking handbags." As we suspected they were something to do with the Special Branch we resisted their attempts to corner and search us.

From the perspective of our *legal defence*, if we admitted that we knew the men were undercover police, it would only have complicated and undermined our defence in Court as it would suggest that we resisted and fought them knowing that they were policemen in civilian clothes. While fighting with the police may have been seen as a 'righteous' and even 'virtuous' act of 'self defence' against police aggression by our supporters and among the youth in our communities, in the context of the dangers we faced from the Court and given we were all Black activists and practitioners of the Martial Arts, it would be a tactical error to take this position publicly, considering the fight. We would have certainly been asked in Court *how* we knew they were undercover policemen **before** they stopped us and (as they claimed) identified themselves as policemen. To us as community activists, they 'stood out' as if they were naked. This question would have left us open to the type of questions we were not prepared to answer in Court.

The face-off between Ridgewell and me at the Oval told me that he and his crew were not concerned with showing us any identification at all, but perhaps felt their *mere presence* as white men claiming to be policemen and making demands on us were enough for us to recognise their 'authority' as white (police) men and submit to a search. We were expected to cower and adopt a pose of *subservience* in the face of their bullying. Well, he may have seen that tactic work in Rhodesia but it wasn't going to work with us. Ridgewell's arrogance also suggested that he expected no protest or resistance from us 'coloureds' just submission and compliance. Under his leadership the squad showed little if any respect for black people and, therefore, had no intention of identifying themselves as police officers. I now believe his intention was to surprise *suspects* by the 'steaming tactics' used by him and his 'gang' so as to cause a great deal of confusion among his intended victims.

More importantly, from a Black political perspective, to admit that we knew they were policemen in disguise was to somehow admit that we acknowledged with that recognition the legality and authority of that 'stop and search' and, in so doing, also acknowledged what a refusal would mean. In those circumstances us admitting that we knew they were police could only have served two functions; one, such a recognition by us of them would serve as a cloak or veil behind which to conceal further illegal acts and, two; our acknowledgement of that recognition would have endowed these illegal acts with Crown authority and State legality, making 'outlaws' or 'political outcasts' of those who question, oppose or choose not to recognise such authority and power at the point of its application. As far as we were concerned they had no legitimate reason to stop us much more to demand that we submit to a search.

Our refusal to acknowledge any suggestion that we either suspected or knew they were police was an act of *non-recognition* of them and hence an *act of power* on our part. In refusing to acknowledge that we recognised them was, on the one hand, an *act of disavowal,* a denial of their existence as well as a rejection of how they intended to act and; at the same time, this *denial* was *a positive act of self-definition on our part.* Us knowing they were police officers in no way diminished our right to self defence and resistance to their aggression. We were to find out later that in all of Ridgewell's previous arrests he and his team pounced on unsuspecting youths without identifying themselves as undercover policemen.

This is an important part of our defence as this happened five months before he and his 'gang' did almost exactly the same thing to two black men from Rhodesia/Zimbabwe in August, 1972, the very place in Africa he claimed to have fled because of the Apartheid-like treatment of black people by the police force in that country.

Gaining our 'respect' or establishing control?

The *social control activities* of the police (Hall and others, 1978:42) are said to be more concerned with the gaining of respect than the enforcement of rules. I would suggest that the social *control activities* of the police in black communities during this time were both for the *enforcement of rules* **and** for the *gaining of "respect,"* especially from members of Britain's black community, and in particular its young people. It is in the policing of black communities and interactions with black people that their *social control* and *law enforcement* activities are realised. This much I discerned in the exchanges between us and the 'plain clothes' police officers at the Oval underground as they attempted to gain some form of recognition of and 'respect' for them from us in their guise as 'upholders' of the law and 'enforcers' of rules.

They insisted on us recognising their authority as 'white (police) men' by their authoritative and aggressive manner, that we should comply with their commands. As political activists we all refused. They were keen to establish some form of control over us and the situation from the onset: that we submit to a search, as one way of us showing some 'respect' to their authority-status and to their demands and not to suggest, as we did, that they could be just a 'gang of drunks' or just 'thugs.'

If we had submitted to an unwarranted search by them it would have been seen as an automatic *recognition* of and *respect* for their false claims to be involved in something 'legal' when we all knew they were not. More importantly, it could not even have occurred to them that their black 'victims' would have been outraged at their false accusations, and that our reactions and subsequent actions were based on this outrage rather than trying to avoid what they deemed to be a 'lawful arrest.' It must have been the case therefore that the police could not have imagined that black people had any *feelings* and even if they did have they could not have been ones worthy of any consideration by them.

CHAPTER 2

'A Clash of Evidence'
The Trial of the 'Oval 4'

You wish to prove that Detective Sergeant Ridgewell in the past has wrongfully used violence to young coloured people and, having initiated proceedings in that way, has gone on to improperly extract statements from them.
(Judge Edward Cussens' summary of
Defence Counsel's Submission)

Yes, that is correct...
(James Kingham's reply)

On 26th September 1972, two weeks before the start of the 'Oval 4' trial, the *Daily Mirror* carried a story with the headline: '*A Judge Cracks Down on Muggers in the City of Fear,*' reporting that, "*Mugging is becoming more and more prevalent in London. We are told that in America people are afraid to walk the streets late at night because of mugging.*" This was the *Daily Mirror's* version the *Evening Standard's* report of the previous evening, 25th September, making much the same point but quoting Judge Alexander Karmel's actual sentencing remarks:

> Mugging is becoming more prevalent, certainly in London. As a result, decent citizens are afraid to use the underground late at night, and indeed afraid to use the underpasses for fear of mugging. We are told that in America people are even afraid to walk the streets late at night for fear of mugging. This is an offence for which deterrent sentences should be passed.

The thrust of both reports was that 'muggers' operate almost anywhere: *on the streets* **and** *under the streets* (in "underpasses" and on "the underground") producing a situation where "decent citizens" fear to venture into these places late at night. Such reporting signalled the start of the circulating and expanding use of the term 'mugging' by the press, especially the *Daily Mirror* since it was they who first introduced it to the British public in the previous month, August, 1972. The 'muggers' sentenced by Judge Karmel included Courtney Harriott given a 3 year 'deterrent' prison sentence as one of the 'Stockwell 6,' arrests in which Detective Sgt Derek Ridgewell played a key role.

On Friday, 6th October, three days before the start of the trial of the 'Oval 4,' Judge Hines sentenced three youths for street robberies, and in so doing adopted the term to refer to crimes that were not called a 'mugging' before the *Daily Mirror* introduced the American slang. The Judge cites the 'public interest' as his rationale for the sentences: "*The course I feel I am bound to take may not be of interest to you young men individually, but is one I must take in the public interest.*' The *Daily Mirror* then invoked the Judge's words to anchor and authorise their own campaign, announcing: "*The Judge is right. There are times when deterrent sentences which normally would seem harsh and unfair, MUST be imposed.... if mugging is not to get out of hand as it is in America, punishment must be sharp and certain.*" What the authors of '*Policing the Crisis*' (1978: 74) termed the "*relations of reciprocity*" was beginning to emerge between the judiciary and the press and went on to characterise the ways in which the judiciary and the media worked together and, in many ways, relied on one another to recruit the general public to recognise and accept the *new term* 'mugging' as both a *new strain of crime,* and a *new code-word* for a *black crime*; that is, crime committed by mainly *black criminals.*

By the end of the first week of the 'Oval 4' trial, Friday 13 October, the *Sun* in an editorial entitled '*Taming the Muggers*' presented itself as defending the 'public interest'—as previously invoked by Judge Hines, where they asked:

> WHAT ARE the British people most concerned about today? Wages? Prices? Immigration? Pornography? People are talking about all these things. But the Sun believes there is another issue which has everyone deeply worried and angry: VIOLENCE ON OUR STREETS.... Nothing could be more utterly against our way of life, based a on common sense regard for law and order...if punitive jail sentences help to stop the violence—and nothing else has been done—then they will prove to be the only way. They will, regrettably, be the RIGHT way. And judges will have the backing of the public.

FASIMBA FOUR ON TRIAL

On Monday 9th October, four brothers from the FASIMBAS went on trial at the Old Bailey charged with a total of 17 counts ranging from attempted theft to assault on police, robbery and conspiracy.

Police Assault

These charges arise from an incident that took place at 11pm on Thursday 16th March 1972. The brothers, who were on their way home from a meeting in N. London got off a train at Oval tube station and as they got to the top of the escalator they were set upon by a gang of drunken thugs who started cursing, kicking and punching the brothers. When the police arrived it turned out that the gang of drunks were plain clothes transport police.

Forced Confession

Three brothers were dragged off to Kennington Road police station but the fourth managed to escape. He was chased and recaptured by police with the aid of a police dog that bit him badly in the face. In the station, the four were beaten up for several hours until they signed up statements. At the time of arrest they were told that they would be charged with the attempted theft of a policewoman's handbag but later the police went through their BOOK OF UNSOLVED CRIMES and made up statements for all four about crimes that they knew nothing about.

Sgt. Ridgewell

This policy of fake arrests and signed "confessions" is characteristic of the officer involved, the notorious Sgt. Ridgewell who is the Transport Police equivalent of P. C. Pulley. He and his gang spend their time lurking in subways attacking individual or groups of black youths that may pass.

Cover-up

The prosecution is trying to cover up this outrage by making the case look like a "mugging" about which there has recently been widespread publicity and heavy sentences passed. The Oval 4 brothers, Winston Drew, George Griffiths, Stirling Christie and Constantine Boucher are being railroaded to prison. Their trial is now going on every day in Court no 13.

HANDS OFF BLACK YOUTH !!

OR FACE THE WRATH OF AN ANGRY BLACK COMMUNITY.......
THE FASIMBA

The Sun's use of the terms 'violence on the streets' and 'our way of life' act as a link to this *new strain of crime.* By such reporting the press claim to speak not only on behalf of the *public,* they claim also to speak on behalf of the *police.* In the previous week the *Times* (5/10/72) reported that: 'Police may seek new powers on 'mugging', that: "Police superintendents, alarmed by the increase in violent crime, particularly by young people, may ask the Home Office for stronger powers to combat 'mugging.' Here the *Times* seems to more than just *echo* the call from the police for *new powers* to tackle *a new strain of crime.* Thus by the start of the trial 'Oval 4' on 9th October, 1972, the 'British public' i.e. "decent citizens" had already been trained to regard *ordinary* 'street crime' as a *new strain of crime,* a 'mugging,' more violent and prevalent than before and committed by black youngsters in inner-city areas. Such areas were places that members of the public, 'decent citizens,' were afraid to venture into at night.

Going on the Offensive

Given the violent and controversial nature of our arrest and the charges we faced, it was decided that *in Court we* would mount a *legal campaign* against the criminal charges but *outside Court* mount a *political campaign* not just to expose the lies of Ridgewell and his 'gang' and highlight the violence he applied in his other arrests, but to also call into question the whole idea of 'mugging' and suggest that the label was really a shield behind which the police were hiding to criminalise black young people like ourselves and, by extension, undermining our work in black communities in London. As a Fasimba publicity leaflet, 'Fasimba Four On Trial,' pointed out at the start of the trial, reversing the imagery in press reports:

> This policy of fake arrests and signed "confessions" is characteristic of the officer involved, the notorious Sgt. Ridgewell who is the Transport Police equivalent of P.C. Pulley.[1] *He and his gang spend their time lurking in subways attacking individual or groups of black youths that may pass.* The prosecution is trying to cover up this outrage by making the case look like a "mugging" about which there has recently been widespread publicity and heavy sentences passed (*emphasis added*).

Our defence in Court was a difficult and complex one, not least because we had little independent evidence to counter what the police said they saw us doing on the night. They could all rely on one another to back-up their witness statements but felt more confident, however, about the 'confession' statements as we knew these were really fiction and would be proved impossible for them to be substantiated. But for what happened at the Oval station, the police had one another's 'testimony' to rely on as well as the implicit confidence of the trial Judge. It was as I had expected: it would be *our word against theirs*.

The case for the Prosecution

The police case was presented to Judge and jury by Mr John Rodgers, prosecuting counsel acting on behalf of the Crown, claiming we were part of a 'mugging gang' who toured the underground system and local markets stealing purses and picking pockets. Much of his opening speech was quoted from statements taken from the accused, he said, by Detective Sergeant Ridgewell, the officer in charge of the 'anti-mugging' squad that night. The jury were taken through the events that led to the arrest of the four and their making of 'confession' statements:

> "On the 16th March London Transport Police were keeping observation at the Oval station when they saw the four accused hanging around and it was clear that they intended to pick the pockets of passengers. The four were observed standing behind an elderly man, aged 60, white haired and wearing a tweed suit, who was waiting for a train. As the doors slid open three of them pushed into the man while the fourth, Trew, ran his hand over the man's hip pocket. Nothing was taken. After this attempted theft, the four got off the train and started up the escalator, followed closely by police. On the escalator the four made a similar move, standing behind an elderly man wearing a sports jacket and the police officers saw one of the four, again Trew, put his hand into the man's right hand jacket pocket. Nothing was taken.
>
> At the ticket barrier the London Transport Police moved in to make their arrests after identifying them-selves as police officers in plain clothes. Griffiths said "Fuzz, Split"

and the four attempted to evade arrest by attacking the police officers, resulting in a violent struggle between the four and the police officers in the Booking Hall. As one fled the scene he stole the policewoman's handbag. Uniformed officers arrived and the remaining three of the accused were arrested. The three accused were taken to Kennington police station. Uniformed police caught the escapee and bought him to the same police station where all four of were searched, and interrogated separately. The missing handbag and its contents were not found as the escapee, Christie, threw it away. Each were interrogated separately and consequently confessed to having carried out a series of thefts and robberies in markets and tube stations across south and central London. At no time were the men coerced into signing the statements. They were all voluntary. The prosecution alleges that during the interviews, Boucher was the first to make a statement, admitting to the police account of that evening. This was shown to Trew who, after reading its contents, began to cry and also volunteered a statement. These documents were then shown to Christie and he too made a statement. Griffith refused to believe the statements were made voluntarily and Christie agreed to go to convince him that he had indeed volunteered the statement."

The 17 charges

The charges resulting from the confrontation at the Oval station were numbered 8 -17 and the charges numbered 1-7 came as a result of the controversial 'confessions' to the police. We questioned the reverse order in which these had been set out but were told that it was part of the way the Crown designed the case so as to make it seem that we were already thieves and criminals before we were stopped at the Oval station, justifying that attempted 'stop and search.' Below is how the 17 charges were set out in a 'narrative form' by the Prosecution:

1. Counts 1 to 7 arose from the 'confessions' made by all of us but especially by Trew and Christie.

2. Counts 8 and 9 were the 2 Counts of 'attempted theft' charges levelled at all four of us.
3. Counts 10 to 16 were the assault charges against all four of us
4. Count 17 against Christie alone for the theft of WDC Wood's handbag containing £30.

Case for the Defence

Our defence was conceptualised and divided into two parts. First, we had to counter all the charges numbered **8-17** that came as a result of our encounter with the Transport police at the Oval underground on the night. We had each been charged with two counts of 'attempted theft from "persons unknown" and each with various counts of "assault on police officers" and *Chris* alone with assault on the woman detective, Wood, and the theft of her handbag with the £30 it supposedly contained.

Second, we had to counter the charges numbered **1-7** that arose from the 'confession' statements. This last task seemed easier than the first as I had initiated the 'confession' in the knowledge that I had independent and unshakable alibis to counter those charges and would prove impossible for me to have committed. I calculated therefore that this would raise questions about police conduct on the night. Conspiracy charges were also added that were derived from the combined charges against us by the Director of Public Prosecution (DPP). The problem we faced was therefore countering the charges arising from what police accused us doing at the Oval underground that night, and it would be was our word against theirs, which we stood little chance of countering without independent witnesses. It was my hope that the 'confessions' would emerge as totally *unproven* that this would consequently raise fundamental questions about police honesty and *poison all* of the evidence in the rest of the police case against us. The obstacles to our acquittal are therefore set out as follows:

1. Countering the charges of attempted theft and assault on the police applied to all four of us at the Oval underground
2. Countering the charge of theft of woman detective's handbag that applied only to *Chris* at the Oval underground

3. Countering the conspiracy charges against all four of us applied by the DPP
4   Countering the charges of theft and robbery arising from the 'confessions,' principally against *Chris* and myself taken at Kennington Lane police station

As already indicated a major difficulty was that we could not contact any potential witnesses who rode the escalator with us, witnessed or overheard the men's approach to us, our reactions to this approach and the verbal exchanges between us except, of course, Mrs O'Connor. She was the woman I saw lying on the Booking Hall floor and whom I saw being hit by the woman detective inside the police van. *It was going to be our word against theirs,* and after the prosecution had set out their case, and we had given evidence in our defence to counter the police claims, the trial Judge described the case as characterised by a 'Clash of Evidence' between that given by the police and the defendants.

A 'Clash of Evidence'

What was to be termed a 'Clash of Evidence' emerged at every stage of the trial. The first 'Clash' came as a result of what the policemen said in evidence. Their account was that we were observed 'hanging about' on the platform and when a train arrived we crowded around an elderly man and I tried to pick his pocket while the others impeded him as he got onto the train. Nothing was taken.

Our evidence was that this was untrue, that we'd got out of the last carriage of the train and walked along the platform towards the exit. We passed a man standing there, as if he was waiting for someone. There were no other passengers behind or immediately in front of us and no other train pulled into the station while we were there.

The police evidence was that on the escalator we crowded another elderly white male and again I tried to pick his pocket but got nothing. Following us to the top of the escalator, the policemen said they identified themselves and attempted to arrest us when *Bunny* was said to have shouted "Fuzz! Split!" and we attacked the policemen in an attempt to escape.

Our evidence contradicted this account; instead, the three of us walked up the escalator leaving *Omar* behind as he had chosen to read and ride the escalator.

Chris gave evidence that halfway-up the escalator we found our way blocked by two men who would not move, so we too rode the escalator to the top. As we turned left toward the ticket barrier to exit the station, a group of men suddenly pounced on us shouting, swearing, shoving and pushing each of us roughly up against a wall claiming to be policemen.

In evidence we said we asked for identification but they refused, saying *"Never you bloody mind; you lot have been nicking handbags and we're gonna search you lot."* On hearing this we couldn't understand what they were saying and demanded that they identify themselves if they were really police. We attempted to leave and were forced back by the men and an argument started which, before too long, broke into a "tremendous struggle" between the four of us and the seven men in the Booking Hall. This was witnessed by crowds of people who were either leaving or entering the station.

Among the people watching the fight was a Mrs O'Connor and evidence was given by her for the defence. Her evidence was that she saw a *"lot of fighting between coloured and white people"* at the Oval underground and as she moved in closer to try and stop the fight she found herself being "roughly handled" by a white woman onlooker who mentioned something to her about the police. Imagining the woman was going to phone the police, she moved in closer to try and stop the fight until the police arrived but found, to her shock, that the white woman *was* a police officer and the white men fighting the 'coloured men' *were* policemen. Mrs O'Connor was arrested and charged with obstruction and assaulting the female police officer, Wood.

Evidence against *Chris* was given by the policewoman who claimed that he attacked DC Chapman, and as he attempted to run off was grabbed by her but he pushed aside, hit her and grabbed her handbag as he continued to flee the scene. This account was partly supported by evidence from DC Bates and DC Chapman. However, cross-examination by George Davis revealed inconsistencies in these accounts of what they said they saw of the assault and theft. First, defence pointed out that the police did not call any independent witnesses from the crowd who could have supported the police account of the attack and theft of the policewoman's handbag. Counsel then drew attention to the differing accounts of the officers who claimed to have witnessed the handbag theft, where one officer denied under cross-examination what he said he'd seen.

Bates had given evidence that *Chris* had the handbag over his shoulder but this was contradicted by Chapman who said he saw him running with the bag under his arm. Bates said *Chris* punched WDC Wood in the face and Chapman said it was her shoulder. But during this time both Wood and Chapman claimed to have been holding on to both of *Chris'* arms. Then Bates was forced to admit that he did not actually see *Chris* carrying a bag as he ran but then claimed that he heard Chapman shout '*Stop him Robin, he' got her bag*'(*Time Out*, 27th October-2nd November 1972). Counsel pointed out that his was not an eye-witness testimony but *hearsay*. For us, enough doubts had been cast over the veracity of police evidence and its glaring inconsistencies warranted directions from the judge to have that charge removed. But it was not. In Chapter 3 accounts from Mrs. O'Connor and her two companions were put before the Appeal hearing as 'new evidence.' It was illuminating. But more illuminating also were the Appeal Court's reactions to this 'new' evidence that cast doubts on the *honesty* of the police in making case against us.

True Confession?

It transpired that the 'Clash of Evidence' between the 'Oval 4' and the Transport police testimony was not just about the very different accounts of the incident on the underground platform, on the escalator or in the Booking Hall but characterised the whole case. The 'confession' was to become the centre of this 'clash.' **First,** doubts raised about police *truthfulness* began to emerge and came to hinge on the 'confession' statements taken by the police, raising the fundamental question: were these *voluntarily* made by us or were concocted by Detective Sergeant Ridgewell, as we said in evidence, to unlawfully incriminate us and which were only signed as a consequence of violence and threats of violence? A tactic agreed among us previous to the trial was to blame Ridgewell for everything, particularly for the contents of the 'false confessions.'

Second, the issue of police truthfulness was again raised when the 'modus operandi' of Ridgewell's team was called into question when we asserted it was one consisting of violence against accused persons, forced confessions and perjured evidence by him and his team in the 10 arrests previous to ours. In other words, was there evidence that Ridgewell had behaved in a similar fashion on previous occasions? These questions were raised in the course of two instances of what Justice James called a 'Trial with a Trial.'

During the first 'Trial within a Trial,' James Kingham for the defence made submissions before the trial Judge, without the presence of the jury, directed to the *admissibility* of the 'confession-statements produced by the prosecution as *evidence* of our prior guilt. The evidence refuting the 'crimes' in the 'confession' came when James Kingham produced alibi evidence that cast serious doubts about the truthfulness of the contents of the 'confessions.' What led to the second 'Trial within a Trial' was when James Kingham was halted by the trial Judge from putting questions to Ridgewell about his other arrests and, therefore, had to seek permission from the trial Judge to question him about his past behaviour in another session closed to the jury.

'Trial within a Trial,' 1

On this first occasion the defence team made a submission to the judge to dismiss all the charges arising from the confession statements. A key witness statement submitted by defence counsel James Kingham provided alibi evidence covering all of the occasions I was supposed to be out robbing and handbag snatching. John Rodgers, prosecuting counsel, must have listened to the submission with some unease as James Kingham went through selected aspects of this rebuttal statement from the manager of the Peckham labour exchange. But Judge Edward Cussens ruled that the charges arising from the 'confession' statements **should** go before the jury to consider.

Our reactions were initially ones of shock and surprise but then we realised that to dismiss them would have, I believe, called into question the whole police account of how these statements were obtained and open up question as to why anyone would admit to crimes they could not have committed, in fact knew to be untrue. When the jury returned and the main trial resumed and after we had given evidence in our defence, John Rodgers' cross-examinations of *Chris* and myself was directed to what he phrased as "the incredibility" (Transcript of the Appeal Judgement, 31/7/73, p.7) of our evidence relating to the controversial 'confessions' because their contents **could not** be believed.

The manager of the Peckham labour exchange appeared as a defence witness and confirmed that I had 'signed on' as unemployed every Thursday morning at 10.30am without fail and had even 'signed on' the morning of the arrest, and on this basis described the admissions in the statement as "meaningless" (*West Indian World*, 4/5/73; *Time Out*, 11-17 May, 1973). In an attempt to salvage the case, the prosecution actually timed the journey from Peckham to Brixton on a 37 bus on a Thursday morning at around 10.20 and found that it took over 30 minutes to get to Brixton. Similar journeys to get to Kennington on a 36 bus and to Oxford Circus on a 12 bus were also attempted and proved impossible to have been done within that time allocated.

What seemed to puzzle John Rodgers was that when the 'confession' statement was tested by their 'rules of evidence'—that the statement must have been obtained *voluntarily* (lawfully, without duress) and that it was *truthful* (the contents can be relied upon), if the answer to the first question was 'YES' then the answer to the second could only be 'NO' because alibi evidence was bought to show that they could not possibly have been committed by me, making these admissions "meaningless." Not only were the incidents described in my 'confession' *untrue* they were also factually inaccurate and, according the manager of the Peckham labour exchange, meant nothing. They could not be relied upon and were not evidence of my guilt as the prosecution had intended them to be. This shifted the attention of the trial to the *truthfulness* of the police evidence. Because the prosecution had presented the *crimes* arising from the 'confessions' as *prior evidence* of our *guilt,* the question was therefore raised as to **how** was it that this 'evidence' proved to be untrue? John Rodgers must have realised that a 'trap' that had been laid for the police, and quickly changed his tactics, shifting the attention of the jury away from the 'truthfulness' of police evidence to the 'truthfulness' of the defendants when making those admissions to the police.

Both he and the Judge could not follow the line of thinking that as the statements were *untrue* to ask themselves why would someone admit to offences and sign statements confirming those admissions as 'true' when they knew the contents to be untrue. Rejecting the idea that we had been assaulted and signed them in a state of fear, and fearing the prosecution might lose the case as a consequence of that alibi evidence, he directed his questions to *Chris* and me on whether **we** were telling the truth when making those admissions.

In his summing up, John Rodgers suggested to the jury that we must have lied to police about the events at the Oval underground and then lied to police when we made those statements at the police station. In his final speech to the jury, he invited them to approach the matter in this order—reversing the order in which they were originally presented. He asked them:

> ... [T]o consider first of all, whether they were satisfied on the evidence relating to Counts 8 to 17 and then go on, if they were satisfied with that, to consider other matters, bearing in mind that they might find that if they rejected the evidence of the accused persons in relation to Counts 8 to 17 they might also find that the content of the statement of the statements [Counts 1-7]

that were first put in by the Crown so was so unreliable that it could not safely found the basis of a conviction (Transcript of the Appeal Judgment, 31/7/73; p 7).

The prosecution did not, therefore, follow their original tactic of taking **first** the evidence of our prior involvement in crime in counts 1-7 from the 'confessions'—as certified by them as true, but as these had been shown to be 'meaningless,' John Rodgers, in a change of tactics, asked the jury instead to look at *our account* of the fight at the Oval station and if the jury did not believe what we said about that fight, then they were entitled to disbelieve the 'truthfulness' of what we said about committing other crimes in the 'confessions.' A 'negative' approach was adopted by the prosecutor in his summing up by asking the jury to consider first what they **did not** believe, and what was left was what they **could believe.**

'Trial within a Trial' 2

In the second episode of the 'Trial within a Trial,' the defence team raised questions about 'truthfulness' again when the *integrity* and *honesty* of Det. Sgt Ridgewell was called into question. In a session closed to jury members, permission was sought from the Judge by defence counsel, James Kingham, to question Ridgewell on his past behaviour. Here are the questions to Ridgewell in open Court that led to the second 'Trial within a Trial.'

James Kingham: It has certainly been alleged in Court against you this year in other cases that you used excessive violence with coloured defendants.

Ridgewell: That is correct

James Kingham: In fact, as recently as a couple of weeks ago.

Ridgewell: Yes. In Court number 6.

James Kingham: See if I can help your memory a little more. You were the officer in charge of the squad that arrested four coloured boys by the names of Morgan, Gordon, Freeman and Morris....?"
(Transcript of the Appeal Judgement, 31/7/73; p 9)

James Kingham was about to question him about the case of the 'Waterloo 4' (who complained of violence and perjury by Ridgewell and his team and were acquitted by the Magistrate) and then about the arrest of the 'Stockwell 6' (who also complained of violence and perjury) when the Judge intervened, saying *"I am going to ask you the matter which you propose to touch upon. I am going to ask you to be good enough to tell me the way in which you are going to do it. I am going to say no more."* Mr Kingham replied that he accepted that the issue of *character* may be what the Judge had in mind, but the Judge replied it was not: what was on his mind was the issue of *relevance.* Mr Kingham said *"It is credibility."* The Judge replied *"That is a matter you will be kind enough to explain to me before we go further, a matter which should be dealt with at this time and we will do so."* He then asked the jury to go out. After a series of questions and answers between the trial Judge and James Kingham, the outcome of this second 'Trial with a Trial' was that the Judge gave the following ruling:

> ... [F]irstly, no questions should be put to the present witness, Detective Sergeant Ridgewell, as to what took place when he was giving evidence in any trials previous to this one. Questions should not be suggesting that allegations have been made against him in the course of questions put in previous trials by defence counsel. Questions should not be put as to evidence given in those trials by witnesses, be they for the prosecution or for the defence..... Thus the position is that I exclude questions based on what happened at any previous trials ...
> (*Transcript of the Appeal Judgment*, 31/7/73: p 11-12).

Judge's final directions to the jury

James Kingham seemed to have been diverted from his original line of questioning to Ridgewell as a consequence of the Judge's ruling, and was not permitted to question him about his behaviour in the two cases previous to ours.

Concerned that the issue of *police truthfulness* had become central to the 'Clash of Evidence' between the police and the defendants during the trial, this is how the Judge put those matters to the jury as the 'confession' statements continued to baffle them: *"Of course, as you know so well by now, the Counts earlier than count 8 are all dependant one or other statement."* He then uttered a note of caution:

> ...when you are considering those counts which are based

on the statements of one or other of the defendants you must approach the matter with caution, because not only must you be satisfied that they are *free and voluntary,* you must be satisfied that you are sure that any confession to any particular offence named in any particular count is to be *relied upon. In other words, they must be true, and you must be sure of that.*
(Appeal Judgment, 31/7/73: p 7-8, *emphasis added*).

These final directions to the jury should therefore be seen in the context of what the Judge saw as 'pitfalls' for police and the prosecution by their inclusion of the 'confession' statements as evidence against the four of us. In the same manner the trial Judge also directed the jury, in reaching their verdicts on the charges arising from the 'confessions,' to "*consider carefully*" whether "*these statements are really fiction made up by Detective Sergeant Ridgewell.*" He then made it plain to the jury what the implications of the 'Clash of Evidence' were: "*It can be but one way,*" he said "*either the defendants are lying or it is the police.*" On hearing this I looked at the jury and asked myself several questions: What verdict would they come to regarding the statements? Would they, could they, see the police case as full of contradictions? Could they accept that the police were lying? Would they condemn the four of us or condemn the police? We were soon to find out.

The Verdicts: Not Guilty ...but Guilty?

The jury of 12 people, made up of 10 white and 2 black (males), took 4 hours to return with **unanimous verdicts of not guilty** on all the counts of theft and robbery charges, counts 1 to 7, arising from the statements. *We were delighted on our acquittal of all those charges, but* they could not agree unanimous verdicts on the remaining charges, numbered 8 to17, as the trial Judge had requested. He sent them back to deliberate and agreed to accept a majority verdict. It took a further hour and a half for them to return with **guilty verdicts by a 10 to 2 majority**.

In total it took 23 days for the trial, and the jury took five and a half hours to arrive at their verdicts. We were each found guilty of 2 counts of "assault on police" and guilty on 2 counts of "attempted theft from persons unknown." *Chris* was also convicted of assault on a policewoman and theft of her handbag. We were found guilty of all the offences where the police were the only witnesses to these events, even though these were part of the same 'confession- statement' that we were found not guilty of all the 7 charges of actual theft and robbery arising from them, to which the police were not witnesses. This contradiction would later form one of the grounds for our Appeal.

And with those *guilty verdicts*, the 'door' leading to 'outside' and to my home closed, literally and metaphorically speaking while, at the same time, the doors leading to prison—the 'inside'—opened to receive me, well all of us. I was back at square one; well, even further back than 'square one.' Before the trial I existed in a state of 'minimum security' and was conditionally 'free.' But after the trial I moved to a state of 'maximum security' as I was in prison. It seemed that what I intended my 'confession' to count for had not happen in the ways I had imagined it would. My 'confession' was intended to be a trap, a 'pit' into which the credibility of the police and their evidence would fall. Two of us had provided unshakable alibi-evidence to counter the charges arising from the 'confession-statements' to the dismay of the prosecution and the Judge. I had hoped that the space opened-up by the diminished credibility of the police's 'truth claims' would be filled by our own testimony concerning the disputed 'confessions.'

But in spite of our offensive against the police testimony and the 'impossibility' of the 'confession' statements, their credibility seemed to remain intact, though somewhat battered, as the political campaign to 'Free the Oval Four' would later reveal.

As it turned out, 2 members of the jury refused to endorse or had grave doubts about the "truthfulness" of police account of the events at the Oval underground, and all of the jury did not believe the police account of the 'truthfulness' and 'accuracy' of the 'confession' statements the police had secured as evidence of our prior guilt. But we were found guilty on some and that seemed enough to put prison sentences before all of us

Remanded in custody overnight...

I knew we'd be in for a rough time when it came to sentencing. The Judge remanded us in custody overnight on 7th November to face sentencing the following morning, 8th November, 1972. The night I spent in a prison cell was not a comfortable one. I was alone with my thoughts and, most of all, my anger and fears. That night passed as a dream-come-nightmare and it was something that I could not

KIDNAPPED

Sterling Christie | Windston Trew | Constantine Boucher | George Griffiths

THE OVAL 4
sentenced to

Sterling Christie	**TWO YEARS**
Winston Trew	**TWO YEARS**
Constantine Boucher	**TWO YEARS**
George Griffiths	**BORSTAL**

THESE FOUR BROTHERS WERE BRUTALLY BEATEN UP FRAMED
ON TRUMPED UP CHARGES, AND JAILED...
WE HEAR A LOT OF TALK ABOUT LAW AND ORDER BUT NOTHING
ABOUT JUSTICE

WE WANT JUSTICE !!

For further information and contributions to
the Defence Fund write to:
Oval 4 Defence Committee
203 Malpas Rd London S.E. 4

COURT ROW AS MEN ARE SENTENCED

By GEORGE GLENTON

EXTRA police were called to an Old Bailey court yesterday to halt a protest in the public gallery.

The demo came as four men were sentenced for attempted robbery and assaulting police.

Relatives of the men were escorted from the public gallery after they shouted down at the court.

One woman relative collapsed and had to be carried by police.

The four men were said to have fought with railway police after trying to pick pockets at The Oval underground station last March.

Three were each jailed for two years—Winston Trew, 21, of Furley Road, Peckham; Constantine Boucher, 25, of Thorncombe Road, East Dulwich, and Sterling Christie, 21 of Ermine Road, Lewisham.

The fourth, George Griffiths, 19, of Grove Hill Road, Camberwell, was sentenced to Borstal training.

All four were acquitted on charges of conspiring to rob underground passengers.

Do not use the word 'mugging' in my court, says judge

By C. A. COUGHLIN, Old Bailey Correspondent

A JUDGE who said that he did not like the word "mugging," yesterday told four coloured men who attempted to steal from travellers on the Tube: "Interference with citizens using the Underground will not be tolerated by our courts."

During the trial of the four at the Old Bailey, Judge CUSSEN reproached counsel for one of the men for referring to "mugging."

He told him: "The first use of this word in this case came from you.

"I have been regarding it as a very good thing that the word had not been used in this case if only for no other reason than that the resources of the English language are not so meagre as to require yet another trans-Atlantic importation.

"This may seem a light-hearted observation but I say this to the jury, 'cast that word right out of your minds. It is a word receiving constant use outside this court. I am most anxious you should cast it from your minds.'"

He jailed three of the West Indians for two years and sent the fourth to Borstal.

CONSTANTINE BOUCHER, 25, of Thorncombe Road, East Dulwich; WINSTON NEVILLE TREW, 19, of Furley Road, Peckham; and STERLING HECTOR CHRISTIE, 22, of Ermine Road, Lewisham, were jailed for two years for attempting to steal and assaulting police.

GEORGE GRIFFITHS, 20, of Grove Hill Road, Camberwell, was sent to Borstal for similar offences.

Purses snatched

Mr JOHN RODGERS, prosecuting, said their arrests followed a series of robberies and thefts on the Underground and markets by a gang who stole from passengers or snatched the purses of women shoppers.

London Transport Police saw the accused come from the Oval station last March and hang around. After seeing attempts to pick pockets the police moved in to arrest them and a fight followed.

Trew is alleged to have told the police that Thursday was their best day for going out stealing as "that's the day when the women go out shopping."

He was alleged to have said that he had done "lots of jobs" not only at the Underground stations but at bus stops and street markets. He worked the Oval Underground station on Thursdays.

"It was my idea because I was out of work and have a wife and three children."

FOUR CLEARED OF MUGGING

FOUR youths were cleared of mugging charges last night when an Old Bailey jury failed to agree.

The youths were alleged to have conspired to rob people on trains, in railway stations and at suburban market places.

But they were found guilty of assaulting police, and will be sentenced today.

The four are Winston Trew, 21, Constantine Boucher, 25, George Griffith, 19, and Sterling Christie, 21, all of South London.

Vengeance threat by jailed man

A MAN, jailed with two others, shouted from the Old Bailey dock yesterday: "These atrocities will be repaid when we come out."

The three and a youth had been found guilty of attempted theft and assaulting police.

The man who shouted the protest was Constantine Boucher, aged 25, of Thorncombe Road, East Dulwich, London.

He and Winston Trew, aged 21, of Furley Road, Peckham, and Stirling Christie, 21, of Ermine Road, Lewisham, were jailed for two years.

George Griffiths, aged 20, of Grove Hill Road, Camberwell, was sent to Borstal.

S.W
Thur. 9/11/72

THREE JAILED FOR TUBE THEFT BIDS

Women screamed and fainted at Old Bailey today when three London men were jailed for two years and another sent to Borstal for attempting to steal from passengers on London Underground, and assaulting police officers.

even wake-up from. The following morning I had to put on the same crumpled and sweaty clothes I had on the night before, was taken from the cell and put in the single cubicle of that blue van with high, part-misty-part-clear windows. It was rumoured that inside those double panes of glass were some sort of 'sleeping gas' crystals in case it was broken in an escape-bid.

We waited in the bowels of the Old Bailey with dread anticipation. Our Barristers came to see us and said they would plead to the Judge for leniency, as was the procedure, before sentencing. Little hope, I thought, as I knew he was going to punish us. I wasn't long before we were all taken upstairs and learn the manner of our punishment. As I entered the dock I looked up to my left and the Public Gallery was full of our supporters and quite a lot police as well. The well of the Court was also crowded with people, with many barristers from other hearings in the Old Bailey. What were they all doing there, I wondered? Had the case caused so much controversy that they had assembled to hear our sentences? It seemed as if they had gathered to hear an important announcement. This caused me more anxiety. Our barristers each said what they could and character witnesses were called on our behalf. James Kingham told the trial Judge I was a married man of two years with two young children and family responsibilities. He listened but didn't seem to care. He appeared anxious to get those formalities over with so he could sentence us. The prosecution said their bit, emphasising the attempted thefts on two underground users and violence against police in the course of their duty, and *Chris'* violent theft of the policewoman's handbag during his attempted escape.

This was it! Now it was the Judge's turn. There was a heavy silence ... then Judge Edward Cussens, QC spoke....

... for sentencing the following morning

"Interference with citizens using the Underground will not be tolerated by our Courts," he intoned, and with those words began announcing our sentences: three of us, *Chris, Omar* and me to 2 years imprisonment each for the counts of attempted theft, and 2 years for the assaults on the police. *Chris* was also given two years for his theft of the policewoman's handbag. The youngest of the four of us *Bunny* was sentenced to 2 years Borstal training. My mother collapsed in Court and *Chris'* mother screamed, while Fasimba members and other supporters shouted protests about our innocence, the corruption of the police, and the injustice of the verdict and Court system. Police seemed to crowd the public gallery and the Court as they did that fateful night when they crowded us at the Oval underground. It was ending like it began; *we were surrounded by police.*

Outraged at this *Omar* said something that would be misquoted by the press but still summarised our rage. I was in a state of shock! I couldn't believe what was happening to me! I was actually being sent to prison for something I didn't do? I wasn't going home that night, nor for hundreds of nights to come? I even thought I was given a total 8 years in prison, 2 years on each guilty charge. I was dumbstruck. Later in the cells below the Court the solicitor and barrister explained that the 2 years on each charge were concurrent not consecutive sentences—they would run along side one another not after one another. My immune system must have also collapsed. I came down with a heavy cold which I must have caught in the prison the previous night and spent most of the time in the bowels of Old Bailey cells, before and after sentencing, with a high temperature, sneezing and coughing.

Three of us were sent to Wormwood Scrubs Prison in London (and then on to Eastchurch on the Isle of Sheppey in Kent four months later). *Bunny* was sent to Hollesley Bay Borstal in Sussex where he remained until released in August 1973. Because I had caught a bad cold, I woke up in the Hospital Wing of Wormwood Scrubs prison on the mornings of the 9th November. I remembered that it was my son, Mark's, birthday on that day and that my other son, Malcolm, had his birthday during the trial in October. I cursed my situation. I was still in a state of shock.

I looked for newspapers to see what was in the press about the trial and sentencing. The following day, 10th, I looked around for all the newspapers I could find, searching for press reports of our ordeal. What reports I could find were varied and provided some indication of reactions to our sentences by our families, friends, supporters and sections of the national press.

'*Court row as men are sentenced*' was a how the *Evening News* (8/11/72) reported the sentencing and reactions to it. "*Extra police were called to an Old Bailey court yesterday*", the report said, "*to halt a protest in the public gallery. The demo came as four men were sentenced for attempted robbery and assaulting police. Relatives of the men were escorted from the public gallery after they shouted down at the court. One woman relative collapsed and had to be carried by police.*" The *Evening Standard* (8/11.72) carried a small piece in a late night edition, entitled '*Three jailed for Tube theft bid*', reporting that "*women screamed and fainted*" at the jail sentences. '*Four cleared of mugging*' was how the *Mirror* (8/11/72) reported the convictions in a small piece on the case emphasising that the *'jury had failed to agree"* on the charges of attempted robbery and theft. How the Mirror worked out that we were cleared of 'mugging' offences is perhaps related to them introducing the term to the British public earlier in the August.

'*Vengeance threat by jailed man*' was how the *Sun* (9/11/72) reported a remark made by *Omar* at his disgust about the sentences. "*These atrocities will be repaid when we come out*" was what he was reported to have said. But later he told us that wasn't exactly what he did say but if they wanted to take it as that then let them.

The *Daily Telegraph's* (9/11/72) reporting on the trial and sentencing headlined "*Do not use the word 'mugging' in my court, says judge.*" Judge Cussens had rebuked defence counsel, James Kingham, for using the word 'mugging' to refer to the public perceptions in the press of the activities for which the four of stood accused. The *Telegraph's* report is worth pausing over for a moment to attempt a small *deconstruction* of the pre-sentencing statement by the trial Judge, which was designed to be picked up and quoted by the press. Already mentioned above are the remarks made by the trial judge prior to sentencing, that: "Interference with *citizens* using the Underground will not be tolerated by our courts." Is it because we were black and the 'fictitious victims' white that the category 'citizen' should be deployed to try and distinguish the 'offenders' as 'non-citizens?'

The 1971 Immigration Act became Law on 1st January 1972 and had been the subject of massive public protest and mass media coverage as it was seen to divide migrants to Britain into *Patrials* and *Non-Partials*, with *Partials* having a 'natural' right of entry and abode and therefore access to the 'natural' identity 'citizen.' The trial Judge, already identified as integral to Court's legal structure and procedure, seemed to also identify himself with the 'citizen-victims' by his ambiguous us of the term 'our courts.' On the one hand, the reference to 'our courts' could mean as he is a 'citizen' as much as are the fictitious 'victims' and that both he and the 'victims' are subject to the same protection of the law, which 'our courts' both denotes and connotes. So his use of the exclusive '*our courts*' could mean that the Courts of Law belong to both he, the Judge and the 'victims' of crime—'interference' with whom by offenders such as we would not be tolerated by '*our courts*'. He is, above all, identified as an eminent *citizen,* a part of the national *We* that in terms of race includes the '*victims*' as well.

However, *within* the context of the racism that the Immigration Act institutionalises, the deployment of the category *citizen* to imply the 'white victims' and the absence of this category associated with the 'black offenders,' the Judge's remarks play into the statistical racism which explicitly defines the 'victims' of crime as 'white' and the perpetrators 'black.' Judge Cussens may have rebuked defence barrister, James Kingham, for using the word 'mugging' during the trial but, but as I have suggested, Cussens subtly deployed a language-strategy that located black subjects as *external to* and *outside of* the category 'citizen' so crucial to the *new* and *racially exclusive* understanding of 'Britishness' which had become institutionalised with the passing of the Immigration Act.

NOTES

[1]   PC Pulley was a 'notorious' policemen who was based in Notting Hill during the 1970s. He became infamous among the black and white residents in the community for trying to frame the 'Mangrove 9' on for false 'riot' and 'affray' charges following a demonstration against police brutality in Notting Hill, August 1970. The local press, *Kensington Post* and a National Sunday newspaper, *The Sunday People,* carried a series of report and article on his activities and the call for his removal from policing in the area.

On 29 October, 1971, the local press, the *Kensington Post*, reported that the trial judge ordered Pulley from the Court after he was seen trying to signal prompts to a fellow officer as he gave evidence against the Mangrove 9. PC Pulley was accused of fabricating evidence against those arrested and consequently all were found not guilty of the principal charges of 'riot' and 'affray.' Previous to this incident the *Kensington News* (21/8/70) reported that the transfer of PC Pulley from policing in Notting Hill was 'Unlikely.' This was after calls increased for his removal from policing in the area as a consequence of widespread hostility to his presence. Towards the end of 1969, graffiti appeared on walls in the area accusing PC Pulley and other police officers of brutality. This was on the back of rumours that had been spread about their corruption and had been known locally as "the heavy mob." *The Sunday People* picked up the story and called for his removal, commenting that PC Pulley "is the object of such widespread hostility that his effectiveness as an officer in this area with its special problems is gravely prejudiced."

The Mangrove 9 were acquitted of the 'state of war' charges of *affray* and *riot*, and included:

> Frank Critchlow
> Darcus Howe
> Roddy Kentish
> Rhodan Gordon
> Althea Jones-Lecointe
> Barbara Beese
> Godfrey Millet
> Rupert Boyce
> Anthony Innis

The trial took place at the Old Bailey and the 11 week trial lasted from October to December, 1971.

The connections between PC Pulley and Det. Sgt. Ridgewell are obvious. Both were the subject of widespread hostility in the local black communities; both were accused of fabricating evidence against black defendants and of inflicting violence; and there were calls for both to be removed from duties that involved contact with the black public.

CHAPTER 3

'Bars could not hold me; force could not control me now': Campaign to free the 'Oval 4' and the Appeal

Yes me friend, me friend,
them set me free again.
Yes me friend, me friend
me dey pon street again
The bars could not hold me,
force could not control me now
they tried to keep me down but
God put me around
Yes, I've been accused
wrongly abused, now
But through the powers of the Most High
They got to turn me loose, mmm
Don't try to cold me up on the bridge now,
I've got to reach mount Zion, the highest ridge yaw
if you are a bull bucker
I'm a duppy conqueror, conqueror.
('**Duppy Conqueror,**' Bob Marley & the
Wailers 1970, Upsetters)

Even as we were settling into prison life, the Fasimba lost no time in starting a Defence Campaign to defeat the accusations and 'Free the 'Oval 4' from prison. Following our sentencing on 8th November, the Defence Committee,' drawn from SELPO and Fasimba members and legal advisors, circulated publicity seeking donations to fund a Freedom Campaign. The Campaign began on Sunday 10th December when the Fasimba held a public meeting at St. Catherine's Hall, Kitto Road, New Cross, south-London, to both publicise our case and to recruit community support for the fundraising drive. Black organisations in London, such as the Lewisham based *Black Unity and Freedom Party, the Black Panthers* from Brixton, *and the Black*

Liberation Front from Ladbroke Grove attended the meeting, with Fasimba and other supporters from the locality and afar.

The following Friday, the South *London Press carried* a report: *'Fund started in bid to free four black men'* (15/12/72) and told that support was being sought throughout Lewisham to fund an appeal against the convictions.It went on to report on the Fasimba publicity flyer that a meeting was planned for the New Year, on 26th January 1973, at Brixton Town Hall, headed *'Cause for Concern.'* At the Kitto Road meeting, the father of a Fasimba member told the Press: "*We feel the boys have been treated unfairly. We intend to get the best barrister around for them so that their innocence can be proven.*" People like Jessica Huntley from publishers *Bogle L'Overture* were contacted to support the campaign and wrote to *Omar* while we were in the 'Scrubs.' Many other people wrote letters of encouragement and sent messages of support to all of us and we received cards and books from many people. These gifts helped to keep our spirits up as we tried to settle into prison life. We had settled into 'B' Wing and met quite a few black prisoners. I was in a cell with a black man from the East End, and *Chris* and *Omar* were next door.

Press reports of the Meeting at Brixton Town Hall

In the New Year the meeting called 'Cause for Concern' was organised by the Defence Committee of the Fasimba at Lambeth Assembly Hall on 26[th]January 1973 in which London-based Black organisations such as the *Black Panthers, the Black Unity and Freedom Party* and the *Black Liberation Front,* as well as the *International Socialists* and many other organisations were represented at the meeting. This event was reported as "*Clenched fist support for 'victims of police muggers'*" (*South London Press* 30/1/73) and told that the meeting was attended by more than 300 people as well as the local and national press and 'plain clothed' detectives posing as reporters. Pictures and propaganda posters with images of the 'Oval 4' lined the walls, some with the slogan: '*Indiscriminately imprison our warriors but the spirit of resistance still lives.*' This poster was designed and produced by a Fasimba member, Sister Desrie Adams, for the 'Oval 4' cause.

The activities of Det. Sgt. Ridgewell against other black youths were being circulated by Fasimba members in Lewisham, in Brixton and beyond, with one leaflet reporting that parents in south-London advised young family members, particularly young males, to avoid underground stations at night. This was picked up by the *Evening News.*

THE OVAL FOUR

CAUSE FOR CONCERN
Public Meeting
& Film Show

In solidarity with the victims of police muggers

**WINSTON TREW
CONSTANTINE 'OMAR' BOUCHER
GEORGE 'BONNY' GRIFFITHS
STERLING CHRISTIE**

**FRIDAY 26 JAN.'73 7.30pm
LAMBETH TOWN HALL Brixton SW2**

sponsored by

The Fasimbas
Black Liberation Front
Black Unity & Freedom Party

Black Panther Movement
International Socialists
and other organisations
and
FILM 'I am a Man'

Protest campaign for four convicted black men

SUPPORT is to be sought

Fasimbas —and a glossary of violence

By MAX WALL

THE FA
organisat
black
about fo
the Br
Lewisham
name fr
African
Just ov
circulated
advice o
questioned
the polic
glossary
language
Definitio
ling," an
"Steel,"
"Kyan,"
the police
from or s
The b
schools c
large-scale
police out
the summ
of black
schoolboy
ments an
crowds.
Last
made one
ganda a
combined
Panthers
mated B
Liberatio
beth Ass
meeting
The O
The Fo
Kenning
port poli

Black youths 'travel in fear'

BLACK children are
being warned to stay
away from a
stations becau
asment by
police.
And, it is c
regard all blac
potential "mug
The allegation
at a Brixton
called for a
into the conv
muggers.
Sterling Chri
ston Trew, 2
Boucher, 23; a
riths, 20, were
the Old Baile
and given
from Borstal
The case a
cident involv
transport poli
side The Ov
in Kensingto

STAT

After their
signed state
attempted t
unknown.
But at le
at Lambeth
Roy Francis
Fasimbas on
the stateme
weeks durin

POLICE ATTACK ALLEGED BY BLACK YOUTHS

By Our Crime Staff

An inquiry into allegations
that seven British Transport
police attacked four coloured
youths at an undergroundg
station and later forced them
to sign false confessions is
being demanded by an organisation of young black people in
South London.

The organisation, Fasimbas,
claims that the youths had
their heads banged against
walls, were kicked in the groin
and bullied by transport police
at the Oval underground station
on March 16, 1972. It is alleged
that they then signed confessions already prepared by the
police.

The four, Sterling Christie,
Constantine Boucher, George
Griffiths and Winston Trew, all
from South London, were each
jailed for two years for assaulting police and attempted theft

Clenched-fist support for 'victims of police muggers'

of "The Oval Four" was demanded at a
Friday night sponsored by the Black Pan-
Black Unity and Freedom Party and the
gamated Black Liberation Front and the
all militant groups representing black

0 attended the meeting, at Lambeth Assembly
jority of them black people who stood with
above their heads in response to a call from
to show "solidarity with the victims of police

of "The Oval Four," all Fasimbas members,
s of the hall with the slogan, "Indiscriminately
warriors but the spirit of resistance lives."
; Winston Trew (21), Sterling Christie (22),
Boucher (23) and George Griffiths (20), were
at a month-long trial at the Old Bailey in
'ear of purse and handbag snatching at the
ation.

was sent to Borstal for two years and the
iled for two years.
members told the meeting on Friday that the
trumped up as an excuse for Kennington police
Transport detectives "to brutally mug and
ur brothers."
med the four had been forced to sign state-
hreat of beatings and that the Old Bailey trial
l of discrepancies, ridicules and absurdities."
nbas member, introducing himself as Brother
the four had been returning from a meeting
don and were followed by Special Branch
etectives.
val tube they were "set upon by seven mug-
lice."

d of stealing handbags
ce station "it was like

unched and threatened
would walk out of the

'LKER'

ace said "Brother Trew
w he mugged a couple
hite guys and normally

the beating, said yes,
ne in the morning he
e and so those charges

ld the meeting, "We
nd we are not fighting
hting everyday issues
to resist the various

s one of a chain of
k people. We are not
we are not going to

e?' Some of our black
ain. They haven't got
to go back to. This is

of frustration among
60 per cent of them

ave no use for us, in
So we've got to fight
that build the roads
them

Fund started in bid to free four black men

SUPPORT is being sought throughout
Lewisham in a bid to get four local
black men freed following convictions
for theft earlier this year.

Donations are wanted by Fasimbas, a
group operating in the northern part of the
borough and a base has been set up in a
two-storey house at 203 Malpas-rd., Brockley.

Lewisham Council for Community Relations is looking into their case before
deciding whether it will offer financial
assistance.

The four men—Sterling Christie (22)
Winston Trew (22), Constantine (25) and
George Griffiths (20)—were arrested at the
Oval underground station, Kennington, and
charged with purse and handbag snatching
in January.

All of them pleaded not guilty at the
month-long trial at the Old Bailey. But the

years and Griffiths was sentenced to two
years' Borstal training.

Spearheading the "freedom" campaign
is West Indian-born Sherman King and his
19-year-old son, Cecil, who are personal
friends of the four men.

They are sure all of them are innocent
and intend to raise as much money as
possible for an appeal.

Mr. King said. "We feel the boys were
treated unfairly. We intend to get the best
barrister around for them so that their
innocence can be proven."

Some funds have already been for-
warded. But the Kings have not set themselves a target.

Mr. Asquith Gibbes, Lewisham's community relations officer, said, "We are
aware of this case and are following developments with interest.

"We need a lot more information. But
we will give them both moral and financial

"Black youths 'travel in fear' was how this appeared in the *Evening News* (27/1/73) as they reported this turn in events, with Ridgewell's name becoming synonymous with danger for black males. *"Black children are being warned to stay away from Tube stations because of harassment by transport police. And, it is claimed, police regard all black youths as potential "muggers."*

The press were at last beginning to take notice of the 'Oval 4' publicity campaign. However, the most *interesting* and *telling* newspaper report on the Brixton publicity meeting was the *Evening Standard* (27/1/73) piece entitled *"Fasimbas—and a glossary of violence."* The report was *telling* because it revealed that the Fasimba were being watched, at least by the press, who reported on one of our publicity leaflets. Collecting samples of publicity leaflets is one way the Special Branch is reported to collect data of 'black militant' organisations to ascertain what they supported and why (Bunyan,1975). It was *interesting* because it spoke about the Fasimba in specific terms. According to the reporter, Max Wall, the Fasimba derived their name from a "once fierce African tribe". History recognises the Fasimba as Shaka Zulu's most disciplined and feared warriors, the *Fasimba Regiment* (Ritter, 1968).

The particular leaflet upon which the report was partly based was one produced in 1971 by members of the Fasimba Propaganda Committee, called 'A Message to Tabby' and aimed at young black young people after they had to defend themselves from attacks by white fairground workers and the police at Peckham Rye Fair in the summer of that year (see *South London Press*, 14th, 17th, 21st September 1971). Readers were told in the *Evening Standard* article that: *"Just over a year ago, the Fasmbas circulated to local schools advice on what to do if questioned or arrested by the police and added a glossary of their slang language for violence. Definitions include: "Hacklings," an affray with the police; "Steel," a knife; "Wicked" and "Kyan," alternatives for the police; "Hustle, to take from or steal."*

The *Evening Standard* further reported that *"the Fasimbas made one of their rare propaganda appearances"* when they combined with other Black Power organisations to demand a *"retrial of the Oval Four."* Effectively, the report suggested that the Fasimba are not only an organisation that derived its name from a *"once fierce African tribe"* and whose publicity addresses young people in the *'language of violence'* they are also a 'secretive' organisation, making a *"rare"* public appearance to defend some of their "warriors." This information alone would have bought the Fasimba to the attention of the Special Branch but they already had information on the organisation, who was involved and their connections to other groups in London and overseas. Certainly the reporter, Max Wall, would have been briefed about an interpretation of the 'street slang' it supposedly used. Both the *Evening Standard* reporter and the Special Branch would have obtained a copy of the leaflet and it is almost certain that we were under surveillance before and after the meeting at Whyteman Road, with the Special Branch already knowing us as Fasimba members and Black Power activists. *The public revelation* that the 'Oval 4' were Fasimba members coupled with our physical resistance to the police at the Oval would have made the 'Free the Oval 4' campaign of interest to them and, as noted above, warranted plain clothes detectives from the Transport and/or the Metropolitan police attending the meeting.

However, the language reported to have been used in the leaflet were the very terms of the so-called 'street slang' used by black youth at the time and as Fasimba we used these terms in addressing the young black people about the dangers they faced at Fun Fairs and on the streets when confronted by the police and/or white thugs. In any event, typical of newspaper journalism, their reports tend to isolate these terms from the issues they seek to address and from their original context. For example a youth told me in 1971—after reading our first 'Black Psalms' leaflet—that the word 'Babylon' was no longer used by youth to identify the police: the "Kyan" or the "Wicked" were the *new* alternative names (nor was the 'Fuzz' used—as Ridgewell had 'verballed' Bunny as saying). So in 'A Message to Tabby' we used their terms because the Black American slang for the police 'the Pigs' was not popular amongst young people at that time. Even the working class white youth whom I met in prison did not use the 'Bill' as an alternative for the police; they were described instead as the 'Filth.' If the word 'copper' was used, it was found on the walls of police cells or prison cells as part of the acronym: **'ACAB'** (**'All Coppers Are Bastards'**).

We all settled into 'B' Wing and found that some sort of 'credibility' for us existed amongst some prisoners as it soon circulated that we had a 'big fight' with the police before our arrest and that our convictions were the result of a 'fit-up' by them.

Nobody we came across in prison had anything good to say about the 'Filth.' Among the black prisoners we were held in some regard not only for fighting the police but also because we belonged to a Black Power organisation, one that promoted the interests of black people. One black inmate with whom I had first shared a cell asked me why our 'brothers' didn't storm the prison and free all of the black prisoners. I suppose he remembered Jonathan Jackson attempting something similar in 1970 to free three 'brothers' from Marin County Court in California, USA. "If only" was my answer.

Prison Life: meeting Jake Prescott

After settling into 'B Wing' of Wormwood Scrubs, I met and made friends with Jake Prescott who occupied a single cell on the second landing, known as a 'strip cell'—as it was sparsely furnished. Jake was accused of being a member of the 'Angry Brigade' and the person who had bombed the Home Secretary, Robert Carr's, London home in 1971. He was sentenced to 15 years by the 'hanging judge' Mr Justice Melford Stevenson. When four of the 'Islington Eight' (with whom we exchanged acknowledging glances and nods with in the bowels of the Old Bailey in October) were sentenced to 10 years each, Jake consequently appealed and had his 15 year sentence reduced to 10 years like the others. He was a 'Category A' prisoner and we were 'Category B.' I visited him regularly in his cell on the '2s' (2nd landing) and had many discussions and made lots of jokes about prison life, but we did not, as a matter of course, discuss our convictions—though I did tell him who I was when we first met; that I belonged to a Black Power organisation and that we 3 had been framed by the police. I also told him that I knew about his case but did not ask him about any bombings he was accused of by the police or security services. On a few occasions I would be ordered from his cell and back to my own cell on the '3s' by a 'Screw.' As a category 'A' prisoner, Jake was not allowed to leave his landing or go anywhere in the prison without a prison guard escort and a 'movement book—his 'passport.' Whenever possible we would walk the Exercise Yard together talking about 'this and that.'

I knew that my association with Jake would be noticed by the prison establishment but I didn't care. *Chris* told me that he and *Omar* watched my friendship with Jake develop and commented that this was probably reported to the prison Governor who would have most certainly told the Home Office about our association. Perhaps the Home Office saw political connections and connotations in it all and I suspect the Special Branch suspected or assumed some sort 'revolutionary' pact with Black Power activists and Anarchist groups, such as the 'Angry Brigade' and the Fasimba. But in saying that I was not prevented from meeting, visiting his cell or 'reasoning' with him whenever I could. I found him a warm, friendly, serious and, above all, a quiet person. It was refreshing to have known someone like him in a place like Wormwood Scrubs.

The 'big fight' over a football game

At that time of press reports and the news of our publicity campaign circulated in the prison during January and February an incident occurred in the Exercise Yard between me and one of a group of white 'East End' inmates over a game of football. On the day of the 'big fight' in the exercise yard black prisoners had been complaining to me that the white prisoners 'hogged' all the football games and among them won all of the tobacco.

"They're all friends and we (black prisoners) get left out," they complained.

The answer is simple," I said, "Organise. When this match finishes, form a team and get on the pitch." But unity and organisation was not on their minds; they just sat there muttering amongst themselves. "I'll show you," I said, and when the match finished I went onto the pitch and beckoned to them to follow me to form the next 'five-a-side' team.

A number of white prisoners crowded onto the pitch and were forming the next two teams.

"Come on," I said, beckoning them onto the pitch. But, they just sat there looking at me.

"They've got two teams already," somebody said.

"Well, I'm not moving, so come on." I heard a voice coming from among the white prisoners behind me mutter, "I'll soon have you off."

I turned and looked to where the voice came from. It was from a white inmate whom I recognised as from the 4s (4th landing) in the Wing in which I was housed. I walked towards him asking "what was that you said?" I recall walking towards him confidently but with both my hands in my pockets: I was that confident!

As I bore down on him, he said: "Look out, the Screw's coming!" Falling for his trick, as I turned to look behind me and he rushed forward and gave me a right jab in my mouth. I stumbled backwards on my arse from the surprise blow, but then I jumped up almost immediately and launched a front kick at him; he jumped back. I heard a lot of shouting and from the corner of my eyes I could see *Chris, Omar* and other black prisoners rushing onto the pitch to support me and other white prisoners ran onto the pitch to support my adversary and one another.

In fact a 'big fight' broke out between the black and white prisoners in the Exercise Yard. I rushed him again, throwing more front kicks at him. He kept running back. He was determined to escape me and I was determined to 'drop him.' I heard the alarm bell ringing and then felt an arm grab me from behind firmly around my neck. It was a Prison

Officer. Other Officers ran onto the Exercise Yard to quell the 'big fight.' I was hustled backwards into the prison by two Officers and locked in an empty cell on the ground floor. All other prisoners were returned to their cells and locked in.

Afterwards the Deputy Governor came to see me to ask me what the fight was about. I told him that it was caused by a misunderstanding between me and another prisoner over a football game. That black prisoners had complained to me about their lack of fair access to the football matches and explained why I had intervened.

"I didn't even play football" I told him; "My intervention was solely on behalf of other black prisoners and was a matter of principle." Access to the football games should, I said, be equally distributed between both black and white prisoners, as the winning team would have won some tobacco. "And" I reminded him "tobacco is an important commodity in here." I told him that the other prisoner had said something to me, we argued and the fight started. I was escorted back to my cell to the delight of my cellmate. He asked if I was OK. I nodded and explained to him why and how the fight started.

From then on the Prison Officers organised the football games. I was even invited to form a team for one of the matches. I declined. As for me, well, I was put on report, went before the Governor, found guilty for fighting, fined one week's wages and loss of association. My opponent also went before the Governor and got the same punishment. The Deputy Governor came and spoke with me again and seemed somewhat relieved that the 'big fight' between black and white prisoners wasn't the start of Black Power activity in the prison.

The following day an ashen-faced 'stooge' of my exercise-yard adversary shouted at me in the 'Louvres' workshop where he and I worked. "Come on then" he invited, gritting his teeth and spoiling for a fight. The other prisoners told me not to take any notice of him as wasn't worth losing remission over. He was a 'nutter' they said. I took their advice and ignored him, although I wanted to kick him down. The Prison Officer who ran the workshop told him to get back to his bench and behave.

My black cellmate, who also worked in the 'Louvres' workshop' and from another part of the East End wanted me to 'have a go' at the 'stooge' on the Wing; he and his mates would be keeping a 'dog eye' for the 'Screws' and sort out his other mates. I told him not to bother as I didn't want things to escalate but I told him that if I ever saw the *ashen-faced stooge* outside of prison I wouldn't hesitate to 'deal with him.' I knew he wanted to 'do something' about the 'fight' for his mate—to the point of even spending time 'in the Block' (in solitary confinement). For prisoners like him losing remission for fighting and spending time in the 'Block' was one way of appearing 'hard' in prison. Plus I knew he also wanted 'something' to tell his friends about. Well he wasn't getting any 'free drinks' on my account. After the 'football game incident' my adversary and I never spoke but just glared at one another if our paths crossed anywhere in the prison. It was a sort of a 'stand-off'. Some days after someone from the '4s' where my adversary lived told me that he didn't know I was part of that 'Black Power lot' who were in the papers. My 'adversary' probably knew as well. He was an amateur boxer at some East End gym I found out later; well good for him. I was a student of the Wado Ryu style of Karate. His 'white boy' trick of diverting my attention to close-down the distance between him and me was his way of gaining an advantage. Well, he probably felt he needed it. I just put that incident down to experience.

Transfer to Eastchurch

In March 1973 we were moved from Wormwood Scrubs, a Category 'A' and 'B' prison, to Eastchurch, a Category 'C' and 'D', semi-open prison. Eastchurch was made up of two sections: a 'bottom camp', the 'open prison' and the 'top camp'—98 Block—which was semi-open. We were allocated to Block 98. The layout of the 'bottom camp' reminded me of the POW camp in the film 'The Great Escape.' Unlike the small cramped cells in 'the Scrubs' holding up to three inmates, Block 98 had larger rooms—dormitories—with up to three inmates in each. The Wings had about four dormitories as well as a number of single rooms. On these Wings inmates had access to washrooms, toilets, showers, and baths any time of the day or night. Despite this improvement in the physical comforts of incarceration, the summer I spent at Eastchurch was not a happy one. For one located on the isle of Sheppey in Kent it was far outside of London, making it a long journey for family and friends to visit. The sense of distance from London tended to increase the sense of isolation and I was beginning to tire of the prison experience. The feelings of hope I had on entering prison that we all would soon be free turned into despair. To make it worse time seemed to move slower at Eastchurch than time did in the 'Scrubs.'

The link between the concepts of 'time' and 'space' and between the *past, present and the future* was an issue for me, as well as issues about 'being' and 'consciousness.' In Eastchurch in 1973 this is how it played out for me. One thing I found prison tendedPri to do was to suspend 'outside time' and introduce 'prison time.' In 'prison time' all systems seemed to operate at a much slower pace and given it was nearly summer, with the extra daylight some prison days seemed an eternity. For most inmates at Eastchurch 'prison time' was marked out by events such as visits, letters, work, pay-day, association (including TV time) and lock-up. It was necessary therefore to avoid experiencing prison in terms of hours or even days. Instead inmates were thinking in terms of weeks and months, to the next pay-day or the next visit or any other event. It was on visits with loved-ones, family and friends where 'prison time' clashed with and was overcome by 'outside time,' and the time would pass quickly. The visit was over. On such visits you wanted to measure time in seconds and minutes in order to experience each moment.

Behind the scenes of the publicity campaign the 'Oval Four Defence Committee' and George Davis, from our original defence team, began the putting together the basis of our Appeal. Information had been collected and collated on Ridgewell's activities in the two cases before ours. In April 1973 were hit by a 'bombshell' as we read in the *News of the World* (15/4/73) that a trial Judge at the Old Bailey had rejected Ridgewell's evidence in his latest attempt to send two more black men to Prison. "*Judge Raps Swoop by Police,*" describing how a trial in which Ridgewell was the main prosecution witness was halted suddenly. We were elated as now more evidence had become available to undermine Ridgewell's credibility and the police case against us and pave our way to freedom. We had been sent copies of *Race Today* and *Time Out* with articles on our case but the prison censor cut-out our photographs before we got to read them. Things started to look up after I had fallen into some depression when it looked that I might serve the whole sentence. I remember an issue of *Race Today* that we were sent. It had an image of Tory MP, Gerald Nabarro, on the cover after he had escaped a speeding conviction after appealing his guilty verdict. His comment was that "*you can have justice if you can afford to pay for it*".

'Fist of Fury' and the TV debut of the Nunchaku

One Saturday in early July the three of us were watching a sports programme on BBC TV in the television room as it reported on the sudden death of Martial Arts film star, Bruce Lee. During the item they showed an excerpt from his latest film, 'Fist of Fury.' It was the Gym scene where Bruce used a Nunchaku ('rice-flail') to devastating effect on his enemies. The three of us looked at one another and laughed.

We laughed and laughed. He used a metal version of the very wooden Nunchaku I had in a carrier bag ripped open by Ridgewell at the Oval; and he didn't even recognise what it was! I even gave evidence during the trial, telling the Judge and jury at Old Bailey that it was an 'exercise stick'—the use of which I demonstrated in Court for all to witness. I had invented a tension-based exercise where I held the two wooden 'flails' in either hand and pulled on the nylon cord that joined them together to create a tension that strengthened the arm and chest muscles. This 'Shaolin Monk/Ninja weapon' was accepted by the Court as an *innocent* 'exercise stick' and not as an 'offensive weapon.' In our laughter, we tried to imagine what the prosecution's reaction might be when they realised that they had been *misled* as to what it was for and its proper use, and that we all might have been practiced in the Martial Arts.

The background to me owning a Nunchaku is also part of the Fasimba Black Power story and goes back to the time we had a base on Tressillian Road, Brockley. We had obtained the prototype from a black American soldier from Vietnam whom some of the Fasimba had met in the summer of 1971. Two of the Fasimba who were advanced in Karate and part of the Fasimba 'Security Group' also learnt some 'street fighting' techniques from him. He allowed us to make about a copy of this weapon, from which Brother D made about dozen or so copies. These were distributed to other interested Fasimba of which I was one. The 'street fighting' techniques he passed on to us were, in turn, passed on to others in the Fasimba in the extra Karate classes we held on Wednesdays. Although I didn't spend any time reasoning with him that summer in Hilly Fields Park and had met him only once, the fruits of our meeting with him greatly assisted in our self defence training and our self confidence as Black activists. This was a year before Chinese Martial Arts films became a Cinematic genre in itself.

We did not want any information about our Karate training as Fasimba to be included in the profile of us emerging in the Court as it would have given the fight at the Oval an altogether different meaning. *One thing we did discuss afterwards was what might have happened if we really were the outlaws and robbers the police accused us of being or were a different type of black men. Well for one thing there would have been less talk and more action. No asking for their ID! They would have been dealt with devastatingly and decisively, resulting in more serious injuries to them than what happened to be the case. And we would have disappeared into the night.*

In those circumstances, being captured was not an option as the stakes would have been much higher. But I had to admit that we might have been both helped and hindered by our training as political activists and as people with family and other responsibilities. One thing we were taught was not to lose control of the situation and that is exactly what those (police) men were trying to get us to do: lose control. Inspired by the news report, we continued to practice our Karate in secret and indulged in lots of strength exercises and fitness training with other black inmates there. We received the expected information from a Prison Officer who dealt with 'legal matters' that the date set for our Appeal was 30th July, 1973 at the Royal Courts of Justice at the Strand in London. We would be attending the hearing. Were we happy and were looking forward to seeing *'Bunny,'* whom we had not seen since November, 1972, although we had heard that he broke an inmate's jaw in a fight at the Borstal.

The Appeal: 'Battering down sentence, fighting against conviction'

The Appeal was heard before Justice Sebag-Shaw, Justice Phillips, and Lord Justice James on 30th July, 1973 at the Royal Courts of Justice, the Strand. The three of us were taken from Eastchurch that morning to attend the hearing. *Bunny* was not. We sought leave to appeal against our convictions and sentence, with John Platts-Mills, QC as lead barrister with George Davis in support, and Mr. John Rodgers for the Crown. John Platts-Mills, QC, and George Davis came to see us before the hearing to re-assure us that things 'looked good.' Once in the Court and in the Dock we could see our family and supporters in the Public Gallery and the legal teams in the Court before us. We saw John Rodgers who was back again to defend Ridgewell and the Crown. In 1976 Bunny Wailer released a 45 single on his *Solomonic* record label called *'Battering Down Sentence,'* and that song sums up exactly what our journey from prison to the Appeal Court would amount to: we'd come to 'batter down' our prison sentence and 'fight against the conviction' that put us in prison.

The Grounds of Appeal

John Platts-Mills, QC, for the defence, proposed the following framework to make sense of the activities of Det. Sgt. Ridgewell and his 'anti-mugging squad': "If I can show a system by the police", he said "it does show a diabolical innuendo—because they are coloured, because they are young, because they are out late, they are arrested" *(Sunday Times*, 5/8/73). John Platts-Mills likened the behaviour of Ridgewell in the 'Oval 4' case to that of the infamous Sergeant Challenor case in 1963. Sgt Challenor was a policeman at West End Central police station who had planted two half bricks on demonstrators in order to gain convictions. It so happened that the demonstrators were on different demonstrations and had never met and was thus impossible for them to have two halves of the same brick. The link between the two men was, or course, Challenor who, after having been found out, had to depart the police force for supposedly 'mental health' reasons *(Sunday Times*, 5/8/73). The link between all the current disputed cases was, of course, Det. Sgt. Ridgewell, and his intention, it is suggested, was to gain as many convictions on as many innocent black underground travellers as possible.

To develop this framework he put forward **three** grounds of appeal. **First,** the verdicts upon which the convictions of the 4 rested were "not safe and not satisfactory" because of a number of *discrepancies* in the evidence of individual police officers and to inconsistencies in the evidence of lone witness for the prosecution. These are such that they cast doubts on the reliability of the jury's verdict. In particular there was *inconsistency* in and between the evidence of various police officers about Christie's theft of WDC Wood's bag as he fled from the tube station. He was said to have snatched Wood's bag while held by both arms by DC Chapman and WDC Wood and was, at the same time, slipping out of his jacket to make his escape. One Officer said that Christie punched her in her face and had the bag on his shoulder while another said in evidence that that he had punched her in her chest and had the bag under his arm.

John Platts-Mills suggested also that a further inconsistency existed between the not guilty and guilty verdicts, since the jury had acquitted us on seven of the seventeen charges and since the evidence on the remaining ten charges were given by the same police officers and from the same disputed statement, this provided a further inconsistency. The convictions were therefore unsafe and unsatisfactory. The inconsistency in the jury's verdict on counts 1 to 7 with verdicts on counts 8 -17 was summarised by Justice James as follows:

> [John Platts-Mills] says the verdicts of not guilty on Counts 1 to 7 are inconsistent with the verdicts of guilty on Counts 8 to 17, inconsistent for this reason ...if the jury were not satisfied that guilt had been proven on

Counts 1 to 7 the jury could not have been satisfied with the reliability of the Officers who were responsible for the presentation of the alleged voluntary statements admitting the offences. All four officers in each case had been present at the time when those statements were taken and must be held responsible in part for the presentation of that part of the evidence, apart from the signatures to the statement. If the jury were not satisfied with those officers in that respect then the jury could not be satisfied with the same officers upon whose evidence the convictions on Counts 8 to 17 rested.

Second that the verdicts were *unsafe and unsatisfactory* for the "total exclusion" of material which the defence wished to bring and which was based on previous trials of black youths in which Ridgewell was involved—the 'Stockwell 6' and the 'Waterloo 4'; that the judge at the original trial had been wrong not to allow the defence to bring to the attention of the jury Ridgewell's behaviour in evidence from other courts and matters relating to his conduct in other cases in particular. The defence was now in possession of facts about a recent case in which Ridgewell was also involved where remarkably similar to the evidence in the 'Oval 4' case was given by him to the judge and jury. In this most recent case—the 'Tottenham Ct. Rd. 2'—the trial judge, Gwyn Morris, stopped the trial and ordered the acquittal of the defendants, rebuking police behaviour with the words: "I find it terrible that here in London people using public transport should be set upon by police officers without so much as a word that they are police officers." Platts-Mills argued that the same system was used in all four cases.

Finally the defence now had the evidence of two witnesses, unavailable at the original trial, who had seen the incident. Unbeknown to us at the time, Mrs O'Connor was accompanied by two young women and all three would give evidence that they did not see Christie clutching *anything* under his arm or on his shoulder as he ran. He was not only "losing his shirt," he was also "running for his life." Daphne Statham would also say that she was approached by WDC Wood, after Christie had fled, asking if she had seen a bag that had been lost on the station platform. The story about it being stolen was not mentioned at all to her. This 'new' evidence would therefore cast serious doubts on the evidence of the policewoman and other officers, and thus the consistency of the whole police case. John Platts-Mills argued that this *"evidence should be allowed to be introduced now and had it been before* *the jury it would have been material evidence on an issue in the case and may well have affected the verdict of the jury."*

Upholding or quashing the Convictions?

Taking all of the points put to him and not in the order in which they were presented, Lord Justice James said that it would serve "no useful purpose to have allegations made against a witness in one trial repeated during another." The trial Judge, he said, had been right to exclude evidence based on transcripts of evidence in other proceedings. According to Justice James witnesses can be questioned about their behaviour or misbehaviour in previous cases to determine their credibility. "But what cannot be of assistance to a jury is the fact that the alleged accusations have been made in the past against a witness". (*Guardian*, 31/7/73). John Platts-Mills commented that, as a consequence of this ruling, the defence team, particularly James Kingham, seemed to have been thrown off their course in their questions to Ridgewell about his previous behaviour. "Further," said Justice James, "there was **no** inconsistency in the jury acquitting the applicants on seven charges and finding them guilty on 10." In arriving at this decision, Lord Justice James reminded the Court of the original trial Judge's summing-up to the jury, and went on:

> Bearing in mind that direction, which we consider to be a proper direction, and bearing in mind also that at least one of the Applicants was able to put before the Court evidence to attendance at the labour exchange at the time which he had said in his statement was the time he used to engage in these activities, the jury could well have felt safe in relying on the evidence of Crown witnesses in counts 8 to17 and could have been so dissatisfied with the Applicant's evidence that they could not believe the truth of what they had set out in the statement which they made to the Police Officers even if they accepted them to be voluntarily made. On that basis the jury could well arrive at a conclusion of not guilty on the first series of Counts and guilty on the second, and we find no inconsistency between those verdicts.

Nor did he accept that the verdict was altered by the fact the jury took a long time (five and a half hours) to arrive at their verdicts, and when the guilty verdicts were delivered, it was a *majority* and not a *unanimous* verdict.

Two 'new' witnesses

The Court of Appeal seemed to reserve its most decisive ruling on the production of two 'new' witnesses by the defence to the incident at the Oval station. These 'new' witness statements were aimed at the *credibility* of witnesses for the prosecution in general and in particular to the credibility of witnesses for the case of *Chris*. Lord Justice James made observations on the 'new evidence,' namely the evidence of two young women, Bernice Stratham and Freda Stearn, who did not give evidence at the trial. Mrs O'Connor gave evidence at the original trial but only about the fight at the Oval and not about the 'theft' of WFC Wood's handbag. All three appeared in the BBC's *Nationwide* programme, 'Cause for Concern,' transmitted the evening of the Appeal hearing on 30th July 1973. Justice James' observations and ruling are drawn from the transcript of the Judgment of the Appeal against the convictions, and is quoted at length as I think it is necessary for readers to get a flavour of the thinking behind that Judgment. According to Justice James:

> It appears from the witness statements available to the defence that Mrs O'Connor had indicated in her statement that she was accompanied by others and there is evidence from Police Officers in the form of statements which indicated that they had knowledge of two ladies, one of whom was referred to as the daughter of Mrs O'Connor. Mrs O'Connor said in her evidence at the trial that there was a lot of fighting going on between coloured and white people and someone white had pulled her about. She heard a woman saying it was the police and she assumed that the woman Police Officer was trying to break up the fight between black and white ....
>
> Mr Platts-Mills now seeks leave to adduce the evidence of the two ladies who were Mrs O'Connor's companions on that occasion. *Their evidence relates first of all to*

the credibility of the police witnesses for the Crown and secondly in particular to the case of Christie ....

The evidence of Statham ... (is) ... that after the struggle she had seen the white woman who was engaged in the struggle and whom by then she realised was a Police Woman come up to her and asked if she had seen the handbag anywhere on the station and she had replied no. She says that the Police Woman also complained that the handbag had £20 to £30 in it. That person was alleged to be Woman D/C Wood.

There is a reference to this in the course of the trial when Boucher was cross-examined on behalf of Christie and he spoke of an occasion in the Police Station when he heard a conversation between Wood and another officer as to the missing handbag and at that time Wood was saying there was nothing in it. But in totality what is urged is this, that Christie denied that he assaulted Wood or stole her handbag and there was some evidence at the trial that Wood had not lost her handbag by theft but may have left it on the station, and evidence of someone going to look for that handbag was inconsistent with the allegation of theft and which went, of course, to the credibility of the Crown case.

In arriving at a decision on this **substantive** point, Lord Justice James said while there may be "validity and accuracy" to the points John Platts-Mills makes about the *'imperfect'* legal representation of the Applicants at the original trial, he was not satisfied that there is a reasonable explanation for failing to adduce that evidence at that trial. Dismissing the Appeal against the convictions, Justice James observed that: *"Reasonable diligence would have resulted in that evidence being available and for that evidence being adduced if those advising the Applicants at the time advised that it should be adduced in the trial ... [T]his Court finds that ... there was nothing unsafe or unsatisfactory, nothing in the substantive grounds, which would justify the granting of leave in this case. For those reasons the application for leave to appeal against the convictions in the case of each of the Applicants are refused."*

BLACK FOR A CAUSE ...

Allowing the Appeal against Sentence

Echoing Judge Edward Cussens' observation, Justice James agreed that: "There cannot have been a greater case of head-on collision of evidence" between the Applicants and the Crown. However, he was allowing the appeals against sentence because the original trial Judge, Edward Cussens, after being "immersed" in the details of a five-week trial, had not taken "proper cognisance of the acquittal of the defendants on the seven of the seventeen charges". The two year sentences were quashed making it possible for us to be released from prison the following day. Justice James turned to us in the dock, appearing to caution us, and said that we should not take the "*Court's decision (to release us) as a sign of weakness.*"

In a statement volunteered at the end of the Appeal hearing, Mr John Rodgers for the Crown, confirmed—as the Fasimba had stated in their propaganda (see *Time Out*, 2nd-9th August, 1973) that Detective Sergeant Derek Ridgewell had indeed been a former member of the British South Africa Police in Rhodesia, but had deserted after three weeks in 1965 because he *did not agree* with the Apartheid-like policy on the treatment of 'coloured people.' At this loud laughter came from our supporters in the public gallery. Lord Justice James expressed his displeasure at this interruption, remarking that *"race relations were not helped by such behaviour"* (*Guardian* 31/7/73). *Time Out* (2nd-9th August, 1973) commented that Justice James' remark at the laughter and his comment about freeing the 'Oval 4' not being a '*sign of weakness*' (*South London Mercury*, 3/8/73) shows that the Appeal Court was well aware of the background to the case and the resentment it had caused in black communities for the police and the judiciary. This also indicates that the 'authorities' knew and accepted that we were Fasimba members, had been reading our propaganda and from that understood that we were prepared to engage in a protracted struggle to gain our freedom.

In commenting on the 'truthfulness' of the much disputed 'confession' statements, Lord Justice James said that "*it occurs to me that some of the defendants deliberately misled the police in those statements and I don't know why.*" Well, I am not surprised he is at a loss for an explanation for this action on the part of two of us. Two historical traditions had clashed. As already told, yes, I did "deliberately mislead" the police with my false 'confession' and then I used the police to pass this tactic on to *Chris,* who then used it and tried to pass it on to *Bunny*—after the police admitted to him that

Bunny had been injured in the police cell during 'questioning.' He asked to see Bunny to find out how he was and to tell him to 'make up a statement' but 'cover' himself by it.

Who has the 'Handle' and who the 'Blade??'

In the Kennington police station Ridgewell and his 'gang' must have felt that they had gained the 'upper hand' when I made a 'confession'; that they 'held the handle' and I 'held the blade'. Well, as I said before, maybe I didn't know what they knew but they certainly didn't know what I knew. *As I will suggest in the Section 2, part of our training as Fasimba was to know what your opponent or enemy did not know, and to know that they did not know it.* Ridgewell was so convinced that he had 'buried' us he didn't even bother to check out any of the places named in my 'confession' as places for my fictitious stealing trips. For example, had he been "reasonably diligent " to have checked out a street map of the Peckham bus garage area, he would have seen that it was not far from Furley Road, where I lived at the time, nor far from Rye Lane indoor market where I might have been recognised during the fictitious acts of theft. However, the 'confessions' strategy didn't bring about the immediate results I had anticipated but that move was to result in the disbandment of the 'anti-mugging squad' and had a devastating effect on Ridgewell's future career and life, as we will see in Chapter 4. His apparent 'triumph' over the 'Oval 4' was a 'hollow victory' as it gave him so much of a false confidence, an inflated ego and a displaced sense of self, that he made grave mistakes in his next arrest attempts.

The irony is that this time his 'victims' would be two black, young African men from the very country he was supposed to have run away from seven years earlier in 1965, claiming he disliked the Apartheid-like orders given to him on the treatment of 'coloured' people. But that is exactly what he did in London on the Underground, showing delight in using the same Apartheid-like thuggery on black people, so much so that Judge Gwynn Morris stopped the trial, rebuked Ridgewell and freed the two black men. This false confidence 'sowed the seeds' of his downfall and his shameful demise as a Detective Sergeant in the British Transport Police, as the BBC Nationwide programme investigated all of the 'suspicious' arrests in which he played a key role.

The BBC Nationwide Programme: 30th July, 1973. 'Cause for Concern'

On the night of the 'successful' Appeal against the sentence, national BBC television aired a 'Nationwide' programme called 'Cause for Concern' that dealt with the cases of arrest that controversially involved Detective Sergeant Ridgewell, his 'anti-mugging squad' and young black males in south-east London. The programme examined the cases of 16 individuals all black and all occurring in south London on the Northern or Bakerloo Lines and all involving Det. Sgt. Ridgewell.

Case 1: The 'Waterloo Four'

The first case involving Ridgewell and his team was heard in April 1972 at Southwark Juvenile Court and involved Richard Freeman, Errol Gordon, Danny Morgan and Lloyd Morris—known as the 'Waterloo 4'. As will characterise these four cases, the defendants gave an entirely different story to that presented in Court by the police. On 2nd February 1972 the four juveniles caught the underground train at the Oval and when they reached Waterloo, Ridgewell and his squad, who had been masquerading as passengers, grabbed them and shoved them off the train into the arms of another team of waiting policemen, without a word to them that they were policemen (in plain clothes). One youth was injured as he struggled to stay on the train with his girlfriend.

All four were charged with being 'suspected persons' who had been 'loitering with intent to commit an arrestable offence' on the underground. The accused youths signed 'confession' statements but in a later statement to the Court one youth refuted the confessions, stating: "I just signed it because I was frightened that I would get beaten up too." A girlfriend of one of the youth's gave evidence that confirmed their stories and contradicted the confused accounts given by the police team. The Magistrates at Southwark dismissed the case and drew attention to the conflicting police evidence. He also referred the case to the British Transport Police for an investigation. Before the Court hearing Lambeth Council for Community Relations had lodged a complaint about police conduct during the arrest and the police evidence against the 'Waterloo 4'. Det. Chief Inspector RE Jones of the Transport Police's Victoria Division held an inquiry. The outcome as reported to the press was that "no evidence was forthcoming from any witness to support any allegation against any person" (Sunday Times, 5/8/73).

Case 2: The 'Stockwell Six'

The next case involved Everett Mullins, Cleveland Davison, Ronald de Souza, Paul Green, Courtney Harriott and Texo Johnson, all teenagers and all tried at the Old Bailey in September, 1972 in Court no. 6. In this case Ridgewell claimed in Court that on 18th February that year he and other officers were on undercover duty at Stockwell station, when he claimed he acted as a decoy and was followed into an empty carriage by Courtney Harriott and the other five youths. Other under-cover officers went into adjoining carriages. They surrounded him and Harriott pulled out a knife and waved it in his direction, saying: "Give us bread, man. Your wallet or it is this". Ridgewell said that he signalled to other officers waiting in the next carriage to join him, and after a struggle, Courtney Harriott and the other five were arrested.

The youths gave a completely different account; they had *not* been on any train with Ridgewell and his 'gang' at all but were coming up the stairs at the Oval when stopped. Again they claimed that neither Ridgewell nor his 'gang' identified themselves as policemen in plain clothes. *The BBC's nationwide programme did a reconstruction of the false tube journey and concluded that what was claimed to have occurred* **could not** *have taken place in the time the train left Stockwell and arrived at the Oval. The six youths claimed that were beaten up to sign confession statements admitting offences they knew nothing about.* Moreover, hardly any black youngster in 1972 used the slang 'bread' to describe money, as Harriott was supposed to have demanded from Ridgewell. This is an obvious but clumsy 'verbal.' "Bread" is an Americanism and became a popular alternative reference to money during the mid to late 1960s, but it was succeeded by new terms in the 1970s among Caribbean youth in the UK; terms such as "dunzer" or "sheckles" were the mediums of exchange.

Five of the six were convicted with Harriott receiving 3 years imprisonment and the other four sent for Borstal Training. Harriott's sentencing occurred in September, the height of the 'mugging scare' in 1972. The sixth person, Everitt Mullins, was acquitted as he was *largely illiterate* and his signed confession statement was declared as having 'doubtful validity.' Brixton Neighbourhood Centre lodged a complaint on behalf of one of the youngsters, Texo Johnson, and Det. Inspector Jones began another investigation and with a similar outcome as in the previous inquiries. "The complainant declined to make a statement in furtherance of the complaint" (*Sunday Times*, 5/8/73).

Case 4: The 'Tottenham Court Road Two'

The final case involving Det. Sgt. Ridgewell's 'anti-mugging squad' was that of two black students from Rhodesia, Lawrence Swelah and Alphonse Chikuri, both Jesuits and studying at Plater College, Oxford, who were accosted at Tottenham Court Rd underground station in August, 1972. Reported by the *News of the World* (15/4/73) under the headline 'Judge Raps Swoop by Police' the trial Judge, Gwyn Morris, QC halted the trial and told the jury: "It is wholly unsafe to allow this matter to go any further." He then turned to the police and declared: "*I find it terrible that here in London people using public transport should be pounced upon by police officers without a word that they are police officers. One of these men was set upon by police without a single word being uttered about being arrested; only after he had been grabbed, manhandled and wrestled to the ground at the top of a long escalator was he told he was being arrested and that they were policemen in plain clothes.*" Commenting on the contradictory police evidence, the Judge added: "*Six different accounts were given by police officers in relation to the movements of these two men, both of excellent character ... How is one to decide which is the accurate account? How can any possible reliance be placed on these police officers?*"

The 'pit' widens

Hall and the others (1978: 40) in '*Policing the Crisis*' summed up the similarities between the case of the 'Tottenham Court Rd Two' and that of the 'Oval 4.' "The police accused them of 'attempting to steal' and of 'assaulting the police'. The defendants claimed they had been set upon by five men, who produced no identification; after the ensuing fight, the two men were arrested. No 'victims' were produced. There were no other witnesses apart from the police. The group involved were the Transport Special Squad, and the operation was led by Detective Sergeant Ridgewell." The authors asked readers: "Was there a pattern here"? The *National Council for Civil Liberties (now called 'Liberty')* listed a number of 'disturbing facts' which have emerged from all the cases and presented a file to the Home Secretary, Robert Carr, for investigation.

The file included the following information:

1. All the defendants were black.
2. Of the 16 defendants 7 were acquitted.
3. In two of the four cases, judges not only acquitted the accused but cast serious doubts about the propriety of police behaviour (cases 1 & 4)
4. Det. Sgt. Ridgewell was involved in all four cases and a number of other officers were involved in every case, i.e. Clift, North and Mooney.
5. In none of the cases were any independent witnesses called (in spite of the fact that the essence of a "mugging" charge is that whoever is "mugged" is obviously aware of the fact, and no independent complainant came forward).
6. The only evidence in one case (case 2 above) which resulted in conviction was the statements of the accused. In the 'Oval 4' case they were acquitted of charges arising from the 'confession' statements. In both cases the accused said these were given after physical assault by the police and under duress.
7. In every case there is evidence that the police failed to identify themselves when making the arrest and used an excessive amount of violence.

Following the showing of the BBC's 'Cause for Concern' programme, John Fraser, MP for Norwood and Labour opposition spokesman for Home Affairs in the House of Commons, said to the *South London Press* (5/8/73):

> I think this TV programme gives us cause for concern and I have asked the BBC for the script. I feel that this warrants further investigation. I will get in touch with the Home Secretary who has general supervision powers over police forces, and ask him to study the material that has been made available, including that of witnesses that could not be made available and those whose evidence was excluded. It is important to look to into these matters because otherwise public confidence in the police—in this case the transport police—may be lost.

The *South London Press* reported the British Transport police's response to the mounting criticism. Det. Chief Sup. B Nichols at Transport Headquarters in West London was forced to concede this reaction: "We are digesting the contents of the TV programme and I cannot make any further comment at the moment". He went on: "There have been no complaints against Sgt. Ridgewell, other than implied in the programme. When we have seen the script, if there is (?) grounds for an inquiry or investigation into Sgt, Ridgewell or any other officer, this will be done." The report noted that Sgt. Ridgewell was still carrying on his duties but not presently involved in 'anti-mugging operations'.

It seems that the mounting public doubts about the convictions and concern about the methods and activities of the Transport Police's 'anti-mugging squad' led by Det. Sgt. Ridgewell had caused him to be removed from those 'anti-mugging' duties. The campaign started by the The 'Oval Four Defence Committee' to expose Det. Sgt. Ridgewell as 'dishonest' and the 'anti-mugging' squad as based on a 'fraud' seems to have been partially successful. This was 1973. Ridgewell would be moved from his post within months, transferred to other duties not involving the public and begin a downward spiral that would prove devastating for him and the Transport police.

Ridgewell: 'a message to you'

The *West Indian World* (WIW), a 'mainstream' national Black community newspaper serving the Caribbean community in Britain during the 1970s and 1980s, carried a reprint (3/8/73) of an article that appeared in an earlier edition (4/5/73). The article, they state, is a reproduction of the one produced by CIVIL LIBERY, the newsletter of the *National Council for Civil Liberties (NCCL)* "whose efforts to safeguard liberty in Britain have won them the gratitude of many minority groups in this country, particularly the black community." Alongside this *NCCL* article on the background to the 'Oval 4' case was an 'editorial' by the WIW on developments in Ridgewell's career. Its observations on the 'Oval 4' case are self explanatory and are reproduced in their entirety below:

> The sad and disturbing case of the OVAL FOUR which has been compared with the miscarriages of justice in the SOLEDAD BROS. trial in America, is widely regarded as a blot on British justice. Millions of viewers and readers who saw and read accounts of the trial of

the SOLEDAD BROS. were outraged at the cruelty, inhumanity and unfairness of the administrative and legal system that could cause so much pain, misery and eventually engineer murders and assaults. Their outrage was normal and natural for, whatever its faults, they live under a system of justice that would not tolerate such hooliganism and irresponsibility. But there is little doubt that some of the questionable methods used by the American police are finding admirers among sections of the British police who have declared a state of war against young black men. Some of the facts of the OVAL FOUR case have caused grave concern among those working for better community relations and those concerned with the quality of British justice. The four young men, Winston Trew, Constantine Boucher, George Griffiths and Sterling Christie have been in Prison for the last eight months."

Last May the chief witness against the Oval Four Detective Sergeant Derek Ridgewell came out very badly in his case against two innocent Zimbabweans who, according to the findings of the court, seemed to have been the victims of a frame-up. Where there is clear evidence that this has happened, English judges, who rightly enjoy world-wide respect for their impartiality and fairness, will unhesitatingly put a stop to such victimisation. The Old Bailey judge in this case, a stalwart of this great tradition stopped the case of the two Zimbabweans and scathingly criticised Ridgewell and his colleagues for giving false evidence. THERE IS NO DOUBT THEREFORE THAT ENGLISH JUSTICE AT ITS BEST WILL NOT FOR ONE MOMENT TOLERATE QUESTIONABLE EVIDENCE. In view of the comments of the Old Bailey judge in the Zimbabweans case on Ridgewell, the chief witness against the OVAL FOUR, there appears to be grave doubts about the guilt of these young men. OUR READERS CAN SUPPORT THESE YOUNG MEN BY PROTESTING AGAINST THEIR CONTINUED IMPRISONMENT IN THE LIGHT OF THE NATURE OF RIDGEWELL'S EVIDENCE AGAINST THE

ZIMBABWEANS AND THE JUDGES COMMENTS
ON HIS METHODS" (ORIGINAL EMPHASIS).

The Editorial concluded by inviting readers to write to MP's, newspapers, Scotland Yard, High Commissions, London Transport and the GLC about the case and to write to the "four brothers and demonstrate your support for their cause". The prison numbers and addresses were listed beneath for those who wished to take up this offer. The observations by WIW on our case suggest a number of things.'

First, the comments represent a culmination of the 'community-based' campaign to 'Free the 'Oval 4'. The 'editorial' and the reprinted article came out on 3rd August, the Friday after we appeared at the Court of Appeal on the Monday and set free on the Tuesday morning from Eastchurch prison. The reprint and the editorial was probably prepared for publication the weekend before the 'Oval 4' had their Appeal hearing on 30th July, and was published on Friday, 3rd August, when *Chris* and I appeared at a Press Conference at Grassroots Bookshop in Ladbroke Grove.

Second, it was clear to those who followed the case that Judge Edward Cussens was not concerned with the 'quality of British justice' the readers of the *WIW* were concerned with or with inconsistencies in police evidence given at the Old Bailey. Reviewing the same evidence, the Appeal Court judge, Lord Justice James was not only unprepared to overturn the dubious convictions, he did not share the alternative reading of the case as expressed in the WIW or as put by John Platts-Mills, QC, on our behalf at the Court of Appeal. His views of 'community relations' or as he put it "race relations" were directly opposed to our reading of Ridgewell's 'race relations' practices, particularly after Fasimba and other 'Oval 4' supporters at the Court of Appeal poured scorn on Ridgewell's claim to have disliked the Apartheid-like policing practices in Rhodesia, causing him to flee. After seeing the BBC's 'Nationwide' transmission on television, John Fraser, Labour MP for Norwood, expressed his concern about the state of 'community relations' in the light of revelations made about Ridgewell's activities against black young people in the programme *(South London Press*, 3/5/73).

Third, it is important to note is that the Oval underground is in the borough of Lambeth, and the Northern and Bakerloo lines service not only the boroughs of south-east London with significant Caribbean populations, they also service travellers between these boroughs and to the West End for work, leisure or entertainment. That the *WIW* devoted a full-page to our cause indicates that it was a very *important issue* for the paper's readership and for the positioning of the paper in relation to the issues raised within it. The *WIW* was popular among large sections of adults who had migrated to Britain in the 1950s and 1960s and their offspring were the very young people targeted by Ridgewell as 'muggers.'

The Press Conference at Grassroots Bookshop

At a Press Conference at Grassroots Bookshop at Ladbroke Grove ` on 3rd August, 1973, Chris spoke to the *Guardian* and I spoke to *Keep Left Socialist* newspaper. The *Guardian* (4/8/73) reported the view that the Defence campaign and our supporters saw the 'drastic' reduction in our sentences by the Appeal court as a "vindication" of our "persistent claim" we made that "we are innocent." *Chris* reported our true feelings to Peter Cole of the *Guardian*: "*We are most dissatisfied with the verdict. We are not guilty of the crime. We spent nine months in goal for no reason at all, at least no criminal reason.*" The "no criminal reason" *Chris* was alluding to was the political reasons for which we were incarcerated, some of which was made known by the Appeal Court Judge by his reaction to the laughter about Ridgewell's claim to have run away from policing Africa because he thought the Rhodesian police were denying the *civil* and *human rights* of Africans. In the interview with a *Keep Left* reporter I reviewed the outcome of the appeal and our political campaign, suggesting that if the Appeal Court had agreed to what our Defence team had been saying there would have been "one hell of a scandal" as it involved a Det. Sgt of the British Transport police. I went on: "*A lot of people would have been in trouble if our convictions had been quashed. It would have brought into question other British Transport police cases, in fact all the cases of "mugging". The aim of our campaign was to question the word "mugging"* (*Keep Left*, 11/8/73).

The police, the press and the manufacture of 'mugging' on the Underground

In this section I want to try and trace and identify the *conditions of emergence* of the 'mugging scare' that we know reached a peak in September 1972, when five of the 'Stockwell 6' were jailed, the so-called ringleader given 3 years in prison. By '*conditions of emergence*' (Smart, 1968: 76-77) I mean the type of *social and political conditions* that made it possible for the 'mugging' label to be imported and applied to describe a *particular sort* of crime, that was committed by a *particular sort* of people who live in a *particular sort* of area. The *'conditions of emergence'* specific to the 'mugging scare' of the early 1970s included management and organisational changes within the police force (Hall and others, 1978:38); low detection rates for particular inner-city crimes (Smith,1984: Hall and others,1978:49); the existence of widespread antagonism between the police and black communities (*Race & Class*, No.6, 1979; Hall and others, 1978: 44-46); Special Branch interest in the emergence and consolidation of Black Power in black communities (Bunyan, 1976; Hall and others, 1978: 45); police activity in black communities following the 1971 Immigration Act (Bunyan, 1976; *Race & Class*, No.6, 1979); and physical resistance by young black people to coercive policing methods (as indicated in the Introduction).

The assumptions underlying this section of the Chapter are that the police and the media manufactured the 'mugging' label in the 1970s for three principal reasons: **firstly**, to re-brand robbery and market it as a "new strain of crime;" **secondly**, to market the name 'mugger' as a code word meaning 'black criminal' and 'mugging' a code word for a black crime, resulting in *synonym* coming to exist between the label 'mugging' and black people, especially young black males and; **thirdly,** focus the public's attention on a *visible* crime; on the *visibility* of the criminal; on the *visibility* of the police response to the crime and the criminal and; on the *visibility* of crime reduction in terms of *visible* statistics.

The *visibility* of the police in tackling 'mugging' would be found in the *visibility* of the 'special measures' introduced by them, such as a special 'anti-mugging' squads that had been created to tackle this "new strain of crime." This final rationale, *the visibility of crime reduction initiatives*, has been linked to criticisms of the police about the *low detection rates* for a number of inner-city crimes such as burglary, car theft, pick-pocketing, handbag snatches, robberies and shoplifting that reached a peak in the mid 1960s to the early 1970s:

> Between 1955 and 1965, national detection rates for all indictable crime fell from 49 to 39 percent. This did not necessarily indicate a loss in efficiency, since the total annual volume cleared up increased by 108 per cent; but this showed a striking inability of detection to *keep pace* with the increased volume of reported crime. During the same period (1955-1965) the force was consistently 'below authorised strength' (by 13 per cent in 1955, 14 percent in 1965) and 'wastage' became a

growing problem. <u>As with detection rates, the position in London was worse.</u> The Royal Commission on the Police (1962) led to, proportionately, the biggest pay increase for police 'this century', but this failed to offset the growing arduousness of the job and the frustrating sense of losing the 'war against crime' (Hall and others, 1978: 49; *original emphasis*; <u>my emphasis).</u>

The re-branding of robbery as a 'mugging' and the lumping together of pick-pocketing and handbag snatches in 1972 offered the police a crime with a *higher visible* and *higher detection* rate. *But 'mugging' is neither a common law nor a statutory crime and no legal definition of 'mugging' exists in English law (Smith, 1984) but is an invented category.* The authors of '*Policing the Crisis*' identify 17th August 1972 as the date on which the *Daily Mirror* introduced to the British public the 'mugging' label: "*As Crimes of Violence Escalate, a Word Common in the United States enters the British Headlines: Mugging. To our Police, it's a frightening new strain of crime.*" However, according to Hall and others (1978:29):

> Strictly speaking, the facts about the crimes which both the police and the media were describing as 'novel' were not new; what was new was the way the label helped to break up and recategorise the general field of crime—the ideological frame which it laid across the field of social vision. What the agencies and the press were responding to was not simply a new set of facts but a new *definition of the situation*—a new construction of the social reality of crime. 'Mugging' provoked an organised response, in part because it was linked with a widespread *belief* about the alarming rate of crime in general, and with a common *perception* that rising crime was becoming more *violent*. These social aspects had entered into its meaning. *(original emphasis)*

The 'mugging' label therefore had its social origins as a *particularly violent* type of criminal activity that was associated with *declining areas* of the American cities and with the *black and poor populations* that reside there. The 'mugging' label was, therefore, a transatlantic transplant that was grafted onto Britain's policing strategy as a socially and racially defined type of offence that had violent connotations.

The Press and the Police: 'lies, damn lies and statistics'

A further problem lies in the relationship between *statistics* and reports of a *rising crime rate*. Crime has always been seen as *measurable* in terms of the number of incidents reported, their rise or reduction, all by the same criteria – *statistics*. But there are problems with statistics when applied to 'mugging.' In *Policing the Crisis* (1978; 29-52), the authors examined the *statistical basis* of the construction of the crime 'mugging' and found that this "*basis does not stand up well under scrutiny.*" They say:

> We concluded from this examination that the reaction to 'mugging' was out of proportion to any level of threat that could be constructed from the unreliable statistics. And since it appeared to be a response, at least in part, not to the actual threat, it must have been a reaction by the control agencies and the media to the *perceived or symbolic* threat to society—what the 'mugging' label *represented*. But this made the social reaction to mugging now as problematic—if not more so—than 'mugging' itself. When such discrepancies appear between threat and reaction, between what is perceived and what that is a perception of, we have good evidence to suggest we are in the presence of an ideological displacement. We call this displacement a *moral panic*....Since the public has little direct experience of crime, and very few people comparatively were 'mugged', the media must bear some responsibility for relaying the dominant definition of 'mugging' to the public at large (29-30, *original emphasis*; my emphasis).

What the police in the Britain sought to define as essentially a 'mugging' was but **one** type of robbery. Section 8 of the Theft Act, 1968, defines robbery thus: "*A person is guilty if he steals, and immediately before or at the time of doing so, he uses force on any person or puts or seeks to put any person in fear of being then and there subjected to force.*"

The law recognises two kinds of theft, categorised as robbery. **First,** *theft from property*, which includes armed robbery of banks, post offices, trains, as well as theft from homes (housebreaking/burglary). **Second**, there is *theft from the person* where force or the threat of force is used. *It is this second category of robbery which fits the police description of* *'mugging.'* But not all theft from the person involves force or the threat of force. For example, 'relieving' someone of personal property by stealth, such as pick pocketing, was not a "new strain of crime" in 1972, nor was purse or handbag snatching. Yet when the police compiled crime statistics, they included snatches, pick pocketing as well as robbery in the 'mugging' category. The **four** constituents of the so-called 'mugging' as coded by the police therefore become identifiable:

1. There is theft from the person.
2. The theft occurs in a public place, recently the streets—hence the term "street robbery."
3. The victim is white, the assailant usually "black" or part of a "black gang."
4. The 'gang' uses force, violence or threatens the use of force or violence. (Smith, 1984)

The 'mugging' phenomenon and an analysis of Ridgewell's arrests

We will see if any of Ridgewell's arrests fit the above description of the press/police-manufactured crime called a 'mugging.' The first thing to be said is that none of Ridgewell's 'victims' were accused of involvement in any acts of theft—save those they had confessed in the police station to have committed on occasions previous to their arrest and later disputed in Court. Of the 16 *known* cases involving Det. Sgt. Ridgewell no 'person' was robbed and therefore there were no 'victims' to produce in Court. Ridgewell's first four juvenile 'suspects' were charged with 'being a suspected person' and/or 'loitering with intent to commit an arrestable offence.' These were essentially 'Sus' charges that dated back to the period after the Napoleonic wars and the 1824 Vagrancy Act (*Time Out*, 5th-11th August, 1977). None were charged with an actual 'theft from the person' and no stolen property was found on any of them. The first four juveniles were acquitted of these offences and a complaint made to Transport police headquarters. Ridgewell appears to have changed the charges levelled at his next 12 'victims' from 'being a suspected person' to 'attempted theft from unknown persons.' Where this charge was applied the police again produced no aggrieved 'victims' because as with the first four accused no person was robbed and therefore no actual 'theft from the person' had occurred. In fact, the police did not find any stolen property on any of those accused (see *Race & Class*, Vol. XXlll, 1981/82:190 on 'Sus' 1). The additional 'assault on police' charges in the main resulted from the behaviour of the police when approaching the 'suspects'. *Violence is therefore introduced into the equation but not violence towards any 'victim' in the course of any robbery but towards the police themselves in them trying to arrest the 'suspects.'* In the second of the four cases, the 'Stockwell 6,' Ridgewell claimed to have acted as a 'decoy' on a train and one of the suspects pulled a knife on him and demanded money from him during an 'attempted robbery'—thus removing the need to obtain statements from any independent 'victims,' only the evidence from the police themselves becomes available. We recall that Ridgewell gave evidence, claiming that Harriott drew a knife on him and demanded "some bread, man."

But the youths contradicted this story, saying they were never on any train with Ridgewell so these events did not occur; he had made it all up. Moreover, the events described by the police could not have occurred in the time it took the train to make the journey between Stockwell and the Oval, as was shown by the BBC's 'Nationwide' programme.

It is because there were no independent 'victims' to these 'crimes' as such that police had to bolster their encounter with the 'suspects' by actual charges of 'violence' against the police. Here Ridgewell acts as both a *police witness to* and the *victim of* a robbery. The lack of evidence of actual theft by the suspects (not finding any stolen property on them) is overcome by the additional charges of theft and robbery coming from the 'confessions' and thus from the accused themselves, after threats and beatings.

In the 'Oval 4' case, as in the previous cases, the police narrative of the events leading to the arrests was designed so as to remove the need for independent witnesses. Because they were made-up events and did not occur but existed in the conspiratorial minds of the men involved, they had to rely on one another's testimony. In all of the arrests following these made-up encounters the accused gave evidence that they were threatened and beaten to make those admissions, later denied in Court. A modus operandi therefore becomes apparent, as noted by Hall and others (1978); by James Kingham, defence counsel at the original trial in 1972; by John Platts-Mills, QC, presenting our Appeal at the Royal Courts of Justice in 1973; by the *NCCL* in their collation of the concerns raised about the arrests by Ridgewell in 1973; and in the BBC's Nationwide programme's review of the four cases involving Ridgewell, also in 1973. I confirmed this in an interview with 'Keep Left' Socialist Newspaper in August 1973, that in each of these cases: "there is a system used by the police—attack, assault, beating, framing—bolstered up by perjured evidence about stealing from unknown persons with no independent witnesses".

It is police activity, including those of Ridgewell's 'anti-mugging' squad, that produced a 'self fulfilling' prophesy, especially about black involvement in 'urban' crime, from which a number of 'muggers' were manufactured in order to substantiate the existence of what is an *imaginary offence*. But its *imaginariness* is just part of the issue, as this *imaginariness* is socially grounded in and by the utilisation of mainly 'non-victim' offences—'being a suspected person' and/or 'attempted theft from unknown persons'—that act as a magician's 'smoke and mirrors' to produce a 'new strain of crime'.

The use of these 'non-victim' offences becomes part of what will be called the *tactics of preventive policing*, a strategy that targets people **before** they initiate a crime. On this point, Colin Maglashen suggested in *The Sunday Telegraph* (1/10/72) that in their 'War on Muggers' the police have tried to arrest 'muggers' **before** they go to steal. In what is known as *pre-emptive policing*, the police are seen as jumping the gap between "theoretical and empirical guilt" (Hall and others, 1978:41). A belief in the guilt of a suspect is converted into their actual guilt by police activity. Ridgewell's cases are classic examples of this 'quantum leap'. It is to be noted that two of the cases (February, 1972) involving Ridgewell's 'anti-mugging' squad took place months **before** the 'mugging panic' appears, and yet the police had already initiated special squads patrolling the underground. "The organisational response on the ground long predates any official judicial or media expression of public anxiety. The situation was defined by the police as one requiring swift, vigorous, more-than usual measures" (Hall and others, 1978: 40).

The argument at the core of this section has been that the police actually manufactured 'mugging' as a particular type of crime requiring a particular response and in that process created the 'mugger.' What becomes clear in all four cases involving Ridgewell is that together they follow the pattern of a 'focused police response' and we see it is beneath the streets—either on the underground platforms or in the empty tube carriages—that the 'mugging panic' first appears. Now called a "street crime" it in fact emerged first on the underground: beneath the streets and under the jurisdiction of Ridgewell's 'anti-mugging' squad.

In fact, it was not until October 1972, well after the 'mugging scare' was underway and every (other) 'theft from the person' in the inner city was described as a 'mugging' that Home Secretary, Robert Carr, wrote to Chief Constables throughout the country asking them to send him details of "the prevalence of such offences, and ...to what extent special measures are being taken by Chief Officers of police to deal with them." But, according to the *NCCL*, the letter from the Home Secretary to Chief Constables had to include some sort of definition of 'mugging' under which various 'crimes' were (liable) to be grouped and coded before being reported to the Home Secretary as 'mugging' (*West Indian World*, 4th May 1973). His definition of 'mugging' was: "robberies by gangs of 2 or more youths on people alone out in the open" (Hall and others, 1978:8). The Home Secretary's focus was on the streets of the metropolis rather than the underground passages of the railway system.

In Chapter 2, the *Daily Mirror* report defined 'muggings' as taking place in the open spaces while the *Evening Standard* report spoke of the underpasses leading to the Underground system. But the variance between the definitions in stories in different papers and between theirs and the police's definition is perhaps not the issue. The point to be secured is that for the police the plasticity of the 'mugging' label served as a method to assist them in improving their *clear-up* rate for crimes that had once eluded a resolution. In Chapter One I recalled being read incidents from an 'unsolved crimes' register to which I was to admit so to enable the police to improve the 'clear-up rate' for the Brixton area.

The 'mugging' paradox

One measure of police efficiency in the early 1970s was the 'clear-up rate' (Hall and others, 1978: 38) as set against the background of 'rising crime.' Therefore, the pressure to improve 'clear up rates' plus the problems of manpower and resources made it *logical* for the police to concentrate on crimes with 'high detection potential' at the expense of crimes with 'low detection potential,' such as petty larceny from cars and burglaries, which were virtually unsolvable. But this *logical* practice turns out to be an *organising* and *structuring* one in that it *amplifies the volume* of these selected crimes, since the more resources are concentrated, the greater number recorded. As the authors explain:

> The paradox is that the selectively of police reaction
> to selected crimes almost certainly serves to *increase*
> their number (what is called a deviancy amplification

spiral). It will also tend to produce this increase in the form of a cluster, or a 'crime wave'. When the 'crime wave' is then invoked to justify a 'control campaign', it becomes a 'self-fulfilling prophesy'. Of course, public concern about particular crimes can also be the cause of a focused police response. But public concern is itself strongly shaped by the criminal statistics (which the police produce and interpret for the media) and the impression that there is 'wave after wave' of types of crime. Of course, the contribution of criminals to 'crime waves' is only too visible, whereas the contribution the police themselves make to the construction of crime waves is virtually invisible.(1978: 38, *original emphasis, my emphasis*).

In other words, what the police choose to define as a problem ('mugging') and focus resources on it not only heightens police awareness of such incidents in terms of what to look for; Ridgewell said in evidence that on the Northern Line he would be particularly on the lookout for "coloured men." The incidents codified as a 'mugging' and recorded under the 'mugging' label serves to increase the prevalence of this "*new strain of crime*" as policy makers and the public are recruited to use the new label. The label does not define the crime itself, it serves to describe, in dramatic terms, the social anxieties created as a result.

As the authors show, while 'public concern' about a particular type of crime may cause a 'focused police response' public concern is often itself shaped by 'criminal statistics' produced and interpreted by the police—as in the data requested by and sent to the Home Secretary about the supposed prevalence of 'mugging.' The circle was now complete. The Home Secretary was able to report to Parliament that Chief Constables report an increase in 'muggings' and the press would then circulate it to the public, creating 'fear' and the judiciary would respond to those convicted with prison sentences which reflect this 'public concern'.

The authors conclude that an amplifying factor in the 'mugging' issue was precisely the *decision* set up 'special squads' to tackle this sort of *crime*, and that it was "almost certain" to produce more of those *crimes* as an "unintended but inevitable consequence of specialist mobilisation." They go on:

Then there is the question of precisely what it is which these special squads were being mobilised against. In the 'Oval 4' and 'Rhodesian students' cases, the Anti-Mugging Squad bought charges of 'attempted theft', i.e. pick-pocketing. Pick-pocketing is an example of 'petty larceny', not of 'robbery', i.e. involves no use of force. It is quite a different situation, however, when the Anti-Mugging Squad descends on a group, accuses them of picking pockets, and then implies that they are members of a 'mugging gang'. Here 'petty larceny' has been escalated by being relabelled as 'mugging'.

Further there were signs in these early cases of a tendency on the part of these 'anti-mugging' squads to be "so eager to prosecute their task" that they were already prone to jump the gap between "theoretical and empirical guilt"—a belief in someone's guilt *before* evidence comes to light of their guilt. It is in this light that Ridgewell's comments become particularly relevant, where he actually indulges in activity to substantiate his 'suspicions'.

CHAPTER 4

"I just went Bent":
The Demise of Detective Sergeant
Derek Arnold Ridgewell

Is it you? Oh yea
Is it you? Oh yea
Is it you? Oh yea
I say pressure drop
Oh pressure, Oh yea, pressure drop on you
I say, pressure drop
Oh pressure, Oh yea, pressure drop on you
I say, Oh when it drop you got to feel it
Oh but you were doing wrong
I say, Oh when it drop you got to feel it
Oh but you were doing wrong
('Pressure Drop,' The Maytals, 1970)

When you going to dig a pit,
my brother, don't dig one always dig two.
(*'Iron Sharpen Iron,' Culture, 1977*)

This Chapter presents research on Derek Ridgewell who we shall see below was eventually exposed as a 'corrupt policeman' in May 1978, six years after his encounter with the 'Oval 4.' What has been unearthed makes interesting reading and the story it tells amounts to a vindication of what we have always maintained: *that we are innocent of all charges and that Ridgewell was a liar and a corrupt policeman who made up all of the events that led to our imprisonment.* What emerges is as much about him as it is about the organisation of the British Transport Police that he implicated in his deception and *his corruption.*

What I tried to do during the trial was expose *his corruption* and though this move was not *immediately* successful, what it did do was to initiate the process that led to his eventual demise. That demise came on Friday 31st December 1982 when LI8072 Ridgewell was found dead, collapsed by one of the toilets on his landing around 5.20am at HMP Ford. He had a heart attack. It is ironic that Ridgewell died in prison while serving a prison sentence for 'conspiracy to steal,' one of the charges levelled by the DPP against the 'Oval 4,' of which we were all acquitted.

Researching Ridgewell

In carrying out research on Derek Ridgewell's background, I made several requests under the *Freedom of Information Act* to the Headquarters of the British Transport Police in Camden to see what information they held on him. I wrote to Brian Coleman, Freedom of Information Manager (in March and November 2005) and spoke to him on two occasions. He told me that while he remembered Ridgewell the Transport Police no longer kept any records or information as the policy is that once they have reached seven years these are destroyed. What he was saying was that no case papers or files existed on him that date back to 1978. After speaking to him I got the impression that the Transport Police no longer wished to be associated with Ridgewell and if it could be denied he had ever worked for them then they would so deny. I decided to try and get information on him from another source.

On making the same request to the Home Office I received quite a lot of information from the National Offender Management Service (NOMS) which included some important information on Ridgewell's background provided to the Prison service by the Transport Police. I made requests to the Central Criminal Court and they said they no longer held any transcripts from that time. After contacting the Court of Appeal, Criminal Division, I was refused access to information on any investigative proceedings against Ridgewell and on his Appeal. Similar information was requested and refused from NOMS at the Home Office, as *some of this was deemed exempt from disclosure* under the Freedom of Information Act, 2000. That in itself is revealing in that there is information held on Ridgewell which is not for public disclosure. I did, however, manage to find out what some of it might be. The rest remains untraceable. What information I did find is set out below.

Ridgewell's background

Derek Arnold Ridgewell was born on 9th of May, 1945 in Glasgow, Scotland and was the eldest of two sons, Paul being the younger brother. He attended infant's School in Glasgow and in 1952, aged 7, his family moved south to England to live in Bromley, Kent. He received what was described as an 'elementary' secondary education and won a scholarship to attend the South London Technical College. In June 1962 he left College aged 17 with 4 'O' levels. Between July and October 1962 he worked as a Clerk in Brockley, SE4. From October 1962 to February 1963 he was employed as a Clerk in Forest Hill, SE23. From February 1963 to May 1964 he worked with his mother as Assistant Manager at the Earl of Warwick Pub in Deptford, SE8. Now aged 19 he joined British Transport Police as a Constable in May 1964 and remained with them for 1 year and 5 months, until October 1965.

Ridgewell and the British South African Police (BSAP) force

According to Transport police records he left in late October to serve for 1 year as a Police Officer in the Rhodesian police force, known then as the British South African Police (BSAP) force, in Southern Rhodesia. His adventures in Rhodesia were cut short after just three weeks when the political situation between this African colony and Britain changed dramatically. On 11th November, 1965 Ian Smith declared Rhodesia independent of British rule and Harold Wilson, the British Labour Prime Minister, declared this an *illegal act* and imposed sanctions on the white-run African colony. Transport Police records show that he returned to England as a consequence of this Unilateral Declaration of Independence (UDI), and on his return, Ridgewell told the *Bromley and Kentish Times* (19/11/65) that he **had** planned to leave Rhodesia (or "escape" as he put it) and had not *deserted—even though he fled* during the 'State of Emergency' declared by Ian Smith.

In the interview with Tom Mangle from the BBC he implied that 'fear' wasn't his reason for leaving but rather it was that he had been told during his 'military-style' training that if he had to use a firearm on Africans, to 'shoot them dead' so as to save the cost of medical treatment. He claimed also to have witnessed brutality meted out to Africans who had gathered to "greet" the British Prime Minister, Harold Wilson, during his visit to Salisbury (interview with Tom Mangle from the BBC as reported in the 'Nationwide' programme, *Cause for Concern*, aired 30/7/73).

Against the background of reports of brutality on African demonstrators and the general treatment of the black population by the white police, Ridgewell's claim that he did not like how he was being asked to treat Africans may have rested well with the public mood in

Britain about the treatment of 'blacks' or 'coloureds' in 'rebel' Rhodesia. This makes his flight from Rhodesia border on 'heroism' rather than 'cowardice' and he may well have been greeted as a returning 'hero' when he rejoined the Transport Police the following month: "*Bromley man in Rhodesian police drama,*" was the heading of a report in the *Bromley and Kentish Times* (19/11/65). Riding on the wave of 'heroism' on his return to England and to Bromley, after his interview by the local press he went to see the MP for Bromley, Mr John Hunt, (19/11/65) at the House of Commons to thank him for his assistance in contacting the Commonwealth Relations Office at the request of him mother during his anxious 'escape.'

Ridgewell claimed he'd 'tricked' his way out of Rhodesia on the Sunday but was stopped in Beira, Mozambique, by Portuguese officials when he and two others tried to board a London-bound plane. The intervention of the Foreign Office at the request of his local MP aided his flight to Nairobi, Kenya, and from there on to London, arriving the following Saturday (*Bromley and Kentish Times* (12/11/65; 19/11/65)

Running away from 'colonial adventure'

That he could leave Britain and so seamlessly join the British South Africa Police force is telling of the cultural ties and administrative relationship that existed between Britain and Rhodesia prior to Ian Smith making his Unilateral Declaration of Independence (UDI). Ridgewell reported to the *Bromley and Kentish Times* (19/11/65) that he and 36 others had travelled to Rhodesia from Britain but only he and two of them 'escaped.' A consideration is that Ridgewell may well have left the Transport Police and Britain to seek 'adventure' and 'opportunities' in policing in the British South Africa Police (BSAP)— the remnants of Britain's dwindling colonial Empire and one of the last bastions of white rule in Africa. He said as much to the *Bromley and Kentish Times* (19/11/65): that he wanted to join the Rhodesian police force "*to see a bit of the world and get more experience of police work*" but clamed what he saw "disillusioned" and "sickened" him, he told his mother in a letter (*Bromley and Kentish Times*, 12/11/65).

Up to the late 1960s Colonial Service was regarded as one of the sites of and routes to *racial manhood and masculinity* where "'real masculinity' could only be constituted in and through colonial adventure" (Benyon, 2002: 31). As this route to *manhood* was not possible in colonial Africa he sought this *rite of passage* through policing in the Britain's 'internal colonies' instead. The BBC's 1973 review of Ridgewell's 16 arrests showed that he may well have taken these *colonial tactics* with him to policing in the 'inner cities, appearing to be quite comfortable with the kind of tactics he claimed to have disdained but nonetheless absorbed from his brief introduction to policing and in the general attitude toward black people held by Police recruits and officials during his short time in Rhodesia. His attitudes and actions certainly showed that he felt generally that black people had no rights he should respect and because they were black were highly suspect, as the case in Southern Rhodesia and South Africa.

Back to policing in London's 'internal colony'

Now back in the Britain he seamlessly rejoined the British Transport Police as a Constable in December 1965 and, after 5 years service, in January 1971 was promoted to the rank of Sergeant, and not 12 months later, in December 1971, was appointed Detective Sergeant. The 'Robbery Squad' was formed around January 1972 with him as its leader.

With this promotion he began to set the tone for the work of the Robbery, or the *'anti-mugging* squad,' as it was to become known in the Press. And on 2nd February, 1972, Ridgewell and his squad made their first arrests: enter the 'Waterloo 4.' With that 'success' under his belt he, later that month on 18th February, cornered the 'Stockwell 6' at the Oval station using the 'squad's 'emerging *trade-mark: real* brutality, *false* arrest, *false* 'evidence' and *false* 'confessions.' Having lost the first case he won the second after changing tactics (see Chapter 3) and, as a consequence of this arrest, became quite skilled in fabricating 'evidence' that would ensure a conviction. He seemed determined to make a 'success' of his *new* title, his *new* role and the *new* 'responsibilities' attached to this role and needed, therefore, to justify the existence and independence of the 'Robbery Squad,' and key to this was the *arrests and convictions rate*. To improve this *rate* he and his 'gang' set about lurking on the underground stations, on platforms, stairwells and passageways in south-east London on the look-out for more black people to turn into his 'victims.'

On the night of 16th March the 'Oval 4' came into the sight of his 'lookout' on the southbound platform of the Northern line, while he and the rest of his 'gang' posed as tube passengers, hanging about at the bottom and at top of the escalator at the Oval station. As we made our way up the crowded escalator they proceeded with their plan to block our way, pounce on us at the top of the escalator and corner us to prevent us from leaving the station. The rest, as they say, is history. But his plan was to make arrests each month seemed to have stalled after his confrontation with the 'Oval 4.'

It wasn't until 5 months later in the August that he and his squad 'successfully' pounced on the two Zimbabweans at Tottenham Court Road Station. He made no more arrests in the 'steaming" *trade-mark* style of the 'squad' and by the following August (1973) the 'Robbery Squad' was disbanded and Ridgewell moved to 'other duties within the same rank' (South London Press, 5/8/73).

From 'Hero' to 'Zero'

A question which needs asking and answering is why when confront-ed with similar evidence as put before Judge Edward Cussens did Judge Gwynn Morris come to a startlingly different conclusion to that of the Judge in the 'Oval 4' case six months earlier? Gwynn Morris believed the two Oxford-based Zimbabweans; Edward Cussens did not believe the four London-based Caribbeans. The differences may be explained as follows:

1. Ridgewell appeared confused as a result of his confrontation with the 'Oval 4' where, on the one hand, he must have felt he'd 'got away' with his deception, albeit with the help of the prosecution and Judge Edward Cussens yet, on the other hand his actions appeared *cautious, confused and overconfident; cautious* in that he and his 'gang' avoided south London tube stations, choosing instead stations in the West End but sticking to ones on the Northern Line. *Confused and overconfident* in that he tried the same tactics on two Zimbabweans and used similarly *careless and uncorroborated evidence.*

2. The trial Judge recognised Ridgewell's two *victims* as African young men who, according to their back-grounds, were attending a College course in Oxford and not as London-based Caribbean men whom the national press had been identified as 'muggers' during 1972 and 1973. Indeed, in a twist, one of the Zimbabweans told Lynn Lewis from the BBC that when the men pounced on him, he thought they (Ridgewell

and his 'tube gang') were themselves 'muggers' and he and his companion were going to be violently robbed. It must have become clear to the Judge that by the way these men spoke and dressed, and from their backgrounds that they were 'overseas students' and had indeed lost their way, as they had claimed, in the maze that is Tottenham Court Road Underground station.

3. Ridgewell and his 'gang' in producing their weak and contradictory evidence to the Court were *overconfident* in hoping for—even relying on—some assistance from the trial Judge and from prosecuting counsel as he had done in the 'Oval 4' case. None of this occurred and had his latest and final case was thrown out of Court. After the Appeal hearing in July 1973 and the negative publicity about his behaviour in black communities in London, Ridgewell was taken off 'frontline duties' and given a 'desk job,' away from underground stations and the black public, and the 'Robbery Squad' disbanded after only 18 months in operation.

Ridgewell's meeting with 'real criminals'

Having been found a new role away from underground stations and passengers, he was moved from his 'desk job' and transferred to Waterloo Goods Depot to investigate the theft of goods from there between 1974 and 1975, about 12 months. He was then transferred to the Bricklayers Arms Good Depot in the middle of 1976 to investigate the theft of 'goods in transit.' These job transfers were a direct result of his 'failure' in so-called *'anti-mugging'* activities and it signalled his down-fall because at the Bricklayers Arms Goods Depot he decided to turn to crime himself, getting involved with *real criminals.*

Around July 1976 Ridgewell was asked by London Transport headquarters to head-up another 'special squad' of detectives to investigate the 'enormous quantity' of goods being stolen from Bricklayers Arms Goods Depot. His 'team' on this occasion included DC Ellis and DC Keeling and they set to work observing the movement of goods from the Depot, as they claimed to have been doing in the 'Oval 4' case.

In February 1977 Ridgewell and Ellis detained, questioned and arrested of two members of the original Bricklayers 'gang,' Anthony

Jeff and Thomas Pearson, as they were driving out of the Depot with a vanload of parcels. According to the *Daily Mail* report (23/1/80) at the trial of Jeff and Pearson at Tower Bridge Magistrates court, both men were said to have received "more consideration" from the two detectives, Ridgewell and Ellis, than was regarded as "normal," resulting in Jeff being fined £200 and Pearson given a suspended sentence.

After the case, Ridgewell and Ellis met the two 'removal men' at a Pub in Catford, south London, where Jeff told Ridgewell that he could get one third of the 'market value' of goods from the Depot, of which 50% would go to the police and the other 50% to Jeff and sons. Ridgewell and Ellis on realising how easy stealing was went into partnership with them; in fact the detectives gave the 'say-so' about what would be taken, when it would be taken and how it was to be transported from the Depot. One Sunday a van was packed with stolen goods and Ridgewell arranged for the van to be given a 'police escort' from Bricklayers Arms. The goods fetched just under £1600 when sold, £800 of which was the police share. On another Sunday stolen goods were transported from the Depot in a police van. From their arrival at the depot in January 1977, during the 11 months from the May of 1977 to the April 1978, Ridgewell and his police 'gang' actually organised the theft of goods from the Bricklayers Arms Goods Depot.

During these 11 months about 60 vanloads of 'hand picked' parcels disappeared from the Goods Depot every weekend and in one weekend Ridgewell (and two police colleagues) netted £2700, their cut of goods sold. In total the detectives reaped around £47,000 for those 'transactions.' Such was the organisation that to prevent disputes the Detectives provided a typewritten list of what had been taken and its mail-order value, and a University graduate, an articled accountant named Geoffrey Baggott was recruited to act as negotiator. But it all began to unravel when one a member of the Jeff family was arrested by Regional Crime Squad officers in February 1978 in the act of transporting stolen goods out of the Depot. They too had been sent in to see why the thefts were continuing. Regional Crime Squad officers arrested and interviewed Jeff to find out who else was involved in the Bricklayers Arms 'scam.'

The Demise of Det. Sgt. Ridgewell

On Sunday 14th May, 1978, DS Ridgewell was arrested at Bricklayers Arms by Regional Crime Squad officers who had been called in by British Transport Police to investigate the continuing disappearance of parcels from the Goods Depot, even though Ridgewell, Ellis and Keeling had been sent there two years earlier to stem the tide of thefts. While the Transport Police investigated his activities he was immediately suspended from his duties, to later resign from his job as a Detective Sergeant in the Transport Police on 31st July, 1978. He then set-up a Tobacconist/Confectioners/General store in Beckenham, Kent, with one of his Bricklayers Arms Goods Depot *co-conspirators,* former Detective Constable Douglass Ellis.

On 27th June, 1979, Derek Arnold Ridgewell was committed at Tower Bridge Magistrates Court for trial and sentencing at the Central Criminal Court set for 21st January, 1980. He was charged with one count of 'Conspiracy to Steal,' to which he pleaded guilty, and with two counts of 'Corruptly Receiving Gifts,' to which he pleaded not guilty. He was remanded on bail. It was over 12 months between his arrest in May 1978 to his committal in June 1979, and his case took a further 6 months to be heard. During these 18 months Ridgewell, his wife, Jennifer Ridgewell [nee Wilkinson] and Douglass Ellis apparently worked in the shop. As the Central Criminal Court claimed not to hold any information on his trial and sentencing, the national press became a source of information.

On Tuesday 22nd January 1980, Ridgewell was back at the Old Bailey, and on this occasion the Recorder of London sentenced him to 7 years imprisonment, and his co-conspirator in the deception, DC Ellis, given 6 years and DC Keeling, 2 years, after all pleading guilty to *Conspiracy to Steal.* The case and sentencing reported the following day under the headlines: *"Railway Police Join Gang in Depot Looting"* (*Daily Telegraph* 23/1/80); *"Rail Police Robbers Jailed"* (*Evening Standard*, 23/1/80); *"Rail Detectives Joined in Massive Thefts Plot"* (*Daily Mail*, 2 3/1/80) and *"Five Rail Police Goaled for Thefts"* (*Guardian*, 23/1/80).

The case against Ridgewell

According to the public prosecutor, Kenneth Richardson, thefts at the Bricklayers Arms goods depot during 1975 and 1976 had reached a "scandalous figure" that by the middle of 1976 a Special Squad of Detectives from Transport Police headquarters were sent in to investigate how thousands of pounds worth of goods had disappeared from the Depot. The Transport Police's Special 'Anti-Theft' Squad was headed DS Derek Ridgewell and his associates on this occasion were DC Douglass Ellis and DC Alan Keeling, and must have expected that the thefts would decrease, if not cease, with the intervention of

Ridgewell's new 'squad.'

In the 15 months between January 1977 and April 1978 instead of the "scandalous" scale of thefts decreasing they had actually increased, with goods valued at £364,000 'stolen in transit' through the Bricklayers Arms (*Guardian*, 23/1/80). The *Daily Telegraph*'s headline, 'Railway Police Join Gang in Depot Looting' summed up the situation: that the detectives actually joined in the thefts rather than acting to prevent them. In fact, Ridgewell's new team took over the organisation of the thieving from the criminals operating at the depot, and went on to use police resources to ease their transportation from the Depot.

Recorder of London, James Miskin, told Ridgewell and Ellis on sentencing that: "*Without any excuse or explanation you helped others ship out of this Depot Lord knows how much stolen property and I shall never know where it went or who got what from the proceeds,*" and to Alan Keeling said: "*It must be clearly understood by police and public that, when police dishonestly fail in their duty, failure will be met by an instant term of imprisonment.*"

Keeling had become so frightened by the scale of thefts taking place that he asked for a transfer away from Bricklayers Arms (*Daily Telegraph*, 23/1/80). Jeffrey Baggott, an accountant from Beckenham recruited by Ridgewell to ensure that there would be 'honour amongst thieves'— that each would be paid their dues from the sale of the stolen goods, was convicted of theft and sentenced to two and a half years. All had pleaded guilty. The other members of Ridgewell's 'depot gang' were convicted and sentenced to various terms in jail. Ridgewell then underwent the de-personalisation process all had undergone before him, people whom he'd lied about to the Courts to guarantee them being processed as prisoners.

Ridgewell's prison confession: "I just went bent"

Two reports were compiled on Ridgewell whilst in prison; the first soon after he was received at Wormwood Scrubs, dated 14th February, 1980; the other on 12th March just before transfer to HMP Ford. On 14th February at Wormwood Scrubs, identifying information was collected on the *Standard Classification Form* upon which an assessment of his prison category and any safety risks would be based. For example, it held that he was 34 years old, had been married for 84 months (7 years), lived with his wife (Jennifer) in Bromley, Kent, for about 30 months, and both parents were dead. Under trade or profession a 'Clerk' was identified but his last job was as a Shop Assistant earning £90 per week, and his longest job (168 months) was entered as 'Police.' In the final section on 'Reactions to Sentence' it says:

> It is hard to understand why Ridgewell had succumbed to join the criminal element when asked this question he replied *"I just went bent."* He seems to have accepted this sentence with no remorse in fact it's as if he gives the impression of being somebody who has done many custodial sentences. A very confident man who says the only ambition whilst in prison is to work for the parole date. A married man who ... states the relationship with his wife is good he will be expecting visits from her wherever he is allocated. It is too early to know how he will react although with his previous good character should not present any control or security problems (14/2/1980).

Ridgewell's new lies

In the 'Allocation' report completed also on 14th February under the section headed *Criminality*, Ridgewell *told a strange and apparently made-up story* when asked about the offence for which he was imprisoned. He told the Assistant Governor that he "stupidly" *became involved in these offences because of an informant.* The informant, he said, had given him some information for which he asked his superiors for some money to pay the informant. When the money was not forthcoming he told the informant that he would give him some goods as a "present."

Ridgewell claimed that the informant had photographs of him handing over the goods and, from then on, he and his colleagues "had to continue with their dishonesty." I could not find any information to corroborate this account given by him to the Assistant Governor, as it seems to be information that the press would certainly have reported as evidence of the *pattern* of police corruption in his case. But like the reason given for his *flight* from Rhodesia and for his current 'fall from grace' he seems to have implied that both were *reactions to forces and conditions outside* of his control. Given the made-up story about his experiences in Rhodesia, the way he subsequently treated black people in Britain makes the reason given for his flight from organised cruelty in Rhodesia laughable, as was the reaction in the Court of Appeal when this reason was given in July1973.

It is my belief that *Ridgewell was* someone prone to 'making things up' to give a *false impression of who he thought he was or wanted to be seen as,* either in pursuit of *honour* or to suggest he was *forced* into doing what he did. The Assistant Governor's report states that Ridgewell says that he has "accepted the sentence but shows little remorse." But the *'bent copper'* had been deceptive in at least two instances on reception to Wormwood Scrubs, certainly about him being 'forced into criminality' by the Jeff family.

Statements taken on him from two inmates at HPM Ford made after his sudden death suggested that Ridgewell presented an image of himself that was a false one, especially about his failing health—the same false story he passed on to his brother, Paul, that was repeated at the inquest into his death. The other inmate said he *did not believe* everything Ridgewell told him. In other words, other prisoners found him not believable as he seemed to have deliberately misled all whom he had interactions with, both inside and outside prison, including the Government (i.e. Lord Hailsham in 1973), the Director of Public Prosecutions (DPP) who processed the false charges, British Transport officials who did not properly investigate the numerous complaints made against him, the Metropolitan Police force who assisted him, the Judiciary and the Press, and even his own family.

His Appeal against sentence

On the *Standard Classification Form* completed at the 'Scrubs' on 14th February he circled 'Neither' to indicate he was not intending to appeal against conviction or sentence. However, he must have changed his mind and decided to submit an appeal against his sentence, submitting his application for leave to the Court of Appeal sometime in April or May 1980. In 1980 the Appeals criteria are set out in Section 31, Criminal Appeal Act, 1968, which provided 28 days from the date of sentence to submit an application for leave to appeal to the Court of Appeal, Criminal Division.

In submitting form NG (Notice and Grounds) to the Court of Appeal, the Single Judge needed to be persuaded that leave **should** be granted, supported by the grounds upon which the appeal will be based. If leave is refused the Applicant has a further 14 days to resubmit that appeal for a hearing before the Full Court, that is, before three Judges. Applicants had also, in 1980, to consider a ruling issued by the High Court on 14th February (effective 15th February), that the Court should penalise 'frivolous' or 'hopeless' applications, meaning that appeals which stood little or no chance of success, or were not supported and signed by Counsel; then the applicant should lose time (usually the time their application took to process) and that this time should not count towards the sentence they serve. In other words, they should "lose time" already served or have extra time added on for wasting the Court's time. Considering the above rules in relation to what we know about Ridgewell's case, he had 28 days in which to apply for leave to appeal starting from the date of sentence, which was 22/1/80. The 28 days would take him up to 19th February.

We know that he indicated that he did not wish to appeal against conviction nor sentence on a document dated 14th February while at Wormwood Scrubs. After he was transferred to Ford one month later, on 14th March 1980, it was after this date that he apparently submitted his application for leave to appeal, well beyond the 28 day time limit. He would therefore have had to apply for leave to submit his appeal *out of time*. Interestingly enough, the High Court's ruling about 'frivolous' or 'hopeless' appeals was made on 14th February, the same day as Ridgewell indicated that he was not going to appeal

His appeal against sentence was therefore submitted *after* his arrival at Ford on 14th March, probably April or May, *out of time,* and on 3rd September 1980, he received notification that leave to appeal against his sentence had been refused by that Single. Apparently, days before he received his notification from the High Court, he sent a renewed application for leave to appeal which was received by the Court also on 3rd September, 1980, but this time for a hearing before the Full Court, but leave to appeal was again refused. He was informed by the Registrar on 18th September that Single Judge's decision is final, according to Section 12 (4) of the Criminal Appeals Rules, 1968. I requested a copy of the notification by the Single Judge which set out the specific reasons why his appeal against his sentence was rejected and was told by the Court of Appeal that this information was exempt from public disclosure under the s32 of the Freedom of Information Act, 2000, concerning Court records. According to Section 32(3) the Court of Appeal stated, quoting Section 32(3), that *"there is do duty to either confirm or deny whether the information requested is held by the Court Service."* (Correspondence 2/8/06).

A previous request (17/6/06) made to the National Offender Management Service (NOMS) asked if they held information on Ridgewell that was exempt from public disclosure under the Act. The reply (5/7/06) received was essentially the same as that received from the Court of Appeal: that they *"neither confirm nor deny"* whether such information is held by them, but in this instance cited Section 30(3) that related *"to investigations and proceedings conducted by public authorities,"* and this exemption over-rides the issue of 'public interest' to whether there is a duty to disclose or not disclose such information if it were held by them. In other words, they cannot say whether they held such information or not, and as the questioned information related to investigations conducted on Ridgewell by public authorities, their refusal to confirm or deny overrides any consideration of a public duty to disclose such information, even if it were held by them.

I followed-up this request for additional information (5 /9/06) held on Ridgewell while he was in Ford prison and was sent some "redacted" (edited with some names/information deleted) copies of *disclosable* information on Ridgewell but was, again, told that some of the information requested was exempt under Section 40(3), *concerned with disclosure of third party information, and such a disclosure would have been in breach of the Data Protection Act, 1998, because some of the documents requested held third party information, such as names of people other than Ridgewell.*

However, it has been possible to deduce what the reasons could be why Ridgewell's leave to Appeal was refused by the Single Judge, and why the Court of Appeal and the Home Office refused access to this information. Starting with why leave to appeal against his sentence was rejected, one reason could be that it was submitted 'out of time.' Another might be that it was submitted without the approval of Counsel or, according to 1980 rules, was considered 'hopeless' or a waste of time' by the Court. However, I have other information which leads me to believe that the reasons behind the refusal is that the Court Records in question show that the two counts of 'Corruptly accepting Gifts' involved *other* Transport police officers—to which he pleaded not guilty—were to be 'kept on file' and *"Not to be proceeded with without leave from the Central Criminal Court or the Court of Appeal, Criminal Division."*

The documents which support this action by the Court are, I believe, (1) the result of the London Transport Police investigation in 1978 that led to the three charges, *two of which were held on file in Court records, presumably referred to by the Single Judge in coming to this decision and the subject of s30 (2) of the Act* and; (2) the same documents held at the Home Office's NOMS in Ridgewell's file, *actually name the other Transport Police Officers involved and identified* as his *co-conspirator* in the (pre-trial) allegations of police corruption, namely Douglass Ellis. As I requested information on Ridgewell alone, *this would have breached* their responsibilities under the Data Protection Act, 1998, concerned with disclosure of third party information, which falls under s40(3) of the Freedom of Information Act, 2000. But an underlying reason may be that he **could not** appeal against his sentence as he was convicted for an offence for which there was set a standard minimum sentence—7 years, which he got.

Ellis and Keeling received lesser sentences for the same offence but as Ridgewell was the 'ringleader' he got the highest sentence. Also an appeal against sentence must show that the sentence was 'manifestly excessive' which could not be shown by the facts of the case. As the road to his Appeal seemed blocked Ridgewell turned his attention to his chances of Parole. These above events take us to the end of 1980. I not could find any information on his 'prison adventures' for the 12 months of 1981 at HMP Ford.

Protesting about Parole

Between January and September 1982 Ridgewell and other prisoners caused some concern to the prison staff at Ford to the effect that a memorandum, dated 13/7/82, was sent to the Home Office by the Governor at Ford. Its contents informed the Home Office that Ridgewell, "together with a number of other prisoners had been in correspondence" with the National Counsel for Civil Liberties (NCCL) about the policy of non-selection of long term prisoners for parole: specifically "that the LRC (Local Review Committee) at Ford has a rule that they will never grant more than 12 months parole." The memo stated that the NCCL had asked three of those concerned to complete Legal Aid Applications "for a proposed action for "Judicial Review" of the LRC decision to refuse parole to all except those with only 12 months left to serve," and informed the Home Office that these forms had already been signed and returned by the time the prison authorities became aware of the prisoners' complaints. The Governor expressed his certainty that the case bought by the named prisoners and supported by the NCCL has "no foundation."

Ridgewell and Ellis were among those inmates who completed and returned legal aid forms to the NCCL, but what Ridgewell did not know, the memo reports, was that he was recommended for Parole by the Local Review Committee (LRC) at Ford in January 1982, but this recommendation was not accepted by the National Parole Board, and his case was set for review in January 1983. The details of his involvement in this 'campaign' are not important in themselves, only insofar as it provides information as to Ridgewell's character.

A question which needs asking is: was a reason for his involvement in this 'campaign' about he and other prisoners being 'discriminated' against by the Parole system at Ford result from his failed Appeal in September 1980? Another consideration is that by involvement in this action himself attempted to demonstrate some *competence* to other prisoners and the *NCCL,* if only that learnt while serving as a corrupt police detective.

The reports of Ridgewell's death in prison 'are not greatly exaggerated'

Three months after the pursuing his chances for Parole, on the morning of 31st December 1982 at 5.20am, Derek Arnold Ridgewell was found collapsed in a toilet on his landing. On examination by a Night Duty Officer 'no pulse was found.' He was dead. A prison officer was put outside to guard the toilet where he lay and the procedures for reporting the death of a prisoner were set in place. A medical examination found that he died from a heart attack –a *Myocardial Infarction,* and an Inquest later recorded death by 'natural causes.' To understand why and how Ridgewell collapsed and died in prison we need to try and understand his state of mind and his physical health. It is possible to get some idea of Ridgewell's *character* from his discussions with other inmates and with prison staff and information on his *state of physical health* from medical staff records at both prisons.

We turn to his *character* first and then to his state of *health.* After his death statements were taken from inmates who had been with him in the evening prior to his collapse. Two inmates made statements giving their relationship with Ridgewell and their impressions of him. In a statement taken on 4th January 1983, inmate 'A' reported his contact and relationship with the former policeman. This inmate had worked with him on the Estate, became friends and visited one another in their rooms, but, he said, more "especially over the past 2 months" Ridgewell "was losing weight" and "had lost weight very rapidly." Ridgewell told him "he wasn't eating too well" and had been to see the Prison Doctor to "get some medical advice," but when he saw the Doctor Ridgewell said that he told them he was "constipated," for which he was given some "medicine."

On the evening of 30th December they finished work at about 4.50pm and returned to their rooms. At about 7.40 Ridgewell came to his room where they "passed the time of day." During that "passing the time" Ridgewell bought up the subject of his features "becoming drawn" which had been mentioned in a letter from his younger brother, Paul. Ridgewell, he said, appeared to be a little concerned because his in-laws were visiting the coming Friday; but he "insisted he was OK" and that there was "nothing to worry about." The bell rang at 9pm and Ridgewell returned to his room, and that was the last time this inmate saw Ridgewell.

Later that Friday morning, this inmate was "very shocked" when told that Ridgewell had died. "*I was never aware that Derek RIDGEWELL ever had any heart problems, but he may have mentioned about blood pressure problems, but it never sank in with me, and it was only a fleeting mention in conversation.*"

Inmate '**B**' says that Ridgewell came to his room just after the 9pm check was over and they were sitting, just "passing the time of day until about 10pm, or at least before the check." This inmate said he had known Ridgewell for nearly two years, but over the last 5 months "Derek has lost a lot of weight," and went on to say that "the impression Derek gave everyone was that he was fit and well and he had told me put himself on a diet to reduce his weight," but he "never mentioned to my knowledge, I was not aware that Derek had a stomach ulcer, or anything wrong with either of his knees." At about 10pm Ridgewell left and went to his own room, which was next door to his. At about 10.20 he heard Ridgewell and it sounded as if he was not in his bed but at the wash basin "trying to bring up phlegm or trying to be sick, which lasted for 3-4 minutes." He said he was "shocked" to hear the following morning that Ridgewell was dead. This inmate concluded by saying "*I did not believe everything that Derek told me.*"

But did Ridgewell only mislead other prisoners about his health but not the medical staff? Whether or not this was the case we need to turn to their reports to see what information they provide on the state of his health and what he did and did not report to them. The following extracts are taken from a medical history compiled by the Hospital Principal Officer for the purposes of the investigation into his sudden death. It records that on entry to Wormwood Scrubs he was seen by the Medical Officer and graded '1A' *but the records do not mention that he "had any heart problems or blood pressure."* On admittance to HMP Ford (known by inmates in other establishments as the policeman's prison) Ridgewell was examined again by the Medical Duty Doctor who also gave him Grade 1—although on reception to Wormwood Scrubs he was described as 5' 9" in height, "stocky," a euphemism for 'podgy' or 'fat' and weighed 95 kilograms. The Hospital Officer's report continues: "*No blood pressure was taken and inmate Ridgewell did not mention any blood pressure problems.*"

Overall he had not suffered any serious illness or injury since arriving at Ford. The report went on to list his visits to the Prison Medical Duty Doctor, the first being 25th June, 1980, when he "complained of Hay Fever and was given treatment for 2 weeks." This is followed by a list of further visits to the Medical Doctor for minor ailments during 1980:

- 9th October and 6th November, saw dentist
- 13th November, complained of diahorrea and vomiting, and had a day off work.
- 12th December had wax in his ears but ear channels were "normal."
- In the New Year, 23rd January, 1981, had diahorrea and vomiting again and was given medication for three days.
- 24th March, 9th April and 2nd June visits dentist again.
- 8th June, complains of a cold and diahorrea and again given medication for three days.

A search of visits to the Hospital Wing was carried out and there was one visit on 4th November 1982 for a toothache but no other entries were found. *The most consistent complaints were his three visits to the Doctor for diahorrea.* However, the Post Mortem Examination report, dated 31st December, 1982, says that it is *"known that he suffered from high blood pressure in the past,"* and an examination of his Cardiovascular system evidences this, finding the heart *"a little enlarged by hypertrophy of the left ventricle in keeping with a history of hypertension ... The anterior interventricular artery is **totally** occluded (blocked) by a combination of thrombus and arteriosclerosis close to its origin."*

The Inquest held on 27th January, 1983 supported the findings of the Post Mortem that he died as a result of a *Myocardial Infarction, a heart attack, caused* by a *"blood clot"* in a *"diseased artery to the heart."* The local paper, *Evening Argus*, (28/1/1983), reported that his brother, Paul Ridgewell, told the inquest jury (repeating his dead brother's false story) that Derek *"always seemed fit and healthy, but had been on a diet prior to his death and his weight had dropped from 13 stone to 10 stone."* His demise was reported under the heading, 'Prisoner died of heart attack' and the jury returned a verdict of 'death by natural causes.'

Ridgewell may well have had a 'constitutional disposition' to **heart disease,** something that probably originated in his childhood and developed over a number of years, remaining unknown to him in its early stages. He would have been aware of this 'constitutional disposition' at the time of the 'Oval 4' incident *and* on entering prison because one of the symptoms is hypertension—unusually high blood pressure—due to the gradual closing of the artery from a diet high in 'saturated fats' (*Encarta Online Encyclopaedia*, 1988). But in addition to his '*constitutional disposition*' his diet, lifestyle and work-related stress undoubtedly played a part in its acceleration. His hypertension or stress was certainly evidenced by his shouting, excitability and general agitation at Kennington Lane police station after the fight that followed the tense stand-off at the Oval underground.

Chapter 1 has told of his frustration at not immediately getting his way with us that his colleague, DC North, had to whisper something to try and him to calm him down. But it didn't work. He must have been put under enormous pressure by our resistance and at the thought of his plan not 'succeeding' after chaos of our 'arrest'. Luckily for him help came in the form of two Detectives from Brixton police station who were there, seemingly, to get things back under his control, hence the appearance of the 'unsolved crimes' book from which the 'Behemoth' read aloud. His history of hypertension was partly confirmed by the medical records and by the findings of the post mortem.

Derek Ridgewell: 'Bent Copper' or Corrupt Policeman?

We now turn to the question of whether Derek Ridgewell was a 'bent copper' or a 'corrupt policemen'. In the Deputy Governor's Allocation report (14/2/80) at Wormwood Scrubs it stated that when pressed as to why someone of his character should have indulged in the numbers of thefts that took place, Ridgewell replied "I just went bent." This is an interesting colloquialism coming from him and is taken to mean that in his own mind he'd strayed from the 'straight and narrow', had **deviated** from his *professional path* as a police detective. But this is far too loose a phrase to sum up or define his activities. In English, the term 'bent' is a simile used to indicate that something *is not quite right*, dodgy, or a deviation from the norm, as in the term '*bent as a nine bob note.*' In reality because there is no such thing as a '*nine shilling*' or '*nine bob note*' if you ever heard the phrase you would know that it referred to *something not genuine.*

This is a reference derived from the currency used before decimalisation, *old money*; that is pounds, shillings and pence, where shillings (coins) came in ones (a shilling, a 'bob'), twos (two shillings, two 'bob' or a florin) and tens (a ten shilling or ten 'bob' note). The term '*he's as bent as a nine bob note*' applied to a person indicates that the person is *not straight*, is untrustworthy, criminal or 'deviant.' The word 'bent' has in the past used also to refer to someone who is homosexual (or gay), someone once regarded as not conforming to the 'norm' of (hetero)sexual activity. Applied to policemen a 'bent copper' is a policeman who has *deviated* from '*normal policing activity,*' someone who *breaks the law as opposed to upholding it*; is someone who *could be bribed* to 'turn a blind eye' to the criminal activity of others, or someone who is just dishonest for his own benefit.

When asked why he became dishonest, Ridgewell must have shrugged his shoulders and replied, "I suppose... I just went bent"; that as a former police detective he '*went bent as a nine bob note.*' By his use of this phrase he showed that he must have been aware that he had *deviated from normal* police activity—or had been convicted and imprisoned for having done '*what he was under a duty not to have done,*' as we shall see below. *The colloquialism,* 'bent copper' is used, informally, as a euphemism to refer to a policeman as being, formally, a 'corrupt policeman'—*an untrustworthy person* who had strayed from the 'Nine Peelian Principles' of ethical policing.[1]

Defining police corruption

I refer to a paper by Tim Newburn, '*Understanding and Preventing Police Corruption: Lessons from the Literature,*' (1999) for a definition of '*police corruption*' and then go on to apply this definition to Detective Sergeant Ridgewell's activities. Police corruption is defined broadly as 'deviant, dishonest, improper, unethical or criminal behaviour by a police officer' (1999:13). A narrower definition is 'accepting bribes' – a classic form of police corruption, which lies at one end of a scale and at the other end there is 'committing a crime,' such as a burglary while on duty (Newburn, 1999:13). Although accepting a bribe and stealing are both criminal acts by police officers, the point is that stealing is not corrupt as corruption involves the "abuse and exploitation of police authority" in a way that burglary does not" (Newburn, 1999:13). Thus police corruption are those 'deviant' acts committed by policemen in the course of their occupations: "*If police officers steal from the scene of a crime they are called to investigate, they are corrupt: If they steal from their families, their friends, or from stores and homes without the cover of their police role, they are merely thieves*" (Klockars, 1977, quoted by Newburn, 1999:13)

Police corruption necessarily involves therefore an abuse of position as what is 'corrupted' in the 'special trust' invested in that occupation (Newburn, 1999: 5-6). *Police corruption* may be defined as 'the exploitation or misuse of authority' and an abuse of the 'special trust' invested in police officers by the public. Thus Newburn (1999:6) quoting Klockars (1977:334) observes that:

> The 'special trust' enjoyed by police officers may ... be corrupted in two ways. First, it may be corrupted when police commit criminal acts under the cover of such trust. Secondly, it may be corrupted when that trust is employed for illegal reasons such as providing services for money. 'The latter type of corruption perverts the fair distribution of the *ends* of policing; the former corrupts both the ends of policing and the *means* we trust the police to achieve them.' Our second observation, therefore, must be that that any useful definition of corruption must pay attention to both the 'ends' and 'means' of the activity.

A definition of corruption broad enough to include both **ends** and **means** is offered by McMullen (1961:83-4) who states that a *"public official is corrupt if he accepts money or money's worth for doing something he is under duty to do anyway, that he is under a duty not to do, or to exercise a legitimate discretion for improper reasons."* Punch (1985) expands on the above definition; corruption occurs *"when a public official receives or is promised significant advantage or reward (personal, group or organisational) for doing something that he is under duty to do anyway, that he is under a duty not to do, or exercising a legitimate discretion for improper reasons,"* but also *"for employing illegal means to achieve approved goals"* (Newburn, 1999:14). If we apply the above to Ridgewell's activities on the London underground, we know that he and his team were a under a 'public duty' in 1972 to reduce the reported number of handbag thefts and pick-pocketing from travellers who used the Northern Line *(Sunday Times, 5/8/73)*. What he and his 'gang' did was to turn his Office and the criminal justice system into a cover for *illegality as a route to legitimacy*. In other words, Ridgewell used illegal means (wrongful arrest, assault, forced confessions, and perjury) to achieve approved ends (increased convictions, reduced thefts). But these actions did not necessarily result in a reduction in the amount of thefts as all those arrested and convicted protested their innocence of the crimes and accused the police of perjury and assault, **raising questions** about the causal relationship that was assumed to exist between an increase in Ridgewell's arrests and a reduction in the incidents of theft and robbery on the underground, for which the 'Oval 4' and others were convicted and jailed.

According to Hall and others (1978) Ridgewell's activities were part of an *over-reaction* by the control agencies, nothing short of a *moral panic*, a reaction that was *out of proportion* to the actual level of such incidents. *What was claimed to be a defining characteristic of the work of the 'anti-mugging' squad, their impact on offences on the underground, turns out to be a false characteristic, because the squad had no such successes.* The *adverse measure* of their 'success' was that the 'anti-mugging' squad was disbanded after just 18 months in operation, not for any 'success' in *reducing* crime on the underground but more for the *rise in the level of complaints* made against Ridgewell's team by the black community for their violent and illegal methods (*West Indian World*, 3/8/73).

Ridgewell's motives

A motive for corruption is to gain something personally or organisationally and this intention to gain something, in most cases, lies at the heart of police corruption, what Newburn (1999:7) describes as having a "*corrupt motivation.*" A question is, therefore, what did Ridgewell 'gain' from his first phase of corruption in the Transport police? On this Kleinig (1999:166) widens Punch's definition, suggesting that: "*Police officers are corrupt when, in exercising their authority, they act with the primary intention of furthering private and departmental/divisional advantage* " (quoted in Newburn, 1999: 7).

The use of 'illegitimate means to accomplish personal and organisational ends' such as the fabrication or the planting of evidence, perjury or the beating up of suspects in order to obtain convictions, is an important dimension. It is important because the 'corrupt motivation' present in Ridgewell during the 'Oval 4' episode was not driven by financial gain, as in standard examples of police corruption, but probably done more immediately for *accolades* from and the *approval* of colleagues and superiors, and for *improved personal standing* in an area of policing to which public attention had been recently directed by the 'mugging scare.' Further this was bolstered by the fact that he now headed a *special squad* set-up specifically to tackle thefts on the underground, thus any monetary gain would not be immediate but come as a result of future promotion and from the higher profile of the Transport Police in *crime-fighting* on the underground.

As the leader of the newly formed *Robbery Squad* the position had presented him with an opportunity to show what he could do as a *Detective Sergeant* and, perhaps, to make up for the feelings of personal 'failure' and 'disillusionment' that still hung over him from the Rhodesia episode, even though he was greeted as a returning 'hero.' Ridgewell's corruption, therefore, involved the following elements:

1 The misuse of authority, the violation of the 'special trust' invested in his public duty.
2 The doing of something he was under a duty not to do.
3 The use of illegitimate means to achieve approved ends.
4 The presence of a 'corrupt motivation' to gain personally and/or organisationally

Corrupting a public duty

Ridgewell's prison admission that he "just went bent" was an admission of 'deviance' that referred to his *most recent* episode of 'dishonesty' because it meant him acknowledging his deviation from the "straight and narrow" path of "honesty," "truthfulness" and "impartiality"—ethical principles and practices enshrined in his professional role as a 'public servant,' as opposed to his 'private role' as 'Derek Ridgewell.'

The previous incidents of violence and perjury arising from his 'anti-mugging' duties on the underground could not have registered in his mind as *wrong* nor did he regard them as 'acts of corruption' but may well have appeared to him as a *normal* and *necessary* part of what he evidently considered to be attached to his detective work in Britain's *internal colony.* He must have interpreted his *duty* in the following way: to *increase* convictions for the crimes to which he had been alerted but did not connect this activity to a *reduction* in the incidents of theft on the underground. The two might seem to be causally related, but with Ridgewell's intervention they apparently were not. I'll explain why I came to this conclusion below when I look at the parallels between the two episodes, mindful that the first led directly to the second and are therefore causally related.

Connecting the corruptions

According to the police narrative the *special squad* was set up as a consequence of the rise in handbag snatches and pick-pocketing incidents on the underground and their duty was to *detect and apprehend* 'suspected persons' before their acts of theft and thieves after such acts and *reduce the volume of thefts* (*Sunday Times*, 5/8/73). But Ridgewell's squad didn't even bother to detect and apprehend any robbers or 'muggers' on the underground system; because black people were already *racially visible* he decided, immediately, to set about turning that *visibility* into a 'suspected person' status by 'stop and search tactics.' That *illegal move* led to violent confrontations between his squad and those stopped, which then led to the arrest of those *young and visible* underground travellers on *fake charges*. In the first two cases on the underground (the 'Waterloo Four' and the 'Stockwell Six') Ridgewell and his squad began their work by framing innocent black people for the types of crime they were sent out to detect and reduce, if not stop. But things went awry with his contact with the 'Oval 4,' barely triumphing in a high-profile and controversial case.

As a consequence of this encounter he lost his next case, *demonstrating that Ridgewell's involvement had shifted the focus of the Transport police from one of detection and arrest to conviction alone.* This intention to corrupt the *ends* of policing and the *means* by which these ends were achieved fell apart during the trial of the 'Tottenham Court Road 2.' More to the point, Ridgewell's arrests *were not for actual theft but for attempted thefts*, making these arrests *fake or feigned acts of prevention* where no evidence of stolen goods or 'victims' needed to be produced in court; the only *evidence* needed was the 'trusted word' of the officers concerned. As the journal *Race & Class* (Vol. XXlll: 1981/82: 190) observed, with the catch-all 'Sus' and vague 'attempted theft from unknown persons' offences, *"an accused person can be bought to trial on no other evidence that acting suspiciously in the eyes of two police officers. The evidence of independent witnesses is hardly ever used."* In all of the 16 cases, Ridgewell chose offences for which he didn't have to rely on independent witnesses just his team of police officers. In the 'Stockwell 6' case he acted as both the *victim* of and *witness to a fake crime*.

In the second connection, the Bricklayers Arms episode, it was the steep rise in thefts from the Goods Depot that prompted Transport Police chiefs to set up another 'special squad' of undercover detectives that were sent in to detect and apprehend the thieves, to reduce/eliminate the thefts, to protect the integrity of the Railway Board's transit of the public's goods and to prevent further theft. Here Ridgewell and his colleagues did manage to detect and apprehend two people taking goods out of the Depot but only to go into partnership with them when he and fellow detectives, Ellis and Keeling, realised how easy it was going to be.

Conspiring to pervert the course of justice

Detective Sergeant Derek Ridgewell was, therefore, not simply a 'bent copper' but a *corrupt policeman,* as in the 'Oval 4' instance he used and abused his professional status to engage in acts of dishonesty that resulted in the wrongful conviction and imprisonment of innocent people, a corruption and perversion of the criminal justice system. His corruption in the 'Oval 4' case may be likened (but is not similar) to that of the two *corrupt policemen* from Nottinghamshire who "fed information to suspected criminals about high profile investigations." A news report headed '*Corrupt policemen jailed for information disclosure*' states that Charles Fletcher, a former trainee detective with Nottinghamshire Police, supplied details of police investigations to criminals over a two and a half year period between December 2002 and June 2005. In return for his 'services' the policeman received discounts on designer suits from a Nottinghamshire Fashion store. He was jailed for seven years after admitting "conspiracy to commit misconduct in a public office" and "conspiracy to pervert the course of justice." His co-defendant, Philip Parr, a former police constable with the same police force, was sentenced to 12 months after pleading guilty to "conspiracy to commit misconduct in a public office" between November 2004 and August 2006. The activities of those policemen, according to the trial Judge, "undermined the trust placed in police officers by the public" (24dash.com, 26/11/2006). Here we have instances of policemen doing "something they were under a duty not to do" (McMullin, 1961; Punch, 1985).

In the 'Oval 4' case Ridgewell used the public trust invested in his position to *pervert the course of justice* by persistent and consistent acts of dishonesty, to which his role was pivotal in sending the innocent to prison. *Here Ridgewell did what he was under a duty not to do: commit perjury, falsify evidence and use violence, corrupting both the means and ends of policing.* The Judge in the Nottinghamshire police corruption case told the policemen on sentencing: "Corrupt police officers do untold damage to the criminal justice system" when they deliberately set out to pervert its outcomes. And that's exactly what Ridgewell did in the 'Oval 4' case: pervert the course of justice by deliberate acts of perjury. He corrupted the duty to be 'honest' and 'truthful' when giving evidence in court—corrupting the ends of policing so as to wrongfully convict and jail the innocent. In all Ridgewell and his 'gang' perverted the means and undermined the ends of the system of criminal justice. In a similar fashion to that of the Nottinghamshire detectives the Recorder of London, James Miskin, told the London Transport detectives that they had *"dishonestly failed in their duty"* to prevent thefts from the Bricklayers Arms Goods Depot.".

Intending to Deceive

Ridgewell's *intention was* to pervert the *means* and *ends* of his policing to the extent that he was prepared to indulge in the type of amorality and illegality he claimed to have witnessed inflicted on Africans in Rhodesia and which "sickened" him, causing him to take his 'unofficial leave' of his policing role there. If we compare the Oval underground and the Bricklayers Arms instances of *corruption* it becomes possible to identify a causal relationship between them.

Ridgewell must have convinced himself that his efforts on the underground and the 'risks' he took to (dishonestly) increase the conviction rate for thefts and robbery for the Transport Police did not reap any benefits for him, personally or professionally. In fact his actions attracted adverse personal and professional criticisms to him and the Transport police. Having been removed from his duties on the London underground as a consequence of his *undetected and unsuspected corruption* he decided to direct his professional role and it privileges to his personal benefit at the Bricklayers Arms.

The two instances spoken about above are therefore comparable *instances of corruption linked in a chain or a continuum of acts of corruption. His work on the underground did not involve detection only deception* and he took this 'art of deception' with him to the *Bricklayers Arms* Goods Depot. I suggest that rather than regard the *Bricklayers Arms* episode as an isolated and distinct incident of *measurable corruption,* a *'conspiracy to steal,'* it should be more properly be seen as part of a *pattern of acts of deception and corruption* by this officer in his abuse and perversion of the machinery of the criminal justice system in both instances. In the instance of the 'Oval 4' it was a *'conspiracy to pervert the course of justice'* by his deliberate and active contribution to the wrongful conviction and imprisonment of the innocent—a corruption of the *ends* of his policing *duties* and a corruption of the *means* by which those *duties* were accomplished. In us making those claims against the Transport police we were not to know in 1972 that in 1978 Ridgewell would very publicly provide measurable acts of *deceit* and a *conspiracy* to conceal his deception that backed up our original claims but in a different context.

The 'Oval 4:' wrongfully convicted or victims of a miscarriage of justice?

Was the 'Oval 4' case an example of the *wrongful conviction of the innocent* or *a miscarriage of justice*? The answer depends on the application of the rules and procedures governing the conduct of criminal trials that were in operation during our trial at the Central Criminal Court in November 1972 and those rules and procedures governing appeals against conviction at the Court of Appeal in July 1973. *It is a common public perception that the criminal justice system does not exist to wrongfully convict the innocent but many solicitors and their clients know that this often occurs and how difficult it is to overturn a wrongful conviction.* But as I have argued above it was to that end that Ridgewell's deception and corruption were directed and, as Walker has observed, *"a conviction arising from deceit or illegalities is corrosive of the State's claim to legitimacy on the basis of due process and respect for rights"* (Quoted by Naughton, 2006:4). Writing about the 'Wrongful Conviction of the Innocent,' Naughton (2006:4), states:

> A distinction between miscarriages of justice and the wrongful conviction of the innocent …(is that)…a miscarriage of justice is wholly internal to the criminal justice system, wholly dependant on how 'justice' is defined: miscarriages of justice, as evidenced by successful appeals against conviction, derive from technical decisions made from existing rules and procedures of the appeal courts.

Therefore:

> a miscarriage of justice cannot be said to have occurred unless and until an applicant has been successful in an appeal against conviction, and until that time s/he remains an alleged victim of a miscarriage of justice (Naughton, 2006:2).

Naughton (2006:3) concludes that a "successful appeal against a criminal conviction denotes an official and systematic acknowledgement" of what should be termed as a *"breach of the carriage of justice"* but this "breach" bears no relationship to whether or not the appellant is "factually guilty or factually innocent" as the criminal justice system is not interested in such questions only observation of the rules and procedures governing a legal process, such as a 'fair trial.' Accordingly, "*If the trial process is not fair; if it is distorted by deceit or by material breaches in the rules of evidence or procedure, then the liberties of all are threatened*" *(Court of Appeal, Judgement of Lord Justice Roch ,30/7/97, quoted by Naughton, 2000:4)*.

Therefore "*...for convictions to be overturned they have to be thought to question the integrity of the trial in which they were given and, thus, be rendered unsafe*" *(Naughton, 2006:4)*. As the 'Oval 4' was unsuccessful in their appeal against conviction they remain, therefore, alleged victims of a miscarriage of justice.

Wrongful conviction of the innocent

Having noted that a miscarriage of justice "is entirely **internal** to the working of the criminal justice system" and "wholly dependant on how 'justice' is defined" and is not concerned with the *guilt* or *innocence* of the appellant, were the 'Oval 4' then victims of a *wrongfully conviction and imprisonment* for charges of which they were innocent? How is a wrongful conviction of the innocent to be defined? Naught on (2006: 4) states that concerns about the wrongful conviction of the innocent are "wholly external" to the workings of the criminal justice system. Concerns about a wrongful conviction occur when "external" perceptions of the "internal" working of the criminal justice system become incompatible with public perceptions of how the system should work: that the innocent should not be convicted. In such cases the Court of Appeal exists because errors occur where the innocent are wrongfully convicted, and these convictions do not serve the interests of justice.

Questions about the *wrongful conviction of the innocent* are, therefore, concerned with *the wider social and political issues of justice* (or injustice) while questions about miscarriages of justice focus only on *the rules and procedures that govern criminal trials*. Issues of the wrongful conviction of the innocent arise directly as a result of campaigning groups (e.g. the 'Guildford 4' & 'Birmingham 6') bringing those concerns to the attention of the public and pointing out **where** and **how** the criminal justice system has erred by that wrongful conviction. Such was the case in the 'Free the Oval 4' campaign during 1972 and 1973 (see Chapter 3) that resulted in a BBC nationwide transmission,

'Cause for Concern' high-lighting the dubious and violent character of Ridgewell's 16 arrests during an eight month period (January 1972 to August 1972) and the numerous complaints made against his leadership and the operation of the 'anti-mugging' squad on the London underground.

NOTES

[1] According to the British Transport Police (BTP) website under *Historical and General Interest* is set out 'Sir Robert Peel's Principles of Policing' which are introduced as follows: "In 1829 before the passing of the Metropolitan Police Act, Sir Robert Peel laid down nine principles of policing to govern the conduct of the police. These are as applicable to the police service today as they were in 1829."

   i   The basic mission for which the police exist is to prevent crime and disorder.

  ii   The ability of the police to perform their duties is dependant upon the public approval of police actions.

 iii   Police must secure the willing co-operation of the public in voluntary observation of the law to be able to secure and maintain the respect of the public.

 iv   The degree of co-operation of the public that can be secured diminishes proportionately to the necessity of the use of physical force.

  v   The police seek and deserve public favour not by catering to public opinion, but by constantly demonstrating absolute impartial service to the law.

 vi   Police use physical force to the extent necessary to secure observation of the law or to restore order only when the exercise of persuasion, advice, and warning is found insufficient.

vii   Police, at all times, should maintain a relationship to the public that gives reality to the historic tradition that the police are the public and the public are the police; the police being the only members of the public who are paid to give full-time attention to duties which are incumbent upon every citizen in the interests of community welfare and existence.

viii Police should always direct their actions strictly towards their functions, and never appear to usurp the powers of the judiciary

ix The test of police efficiency is the absence of crime and disorder and not the visible evidence of police action in dealing with it.

Found at: http://www.btpspecials.org.uk/thebtp/peelianprinciples.xpp

The fern ("aya") is a symbol from the Andinkra Tribe in West Africa. "The fern is a hardy plant that can grow in places where others cannot. 'An individual who wears this symbol suggests that he has endured many adversities and outlasted much difficulty.' (W. Bruce Willis, *The Adinkra Dictionary*)

Extract of an interview given by Winston Trew to Keep Left Socialist newspaper, at the Grassroots bookshop, Ladbroke Grove, 3rd August, 1973, after the release of the 'Oval Four" following their appeal.

"We don't think the police will ever change their behaviour ... Nothing short of revolution will change it. If they make a scapegoat out of an individual like Ridgewell, it will not do any good. Rather than wallow in the fact that I am out of prison, we've got to bring the campaign to a successful conclusion."

SECTION 2

'Black for a Cause...
...Not Just
Because'

CHAPTER 5

The Journey to Find My Self

I want you to know that I am the man who
fight for the right, not for the wrong
Going there and staying here;
Talking this and talking that;
Soon you will find out the man I'm supposed to be.
(**'Bam Bam,' Maytals, Doctor Bird Records,
1966 Festival Song).**

The river crosses the path; the path crosses the river.
Which was first?
-African proverb

The Start of the Journey

My journey to the Oval underground did not begin on that fateful day in March 1972, but originated some two years earlier in the spring of 1970 at my home in Peckham. Its origins lay in part in a visit from my brother one Saturday afternoon who told me he had been going to Black Power meetings in New Cross. There was excitement in his voice a sparkle in his eyes as he then began to reel-off all that he has learnt there: that Africa was the cradle of civilisation; that the Egyptians were black; the Moors were black; that Timbuktu was a seat of learning in Africa, with a library; that the Greeks learnt philosophy and science from the Egyptians; that Jesus was black; that Beethoven was black. What? My mind was racing. The Egyptians, the Moors, Jesus—black? I just sat there staring into space trying to imagine what he was telling me. I remembered Sidney Poitier in 'The Long Ships'. He played a Moor. I thought about Charlton Heston in the film 'El Cid' fighting the Moors. So it was black men who defeated him, I laughed to myself? Well, well! He said he was going tomorrow and that I should come along. I agreed. I had no idea what to expect but I was excited.

When I entered the meeting place that Sunday afternoon, I was overwhelmed. It was being held in the basement of a house that had been converted to run as a 'she-been,' a dancing/drinking/gambling house. It was full of young men and women like me, all black; some of whom I knew, others I'd seen around, others I didn't know. Many of the young men and women were dressed in all-black, or wore Dashiki shirts/African-print warps. The Afro hairstyle was the order of the day for both men and women. Some of the women had their heads wrapped in African print, while others wore their plaited hair in corn-row. There were a few with black berets, decorated with a Black Panther or Malcolm X badge. People were smiling and saying hello, addressing one another as brother and sister. It was beautiful as it was breathtaking. The low ceiling and the body heat generated by everyone contributed to the feeling of closeness and togetherness. The walls were decorated with posters of Malcolm X, Marcus Garvey, Che Guevara and figures from the American Black Panthers.

I recall seeing the famous icon of Huey P Newton for the first time, sitting in that Wicker chair staring at us with gun in hand. Maps of Africa, the Caribbean and of Jamaica also decorated the walls. A speaker addressed the congregation, and talked about the reason we all had assembled there that afternoon. It was as a consequence of a history of brutalisation inflicted on us by British slave masters during capture and enslavement, of the experience of poverty and contract labour after Emancipation and Independence, the forced migration and the racism that met our parents on arrival to Britain, he said. This history showed that we had common origin and history of suffering and resistance in the West, and this was the basis of our identity in opposing a common enemy: the 'white man'.

> We've been exploited and oppressed for over 400 years.
> It is time for us to unite and organise and stand up for
> our rights. Black Power! Black Power! Black Power!

Everyone clapped, cheered or gave the clenched fist salute. The hairs on the back of my neck stood up and electricity shot through my body. There I stood in the basement looking around at the people in the room. It was electrifying. It was awesome. I had fallen in love with it all, and in those moments found something I could believe in, something that I could become, and a place where I could belong—in a *congregation* of young black people who had a *purpose* and were part of a new *perspective* on life.

Sitting at home later that Sunday night, I began to see things differently and was able to reorganise the jig-saw pieces of my life into some sort of narrative. Coming to Britain with my brothers aged 6 to join my parents in 1956; my father killed at work in 1959 when I was aged 9 years old; separated from my family and sent into Council Care until age 11; followed by my self-elected exclusion from post-16 education following my refusal to be downgraded in school. This attempt to downgrade me followed my heightened visibility in school after a Juvenile Court appearance in the winter of 1966, about which I had spoken the 'forbidden' by telling the Headmaster that my Court appearance was the result of a wrongful arrest and a beating by the Brixton police.

Their view was that I had bought the School into 'disrepute' and, with other incidents in school (of which I was innocent) saw my down-grading into a lower year as a way of keeping me under surveillance. I couldn't believe what I was hearing. I thought, I had agreed to stay on in the 6th form to extend my education, but it was explained to me that the 6th form timetable offered me too much 'free time' in school; they needed to know where I was at any time of the day. I protested that I was not mentally subnormal and I refused go down one year. To me it was a further humiliation after all that had happened. I was burning with anger and remember looking at the Head of Year with all the contempt I could muster as he said these things, causing him to exclaim: *"Did you see the way he looked at me, Headmaster; did you see the way he looked at me"*? I walked out of his office and out of the school.

At once my story became part of that early migration to and settlement in the 'Mother' Country and, at the same time, part of a struggle of resistance against overwhelming forces in the land that once held the fragile hopes and dreams of my parents. Arriving with my brothers in 1956 to join my parents, the privations we suffered as a family because my mother was a widow, and the liberties taken with me by the police and the school were only militated against by the sacrifices made by my mother and my own determination not to give in. These experiences, I perceived, were no longer a series of unfortunate, personal life events, but part of a 'bigger picture'.

I returned to the basement the following Thursday, joined the Fasimba, and from then on became part of the Black Liberation Struggle, part of this 'bigger picture' I had heard spoken about. With Black Power I had found answers to some questions, and those answers led to other questions. Prior to that Sunday afternoon, such questions, as there were, lay dormant and voiceless, as what Claude MacKay describes in his poem, 'Outcast,' as *"words felt, but never heard."* They were questions locked inside with no language with which to speak or to give them form or voice.

After that Sunday I was able to access a new language and a framework that enabled "my lips to frame" and 'speak' words that once were only "felt, but never heard." I was not only able to speak I could also hear a bit more clearly. The music being played in the local record shops and in dances at the time also raised questions about being black, as in the reggae version of Nina Simone's (To be) *'Young, Gifted and Black,'* sung by Bob (Andy) and Marcia (Griffiths). The lyrics seemed to sum up a series of unasked questions and expressions of sentiment that could now be uttered in public. There was a 'more rootsy' DJ version from Rupee Edwards called *'Herbert Spliffington'* being played on 'pre-release' by Sound Systems. The pre-start jingle ran: *"This is the return of I Dread, Herbert Spliffington; still young, gifted and black. Where do you stand brother?"* Where did I stand? I stood with the Fasimba (the organisation) and for Black Power (the political philosophy) and, as CLR James once put it, "on the shoulders of my ancestors."

The Fasimba: 'The Young Lions'

I joined the Fasimba in the spring of 1970 around the time Edward Heath won the General Election for the Conservatives, to become the new Prime Minister replacing Harold Wilson and the old Labour Government. There was a general sense that the new Government was not in favour of black people being in Britain as this was the same party to which Enoch Powell belonged when two years previously he had referred to black children as 'grinning piccanninies' pushing excrement through the letter boxes of old ladies' front doors. The enforced repatriation of black people to their 'native lands' by the new Government was one of the rumours being circulated that was to be enshrined in the new Immigration Bill under discussion, certain to become government policy. The air of uncertainty hanging over the status of black people in Britain was one of the drivers fuelling Black Power activism, driving the need to try and create some certainty about who we were and what we wanted.

The Fasimba was the *Youth Wing* of the South East London Parents Organisation (SELPO), an organisation set up in 1969 by a group of black people concerned about the mis-education of 'West Indian' children in British schools (Coard, 1971). The four founders of the organisation decided to set up and run a Saturday School in New Cross and took in black children bought there by their parents, carers or collected by SELPO members for 'Supplementary' education. The Saturday school was staffed by trained and concerned black teachers who gave their time as they saw this as a personal if not political duty. Every Saturday morning SELPO members, Fasimba and other volunteers would set out the desks chairs in that same basement, *transforming the 'political space' into a classroom, an 'educational space.'*

The walls of the classroom were decorated with posters of black heroines and heroes who organised resistance to slavery, black scientists and inventors, African Kings and Queens, while others depicted scenes from Black history, such as Hannibal crossing the Alps on African Elephants to defeat the Romans. The emphasis of the Saturday school was on the '3 R's. English language and grammar were taught, writing skills and practice as well as mathematics and, where possible, African and Caribbean historical events were woven into the teaching of these lessons. There was storytelling using European and Caribbean stories and folktales, including the telling of Anansi stories which caused endless amusement to the children who attended. Meals were prepared on premises for the young people who came for the extra lessons.

The Saturday school was well established and had been running for about a year when I entered that same basement on that Thursday to meet a group of young people calling themselves the Fasimba. They were meeting there to rehearse a play called 'The Black Experience." I joined this group. Thursdays functioned as a time for both the rehearsals and for political discussions. Routinely, I began attending the Sunday and Thursday meetings, met new 'brothers' and 'sisters', where I continued to develop a new language with my new vision. I would discuss books I had read on African history and the Slave Trade. At home in Peckham, I adopted new cultural practices: wearing black, plaiting and then combing my hair out in an 'Afro,' adorning my bedroom with Malcolm X, Marcus Garvey and American Black Panther posters. As well as continuing to collect records, I started a collection of books on Black history.

I even joined the library in Camberwell to see what titles were on a booklist I got from either George or Dudley. I sought out titles such as 'The Autobiography of Malcolm X'; W.E.B. Du Bois' Africa and the World', 'The Negro' and 'Souls of Black Folk.' I read journals like *'The Black Scholar'* and the US *Black Panther Party* newspaper, the UK's Black Panther paper, *Freedom News*, the *Black Voice*, and *Grassroots* community newspaper. As the lyrics of *'Young, Gifted and Black'* expressed "*I longed to know the truth.*" It had felt good when I first heard the lines: "*... to be young, gifted and black, your soul's intact.*" I saw myself as part of the new generation of young people who **were** *"young, gifted and black"* **and** *'rough and tough.'*

This was not an easy time for my family. My wife, Marie, was not pleased about my conversion to Black Power; my father-in-law less so.

For him, like for many of his generation, black people lacked the ability to organise and accomplish anything worthwhile. He and his family had left Haiti for Jamaica in the mid-1960s, where they lived for a while before coming to Britain, like many other Caribbean migrants, looking for new start. Other family members left Haiti for America. He often said that the only 'progress' black people can make in the white man's world was to work hard and make money. He was a welder. His work was tangible; *he worked with his hands.* I had once followed him to where he worked and watched him at his craft; welding some iron railings. *I couldn't do that, I thought. I was never any good at technical drawing or metalwork at school.* His work was typical of the craftsmen of his generation and made him regard me as idealistic. As far a Black politics was concerned, he felt black leaders worked on 'people's head'—'brain working them'—tricking and eventually betraying them, running off with their money, sometimes with white women. This he portrayed as a double betrayal and a weakness in black men who get into 'politics.'

On one occasion when we were sitting in the front room in Peckham, I was going through my albums looking for James Carr's to the play tracks, 'Freedom Train' and 'Dark End of the Street' and passed Otis Redding's Album 'Otis Blue,' on the cover of which was a picture of a white woman. He asked me to explain why a black man would want to have a white woman on his album cover. I said it was probably not his decision, probably the record company's. He looked at me and laughed sarcastically. I was fascinated as to why he should think this way when his country, Haiti, was the first in the Western hemisphere where slaves mounted a successful overthrow of the slave system and defeat the French, Spanish and British and set up the first independent black nation. These events seemed far from his mind. He only spoke about the corruption and poverty in Haiti nowadays, which was more immediate. Given the 'failure' of the revolution, I took it that there was a *material basis* for him feeling the way he did. The 'black revolution' had long since gone and *Papa Doc's* rule was more immediate. I never mentioned the subject to him again as *Papa Doc* became a sort of a 'forbidden' name to utter in the household.

My mother had told a family friend that I had "taken up black power." One Sunday, when I visited her, Mr. S was also visiting. He saw the way I was dressed, and cautioned me, saying: *"You see how you take up this black power thing pon you head? Mind, yu'self yu' know bwoy, mind yu'self."* Mind myself from what? I asked myself. Like most of the advice given by my parents' generation to young people like me, their counsels always came tinged with 'dark sayings,' things beyond the obvious: things that cannot be 'seen' or 'heard,' only 'known.'

To me his caution about "taking up this black power thing on your head" and that I should "mind myself" were 'dark sayings' whose meanings eluded me at the time. I came to understand the multiple layers of its 'dark meanings,' that is, *obscure* and *hidden* meanings many, many years after being released from prison in 1973, and after re-reading Countee Cullen's poem, '*Heritage*' many times. Looking back at what he said I believe Black Power to him meant a sort of 'forbidden knowledge,' something that the *knowing* of would eventually lead to trouble. Although he did not use that all-encompassing word 'trouble' his caution "mind yu' self" nonetheless, had all the echoes of that word. He could have said "Don't trouble trouble" or "Trouble deh a bush nuh bring it a yard." His term "taking up" and "pon your head" carry two meanings in my understanding of Jamaican folk wisdom. Carrying a load on your head, as the rural and urban poor do all over Jamaica is also, symbolically, carrying your low social status and its personal burden on your head in public.

"Taking up things *pon you* head" refers not just to carrying a physical burden, like a lowly status, but to carrying a 'mental burden' (like *forbidden knowledge, such as Obeah*) that would eventually lead to *destruction* (madness and even death) if you didn't "put it down." The rebuke for "taking up" something, in this chain of meaning, implies that it is a 'thing' or 'activity' you ought not have 'taken up' with in the first place, more because of it perversity rather than its illegality— though it might lead to confrontation with the authorities, especially the police, in the long run (such as taking up '*bad company*'). In short, he was saying that '*taking up this black power thing on you head*' could only lead to trouble. The Maytals' reggae hit, '*Don't Trouble Trouble*' of 1969 draws from the same pool of Jamaican folk wisdom.

To me Black Power came to mean not just wrestling with the *external* and *visible forces* and *institutions* of a society pitted against you but also those *external* forces that had become *internal* to black psychology and language, somehow indivisible from the traditions of family, community, culture and history into which you had been born. In that tradition, 'black' not only meant 'trouble' it was also a 'forbidden word' when prefixed to nouns such as 'people,' 'power,' 'protest' and 'art' or used in close proximity to adjectives such as 'goodness' and 'rights.' At the end of the 'taking up black power' caution from Mr. S, I mentioned to him that I thought that black people had been wrongly treated by white people. "*Black people nuh good,*" he declared. "*We are the sons of slaves. Noah cursed Ham for looking at his father's nakedness, saying 'thy seed shall be black and thy sons shall be servants of servants,'*" he said, as if to quote the Bible verbatim. I was taken aback. He was black. I was black, so how could he say this? I excused myself and left the room. Later on at home in Peckham, I picked up a Bible and looked up the relevant passage. Noah's 'prophetic declaration' is made in Genesis Chapter 9, verses 20-25, especially verse 25:

20. And Noah began to be a farmer and he planted a vineyard.
21. And he drank of the wine, and became drunk; and he was uncovered within his tent
22. And Ham, the father of Canaan, saw the nakedness of his father, and told his two brethren outside.
23. And Shem and Japheth took a garment, and laid it upon both their shoulders, and went backward, and covered the nakedness of their father; and their faces were backwards, and they saw not their father's nakedness.
24. And Noah awoke from his wine and knew what his younger son had done unto him.
25. *And he said, Cursed be Canaan; a servant of servants shall he be unto his brethren.*

What is important is that it didn't matter that the text did not read as he had quoted it to say, nor referred to the meaning he attached to it to be an obvious one. In the Bible version no mention is made of slaves being 'black.' But it was the case that it had been made to have the significance he attached to it, as **the** interpretation of the Christian story offered to ex-slaves in post-Emancipation society and continued into post-Independence Jamaica and served as a justification of racial slavery. To him and other believers of this teaching the slave trade and slavery could only be explained by reference to this prophecy.

Slavery was therefore on account of the wickedness and 'sin of the ancestors of black people rather than the wickedness and 'sin' white people's ancestors. Because black people 'nuh good,' the term 'black' as a self referent was not usually uttered in public or polite conversation. *'Coloured people' was the accepted currency of recognition for white people to and about black subjects, and used by black subjects to and about themselves.* Perhaps, more to the point, 'black' carried with it something decisive, abrupt and non-compromising: in a word, it sounded 'threatening.' 'Coloured' was softer and less threatening. I remember my mother using a similar phrase, saying "anything too black nuh good." But I think that for Mr. S. and for many of his generation, including my mother, the word 'black' also carried with it the feared threat of opening doors that had long been locked. Behind these doors were stored the memories and experiences of frustration, suffering and thwarted ambitions that could only lead to further torment and 'self-destruction' if opened and stirred. So that door had to be kept locked. Shut.

This is where Countee Cullen in his epic poem, 'Heritage,' (Bontempts, 1974:86) offers insight. As if to speak of and to this inner torment and anguish, he cautions himself thus:

> All day long and all night through
> One thing only I must do:
> *Quench my pride and cool my blood*
> *Lest I perish in the flood*
> *Lest a hidden ember set*
> *Timber that I thought was wet*
> *Burning like the driest flax*
> *Melting like the nearest wax*
> Lest the grave restore its dead
> Not yet has my heart or head
> In the least way realized
> They and I are civilised

I think it is these 'torments' he may well have been alluding to in that 'dark warning' about me "taking up black power on my head," cautioning that I should "mind myself." Well, I didn't know it then but that is exactly what I did. His warning was prophetic for many reasons, including the personal and political ones he alluded to; but he could not have foreseen the personal triumphs as well and the social, cultural and political change that would take place as a consequence of legions of black young men and women in Britain "taking up Black Power."

'Taking up' Black Power

I spent the early part of my 'induction' into the Fasimba reading about the Atlantic Slave Trade, African history and in discussions with other Fasimba on the same. On some Saturday afternoons I would go up to Ladbroke Grove and to the Mangrove Restaurant on All Saints Road. There seemed to be black people everywhere. Like many other young people I was decked in Black 'militant' regalia— black trousers, black shirt or jumper, black (leather) jacket, complete with a Malcolm X or a US Panther badge, and the Black Panther-style black Beret.

Other young black men and women were decked in the apparel of an 'African' identity such as a Dashiki shirt or dress, African print dresses and wraps. Others were dressed in 'military-style' garments, reflecting the anti-colonial wars in Africa and Vietnam and in other parts of the world, and in different ways signified an allegiance to the prospect of 'change' on the one hand, and Black Power militancy on the other.

During the 1970s Black Power and 'Internationalism' were closely related political ideas and practices. *The Mangrove Restaurant* in Ladbroke Grove was both an eating and a meeting place for black people who wanted to be 'at home away from home': that is 'in the Caribbean' in England. *Black food* was being cooked and served by *black people*, while in the background *black music* played and you listened to the *'black talk'* of the diners and passers-by. *Black talk* does not just refer to talk about black culture, history and black politics and contemporary issues, but talk in the harmonious accents of the rich languages spoken in the Caribbean and in black communities across London.

It began to dawn on me that 'taking up' Black Power meant more than just fighting against racial discrimination in education, jobs and housing, the lack of recreational facilities, and against increasing police victimisation and brutality, equally important was the fight to rebuild your sense of blackness and selfhood in the *present* and well as fighting for the *past* and for the *future*. It was not just a fight for 'equal rights and justice' **in Britain**, but fighting for a just place **in history** *against history*. What I mean by this is that fighting **for** history *against* history is fighting *against the flow of Western history **for** your own history*. As Amilcar Gabral (1976) once observed, *'the moment imperialism arrived in Africa we left our own history and culture, and entered European history and culture.'* (Bulhan, *Race & Class*. XX, 3 (1979:247)

The Black struggle, as I beginning to envision it, was **at least a two dimensional** struggle: on the one hand, it was *to wrestle **against** those external and visible forces and institutions of a society pitted against you **and,** on the other hand, **against** those external forces which had become internal to black psychology and language, and indivisible from the traditions of family, community, culture and history into which you had been born. **Black Power** was, in a sense, a fight both **for** a human identity **against** a non-human identity; a fight **against** yourself **for** yourself.* Some of these dimensions had been inherited from past struggles but in the 1970s it had a new urgency and took on a new characteristic. *Unlike previous forms of struggle, this one was essentially youthful.* In fact, reggae music would characterise the 1970s as a period for youth and of youthfulness.

Black Power in 1970s Britain

At this point I wish to break with what I see as *orthodox accounts* of the emergence of Black Power activism in Britain. In my view, it is erroneous to believe that British Black Power drew its energy from American style black protest, a constant feature of news from across the Atlantic during the mid to late 1960s—with images of 'burning and looting' as expressions of black anger. This Chapter challenges the widely held view that British Black Power was imitative of Black Power activism in America, seemingly inspired, principally, by the visits of Martin Luther King, 1964, Malcolm X , 1964/1965, and Stokely Carmichael, 1967, (Philips & Philips, 1998; Cashmore, 1979), and the setting up of new Black organisations as a consequence.

It is the argument of this book that although black people in Britain were inspired **and** appalled by compelling images of black women and men standing up to police intimidation and violence, **the conditions** and **forces** that produced Black Power activism on this side of the Atlantic were specifically British, post-colonial, urban and youthful. A number of authors (e.g. Cashmore, 1979, Philips & Philips, 1998) have tended see the 1960s as the **only** period of Black Power organising and activism in Britain, completely ignoring the 1970s. *This Chapter intends to try and show this belief is in error.* The **conditions** and **forces** which led to the joining of Black organisations by young people in the early 1970s across London and other urban conurbations in Britain were quite British and did not require any trans-Atlantic imports. To understand how **Black Power** in 1970s Britain **broke** with its 1960s antecedents, and to try and **identify** the demographic, social and cultural constituents of its **emergence**, we need to look again at the *1960s and conceptualise this as a period of 'seasoning'—a period of 'conditioning' and 'preparation'— for Black activism in the 1970s.*

The Caribbean connection to British Black Power

To begin to make these essentially British, Caribbean and youthful connections, it is necessary to revisit briefly the social, cultural and political conditions of the late 1960s as *experienced and negotiated* by the so-called 'second generation' of young black people who either arrived with their parents in the mid-1950s or were born in Britain in the early 1950s and 1960s. It is to be noted that although the vast majority of Caribbean migrants arrived during the 1950s and early 1960s, *their children became a significant presence in the school system only in the 1960s and 1970s.* The main reason for this was because those couples who already had children prior to migrating would have taken a few years to settle down, find a job, save enough money, initially living in a single rented room in a house of *multiple occupation,* then renting double-rooms or bought a house, **before** sending for their children (Coard, 2004).

As noted above, while some relocated to Britain *with* young children in the 1950s, others started families only *after* arriving in Britain in the 1950s, early 1960s, either way this would have meant a gap before such children would reach primary/secondary school age and become **sutured** into the British education system. We will return to the issue of Caribbean children's education and black re-education in the origins and Programme of the Fasimba in the next Chapter.

These British-educated or British-born descendants of Caribbean migrants would have, therefore, *experienced and negotiated different social forces and institutions from their parents and other Caribbean adults.* Whereas adult migrants experienced discrimination in jobs, housing, and on public transport and public places such as churches, clubs and pubs—to which the development of alternative social, religious and cultural institutions were testimony; their children, on the other hand, were subject to discrimination experiences in different social institutions: in child minding (Jackson, 1972/3?), education in primary/secondary schools and their psychological services (Coard, 1971), in encounters with white boys in schools, with 'teddy boy' gangs and the police on the streets (Brake, 1980).

At the same time, Caribbean families lived in crowded, cold and damp conditions, and with all of the tensions and problems these conditions produced as a consequence. Jackson, (1972/3: p.4), in a survey of *unregistered childminders* in West Indian communities, described the living conditions experienced by Caribbean families during the 1960s:

> West Indian families are likely to be poorly housed and overcrowded, partly because the cities and towns they found work have often been those which, because of their attraction for labour, have severe housing shortages. Over half live at a density of more than one person per room, as compared with 12 per cent

of the population. They are ten times likely to be sharing accommodation, which will probably be rented furnished. In London only 4.2 per cent, and in the West Midlands 7.7 per cent, have council houses.

West Indians, like other immigrant groups, must either pay a high price for rented accommodation or buy a large house, usually in a decaying inner city area, and fill it with lodgers to meet the mortgage payments. Often the owner can afford to keep no more than one room for himself and his family, and they are as over-crowded as many of his tenants.

To set in context further the overcrowded conditions in which Caribbean migrants lived, Peach (1968) observed that although the labour shortage made migrants *economically acceptable*, the housing shortage made them *socially undesirable*. He adds: *"The colour prejudice of landlords and landladies coupled with the shortage of houses made the crowding, and in some cases the overcrowding, of much of the accommodation available to migrants inevitable and this, in turn increased their image of undesirability"* (quoted in Sivanandan, 1976: 350). As will be shown below, this situation produced an endless stream of school-boy 'jokes' about overcrowding in the houses where 'West Indian' families lived.

Britain's young migrant population

A striking feature about the black population in Britain was that, compared to the UK white population, it was a 'young' population, reflecting the 'youthfulness' of the original migrants. In 1971 the black British population stood at 1.4 million, 70% of whom were aged between 15 and 44 years, with the remaining 30% under 15 years of age. However, the 1.4 million included 500,000 (0.5 million) who were British-born, and 90% of that contingent were under 15 years of age also. Therefore in 1971 just under half (41%) of the British black population were under 15 years of age, with the remaining 49% aged between 15 and 44 years (Runnymede Trust, 1980: 9). *Those who were aged 21 years in 1971 would have been leaving school aged 16 in 1966, and those aged 15 in 1971 would be 10 years old in 1966, having been born in 1956.* In the last quarter of the 1960s, therefore, Britain's black population was characteristically youthful but this youthfulness was not distributed evenly across London or across Britain, but concentrated in cities, towns and boroughs, areas with a sizeable black presence such as Greater London and the South East, as well as Birmingham, Nottingham, Leeds, Manchester, Bristol and Bradford. Moreover, Caribbean migrants were found to be concentrated in particular wards in the boroughs of those cities.

For example, in the London borough of Lewisham, Caribbeans are found to be concentrated in the northern and western parts of the borough—Deptford, New Cross and some parts of Brockley, while the eastern and southern parts of the borough are predominantly white, like Eltham and Bellingham (Lee, 1977). This pattern is noticeable in other London boroughs such as Lambeth, Southwark, Hackney, Haringey and Islington. Therefore although there was a general movement into working class areas, not all working class areas were open to migrants (Sivanandan, 1976). Bermondsey, Rotherhithe and Surrey Docks are examples of areas that resisted significant black settlement (Lee, 1977).

A focus on the years between 1966 and 1969 when large numbers of the youthful contingent were leaving school would show this period to be a time of change, a time of both optimism and tension. Optimistically, it was a time when black migrants were settling into and changing the social-demographics, culture and local economy of the urban areas of Britain's major cities and Industrial centres (Hiro, 1973). These same areas were suffering not only from a shortage of labour, it was a shortage bought on by the rapid decline of the local white population, moving from these 'twilight' areas into better housing and jobs in New Towns (i.e. Milton Keynes) and Council Estates. It has become clear that, occupationally and residentially, Caribbean migrants acted as a *replacement population* (Peach, 1968, 1984; Hiro, 1973; Sivanandan, 1976) in the areas most experiencing an exodus of the white population into the new towns.

For example, Haringey's population had been declining even before the last war, from 307,500 in 1931 to 259, 200 in 1951, in spite of a post-war influx of Cypriots and Caribbeans. North Paddington had also been losing about 1000 voters a year. In 1966 its population stood at 254,000 and despite an influx of Caribbeans it fell to 245,000 in 1969 (Hiro, 1973: 8). Whatever housing remained in these localities, it was these Caribbean migrants occupied. As Hall and others (1978:351) observed, during this period, there:

began the 'colonisation' of certain streets, neighbour-
hoods, cafes and pubs, the growth of revivalist Churches,
mid Sunday hymn-singing and mass baptisms in the
local swimming baths, the spilling-out of Caribbean
fruit and vegetables from Indian shops, the shebeen
and the Saturday night blues party, the construction of
Sound Systems, the black record shops selling Blues,
Ska and soul, the birth of the 'native quarter' at the
heart of the English city.

It is my argument that these *new* Caribbean social and cultural
institutions catered mainly for the needs of adults and not necessarily for
young people and teenagers who were emerging as a needy social group.
Alternative black social and cultural institutions would be required to
figure in the development of 'self awareness' and 'black' group awareness
as Caribbean descendents in urban Britain, needs which were not able
to be met by existing forms of Church-based family or 'community'
entertainment, or the West Indian-type associations being formed.
Young adults seeking entertainment would have to *negotiate entry* to
these local *she-beens* or all-night blues parties, principally because
these were forums of adult entertainment and catered only for adult
men and women. In any event, the music was dominated by Ska, R&B
and Soul, which did not reflect their own particular experience, needs
and wishes. In short there were few recreational *places* or *spaces* for
young people to meet and congregate, to forge and perform their '*new
awareness*' through dress codes, youth talk and dance performance.

As music, dance and dress contributed to the development of white
youth sub-cultures in the post-war decades of the 1950s and 1960s
(Brake, 1980: Hebdige, 1978; Hall et al, 1978), black music, dance and
dress were a distinguishing and identifying element in the development
of black '*youthness*' during the 1960s. The new clubs playing this
kind of 'youth' music reflected the *place* and the *space* where young
people could and would meet and, in turn, assisted in the *emergence*
and *consolidation* of this *self conscious* grouping (Hebdige, 1978). The
limited range of choices facing black teenagers oscillated between
staying in during the evenings or to attend Church-led recreational and
social activities at the weekend. The only other alternative was to 'hit
the streets' to 'win some space' or to meet friends from school in a local
Park. Taking friends home due to lack of space there was not an option
for many young people.

The 'Big Freeze' of 1963

An important environmental factor requiring some consideration is the inclement weather experienced by Caribbean migrants on arrival to England during the 1960s and its impact their living circumstances. The 'big freeze' followed a 'beat the ban' rush of immigration from the Caribbean as a result of the 1962 Immigration Act that was designed to 'close the doors' to primary immigration. Those aged 50 years and over will be able to recall the memorable 'big freeze' of 1963, the coldest winter in 200 years when much of England was quite literally *frozen solid* under a "blanket of snow."

The snowfall began in the year preceding the 'big freeze' in December 1962 when, just before Christmas, snow fell suddenly in London and the South-East, accompanied by 'biting winds' and snow blizzards, lasting from Boxing Day 1962 to March 1963. As well as the country 'blanketed' under snow the temperature did not rise above zero for three months. The effects were that London had 12 inches of drifting snow, the River Thames froze over, rail and road transport services were severely disrupted, and airports closed. Near Gatwick Airport the temperature fell to *minus* 16 degrees below zero. Rubbish remained uncollected for months and because water pipes froze householders had to collect water from road tankers in the street. Factories that relied on coal for power had to be closed because the disruption to road and rail traffic meant no deliveries to factories or to power stations. Power cuts soon became the norm. Many schools, unable to be reopened, remained closed after the Christmas break. A knock-on effect of the 'big freeze' was an increase in the price of food, especially fresh fruit and vegetables and imported produce.

Considering that migrants who arrived in 1962 came from tropical countries and came dressed in only thin summer-wear, the freezing weather was both a shock and great discomfort to their physical and emotional systems. Coats, warm clothing and blankets had to be bought as in the houses where rooms were rented there was no central heating and few had running hot water so the only sources of heating were paraffin oil heaters and coal fires. As these heaters and fires had to be kept alight all evening until bedtime, keeping warm was expensive. It often became so cold you could see the steam coming from your breath when visiting the freezing toilet or bathroom. I remember going to bed many times in socks **and** pyjamas, and having to sometimes wash in cold water in the morning as running hot water was not the norm.

There was also waiting at bus-stops in the freezing cold to go to school, with buses always full-up because so many had broken-down on the icy and snow-bound roads.

As well as being bitterly cold it was also a miserable time. At home the whole house used to smell of paraffin and it made your clothes smell also. I was a teenager during the 1960s and as the eldest among the siblings in my family it was I who was always sent out to buy paraffin, either at the local Garage, Hardware store or Ironmongers. Having bought the *precious* heating fuel (*Esso Blue or Alladin Pink*) and carried it to the house with frozen fingers, the next job was to try and open the front door with those frozen digits, using that small and awkward Yale key given you by your parents to let yourself in. You couldn't do it. Even if you managed to put the key into the lock, your numb fingers couldn't hold onto it to turn it and open the front door. A *false* remedy for cold and numb hands and feet tried by many was soaking them in hot water; it was a *false remedy* because this resulted in another common health complaint among Caribbean families: 'chilblains'—itching and swollen hands and feet caused by bad circulation. Many found it quite difficult to walk.

Paraffin heater fire deaths

News of Caribbean family members, adults and children, being burnt to death or horribly scarred in fires started by such heaters was becoming common and widespread in black communities, particularly in households of multiple occupancy. In these dwellings one of the effects of trying to combat the cold weather was the reliance on cheap and portable paraffin heaters by many families for warmth and cooking. Their use was to become a standard practice. The following figures help to illustrate the conditions of existence of many black families during the 1960s, especially during the 'Big Freeze' of 1962/3 and the long and sustained snowfall and low temperatures of 1965/66.

During the 'Big Freeze' of 1963 and as Caribbean migrants struggled to heat their homes, on 7th February, 1963, the MP for Nottinghamshire Central, John Cordeaux, asked a parliamentary question about the number of fires caused by paraffin heaters reported to the fire service over the past three years, and how many deaths resulted from them. The Secretary of State for the Home Department, Christopher Woodhouse, answered as follows:

In 1960 2,988 fires caused by paraffin heaters were reported to fire brigades in England and Wales and in 1961 3,004. The statistics do not show how many deaths were caused by these fires, but it seems from sampling that there were fewer than 30 in each year...figures are not yet available for 1962.

The MP told parliament that in Nottingham these heaters were "very much used by Commonwealth immigrants," and there had been, on average, about one fire a fortnight over the past two years (*Hansard*, 7th February, 1963: Vol. 671 cc 656-657). In answer to another parliamentary question on the recent increase in fires in domestic premises and the loss of life involved, the Home Secretary replied that "between 1958 and 1961 ...the number of fires attended by fire brigades in dwellings in England and Wales rose from 22, 736 to 28, 532, an increase of approximately 25 per cent. The number of deaths was 579 in 1958 and 564 in 1961." And the fires were caused chiefly by electricity, oil appliances (paraffin heaters), smoking materials (cigarettes), chimney fires and gas appliances, in order of relative importance, with fires caused by paraffin heaters coming second only to fires caused by electricity (*Hansard*, 7th February, 1963 Vol. 671 c 657).

Paraffin heaters and 'multiple death fires'

Published in the *Royal Society of Health Journal* (1970) are the following figures from a *'Fire Research Technical Paper'* on *multiple death fires* in the United Kingdom over the previous ten years. This is quite revealing in that the data places the incidents of paraffin heater fires and deaths in a socio-economic and geographical context. *Multiple death fires are fires that kill five or more people in a residential property or three or more in a non-residential property.* Between 1960 and 1966 there were **368** incidents of multiple death fires in the UK, 237 of which were in dwellings resulting in 1000 fatalities, of which 359 were children aged 5 or under. Around 10% (36) of the *multiple death fires* were caused by oil heaters and this factor accounted for 20% of all domestic outbreaks, with the other 80% caused variously by electricity, smoking, coal fires and gas appliances. The Journal points out that *multiple death fires occurred most frequently in more densely populated areas where multiple occupancy is common and where overcrowding in old property is an important factor and occurred most frequently in the winter months.* *Multiple Occupancy* is defined by the Government as 'entire houses or flats let to three or more tenants who form two or more households and who share a kitchen, bathroom or toilet.'

During the same period the numbers of fires "increased most markedly in the London area, northwest England" as well as the Scottish lowlands. "In London and the southeast the number of fire fatalities over the seven-year period was 26%," more than a quarter "of the total for England, Wales and Scotland, and nearly double that of northwest England which had the highest number. In the same way, the number of multiple death fires doubled." The 1966 census records 1,159,170 *shared households* in England and Wales, nearly 60% of which were in Greater London, and such households represented nearly one quarter (24.4%) of the total households. The inhabitants of those shared households were living at a density greater than 1.5 persons per room. In some London Boroughs the situation is much worse. In Kensington & Chelsea, for example, shared households were 46.9% and represented 7.3% of households in the borough and this position is accentuated in areas with "a large immigrant population who mainly occupy furnished accommodation in *multiple occupations.*" Ladbroke Grove and Notting Hill are located in this borough and in those circumstances many of "the occupants have elected to have portable paraffin heaters for perfectly valid reasons."

Seasoning Time: 1960-1969

It is against the demographic background and environmental conditions as described above that I intend to develop my argument. To do this it is necessary to attempt a re-conceptualisation of the *motivations* and *forces* which I believe were contributory factors in preparing young black people for change; to make them receptive to the new social, cultural and political environment which, in the 1970s, emerged as distinctly 'youthful.' To re-conceptualise the nature of their progression into this new social environment, I have *adopted* the term *seasoning* which I have drawn from the mechanics of slavery in the Caribbean and *adapted* it for use as an analogy to explain and describe the process of that progression.

Seasoning was a term used during slavery to describe a two dimensional process. At the one level, it was one by which newly arrived African captives were put through a system of 'behaviour modification' to get them to accept their new status as things— 'tools'—set to *en-forced labour* to ensure their functional survival (It was Aristotle who advanced that slaves were mere *things*, no more than tools: see Marsh,

1974). At the other, it was also a process of 'acclimatization' to see if the constitution of the African could withstand the dramatic change in being removed from the climate of Africa to that of the Caribbean, and from one part of the slave Island to another. This dual *seasoning* process was integrated into the general transportation of slaves and into the slave economy and is described (Higman: 1976:131) as follows:

> ...(T)he process of seasoning followed for newly arrived Africans was **also** thought to be necessary in the movement of slaves from plantation to plantation within the island; heavy mortality was said to occur when slaves were 'removed to a climate which did not suit their constitution'. Such cases were said to result from the removal of slaves from the dry lowland areas to damp inland situations, where tetanus, catarrh, rheumatism and colds were prevalent. Examples of heavy mortality consequent to removal were certainly found, but it is doubtful that the adjustment to a new climate was the only factor involved.

The other factors involved were, of course, overwork and cruelty as well as environmental illnesses and disease. Put differently, during the *seasoning* period, which lasted between 1 and 3 years, there was a heavy loss of life among the slave population—between a quarter to one third perished mainly from a combination of overwork, disease and cruelty (Patterson, 1973:98). Those who survived the 'seasoning stations' were moved from plantation to plantation on those islands, or shipped to other islands across the Caribbean or sent to American plantations in the 'deep south.'

Whereas in the history of slavery *seasoning* referred to the process of preparing black captives to *accept and adjust to* subjugation, my use of the term here is to describe, analogously, the *conditions* and the *ways* in which black young people in 1960s Britain were *prepared* or *seasoned*, if you will, by environmental and institutional conditions and forces to make them receptive to the cultural politics of black liberation which were to emerge in the 1970s. A reversal of the *logic* of the slave-making *seasoning* process was therefore the outcome of the 'conditioning' and 'preparation' black young people underwent *in the urban crucible of post-war Britain.*

Unemployment and underemployment and 'seasoning'

This preparation, I want to suggest, occurred in a number of contexts and in a number of ways. Before I examine music, dance and post-war black youth subculture as a **force** in the *preparation* of black young people which I typify as constituting a 'pull' factor in the *'seasoning'* process, I will examine, first, the **forces** typified as 'push' factors that contributed to the social and cultural development of black young people in Britain. Hebdige (1978:150) observed that the "parting of the ways" between black and white school leavers *"had been preparing for years"* in the world of school and work during the 1960s. Hebdige (1977: 151) cites Hiro (1973) to point out that the *close proximity* into which black and white children were cast at school tended to break into crude racial stereotypes and myths, problematising the illusion of English 'racial' superiority engendered by the colonial education received by their parents' generation in the Caribbean. Contrary to their parent's experiences and expectations school was where their children were called *'wogs,' 'niggers,' and 'coons'* as a matter of routine, or referred to as *golliwog, sambo, rastus or,* simply, as *a black bastard* by white pupils.

Some were even told to *'get back to your own country'* even though they were born in England. Moreover black pupils could not get away from being described by the anonymous term *"you lot" (the Jamaican oo'nu) and told that "you lot live in houses packed with families of ten to a room"*—as is illustrated by the following 'jokes' about overcrowding:

> *Hey, (your name) did you heard the news?*
> *No, what news?*
> *Ten wogs died last night?*
> *(Recognising 'wog' as a code word for black people, you ask):*
> *How? What happened?*
> *The bed collapsed!*

Or, the not-funny one about house fires:

> *Hey, have you heard the news? No, what news?*
> *20 wogs died last night*
> *How?*
> *The house burnt down!*

And on those punch-lines, the *joker* would walk off laughing with his friends. Black pupils were both the butt of *jokes* as well as the listeners of them. In fact, part of the *joke* was to see the reaction on **your** face as it was being told; because *their laughter* and *your humiliation* were the aims of telling **you** the joke, once laughter broke-out, the humiliation was reinforced. In line with the 'Othering' effects of such jokes, a regular chant would be:

> *God made little woggie men*
> *He made them in the night*
> *And in his haste to make them*
> *He forgot to paint them white.*

When black pupils complained to their parents the reply would usually be the familiar: *"Sticks and stone may break my bones, but words will never hurt me."* Well, those words did hurt; they cut deep on the inside. Fights were inevitable. For some black pupils going to school on a Monday morning was a time to dread if a *Tarzan* or *Bob Hope* film had been on television the previous Sunday afternoon or evening. There would be no let-up on being asked if it was your relatives they saw on television last night or if *"you lot* really eat people?" I remember being told as a matter of course that *"you lot* eat Kit-e-Kat?" (i.e. Cat food). More denials, more arguments, more fights. That was during school. And on recognizing themselves as part of a *minority* in the school playground and on the streets, sticking together would ultimately become the norm, giving way to *group cohesion* and *solidarity*.

On leaving school black teenagers were often met by a more subtle discrimination by the *Careers Service* and prospective employers. As unemployment rose the impact was uneven and black school leavers lost-out to white school leavers, and even when black school leavers showed more ambition and sought skilled work or an apprenticeship, they met with disappointment. *When in 1966 asked by a Careers Officer what I wanted to do after leaving school, my reply was to train as an artist; his reply to me was that vacancies at London Transport seemed a more realistic option rather than the years it would take for me to undergo training. I decided to stay on in the 6th form instead, but this did not improve my job prospects any.* A report in the *Observer* (14/7/68) showed that white youths in deprived areas of black settlement, like Paddington and Notting Hill, were almost *five times more likely* to get skilled jobs than 'coloured' teenagers. In 1967 Michael Banton estimated that by 1974 "one in six of school leavers in the inner London area will be coloured" (Banton, 1967 quoted by Hebdige, 1977: 151).

This predicament, according to Hebdige, encouraged many black teenagers to review their situation in relation to the assumptions of their parents' generation, on the one hand, and to also review their experiences in the light of the discrimination they faced when compared to their white peers, on the other. A new **awareness** of their *particular situation* began to **manifest** in the **options** chosen by teenagers from the late 1960s, and with this new awareness began to recognize themselves as not being valued, as *being pushed* away from economic, social and cultural inclusion **in** British society, rejected by a society into which they had either been born, or in which they had grown up. Looked at another way it was more 'marginal inclusion' than total exclusion, or as put by Hall and others, (1978:350) their "differential incorporation" led to uneven distribution and to informal segregation.

When to run not whether to run

Running away from trouble was a prime **act of agency** used by young black people in developing *sub-cultural response*s to a range of problems encountered by them in urban Britain. On the streets in particular *where space had to be won and defended*, young people faced conflicts with local white youth 'gangs' and antagonisms with the local police over their presence on the streets and, as a consequence, a number of street tactics were developed for such eventualities. So by the time many of us became Fasimba and BUFP members, we all had a collective repertoire of responses to any number of confrontational situations.

Being stopped by the police was a routine and not an extraordinary event throughout the 1960s. By the late 1960s for all of us any contact we had with the police should avoid us being taken to the police station. Police stations were places to be avoided at all costs, and even if you had to leave clothing behind escape was paramount. This was necessary for two principal reasons: **first**, in the police station we knew that we get called any number of abusive names, get a few boxes or punches or a knee to the groin, or even planted with a knife or 'hash'—depending on *how* and *why* you'd been 'taken in': **second**, none of us wanted to explain to our parents why the police wanted to talk to us or what we were doing in a police station in the first place, as we feared admonition from them and other adult relatives. Running was therefore a prime strategy to escape police captivity and a possible beating and, more importantly, to avoid your parents' displeasure.

If a group of us were stopped by the police on our way out or on our way home, each of us had a false name, address, date of birth and school ready to offer. Because these were made-up names, we knew that they would not emerge in any checks made as the names had no criminal record attached to them. Moreover, we could also describe where the address was and that it was an address occupied by 'many West Indian families,' relying on their own stereotypes for its authenticity. We knew also that they could only check if the address actually existed only by visiting it; but that would only happen *after* you had been arrested.

In the 1960s personal radios were not common amongst the police so they could not immediately make any checks if that name was 'wanted' or had a conviction listed on the police national computer. In any event, we all had a made-up story that we'd met at a youth club like, for example, the West Indian League on Grove Lane in Camberwell, and that we only knew one another by nicknames learnt at the club. Whilst giving this information to the police as politely as possible, each would be surveying the scene for a route to run if the police said they were going to use the car radio to call for a Black Maria van to take us to the police station. If that seemed a possibility, then it only took a moment for us to all run in different directions simultaneously, or take the lead from the first person to make a move. To do this successfully, we had to know the area.

This act of agency may be illustrated by recalling an incident in a *late session* at the *Ram Jam* in Brixton in the summer of 1968. The *Ram Jam* was a club on Brixton Road where young people would meet, eat and dance to Soul, Rock Steady and Ska music. It held two sessions on a Sunday, an early one between 3 and 6pm and a *late session* between 7-11pm. I would normally go along to both sessions with a group of friends from Peckham where I attended school. The club itself was a mixed venue attended by black and white, male and female teenagers; it had a resident DJ too. International black artistes made regularly appearances and I remember seeing the *Supremes* and *Prince Buster* there. There were the inevitable clashes between white and black males where the knifing ('wetting') of white males was a regular outcome of these antagonisms (see Hebdige, 1977:149).

On that particular Sunday evening, I was sitting upstairs in the 'restaurant' and was found with an ornamental paper knife in my possession; the Bouncer took me to the club Manager who then called the police. *Shit! I thought. I'm in for it now.* Two plain clothes policemen arrived and escorted me down stairs, but on the way down I noticed that my 'escorts' weren't holding onto me. Once outside the Club one directed me to get into the open back-door of the Rover squad car. I could see Brixton police station across the road to my right, and knew what would happen once there: I was found with a knife and white youths had been cut-up in the Club! I noticed also that the squad car was facing towards Kennington. *It was now or never, I thought.*

In an instant I took off, running across the main road towards the direction of the road on the right of the police station. I could hear my 'escort' running behind me and his pace was quickening. I knew that if I continued to run in a straight line I'd have to work harder to out-pace him, so I swerved suddenly to the right and as he tried to match my move, he slipped and fell over. Leaving him on the ground, I ran as I'd never run before, ran and ran as *swiftly* and as *far* as I could up that road, jumped over a wall by some flats and lay there, still, on the ground near a bush. I could hear police cars racing by. My heart was beating so fast and so loud that I feared it could be heard far out in the street. I must have lain there for about 30 minutes or so listening for any activity on the street. I heard nothing, felt it was safe, left my hiding place and made my way from Coldharbour Lane to Peckham.

Once there I met some of the friends who were with me at the *Ram Jam* and had seen me take-off. They were *happy* to see that I hadn't been caught as I explained how I'd got away from the police, and from the beating I might have got if I didn't run. I didn't go back to the *Ram Jam* for weeks, and my mother knew nothing of this incident. As a consequence of this routine street tactic, the response of police patrols from the late 1960s was to routinely have a 'runner' or two with them. He or they could be identified as the one or two plain-clothes policemen *standing apart* from the 'uniforms' questioning you; they would be watching you, ready to chase and intercept anyone who tried to run-off. They'd be the ones wearing worn 'hush puppy' suede shoes. *Chris* made the same move to leave the British Transport police at the Oval underground station. It had been a tactic he'd developed in the years of his *seasoning* on the streets and in British institutions, prior to him joining the Fasimba.

The entry, therefore, of 1960s Caribbean teenagers into the *black cultural* politics of the 1970s would come only after another important *social and cultural process* had taken place: their experiences of institutional racial discrimination and police aggression countered by cultural and social agency, group consciousness and group solidarity. This was a self-generating consciousness and self-directed agency which, on the one hand, began to pull black teenagers **together** and **toward** a new cultural and social awareness/consciousness and **group**

cohesion and, on the other, was pushing them away from what they were beginning to perceive as an unjust society. These important social and cultural changes were not led by a single cause but driven by a combination of forces, social, economic, cultural and political, mediated partly by the flow of people, news, music, information and cultural exchange between the Caribbean and the circumstances of the Caribbean Diaspora taking shape in Britain.

All this led to the emergence of a *new social grouping* in British society who were not only racially, culturally and socially distinct from their white counterparts they were also socially and culturally differentiated *by age* from their parents' generation: *they were becoming urbanized black young people.* Having said that, there was an important social factor which connected these youth with their parent's generation and separated them further from their white peers, and that was *group* solidarity or, as it would become known during the 1970s, *black solidarity.* Brake (1980:125) describes this situation as follows:

> The solidarity of the black community against police harassment and the mutual support young blacks gave to each other in fights was something not found in the working class community.... (T)he breakdown of stable, subcultural identity among the working-class whites, combined with the erosion of the traditional supports of their parent culture, led to white youth feeling particularly threatened by the presence of any socio-cultural group cohesion. White groups were separated by neighbourhood, sub-cultural forms (*i.e. mods/ rockers*), but the very element for which blacks were despised—race—unites them against a common threat, be it white gangs, the police and other authorities.

From Youth Subculture to Black Culture

Already mentioned is the role that music, dance and dress played as defining ingredients in the formation of youth subcultures in post-war Britain (Hebdige, 1977, in Hall & Jefferson, 1977; Brake, 1980). With the development of youth sub-cultures among Caribbean descendents in 1960s Britain, Jamaican music, the most dominant music from the Caribbean, occupied this role. It is in this context that I suggest that very little if any attention has been paid to the influence of a Jamaican popular music style, Rock Steady, in helping to shape a sense of groupness, self-awareness and a 'black awareness' amongst young people of Caribbean descent in Britain.

In the historiography of Jamaican music, a number of text have been devoted to Ska and to Reggae and to the latter's genre of 'roots and culture.' Passing attention has been paid to *Rock Steady* music, with the exception of a section in Sebastian Clarke's *Jah Music* (1980). One reason for this historical distortion is that *Rock Steady* music is rarely seen as carrying a 'political message' when compared to its successor, Reggae in the 1970s. It is argued that this is not the case, as the cultural politics of Rock Steady music has to be seen in the *social context* and *time*s in which it emerged, as well as the conditions and contexts of its consumption by young people of Caribbean descent in Britain.

'People get ready, this is Rock Steady'

The lyrics set out below belong to a *Rock Steady* tune that, to all intents and purposes, signalled a break with the previous era dominated by Ska music and dance and the ascendancy of a new *style* of social and cultural entertainment speaking directly to young people.

> *Do it, do it, do it right now*
> *Do it, do it, do it right now*
> *Do it, do it, do the Rock Steady now*
> *Do it, do it, do the Rock Steady now*
> *We are young and we are strong*
> *And we know we can't be wrong*
> *So let's do it, do it, do it right now*
> *Do it, do it, do it right now*
> *We are young and you are old*
> *Still we know we've got the soul*
> *So let's do it, do it, do it right now*
> **(The Termites, Coxsone Records, 1967)**

Expressing the urgency of youth, it privileged the 'moment,' announcing that 'right now' is the time when youthfulness, strength and vigour should come to the fore and express itself—displacing but not subverting the philosophy of 'patience' and 'wisdom of age' of their parents' generation. *Rock Steady should be considered therefore as 'youth music.'* The youthfulness, vibrancy and optimism expressed in the music were clearly reflected by the youthfulness of the artists, the audience to whom they spoke, as well as the experiences and desires addressed in the lyrics. The Termite's asserted that: "We are young and we are strong/ still we know we can't be wrong/so let's do it, do it, do it right now." *These lyrics signalled also a desire for change.*

The entry of this new *style* of Jamaican music and its dance performance into the parties, clubs and blues-dances in black communities in Britain in the last quarter of the 1960s was to a new generation of youthful dancers. Dance venues were no longer dominated by adult revellers and Ska music and dance, but with the teenage descendants of the so-called 'Windrush' generation. Seen in a historical and social context, Rock Steady came to the fore when young people in urban Britain were experiencing and negotiating the tensions **in** black communities, and conflicts **between** black communities and white society.

Calling all Dancers

The rhyming of the words 'Ready' with 'Steady' may seem a lyrical over-simplification in Jamaican music but that's exactly what music lyrics do: provide short-cuts to the use of ordinary, every-day words and offer new connections and new meanings to how these words were used in the past and are to be used in the future. For example, in the Impressions' spiritually-focused soul-hit of 1965, '*People get Ready,*' the phrase 'Get Ready' functions, in this context, as a call to attention, a preparation for or in anticipation of a 'coming event' or of 'things to come' like a 'change'.

> *People get ready, there's a train a comin'*
> *You don't need no baggage you just get on board*
> *All you need is faith to hear the Diesels hummin'*
> *Don't need no ticket, you just thank the Lord*

There were two Rock Steady versions of the Impressions' '*People Get Ready:*' one by the Minstrels, a Studio One group (that included Cornell Campbell), and the other by Devon Russell, both to Clement Dodd's classic Rock Steady rhythms. Alton Ellis' "*Rock Steady*" and the Soul Agents' "*Get Ready, its Rock Steady*" are two tunes that use the lyrical economy of rhyming 'Ready' with 'Steady,' and the example by the Soul Agents not only *call dancers to the dance floor,* their lyrics take dancers also through the moves necessary to do the new Rock Steady dance:

Get ready, to do Rock Steady
Get ready, to do Rock Steady
Get ready, to do Rock Steady
Get ready, to do Rock Steady
Get in the mood
Face your partner move to the left
shake your shoulder
move to the right
rock your hips
now jerk your body line
rock you, rock in time.
sock it to me
sock it to me
sock it to me
sock it to me

Alton Ellis' hit also exhorts the revellers to do this "new dance when you're ready" inviting dancers to "shake your head, rock your bodyline, shake your shoulders, everything in time." Other Rock Steady hits were 'People Rock Steady' by the Uniques and a version on the same rhythm by Max Romeo; there was 'Stir it Up' and 'Bus Them Shut' (Pyaka) by the Wailers on the classic Wail N' Soul M' Rock Steady label; 'Engine 54' by the Ethiopians, and Jamaican 1966 Festival Song entrant, 'Ba-Ba Boom' by the Jamaicans, telling that: "*people are dancing, teenagers romancing* ..." According to Clarke (1980: 81) without dance there would be no music as from its inception the music was played "almost exclusively" for dancing via the Sound Systems or live performances.

"During the Ska era, because the rhythms were fast and pacy, the accent was placed on the feet, thus the shuffle and the split were the qualitative ingredients of the music." But Rock Steady music worked at a much slower pace than Ska music. It emphasized the bass more than Ska did, over which were laid songs with *vocal harmonies,* concerned themselves with *serious social issues and* expressed through *conscious lyrics.* An example of this is 'Time is getting Hard' by Lloyd Charmers,' who sang about the hard life many people endured in Jamaica and which drove many to migrate to Britain as a consequence:

Time is getting hard, boy
Got to leave this land, now
Time is getting hard, boy
Got to travel on
Pack up everything I own
I got to leave this place
Got to find somewhere else
Where I can help myself, believe me

Rock Steady music arose at a time of both *internal and external migration* set against a background of economic, social and demographic change. As well as people leaving the Island for other countries to seek a viable future, it was a time when young people were leaving the countryside also and congregating into the urban ghettos of Kingston. With increasing unemployment, poverty and homelessness, the emergence of Rude Boy 'gangs' was one consequence.

The 1960 Jamaican Census recorded a heavy drain of population from rural areas to the Metropolitan district of Kingston, where almost 40% of residents there has been born elsewhere in Jamaica (Francis, 1963, quoted by Hebdige (1978) in (eds) Hall and Jefferson, 1978: 155). This new social and political constellation provided the raw material for musicians and singers. Clarke (1980:81-82) identifies and distinguishes between the *physical* and *social* aspects of the *dance* moves in the Ska and the Rock Steady as follows:

> Ska was akin to the traditional expressionism of the free churches, the body could be expressed in whatever fashion, and it bought people together. When the rhythm slowed down, paradoxically, the tension increased, and the body was now responding to an inner rhythmic drive. *The tension of the external society was internalized by the dancer and expressed physically.* Thus in the Rock Steady the dancer could remain on his spot of earth, shake his shoulders, make pounding motion with his arms and hands (at an invisible enemy, an anonymous force), without recourse to or consciousness of a partner. The internal tension was demonstratively and explosively expressed. Because the movement was stylized, its external appearance alone could be interpreted as tension-releasing, violence shimmering beneath the surface.

The lyrics, the nature of the dance moves and their *new* social context distinguished Rock Steady further from Ska. Clarke (1980: 81-82) adds that *"in Ska there was happiness, a joy in the freedom of expression. This is not to say, however, that Rock Steady was not a joyous music but its slow tempo, its intensity and tension building features separated it from Ska."* The change from Ska to Rock Steady amounted to an "indigenization" or 'localisation' of the music as it began to reflect the *new* social and cultural mood and economic conditions **in** Jamaica. Rock Steady emerged therefore as a particularly Jamaican development, losing whatever *rhythmic* connections it once had with African-American rhythm and blues music but embraced the vocal styles of the new black artists singing Soul music, such as the Impressions and Major Lance.

However, what Clarke was not able to explore, and which is explored here, is the influence and impact of the Rock Steady style of music and dance on the sub-cultural styles of Caribbean descendants in Britain during the 1960s. The economic and cultural changes taking place in Jamaican were felt in Britain, principally through migration, and it led to a particular pattern of sub-cultural development among young black people and to separate and distinct social trajectories for black and white young people.

It is my argument that the Rock Steady style became dominant at a time when young black people were beginning to emerge as a *self-conscious social and cultural group* **in British society,** negotiating the tensions about *parental protection, family control and family based patterns of entertainment dominated* by Church gatherings, Christenings and 'big people's parties' while, at the same time, negotiating their *independence* from those, and from 'race' and class conflicts in schools and violence on the streets. The 'freedom of expression' dancers experienced in the Ska of the 1950s were transferred to the youthful revellers during the Rock Steady period of the 1960s.

That this music came to the fore in the London's black communities in mid 1966 is significant as it was to become one of the social and cultural forces binding together a new group of black teenagers in Britain as a self-conscious social group.

New clubs and dance venues were opening up in south London catering only for a new generation of black and young people playing Soul and Jamaican music. One such place already mentioned was the *Ram Jam* in Brixton where black teenagers were dancing to '*Pressure Slide*' by the Tennors, as white youths (mods) danced to Prince

Buster's *'Dance Cleopatra'*—a shuffling and 'toasting' version of a Ska instrumental, *'Jericho Chain,'* by Roland Alphonso. The others were the *Bedford Arms* in Balham where the same youthful contingent was dancing to *'Take it Easy'* by Hopeton Lewis, and the King Alfred in Bellingham dancing to Slim Smith's *'Rougher Yet.'* These new clubs, dance venues and Sound Systems, such as *Neville the Enchanter and Duke Lee*, offered opportunities for young men and women to forge a self-awareness, explore a 'youth identity' and participate in a youth culture and social behaviour not mediated directly by the 'parental gaze' of family entertainment events.

The music called for change, for things to happen 'now' (not to 'meekly wait and murmur not'), to fight for change, to overcome personal obstacles, to 'do good,' to be steadfast and, above all, be 'fearless.' At the same time, it called *for enjoyment, youthful cultural celebration and expression, emotional love and sex.* The audience taking in this music was not so much based on *commercial consumption* related to purchasing power but more on the *social and cultural consumption* of its beat and lyrical content.

Inasmuch as the artists and cultural stylists who came to the fore were themselves youthful, so too were the participants who rocked and sang to the new beat in the clubs and blues dances across south London between 1966 and 1968. Importantly, the social and cultural space created by the Rock Steady music style and dance venues became the forum for social, cultural and **identity development**, all of which took place away from the home and the parental gaze and, importantly, far from the scrutiny of white authority. It was an independence that was theirs to shape and mould in their 'own image' **in Britain.**

One important role this music played was to provide access to the Jamaican language and an alternative meaning system to the youthful descendents of Caribbean migrants, who had either been born in Britain or arrived here as youngsters. Speaking in Patios emerged as one form of cultural resistance and distancing from white society, the English language and culture. It was a 'lingua' which helped them to map and begin to understand their origins, presence and location in British society.

Against the expectations of their parents, they began to reject standard English and started to express themselves in a form of *lingua*, in a youth language mentioned in *'Good Good Rudie'* by the Wailers, or in what is described below by the Valentines in Jamaica as 'Rudie talk."

'Now fellow Rude Boys, stand fast and let us unite'

To illustrate my argument I have isolated three themes in Rock Steady music which I believe impacted on the *consciousness* and contributed to the cohering of Caribbean young men and women in the last quarter of the 1960s. The first I wish to refer to is the 'Rude Boy' genre, a continuation from the Ska era, where stories took place against a background of violence and terror waged by political gunmen in poor communities in Kingston, Jamaica (Clarke 1980). *'Guns Fever'* had been the title of a Ska instrumental by Baba Brooks in 1965, and became that of a Rock Steady vocal by the Valentines in 1967.

> *Did you read the news?*
> *I'm a bit confused*
> *The guns fever is back,*
> *Guns fever*
> *Rudie talk is in*
> *I don't know what it mean*
> *The guns fever is back*
> *Guns fever*
> *Every time you read the Gleaner or Star*
> *Man shot dead', 'Rude gangs at war',*
> *It's the fever*
> *Guns fever.*
> *The simplest thing is blam blam! blam!*
> *What is this on our little island?*
> *It's the fever, Guns fever*
> *You can know a rude chap*
> *By the way he set his cap*
> *The guns fever is back*
> *Guns fever*
> *Rudeness and guns It's*
> *the talk of the town*
> *It's the fever*
> *Guns fever*

Many Caribbean teenagers in British cities identified with the 'Rude Boy' style not just its outward *appearance* of 'badness' but with the *internal* 'fearlessness' associated with Rudies, against the wishes of their parent's but it was one of the few *black identity **styles*** available to them. As the 'Guns Fever' lyrics explained: "*You can know a rude chap by the way he set his cap,*" and many a black teenager *set* or *leant* their caps and hats in a Rude Boy style when going to clubs and dances, or on the street as a mark of group cohesion and distinction. Rude Boy tunes (as most Jamaican tunes did) combined news, reports, local stories and social commentary while others carried warnings about jail and the retribution awaiting those who take-up 'rudeness' using the ratchet and the gun.

Keith McCarthy's '*Everybody Rude*' was a popular Rock Steady Rude Boy song asking Rudies to "cool down," and known popularly by the phrase "*with the 'ratchet 'gainst the ratchet ...*" Stranger Cole's '*Drop the Ratchet*' offered another warning ("Don't let the ratchet find you guilty"). The *Rude Boys* in Derrick Morgan's '*Rudies in Court*' claimed they were "*rougher that rough/tougher than tough/strong like lion/we are iron.*" In the follow-up, '*Court Dismiss,*' the 'roughness' and 'toughness' and the *iron constitution* of the Rude Boys are ridiculed, where this Judge declares: "*I am Black Sulphuric Acid and I melt all iron.*" The lyrics of many tunes at the time spoke both in *support for* and *condemnation of* Rude Boys, their 'roughness and 'toughness" and their anti-authority stance inevitably led to violence, a violence that was especially condemned as it was on defenceless 'black people.'

Two sub-themes in Rude Boy stories are the position of young people —"the youth"—in what was seen as a corrupt and unjust post-colonial society; and the position of 'black people' in a post Emancipation and post Independent Jamaica. Prince Buster's *anti-Rude Boy* 'song/ play' (Clarke, 1980) "Judge Dread" confronts these contradictions in terms of what came to be described in the UK as **'black on black'** crime, but in Jamaica this seen as 'tribal war' and linked to wider political violence, poverty and government indifference to the black poor in post-colonial Jamaican society (Clarke, 1980). At the same time it resonated with an undercurrent yearning for a '*Black Redeemer*' to defend and seek justice for the poor, downtrodden and voiceless. Buster called his 'Prince Buster' label "Voice of the People."

'Isn't it Good to do the Rock Steady?'

Next are those that celebrate the dance itself, the Rock Steady. I have already referred to the 1967 Termites single, '*Do it Right Now.* Introduced with a fanfare of trumpets and Coxsone's distinct Rock

Steady beat, it invited dancers to the floor not only to "do it" but also to "sock it" to one another. It celebrated youth and vitality and evoked a sense of 'feeling good.' Included in this genre is *"Shake it Up"* by the Pioneers and introduced by the lyrics asking: *"Are you ready to do rock steady? ....We gonna shake it up, shake it up, shake it up all night long."* This celebration of dance and the call to 'feel good' was exhorted by Roy Shirley in *"Get on the Ball."* The tune had a hard, driving beat, a solid bass line over which, Roy Shirley's unique voice equates the Rock Steady dance with "feeling good" and with a sort of license to enjoyment unavailable in the present order of things.

> *Get ready, a get steady, a get ready*
> *Oh, there you got to feel nice*
> *Oh there you really feel good*
> *Ooh, feel, you've to move now for me,*
> *Yea, move your best for me, ay ay ay*
> *Oh there you got to feel nice*
> *Oh there you've got to rock steady, now*
> *Rock steady, a get ready, rock steady*
> *There, you've got to feel good*
> *Oh there got to feel nice for me, for me…*
> *A rolling, rolling, rolling rocking,*
> *Oh there you really feel it, Oh yea*
> *Feel again, again, now*
> *Get on the ball now friends*
> *Yea, feel nice.*

'*Get on the Ball*' went on to provide the basis for Roy Shirley's later Rock Steady hits, '*Hold Them*' and '*Be Good.*' Finally, there is the Melodians' '*Last Train to Expo 67.*'

Others tunes invited contact with your body, emotions and sexuality through dance performance, with songs of love, betrayal and heart-break, as well as physical contact and simulated sex. In the emotional vein come Slim Smith's early ballads, '*Let me go Girl,*" '*Love and Devotion*' and '*Conversation,*' Errol Dunkley's popular *"You Gonna Need Me" and "Please Stop your lying,"* and Ken Boothe's original and haunting track, '*Thinking,*" to an early Studio One, slow Rock Steady beat. Derek Harriott produced a succession of bitter love songs, such as '*Walk the Streets*', '*Do I Worry*' (US crossovers) and '*Stop that Train*' by Keith & Tex (the DJ version, '*Draw your Brakes*' by Scotty was released in the 1970s and featured in the film, 'The Harder They Come').

The Rock Steady version of P. P. *Arnold's 'First Cut is the Deepest'* by Norma Fraser, and Marcia Griffiths' classic *'Feel like Jumping'* are among a number of Rock Steady offering by women in Jamaica. Included is Dawn Penn's reply to Slim Smith's *'Let me go Girl,'* in *'Let me go Boy,'* on the same Slim Smith rhythm. She tells him:

> Me never hold you nor try to control you
> Me never hold you nor try to control you
> Go on guy, go out go tour the world, yea
> Safe travel guy, go on and rule the world, yea
> Now you are free from all misery, yea

The genre includes many instances where female artists reply to sexism or misogyny by male artists, such as Ullett's version, *Ten Commandment of Woman*, a reply to Buster's original, *Ten Commandments of Man*. Finally, we have Dermont Lynch's *"Adults Only"* and Slim Smith's *"Hip Hug"* which are among many examples of tunes that invited intimate physical contact: *"Come on and dance with me, come on and hip hug with me, hip hug baby, let's do rock steady."* Clancy Eccles' Rock Steady vocal, *'What will your Mama Say?'* was another tune with its lyrics drawn from the raw material of youthful experiences and spoke of young people's concerns: differences between young lovers about hurried marriage plans which were unbeknown to the bride's parents:

> Have you thought about things that we've been doing?
> Have you thought about things that we've been saying?
> All you talk about is wedding plans
> Those things we don't understand
> What will your mama say,
> what will your mama say?
> When she finds out, oh yes, were in love.

From the USA to JA

Rock Steady music also provided many examples of the cultural flow and exchange between Jamaican and African-American music, with examples of soul tunes given the Rock Steady treatment. These tunes are what I will describe as a 'Lovers Rock Steady" and include Soul songs such *as "Young Wings can Fly"* by Johnny and the Attractions, *"One Fine Day"* and the haunting *"Gypsy Woman,"* by Slim Smith and Prince

Buster's Rock Steady version of *"Dark End of the Street."* Examples of pop covers are *"Sweets for my Sweet"* by Jamaican group, Bobby Aitken and the Caribs, and Ken Booth's *"Tomorrow."* Other soul crossovers include the Impressions' *'You'll want me Back'* which appeared as *'You Don't Care'* by the Techniques, Lloyd and Glen's *'Keep on Pushing,'* and *'Born to Love You'* by Derrick Harriott. Producers Sonia Pottinger (Gayfeet) and Derek Harriott (Crystal) issued many Rock Steady versions of Soul classics.

'They push them around like a old time Slave'

Finally, come those songs that addressed directly issues about blackness, slavery, poverty, and the displacement of black people, the Jamaican poor, codified as 'poor people'. Tunes that spoke of the displacement of the urban poor from 'Shanty Towns' began in the Ska era, with tunes such as Buster's *'Shanty Town'* and other releases on the same theme, telling of the bulldozing of homes occupied by poor people on 'captured' land.

However, principal in this genre is Prince Buster's Rock Steady tune, *"White Power"* (now repressed in Japan as *'Black man must be free.'*). Apart from a few copies that were circulating on pre-release and played in south London clubs and dances, mainly by *'Neville the Enchanter'* Sound System over 1967 (e.g. the Ska Bar), this record was not released and was banned in post-colonial Jamaica—though the instrumental version to this was released in Britain as *'Come Do it with Me'* on a blue 'Fab' label in 1968. In its lyrics, Buster asserted the right to self-determination and to self-definition for black people in Jamaica.

> *Black man must be free*
> *to be what he wants to be*
> *How long will you use?*
> *Your bible and your hymn book*
> *to keep him down in slavery*
> *Love neither silver nor gold*
> *That's what my foreparents were told you*
> *beat them with you whip*
> *You juk them with you sword*
> *And you pitch them out on Spanish Town Road*
> *But me? Ketch me if you want me,*
> *ketch me if you want me, ketch me*

Ketch me if you want me,
ketch me if you want me, ketch me
Me want me real name
Me no want no slave name
Me no want me pickney fe have no white man name
I man must be free.

By wanting his "real name" and refusing a "white man's name" along with the self-deprecation, cultural subordination and economic bondage this naming embodies (Benston, 1984), Buster is privileging black accounts of slavery, displacement and brutalisation in Jamaica, the very colonial lines of descent leading to the youthful Caribbean descendents in Britain who were consuming its message. Jamaica gave birth to Marcus Garvey, the 'father' of Black Power, it is therefore not surprising that these questions should come to form the basis of an inquiry as to **origins** in Jamaican popular music. During the 1970s Jamaican music came to be called 'Black Music', speaking **to** *and* **for** the oppressed and dispossessed in the African Diaspora as it had a handle on 'black subjectivity.' It is to the development and mapping of this 'black subjectivity', 'black consciousness' and 'black awareness' to which, I suggest, Rock Steady music has made a contribution.

Rock Steady music came to the fore in the UK about 1966 and at a time when youthful Caribbeans were emerging as a self conscious group. It coincided also with the emergence of new entertainment genres and venues catering for young people playing Soul and Rock Steady music. Considered principally as 'youth music', it was more than just dance performance; it was a **social** and **cultural** performance where young black people developed a language, dress style, social attitudes and dispositions far removed from the parental gaze.

It offered opportunities for contact with and expressions of emotional love through the lyrics of the songs, invited contact with your body and sensual/sexual experience through close dance, and is a cultural and social performance firmly located in the 'rites of passage' into young adulthood. These, I argue, were necessary developments in and a 'preparation' of 'black subjectivities' through language and a social and cultural awareness of themselves as black young people in Britain, upon which a wider and deeper consciousness could be built by Black Power in the 1970s.

I was 19 years when I entered that *Black space* on that Sunday afternoon and recognised some of the young people there as people I'd seen at blues-dances and clubs in the south-east during the late 1960s. Many of the young people there, I will suggest, had been 'seasoned' as a result of their experiences of marginalization in British society, had *survived* and now had a 'preparedness' about them. The Fasimba offered an ideological site and a socio-cultural venue for this 'preparedness': to engage in a new black cultural performance but this time mediated directly by Black Power politics.

CHAPTER 6

SELPO, the Fasimba and Black Power

In the long run the success of the revolution depends on whether or not developments of consciousness have been set in motion in the oppressed during the first phase of the revolution. Their indignation must be channelled and conceptualised to such an extent that they gain an insight into the mechanics of their own oppression.
(**Renater Zahar,** Frantz Fanon: *Colonialism and Alienation,* 1974:93)

Men must not only be dissatisfied; they must be so dissatisfied they will *act*.
(**Denmark Vesey,** 1767-1822; quoted by Bennett, 1969:113)

'Let us do Something'
(**Joe Higgs,** Elevation Records, 1972)

Who were the Fasimba? What were their origins? What is the significance of the name? What was their 'Cause' in the spectrum of 'Black Causes' in Britain and internationally, and how did they define, organise and propagate this 'Cause?'

The Fasimba emerged from the South East London Parents Organisation (SELPO) in the spring 1970. The origins of SELPO itself was as a response to the ESN controversy and the issue of black children's education, so its main programme was an *educational* one and began with the 'Saturday School' in the early part of 1969 in the New Cross area of Lewisham to counter the effects of the mis-education of black children in British schools. The Fasimba were themselves the 'Youth Wing' of SELPO and emerged from the growing interest in, and attendance to, the organisation by young people who came from far and wide as news spread of its black history classes, education and cultural programmes. But most of all it was a new place to meet other young people outside of the home, of the 'parental gaze' and the gaze of white institutions, to extend the practice of their young adultness and their *elevated* sense of self—their *'blackness.'*

The name 'Fasimba' was Brother Dudley's idea and is Swahili for *Young Lion.* It was used, initially, to describe those young people who formed the rehearsal group for the play, 'The Black Experience.' But the *Fasimba tradition* eventually embraced by the Youth Group was that the name referred in particular to Shaka Zulu's most *feared* and *disciplined* warriors, the *Fasimba Regiment* (Ritter, 1955, 1968) and regarded ourselves, therefore, as *young* and *fearless* warriors and as a *disciplined* group of young people. However, even as the Fasimba grew out of the 'parent organisation' SELPO, this organisation had its origins in a Caribbean tradition, a tradition derived from the teachings of Marcus Garvey. Garvey was an originator and forerunner of **Black Power** (Rodney, 1971) and of Pan-Africanism, an idea said to have been credited in error to the Black Scholar, W.E.B. Du Bois (Tarikh, 1980:31-34), hence the Pan-Africanist political stance of the organisation and the Garveyism underpinning its cultural politics.

The Fasimba also embraced Malcolm X's political philosophy on community self-defence, self-organisation and self-reliance, all of which were based on Garvey's ideas and programmes. The events and the motivations leading to the founding of SELPO lie therefore in the meeting of its four founding members: Dudley Arthurs, George Campbell, Roy Francis and Ronnie Eaton—all Jamaicans and, in different ways, followers of Marcus Garvey's traditions on the 'upliftment' of black people. Caribbean connections, as we have seen, were important to the origins and development of the organisation and to '**Black Power**' itself. According to Brother Dudley, between 1968 and 1969:

> Brother Eddy had this group going on in Peckham. Brother Eddy was an old Jamaican man who was part of the 'Back to Africa Movement' with Garvey. I used to go down there with Roy to meetings on Sundays and there I met Palmer (a Jamaican Marxist) ... I think it was called the Afro-Caribbean Brotherhood. I was introduced to George through my sister, and it was a meeting at George's that I met Ronnie Eaton (a Garveyite from Jamaica) and Roy Sawh (from Guyana). What motivated me to change, what caused me to change—what really got me—was the whole civil

185

rights thing in America, watching TV and seeing dogs being set upon people...But what really grabbed my interest more than any-thing else, and I'll never forget to this day and what spurred me to move on was one of those racist governors in the American south, when he said "in 5000 years of history you name me a city that a Negro had ever built?" And you know I didn't know it. I had no idea. I was dumbfounded!

So we decided to launch this organisation. One of the reasons we decided to launch this organisation, was as a counter to the racism that was going on (in Britain) and what was going on in America—the whole Civil Rights Movement and the whole **Black Power** Movement. But we wanted to focus on questions about education because we were discovering now that some of our children were being sent to these schools for the educational subnormal and felt that was very wrong (Personal Interview, 2005).

The two main reasons for launching SEPLO were, firstly, to combat the racism in the British education system which was the assigning to black children the status of mental sub-normality and; secondly, the newspaper reports and television images from the US of black people fighting for their civil rights in America. But, at the back of Dudley's mind was the broader issue of the mis-education of black people generally and their children in particular, as during his own schooling in Jamaica in the 1950s he recalled having learnt nothing about Black history or even African history, apart from those inherited utterances from Marcus Garvey. It was as if black people had no history before slavery and colonialism, hence the confidence of the racist Governor in the southern states in declaring that black people had made no contributions to world history. It became the strategy of one of the founder members, George Campbell, to build the organisation by focusing on education so as to *attract and involve black parents and young people in their own improvement and social change,* and for the organisation to move away from the 'public show' of militancy that most Black groups had hitherto seemed to display

The Saturday School would encapsulate this focus and do two things: first and foremost, it would provide a material benefit to the children and their parents and, second, tap into the parents' own educational aspirations—those who saw the education of their children as an investment in their own futures. *The message to them was, therefore, that British racism, as manifest in the ESN issue, sought to deny any realization of these aspirations. One of the reasons for migration was to secure a better future for themselves and their children.* Additionally, because the parents knew someone who knew someone connected with SELPO or the Saturday school, and believed in the motives for this work, they were confident to leave the children there most of the Saturday to be taught, cared for and fed. For all intents and purposes, it was like a 'large family.'

As the organisation grew in popularity and influence in and around the Lewisham area, and with a large body of young people, the group began to envision the work of the organisation as to re-educate, motivate and politicise black people, especially the 'youth,' so that they become the force for change. The Fasimba grew from just being the name for the young group rehearsing the play, 'Black Experience' with Bro. Dudley, to become the name of all the young people who flocked to the organisation. The Fasimba as a Black Organisation was thus created. The Fasimba is the Organisation and the Fasimbas refer its members, and the two names are used here alternatively. At the time I visited the meeting place New Cross in the spring of 1970, I was aware that young people joined Fasimba, which was, mainly for the young people, and the adults joined the South East London Parents Organisation (SELPO).

Black Power activism in South-East London

In her book, 'Longest Journey,' Joan Anim-Addo (1995:16), describes the situation in Lewisham with the emergence of more youthful and radical **Black Power** organisations in London in the 1970s, including the 'Fasimbas.' The 1970s **Black Power** 'generation' had inherited some of the programmes from 1960s 'generation,' including holding "meetings and study groups locally and nationally" and 'direct action' through demonstrations, picketing and other forms of 'disruption.' The general aim of all these activities had been to *"raise the level of black consciousness, to politicise the black community into understanding the nature of racism and its impact"* on their daily lives. Of particular importance was how Britain systematically *"kept black people powerless"* and activists consequently sought to *"develop strategies to counteract the entrenched political reality."* The *"political mobilisation"* of black people, it was posited, *"would ensure action on a number of fronts."* The call for **Black Power** was seen as an answer to black powerlessness. Anim-Addo writes:

> Before long, radical groups of politically differentiated persuasion emerged. The Black Unity and Freedom Party (BUFP) became established in the Lewisham area. Known colloquially as the 'black and white unite and fight' Group, BUFP assumed a class perspective on the black struggle, emphasising the radical alliance of working class activists. *The Fasimbas, in comparison, were closer to Pan Africanists.* The North London based Black Liberation Front (BLF) assumed a culturalist/ nationalist stance while the Black Panther Movement, with branches in South and West London, was largely modelled on the highly publicised original in the USA. They were perceived as young Marxists, class warriors verging on the militarised.
>
> Each group organised meetings, social programmes and a published voice. Publications such as Grassroots, *Black Voice*, and *The Black Liberator* became the voice of the new black organisations and were made available to the wider black community whether they were out shopping or had been invited to hear a popular speaker. Membership of the organisations was not simply local. Young people travelled across London and further afield to take up leadership roles in political activities which for many had ousted the ritual churchgoing of their parents' generation.
>
> These new activists radically challenged the role of the church in keeping black people passive or complacent in the promotion of their rights. They also suspended the petty inter-island rivalries characteristic of the older group. The common enemy of diasporic black experience was the rallying force. Black identity was reclaimed and forcibly asserted.

Anim-Addo *(1995:154-155)* also describes the activities, organisation and membership of the Fasimba, who "undertook voluntary supplementary teaching at weekends:"

They stressed the need to relearn black identity and get rid of derogatory conceptions of black identity derived from a racist curriculum as well as from the English language itself. The teaching of black history was given a central place and, contrary to colonial and English educational practice, pride in the connection with Africa was reinforced. The basic tools of literacy were given careful attention.

The organisation elected members and held weekly meetings where Fasimbas from other areas would attend. New members were screened for their level of commitment and assessed initially by their attendance at meetings. It was then put to a full meeting whether the prospective member was acceptable for membership. The Fasimbas were a variety of ages but there was a special *interest in young black people who felt alienated or frustrated with the system.*

As former Fasimba told Anim-Addo about the purpose of the organisation's outreach to and focus on the 'youth':

We are saying to them 'get politically involved' and the way to do it is not through the destructive paths of petty crime but through the constructive outlet that we offer as a black organisation. The Fasimbas have given many young blacks a sense of pride and purpose.

Structure and Organisation of the Fasimba

The organisation was composed of two interrelated groups: **SELPO**, which ran the Saturday School with the help of Fasimba members and other volunteers, and the **Fasimba**, the 'Youth' or 'Political Wing' of SELPO, and were combined and structured as follows: there was the 'central committee' that included the four founders of the organisation: George Campbell, Chairman; Ronnie Eaton, Treasurer/ Secretary; Dudley Arthurs, Arts and Culture; and Roy Francis, Security/Self-Defence. Operating beneath the central committee was the sub-committee, drawn from the Fasimba members and represented both the 'Youth' and the 'Political' Wing of the organisation. It was by way of meetings between these committees that all the policy and decision-making functions of the organisation were carried out.

The membership of the Fasimba was divided into four geographical 'areas' according to where most people lived, each with an 'area leader' who was also a member of the sub-committee and attended sub-committee meetings with the central committee. It was via the meetings between central and sub-committee members that organisational policy and direction was debated and decided, where the needs and wishes of the Fasimba were represented, and the means by which initiatives planned by the 'areas' were given the go-ahead. Central to dispersing the work of the Fasimba was the 'propaganda committee' which included Sister Andrea as well as the Oval Four. It was at a meeting between the central and sub-committee that it was decided that five of us would represent the Fasimba at a meeting to be held in support of Tony Soares on Thursday in March 1972.

The four geographical locations were identified by particular names or an acronym by the members who lived in those areas: *Black Core* (Lewisham, Catford, Lee Green); *Black Acres* (Greenwich, Plumstead, Woolwich); *EDPAC* (East Dulwich, Peckham and Camberwell); and *Marcus Kwame* (New Cross, Deptford, Brockley, and Forest Hill). Fasimba members who came from as far as East, West and North London would join meetings in whichever area was closest to them. From the spring of 1971 the central committee met fortnightly at the new headquarters in Tressillian Road, Brockley, on a Saturday evening between 7.30 and 9.30pm. Prior to the move we all met at a central committee member's home at Peckham Rye on a Saturday evening. 'Area' meetings were every two to three weeks and held at a member's home in that locality, between 7.30 and 9pm (see Fasimba within the Fasimba below).

Fasimba Programmes: Community Outreach

The basic and most important aspect of our work was Community Outreach and was one way of engaging with the local black community, sharing our ideas with them and, importantly, providing a range of services. An integral part of this sharing of ideas was the selling of black books, posters, carvings, badges, Malcolm X T-shirts, African material, and Black Community Newspapers like *Grassroots* and *Black Voice* on a Saturday. Importantly these stalls were set up outside black businesses, including a Grocery shop in New Cross, a black Bakery in Brockley and

NOT JUST BECAUSE ...

a Barber shop in Brixton. This served a number of purposes: **first**, to forge real links with black businesses as a part of the philosophy of self-help advocated by Marcus Garvey; **second,** engage in discussions with shoppers and passers by; and **third**, to promote the use of their goods and services by Fasimba and members of the local community.

Propaganda

A second-hand printing machine was purchased and on it we produced organisational documents and propaganda leaflets and other items, such as a sticker entitled '*Kill the Bill*' opposing the 1971 Immigration Bill before it became the Immigration Act in January, 1972; these were distributed and stuck on buses and other public places in the south London area. Another item of propaganda was the famous 'Message to Tabby' leaflet, designed and produced by *propaganda committee* members from *Marcus Kwame* and *EDPAC* after the week-long clashes between black youth, white fairground workers and the police in the summer of 1971. The *Message to Tabby* leaflet commented on the beating-up of *Radcliffe Carr* by fair-ground workers at Peckham Rye fun fair and, as already discussed in Chapters 3 and 5, spoke to the youth in the *street lingua* used by them at the time, in which we advised them *what to do and what not to do* when confronted by white gangs or the police on the streets of Peckham (*Evening Standard*, 23/1/73).

Black Psalms was another item from the Fasimba propaganda machinery transforming and endowing aspects of black social and cultural practices with new meanings and new connections, again using the terms with which adults and young people would be familiar. An example of this transformation process can be seen in the production of '*Black Psalms—Versions 1, 2 & 3*' in 1971, based on the 23rd Psalm, a popular prayer of 'protection' in Christian Caribbean households. As a member of the '*propaganda committee*' I saw it as my role to find creative ways to get our messages across, working with and *transforming existing cultural mediums and turning them into something new.*

The teenagers and young adults who attended parties and dances at that time were quite used to dancing to a 'musical feast' of 'versions' of popular reggae tunes, to the extent that 'versioning' is now an integral part of Jamaican music culture. As a teenager during the 1960s, I was quite familiar with the verses of the 23rd Psalm and Prince Buster's Rock Steady hit, '*Drunkard Psalm*,' with its warning about over-indulgence in drinking the 'white spirit'—rum. For example, in 1971 I came across another version of the 23rd Psalm as '*The Capitalist Psalm*' in a *Youth*

Forces for National Liberation (YFNL) newspaper from Jamaica. This version ran: *'The Capitalist is my Shepherd and I shall always live in want.'* *'Black Psalms: Version III'* is introduced by the religiously familiar announcement: *'Verily, Verily, We say unto you:'*

> **Black Power** is my Shepherd and I shall **not** want,
> It maketh me to see beauty in myself
> It giveth I knowledge, it giveth I confidence and it
> cleanses my soul
> It leadeth I through the paths of revolution for
> freedom's sake.
> Yea though we tread the streets and alleys of Babylon
> (England)…

Expressed partly in the language of Ras Tafari, our **message** to the youthful black masses in south London was that with **Black Power** as your 'Shepherd' you shall **not** want.

Services to the Community

Organisationally, SELPO and the Fasimba provided a range of services to the local community which were spread by word-of-mouth rather than by advertising. These services included the educational, political, cultural and legal.

GCE classes: These classes were part of the Supplementary education programme extended to any young person about to take their GCE exams , and were run on a Saturday and involved Fasimba members who already had passes in the subjects to be taken.

Plumbing and Electrical repair services: A cheap and efficient service was available to any local black household requiring the services of a qualified plumber, as well as a safe household repair service provided by the qualified tradesmen in the organization.

Electronics classes: This took place on a Thursday where Fasimba members Ossie and Tony took a group of young people through the stages of building a *transistor Amplifier as opposed to the valve Amplifier*. A popular class amongst young males, the Amplifier eventually builtwas used to play at house parties, Christenings and Birthday parties by members of the organization.

Legal Advice: The South East London Parents Organisation (SELPO) had contact with a firm of Solicitors to whom we referred those seeking legal advice or representation. Bruce Pitt, son of Lord Pitt, was one of the Barristers.

Plays: The Fasimba produced three plays: *The Black Experience*, tracing how we were transported to the West; *Black Versions,* and *Malcolm X*, with the Black Arts Workshop. The three plays were great hits and were attended even by those who saw us as 'cultural nationalists' (see below, 'Fasimba and the particular application of **Black Power**').

Thursday meetings: Thursday was the time for political education, study groups, discussions among the Fasimba. For a while it functioned also as a meeting place for those rehearsing the play, 'The Black Experience.' As Thursday meetings developed into a political arena Fasimba members were encouraged to do presentations on topics of their own choosing, honing and sharpening study, presentation and political debating skills. In those study groups, Paul Bogle and the Morant Bay rebellion featured, as well as the political organising of Malcolm X, Stokely Carmichael and Marcus Garvey, and the *Groundings* of Walter Rodney. Studied also were the writings of Marx, Lenin and Mao, as well as the military campaigns and tactics of Hannibal and Shaka Zulu. It was also a forum for national and local news and issues, as well as news from the Caribbean, America, and Africa.

Area meetings: Area meetings were held every third week by each geographical **area** of the organisation's operations and were the forum for the discussion of local issues, activities and initiatives to be undertaken. Local study group initiatives also grew from these meetings. See Fasimba within the Fasimba below.

Sunday meetings: Meetings held every Sunday were open to the black public. It was where talks on major issues were given by the Chairman, George, or by guest speakers invited or had requested to come and address the often huge gatherings. Importantly, it was **a general forum** for the expression of ideas around themes of *black unity and black consciousness* that were central to our **Black Power** organising. It was the policy of the organization that white people were not allowed into these meetings, and was a long-standing policy position in black organisations operating under the umbrella of **Black Power** or Revolutionary Black Nationalism. When Malcolm X was asked in 1964 if his new organisation, the OAAU, was open to white membership, he replied:

> Whites can help us, but they can't join us. There can be no black-white unity until there is first some black unity. There can be no worker's solidarity until there is racial solidarity. We cannot think of uniting with others, until we have first united with ourselves (quoted by Proyect in 'CLR James and Malcolm X;' 1999: 6).

Along the lines of this policy, a number of well-known black people were invited as guest speakers at these meetings, including the Reverend Wilfred Wood; Bernard Coard; GK Osei; Darcus Howe; John La Rose; Obi Egbuna; Roy Sawh, to name but a few. Hakim Jamal, a cousin of Malcolm X, was also a speaker at one of these meetings, as is described further down. Miriam Makeba, at that time married to Kwame Toure (Stokely Carmichael), was invited by Dudley Arthurs to address a Fasimba meeting but was unable to attend.

An original member of SELPO Marilyn Neufville, the Jamaican sprinter, was also a Fasimba member during the time she represented Britain at the European Indoor Championship in Vienna, March, 1970. But she metaphorically 'ran into problems' after deciding to represent Jamaica and not England in the Commonwealth games in Edinburgh in July. Despite being pursued and hounded by the press for "betraying the country in which she received her athletics training" she **did run** for Jamaica and won her race easily by over 20 meters to become the 400m Commonwealth Gold medallist in 1970. What is an unknown is whether her decision to run for Jamaica and not England was influenced by her Fasimba membership and the philosophy of **Black Power** professed by us at that time. She certainly got a lot of support from the Fasimba and her close friendship with *Omar* would have had some influence on her subsequent decision.

Black Power: 'Better Must Come' or 'New Civilisation?'

Black Power activity in the 1970s was much more than strictly prosecuting the *politics* of Black Redemption. **Black Power** envisaged *social* and *cultural* dimensions to Black Redemption. Moral support for Marylyn Neufville's athleticism and her decision to run for Jamaica was one dimension of the activities in which the Fasimba were involved. Her decision to run for Jamaica reflected a new *nationalistic* mood of personal and cultural pride and self-determination that were developing in the consciousness and disposition of Caribbean descendents in Britain during the 1970s, captured in 1972 by the sentiments expressed in Delroy Wilson's popular hit single, *'Better Must Come.'* And that was what drove **Black Power** activism amongst sections of black young people in Britain during the 1970s: a hope for a better future.

Young people came from near and far to take part in new cultural activities and black educational programmes. It was also a place where they could and did meet socially, away from the 'parental gaze' and state surveillance. It was a place where black young people met on their own terms to generate new dimensions of *brotherhood and sisterhood and* explore new dimensions of *sociality.* It was where black young people developed and practiced public speaking skills, gained personal confidence and confidence in one another, which lent itself to discussions of new ideas and old issues, to the exchanging and sharing of information on what they'd learnt as a consequence of engaging with **Black Power**. Importantly, it served as a forum for an increase in literacy among black young people by the increasing availability and exchange of black literature.

New words, expressions, terms and concepts emerged from these literary and cultural explorations as personal, cultural and political vocabularies were enriched. Reading national and international black community newspapers soon became a norm and, as a consequence, an interest in education and self-improvement was resurrected. At the same time an interest in and solidarity with the situation of black peoples world-wide was nurtured. Locally, people joined libraries to seek out recommended books and if they were not there requested that they were ordered and stocked. Some took further education classes while others began to express once-hidden ideas and feelings in poetry. But most importantly, no longer marginalised as a 'coloured' person, the new Black identity now offered a place of centeredness, a place of safety, a sanctuary; it was a place of confidence, assurance, invigoration and growth. With **Black Power** the new Black identity was to become a *Place of Habitation.*

The Fasimba Sunday meetings functioned as an expression of this place of Habitation. It was **the** forum where new cultural practices were expressed, displayed and shared; where men and women presented Black artistry and aesthetics in the plaiting or corn-rowing of hair or the wearing of the 'Afro' or 'Natural.' It was where Black beauty and elegance were displayed and enjoyed. Young men and women adorned themselves with all manner of Black art and artefacts, such as beads, wooden and silver hair jewellery, head wraps, necklaces with Black fists or a map of Africa. An array of badges were used to represent the new Black identity and allegiance to a Cause: Black Panther, Malcolm X, 'Free Huey', **Black Power**, and 'Free Angela Davis' badges were on display. African-print clothes like the Dashiki became the norm and African materials were fashioned into shirts, skirts or dresses. Fasimba meetings and functions were attended by Ras Tafari youth attired in Khaki decorated with the Ethiopian red, gold and green; others came dressed in military style garments while some were kitted-out in all-Black attire, complete with black berets, dark glasses and badges. Dashiki-shirts and Afros were also popular identity choices. In fact every style of dress and presentation were represented by the Fasimba membership.

Not to be ignored were those young men regarded as the 'lumpen-proletariat' or 'hustlers' who came to Sunday and Thursday meetings to see what was going on and, in many cases, attended Fasimba functions. Sub-committee members knew many of them from school but their presence caused some concern amongst some members of the 'parent' organisation, *SELPO*. On occasions it was these young men, with Fasimba security, who would 'hold the door' at packed meetings, dances and plays, and in defence of their presence we argued that if we could not reach out to them, what then was our purpose? As conscious Black activists, declaring a Black identity (as a place of Habitation) was but the first stage in Consciousness-raising; but declaring oneself to be 'Black and Proud' wasn't enough as this new-found identity and consciousness needed to be engaged with a purpose or Cause. A Black identity or a Black Consciousness was, therefore, not an end in itself but a means to an end. It was a Consciousness that needed to be applied as an instrument for the liberation of *black minds* from the tyranny of *mental slavery* and black bodies from economic and political bondage. A Black identity needed also to be a site of constant striving, advancement and upliftment. A Black identity needed to move on from being a *Place of Habitation* to become a *Place of Action*.

Black Music

Music was an important element of social and cultural identity, expression and performance in terms of dance, social and cultural commentary. As discussed in Chapter 5, Black music also confronted political issues, many of which centred on the displacement of black ancestors from Africa via the slave trade and their experiences of slavery, emancipation and the post-colonial politics and economy of the Caribbean. Represented among the Fasimba were the *Soul and Funk* and *Reggae and Roots music* communities. Not to be forgotten were Jazz community members, such as Bro Dudley, who introduced me to the music of Nina Simone, the originator of '*To be Young, Gifted and Black.*' Among classic Soul *message music* was '*Respect Yourself*' by the *Staple Singers*, and *Cutis Mayfield's* timeless and spiritually-*inspired* '*People Get Ready,*' again expectant of a *change.*

An important medium of musical expression and entertainment were the Last Poets, much enjoyed by the membership. The Last Poets dealt with the 'spoken word' and their first album, '*The Last Poets*' (1970) featured the famous tracks, '*Niggers are Scared of Revolution,*' 'When the Revolutions Comes' and '*Wake up Niggers.*' The term 'Niggers' as we understood it's use then was a political definition applied to someone who did not possess or seek to possess himself or herself, a white man's version of a black person. It was the definition of a black person still mentally a slave and the track '*Niggers are Scared of Revolution*' pointed to a person willing to do *anything* except undergo *radical change.* The second album '*This is Madness*' (1971) was a devastatingly black conscious and rhetorical album that subjected *blackness* to self-criticism and *whiteness* to black criticism. '*True Blues*' addressed the slave trade in the *spoken word* accompanied by drumming and humming. 'Singing the Blues,' they contended, emerged as a social, cultural and musical form and expression following the onset of the forced migration from Africa and the founding of America:

> True blues aint no new news
> about who's been abused
> Cos the blues is as old as my stolen soul
> I sang the blues when the missionaries came
> Passing out bibles in Jesus name
> I sang the blues in the hull of the ship
> beneath the sting of the slavemaster's whip
> I sang the blues when the ship anchored the dock
> my family being sold on the slave block
> I sang the blues being torn
> from my first born

And hung my head and cried
When my wife took his life and then committed suicide
I sang the blues on the slavemaster's plantation
Helping him to build his free nation

The third album released in 1973 was called '*Chastisement*' and the fourth released in 1974 named '*At Last.*' The Fasimba too made a contribution to songs talking about revolution—our vision radical change—and was put together in 1970 to capture the *aspirations and methods* of National liberation and revolution as expressed during that period; it went something along the following lines:

Tell me brothers, how to get our freedom?
Tell me sisters, how to get our freedom?
Tell me people how to get our freedom?
We got to fight, O we got to fight
We don't need no evolution
What we need is revolution
We don't need no evolution
What we need is revolution
With an AK47, an AK47
Spitting out the fire, the fire of freedom

Black Power activity in Britain was connected therefore to global political aspirations and to the Black musical forms defining the early 1970s and, as noted in the Introduction, was a period punctuated by songs of protest and the search for blackness, all against a background of armed struggles against colonialism and neo-colonialism in the *Third World*. Black music, following its own historical dynamic, expressed sentiments of personal and cultural pride, self-respect, personal self-determination, and group cohesion. It spelt out a number of personal, social and cultural issues of concern to black people in the Caribbean **and** in the 'mother country.' An example of this is expressed in the lyrics of Bob Marley and the Wailers' 1970 hit, *Duppy Conqueror which was the first tune I played on arriving home after being released from Eastchurch prison. It summed up my anger and my defiance.* As consumers of Black music Fasimba members became identified by a particular expression of that music culture, and this expression went on to inspire a new and permanent element of musical creativity and dance culture amongst legions young people in south London.

'Calling the Youth': Jah Shaka

The Sound System, *Jah Shaka*, was formed by members of the Fasimba around 1970 and is testimony to the organisation's connections to the youth locally and of our youth membership and youth following. Unlike organizations that claimed to have a youth following or to be their 'guardians' the Fasimba didn't need to make such claims. The Fasimba, as we now know, were Shaka Zulu's most feared and disciplined warriors, known in history as the *Fasimba regiment*. The youths who originally formed the sound system were either visitors to or members of SELPO and the Fasimba so it seemed only logical that the name for a Conquering Sound should be called Shaka. The Shaka Sound System is integral to the black history of the New Cross area and the Fasimba are part of that history.

The Sound was known originally as *Shaka Downbeat* and played at Fasimba functions, such as ones held at the West Indian Students' Centre in Earls Court during 1970 and 1971, at the play Malcolm X, and many other Fasimba functions in London. If there ever was a dance involving the Fasimba, *Shaka Downbeat* would provide the *Roots and Culture* musical entertainment. TWJ Sound System played mainly Soul and popular reggae music, as they did at the plays at the Dark and Light Theatre in Camberwell in 1970.

From 1972, *Shaka Downbeat* became the resident sound at the *Moonshot Club*, New Cross. The growing influence of *Ras Tafari* on Caribbean culture and reggae music from the early 1970s made it impossible for black youth in Britain to ignore this cultural and spiritual phenomenon; given the broad rejection of Christianity by the **Black Power** and the *Ras Tafari* Movements, it seemed only logical that these issues should come together in a youthful Sound System that combined the *warrior spirit* and *conquering lion* disposition of Shaka Zulu's *Fasimba regiment* with the spirituality and culture of resistance of Ras Tafari, the *Conquering Lion*.

Around 1977 *Shaka Downbeat* evolved into *Jah Shaka* and once the *Jah Shaka Sound System* went into the recording business, the backing group were called *the Fasimbas, hence Jah Shaka and the Fasimbas*. The inspiration behind the founding of the Ras Tafari Movement was, of course, Marcus Garvey, the 'father of **Black Power**.' Jah Shaka's Sound System is now recognised nationally and internationally, promoting and publicising *conscious* music that reflected and still reflects our political and cultural beliefs, activities and aspirations as young black people in the early 1970s.

199

Contact with Black organizations in London

Black Liberation Front, Ladbroke Grove

In 1971 the Fasimba formed a political alliance with the *BLF* to work together on issues of mutual concern and benefit; the arrest of Tony Soares on 'terrorism' charges was such an issue on which we planned to work together. We sold *Grassroots* as a part of this alliance and the International Black Newspaper printed in Algeria called '**Babylon**.'

Black Panther Movement, Brixton

Fasimbas held a number of meetings with the *Panthers* and worked with them on a variety of issues pertinent to the black struggle of the 1970s.

Black Unity and Freedom Party, New Cross

As many Fasimba members went to school with members of *BUFP*, we would train in Martial Arts with some of their members and sold *Black Voice* on our bookstalls on Saturdays

International Solidarity:

Jamaica

The Fasimba were in regular contact with members of *Youth Forces for National Liberation (YFNL)* a Marxist youth organization with a base in London and Jamaica, who were regular visitors to the Fasimba Sunday and Thursday meetings. They were among those whom I and other Fasimba had in-depth 'reasoning' and groundings about Garvey, Marxism and the contemporary Black struggle at a base in Peckham.

Algeria

The BLF had contacts with Eldridge Cleaver who had departed the USA to live in Algeria, North Africa, from where the International Black Newspaper, **Babylon**, was printed and, as mentioned above, was distributed across the World, including London.

Angola

George Sugumba, a representative of UNITA and one of three Liberation organizations in Angola, was a regular visitor to the Fasimba. It soon transpired, however, that UNITA was in the pay of CIA and were using South African mercenaries to fight against the Portuguese **and** the leading African liberation organization in Angola, MPLA. As a consequence, in 1975 Fidel Castro, Premier of Cuba, in the practice of International Solidarity, sent thousands of Cuban troops to assist MPLA in defeating the Jonas Savimbi's CIA backed UNITA, the South African mercenaries and the Portuguese colonists (see Manley, 1982: 110-117).

Tanzania

Fasimba members visited Tanzania during 1971 to establish links with East Africa. A number of the organisation's members had been taught Swahili by a Fasimba from Tanzania and the visit to the country found to be inspiring, to say the least, happening at the time Julius Nyrerere was leader of the country and 'scientific socialism' was seen as one answer to African social and economic development. The Fasimba had been collecting clothes for a number of months to send there, and those who undertook the visit spent time in village communities sharing their engineering, electrical, teaching and other practical skills with those communities as well as improving their Swahili.

Self-Defense: Wado Ryu style Karate

Under the mantle of 'Self Defence' and in line with discipline and physical fitness invoked by modelling ourselves along the line of Shaka Zulu's *Fasimba Regiment*, the Fasimba had a **Security Group** overseen by Brother Roy. One purpose of this group was to 'patrol' the immediate locality during the often crowded Sunday meetings, stand at the door to 'vet' new visitors to meetings and, with the local youth 'hold the door' at plays and dances put on by the Fasimba. The other purpose of this Group was to arrange self-defence classes for the membership, namely Karate (*'the Way of the Empty hand'*) classes, which was open also to members of the community.

We chose the *Wado Ryu* style (*'the Way of Peace and Harmony'*) while members of other local organisations, such as Black Unity and Freedom Party (BUFP) practised the *Shotokan* style of Karate. The Fasimba held *two levels* of Karate training. The *first* was a Karate class for the general membership where they were taught the basics of unarmed self-defence for up to one hour. This class met on a Friday evening and the Japanese Instructor(s) we hired was for paid by a collection from those who attended. The *second* was the more advanced class and taught by the same Japanese team of instructors from Professor Suzuki's Dojo. This group met on Wednesday evenings and again this class was paid for by a collection from those who attended.

Once these classes became established, those of us who took the advanced classes and had become quite proficient in *Wado Ryu*, in turn taught the classes to the general membership, along with an Instructor. Other Karate practitioners with other styles, such as *Shotokan or Kyokushin-kai,* would often train with us and we exchanged what we knew, as did Omar's brother, who was a Black Belt, and Peter, a Fasimba, already a Green Belt in *Wado Ryu*. After a while we only paid two of Professor Suzuki's Instructors for the advanced classes.

The existence and contents of the *advanced* classes were kept *hidden* from the general membership of the Fasimba, as it was where we were taught 'street fighting' techniques and sought to do as one the instructors would always tell us to do—"*one punch, break bones*" while demonstrating a devastating *reverse punch*. We were told that all the 'fancy' and complicated moves and techniques we learnt in the classes were for grading, for Kata's and for competitions, where rules of *form* and *style* had to be observed. In 'street fighting,' we were told, there was only one rule: stop your enemy and escape. Consequently we were advised that some techniques we learnt should not be used in 'free fights' or in 'playing about' but only in 'street fights' and only when absolutely necessary. After some often tough training sessions those of us that had any energy left we were allowed a 5 minute 'free fight' between one another and, sometimes, between Fasimba members and the instructors. That way we tested our progress, skills and techniques.

The Fasimba within the Fasimba

However, this outward organisational formality concealed a *hidden and revolutionary* cell structure where each geographical area doubled beneath it all as an *independent unit or cell* each made up of two or three Fasimba members. In many ways these *cells acted independently* of the wider organisation like, for example, going on *missions* unbeknown to others in the *area* or to the organisation membership. It was part of the 'security' operations of the group. By way of these *cells* surveillance andreconnaissance work was undertaken as a way of getting to know your own locality; each *cell* also had tasks to complete and specific text each *cell* had to become familiar with. A Swahili class was set up for members and taught by a member from Tanzania, East Africa, so as to enable *cell* members to have at their disposal another language in which to speak, to send and/or receive messages. These *missions* were undertaken during the winter 1971 and during the *power-cuts* of February 1972. Many were planned and undertaken by members of *cells* in other areas, or as joint *missions* between members from different *cells*. Only now are some of those missions being revealed, some thirty years hence.

The decentralised cell structure—the *cell* within a *cell* format— was a hidden feature of Fasimba organisation and served a number of purposes. Already mentioned were the reconnaissance and surveillance missions undertaken by each cell to 'map' the locality. However, this 'mapping' mission also enabled *cell* members to know, for example, how long it would take to move from location 'A' to location 'B' and which would be the quickest route. Chapters 1 and 5 have shown why and how such information would have been of importance. But the *cell* within a *cell* format was also part of a 'game of deception' and 'war of position' in which the 'Fasimba within the Fasimba' positioned and repositioned themselves against those forces, some 'apparently benign' yet fundamentally opposed to our vision of the Black Cause.

Why did the *cells* exist and what were they for? The word was that they were in *preparation* for the 'Black Revolution' which, according to Carmichael, quoting Ernesto Che Guevara, would be "no mere street fight" but part of a "long and harsh struggle" (Carmichael, 1969: 170). Carmichael was referring to the representation of events in the US that gave the impression that the 'Black Revolution' would be akin to a 'street fight' between black youth and white police. In the summer of 1970 Michael X had pronounced that "the battle for the liberation of our territories would be fought on the *streets* of London" (*Evening News*, 2/8/70) even though Carmichael had already cautioned three years earlier that this would not be the case. Michael X had been asked to cover for Carmichael at a talk in Reading later in 1967 but ended up being accused, arrested, charged and imprisoned for 'inciting racial hatred' under the Race Relations Act,1965, for which he served 1 year (Tinaz, 2001: 5).

So far I've described the origins, structure, organisation and programmes of the Fasimba as a Black organisation, but not its Cause in the spectrum of Causes espoused by Black organisations in Britain and Internationally. The question is what was **Black Power** about or, more to the point, **to what did Black Power refer?** It's been over 30 years since the Fasimba operated as an independently funded Black organisation in the south-east area of London, and given that passage of time, *it is necessary now, in the 21ˢᵗ century, to try and delineate the properties of and connections to **Black Power in Britain.***

Black Power as a Caribbean Concept

The thrust of Chapter 5 has been that, contrary to popular belief, the emergence of **Black Power** activism in Britain had Caribbean not American connections. In fact **Black Power**, as a political aspiration and cultural philosophy, *was conceived* in the Jamaican colonial context but *its birth, naming and coming of age* took place in America where it was nurtured and influenced by Black activists in America, but in particular by activists who owed their **origins and connections to the Caribbean.** Three names are associated with the basis, development and emergence of the organisational, social, cultural and political practices associated with the concept **Black Power**: they are **Marcus Garvey**, a Jamaican; **Malcolm X,** whose father was a Garveyite and mother from Grenada, and **Stokely Carmichael**, a black Civil Rights activist and **Black Power** political organiser, originally from Trinidad. It was the work of these people that laid foundation and set out the framework for what became known as **Black Power** in the 1960s that was **fashioned in our own image** in the 1970s to become the basis for the **Black Consciousness** we now recognise as an International one.

CLR James and the 'political imagination' of Black Power

I want to draw on the work of another Caribbean, the renowned Marxist, historian, writer and social critic from Trinidad, CLR James, who helpfully provided the following framework to help in locating the rise and relevance of **Black Power**, *theoretically and historically*, and link it to the stage of development of the International Black struggle. CLR James, having listened to Stokely Carmichael's **Black Power** speech in July 1967 at the Roundhouse, Chalk Farm, London, made the following observations. He said the *vision of the world advocated by* **Black Power** activists symbolised a "new force" in the USA and the world; it was a *new force* because, as he described it, there were "grave weaknesses" in the past and contemporary Black struggle as it lacked a sound *historical* and *theoretical* foundation. It was necessary, therefore, for this struggle to be placed historically and theoretically.

For CLR James, **Black Power** *is* and *is not* a political slogan; rather, it is a *statement* which captures the "political imagination" and "guide the activity of people all over the world," particularly, the *imagination* and *activity* of people of African origin dispersed globally by Western imperialism that began with the transatlantic slave trade. His view was that only by locating **Black Power** *historically* and *identifying* and *tracing its ancestry* that we can see what **Black Power** signifies—avoiding what he termed as "gross and dangerous" assumptions of what **Black Power** is and is not. He made it clear that **Black Power** was **not** a black racism, **nor** was it fostering hatred among black people for white people—a so-called 'reverse racism.' Rather, the struggle for **Black Power** was a legitimate struggle for Black emancipation and a struggle against a history of Western domination. **Black Power** was therefore "*a banner for people of certain political aims, needs and attitudes; a banner around which they can rally; a banner which ... many millions already see today and in the not too distant future will see, as the symbol of a tremendous change in life and society as we know it today*" (James, 1967: 4). By situating the modern *phenomenon* of **Black Power** historically and politically, James suggests that once **Black Power** is connected to the *historical period from which it emerged (Smart, 1989)* it becomes possible to *also* **identify** the *political conditions* and *social antagonisms* that gave rise to it as a *rallying banner for political change.*

The same line of inquiry should focus also on the *ancestry* or *genealogy (Smart, 1989)* of the *historical/political conditions* and the *social antagonisms* generated by these particular conditions to see what form these had taken prior to their *consolidation under the banner of **Black Power***. Situating the origins of **Black Power**, historically, CLR James, who was largely unimpressed by Marcus Garvey's approach, nonetheless, described him as someone who "*opened up a wide avenue in the Negro struggle*" (James, (1967: 6). He goes on to say:

> Before Garvey the great millions of Africans and people of African descent simply did not exist in the political consciousness of the world in general, of the general public, and of politicians in particular. After less than a decade this Jamaican had placed them there. He had placed them there in such a manner that they could never be removed again. Garvey had placed them not only in the consciousness of the oppressors but as a constituent

part of the minds and aims of the great mass of Africans and people of African descent (James, 1967: 6).

It is important to note that Garvey advocated what was essentially a *Black Nationalist* position in a shape and form that was suitable for his **time and place in Black history;** the development of a necessary Black consciousness. On this historicity, Mackie (1987:9) makes two points. First, on his place in the history of the struggle for Black emancipation:

> Garvey changed the way that black Americans saw themselves. He taught them that Africa was their *spiritual* home, at a time when most thought their homelands were in the slave plantations; that Africa was theirs to reclaim by right, while Europe's stranglehold on the continent looked unassailable; that blackness was beautiful, when a black skin was still the mark of servitude and a burden of shame. His ideas spread to Europe, Africa and the Caribbean—to every place where black people lived under the imperialist white rule; and they to responded in their thousands to Garvey's call for a 'universal confraternity of the race'. Garvey's was the first and, as yet, only internationalist, black mass movement.

Second, on the development of Black consciousness:

> ...Garvey... took the emergent theories of black consciousness out of the hands of the closeted (black) intellectuals and delivered them to the people. *Without Garvey's popularisation, the concepts black pride, black solidarity, and blackness as an organising principle in the collectivisation of resistance to racism, would have remained no more than abstract notions.* Garvey gave millions of black people an awareness of their shared history and common interests. The improvements which black people have made for themselves in the decades since his death are all part of Garvey's legacy to the world (1987:63; emphasis added).

These principles were developed further by Malcolm X as *Revolutionary Black Nationalism and Internationalism* and situated the struggle in an *urban* context, followed by the work of Stokely Carmichael, to which James refers. It was CLR James' belief that the advocates of **Black Power** stood "on the shoulders of their ancestors" and were the inheritors of *all the struggles for Black Emancipation* that have gone before and, from where he stood, **Black Power** represented *"the highest peak of thought on the Negro question"* on issues of black autonomy and self rule that had been going on for over half a century (James, 1967: 6), at least since the dawn of the twentieth century.

The so-called '*Negro question*' had been posed in a number of historical forms but the one to which James refers is the American version that posed the following question: was the Black struggle in America part of the *class struggle* for socialism via integration into white society or was it essentially a '*nationalist struggle*,' distinct from the class struggle, which took into account the history of American slavery and racism. It was a struggle in which the impact of the history of slavery on black consciousness and on black unity was seen as crucial and important. CLR James ultimately rejected the idea that the Black struggle in America should be led by American Communists as it had dynamism of its own (see Proyect, 1999). But the so-called 'Negro question' was dismissed by Black activists such as Carmichael by relocating the Black struggle from a **national** to an **international** arena, outside of the historical dynamics and the *political boundaries* of imperialist nation states, such as America, Britain and France. The new allies in the International struggle were not the *white working classes* of the imperialist nation states but the *exploited and oppressed workers and peasants of the Third World, including the Caribbean:*

> **Black Power** *means that black people see themselves as part of a new force, sometimes called the Third World; that we see our struggle as closely related to liberation struggles around the world. We must hook up with these struggles ... There is only one place for blacks in ... these struggles, and that is on the side of the Third World"*
> (Carmichael, 1969: 172).

CLR James therefore acknowledged **Black Power** as an **International phenomenon**, as a trans-global political ideology with the needs and interests of the African Diaspora in mind, pointing out that *"in any political manifestation on a **world stage** there is involved a **general principle** and as far as any particular country or political epoch is concerned, we see it not only in its general but in its **particular application"** (1967: 7). First we deal with the emergence of its *general principles* and, second, go on to look at its **particular application in Britain.**

Marcus Garvey and the 'general principles' of Black Power

Marcus Mosiah Garvey is to be considered the 'Father' of modern **Black Power** as many of its key doctrines, that is, its 'general principles' are traceable to his ideas and practices as expressed by the UNIA Movement and summed up in the slogans: '*Up you mighty race, you can achieve what you will*" and "*Africa for Africans, at home and abroad,*" both of which raised as a consequence of their international dispersal through the transatlantic slave trade. Although the *slogan* **Black Power** had its particular *origins*, principally in the 'Civil Rights' organising and speeches of Stokely Carmichael in the **1960s,** the organisational philosophy, cultural and social practices, and the political goals of **Black Power** are traceable to Marcus Garvey's Black Nationalist doctrine of black self-determination, black self-consciousness and in his 'Back to Africa Movement.' Garvey's advocacy of African unity and Black Nationalism became the basis of Malcolm X's teachings on black unity, black self-determination and black self defence; although Stokely Carmichael propagated the slogan '**Black Power**' while organising in the southern Civil Rights Movement, his political position on Blackness—cultural self-definition, black self-consciousness, black self-determination and political independence can all be traced to Garvey's doctrines (Rodney, 1971).

Marcus Garvey was born on 17th August, 1887, between St Anne's Bay and Roaring River, not far from where Christopher Columbus landed in 1492 to 'discover' and claim Jamaica for Spain. Garvey came to be born into the historical and geographical configuration of the 'Triangular Trade' (Edwards, 1972: 5), a trade that figured in the 'suturing' of Africans into European economies and cultures as chattel slaves, and into a history where blackness was to become stabilised as a sign for both servitude and human marginality.

Inheriting and fighting against the 'demonology of blackness' in the Caribbean and America, much of Garvey's UNIA organising and speeches were intended to combat the negative view of Africans, Africa and blackness by exhorting the black masses to be proud of being black and recognise their racial unity and origins as Africans. Garvey's time and place of birth is significant in other ways. His birth occurred nearly

50 years after the Emancipation of Slaves in Jamaica in 1838, 22 years after the 1865 Morant Bay Rebellion led by Paul Bogle and in the ripples of its brutal suppression by Governor Eyre. Garvey was born about 100 miles or so from the vicinity of that rebellion. According to Gillian (2005:2), being born "*in the repressive, anti-black hierarchical, colour conscious society of newly emancipated Jamaica, Marcus' phenotype, black skin and social background marked him at the bottom of the social ladder.*" As Garvey recalls:

> From early youth, I discovered that there was prejudice against me because of my colour, a prejudice that was extended to other members of my race. This annoyed me and helped inspire me to create a sentiment that would act favourably to the black man. It was with this kind of inspiration that I returned from my trip to Europe to Jamaica in 1914, where I organized the Universal Negro Improvement Association and African Communities League. When I organised this movement in Jamaica it was treated with contempt and scorn by a large number of the highly coloured people and successful black people. In Jamaica the coloured and successful black people regard themselves as white.
> http://www.spartacus.schoolnet.co.uk/USAgarvey. htm accessed (12/9/05)

Gillian (2005) refers to this form of racial domination as "colourism," an institutionalised *socio-economic subordination* and *cultural marginalisation* of the 'dark-skinned' nationals of Jamaica by members of the 'light-skinned' class that had its origins in the racial and sexual dynamics of slavery and colonial society. The well-off 'dark skinned' nationals mentioned by Garvey disassociated themselves from their 'black skins' by identifying with the 'anti-black logic' of the emerging socio-economic order underpinning emancipation.' Garvey's 'Black is Beautiful' initiative against the universal hegemony of the Euro-American 'Blackness of Blackness' was one of the bases upon which the **Black Power** Movement emerged in the UK in the 1970s, to organise around not just the *material conditions of existence* (i.e. economic exploitation) but also against the political, historical and *ideological conditions of existence*. **Black Power** *was therefore as much about the struggle in **ideas** as it was about the struggle against the **material conditions of existence**.*

Black Power activism also effected a reversal of this racialised 'logic' by not only pushing for 'blackness' to become a desired (not despised) personal, social and cultural identity but to also make the rejection of 'blackness' by those who distanced themselves from a *black identity* to be pejoratively identified as 'white'—a 'white man in black skin' (Fanon, 1967). The term 'coconut' is a modern description of such a person who, on rejecting their external blackness and ancestry, is considered 'white' on the inside and as a person who has aligned themselves with the interests of the white West, the international white bourgeoisie, or what Malcolm X called the 'white power structure' (see James, 1967: 6).

On this basis, Marcus Garvey was the first black person in the post-emancipation **but** colonial world to have attempted to *unify and organise* peoples of African descent on a global scale, and to have confronted the canons of the 'Blackness of Blackness" by which Africans were figured by the colonial government as not only lacking 'whiteness' externally but by definition, their 'external' blackness symbolised an *absence of white civilisation*, from which they were barred by their 'internal' blackness. Here the Jamaican colloquialism "too black" is one expression of this 'colonial logic,' a 'logic' that Malcolm X reversed in his analogy about black coffee, *unintegrated* with milk was *"too black, too hot, too strong,"* a view reaffirmed by the popular US rap group, Public Enemy, in the 1990s. Garvey began the work to signify blackness as *presence,* as opposed to its place in black people's psyches, in history and in white society as *marginality* or *absence,* and did this by addressing the aspirations of the working class and black people in Jamaica, the USA, and the aspirations of the migrants who travelled to Britain in the 1950s and 1960s (Garvey, 1970: Chapter 1).

Malcolm X and Radical Black Nationalism

Born as Malcolm Little on 19th May 1925 in Omaha, Nebraska, Malcolm X was the fourth of six children of Earl and Louisa Little. Louisa, his mother was from Grenada, in the Caribbean, and Earl Little from Reynolds, Georgia. Earl Little was a Baptist Minister and a member of Marcus Garvey's Universal Negro Improvement Association (UNIA); he was a preacher on Sundays and the rest of the week was an activist for Marcus Garvey. As a consequence of his black pride teachings and civil rights campaigning, he was routinely threatened by members of the local Klan group. As Malcolm recalls, his mother told him that a party of hooded Ku Klux Klan riders galloped up to the home in Omaha, Nebraska, one night.

> Surrounding the house, brandishing their shotguns and rifles, they shouted for my father to come out. My mother went to the front door and opened it. Standing there they could see her pregnant condition, she told them that she was alone with her three small children, and that my father was away, preaching in Milwaukee. The Klansmen shouted threats and warnings at her that we'd better get out of town because "the good Christian white people" were not going to stand for my father "spreading trouble" among the "good" Negroes of Omaha with the "back to Africa" preaching of Marcus Garvey (see note [1]).

This threat to his family had him move to Lansing, Michigan, where Earl bought a house and continued his preaching on Sundays in local Baptist Churches, and during the week he roamed about spreading the words of Marcus Garvey. As Malcolm recalls:

> This time, the "get out of town" came from a local hate society called The Black Legion (Society). They wore black robes instead of white. Soon, everywhere my father went, Black Legionnaires were reviling him as an "uppity nigger" for wanting to own a store, for living outside the Lancing Negro district, for spreading unrest and dissention among the "good niggers." (See note [1]).

The family home was burned down by members of the Black Legion Society in 1929. In 1931 Earl Little, the "uppity nigger," was found dead by a street railway car track, a death that every one believed was the work of the 'Black Legion Society. It was too much for the family: his mother suffered a nervous breakdown, was confined to a mental institution and the children put into institutional care. Malcolm's early life was therefore characterised by violence and terror and its resistance, and by his family having to move and relocate in an effort to escape persecution. The violent death of his father by a KKK group for his preaching of Civil Rights and the confinement of his motherin many senses led him to his particular educational experience, to his 'drop-out' life, crime, imprisonment and his conversion to a Black Muslim. Consequently the violence inflicted on black Americans and the need to resist it became a *core part* of his philosophy of self defence and integral to his speeches. Such was Malcolm's impact on his visit to Ghana in 1965 that a folk singer wrote the following song in his honour:

> *Malcolm Man, Malcolm Man*
> *You speak a tale of woe*
> *The Red on your face like our*
> *Blood on the land*
> *You speak your tale of woe*
> *Malcolm Man, Malcolm Man*
> *The Anger that you feel*
> *Will unite our people*
> *And make us all so real*
> *Malcolm Man, Malcolm Man*
> (From Norman Richmond, *The Black Commentator,*
> May, 2005)

Stokely Carmichael and the 'emergence' of Black Power

The political ideology and organisational framework, **Black Power**, emerged at a turbulent time in world and American and British history as it stove to express a new racial consciousness among black people during the 1960s and 1970s. It became a call for black people to unite, to recognise their own heritage and build a sense of community, wherever they might be. The call for '**Black Power**' was used to motivate black people to form and lead their own organisations and to reject the values of American and British societies as both were built on the enslavement and exploitation of Africans and their descendents. The concept '**Black Power**' was advocated and popularised by Stokely Carmichael as both an organising principle and as a particular aim of the Civil Rights Movement in the southern United States, but what was to become **Black Power** activism in northern cities soon broke away from the non-violent approach of the southern Civil Rights campaign. It was becoming clear that black people's situation in the USA required more than just a struggle for *civil rights*. In the European anti-colonial context, the struggle was for *human rights*, as advocated in the conclusion of Fanon's '*Wretched of the Earth*' (1963).

Stokely Carmichael was born in Trinidad on 29th June, 1941 (died 15/11/98) and, like most Caribbean young people during that era, his parents migrated to the USA, settling initially in New York where he joined them in 1952, attended high school in a district of the City, thereafter enrolling in Howard University, Washington DC, where he studied and passed a Degree in philosophy in 1964. During his student years, he joined the *Non-violent Action Group (NAG)* in their campaigning for black civil rights in 1960. In 1961, aged 20, he became a member of the Freedom Riders, travelling to the southern states organising disenfranchised black people to register to vote. He later joined the *Student Non-Violent Coordinating Committee (SNCC)* as a field organiser in Lowndes Country, Alabama, where the black citizens were in the majority but 'politically powerless.' Stokely organised the local and all-black *Lowndes County Freedom Organisation (LCFO)* and encouraged them to adopt the Black Panther as their organisational logo, later adopted and universalised by the *Black Panther Party* in 1966 by Bobby Seale and Huey P Newton (see 'Stokely Speaks,' Carmichael, 1971: 187) The origins of what was to be the northern **Black Power** Movement therefore emerged with him from his involvement in non-violent civil rights activity and his organising of disenfranchised black people in the southern states between 1961 and 1966.

The slogan '**Black Power**' first emerged as a rallying cry of Student Non-Violent Coordinating Committee (SNCC) by activist Willy Ricks (aka Musaka Dada) just prior to Stokely Carmichael's elevation of it on the '*March Against Fear*' in June 1966. On 6th June 1966, James Meredith, the first black student to attend the University of Mississippi, attempted to walk across the State to demonstrate the 'freedom won through the struggles of the Civil Rights Movement,' but was shot by a sniper. During the '*March Against Fear*' called by SNCC in support of James Meredith, Stokely Carmichael roused the gathered audience with an attack on Mississippi justice, stating: "*This is the twenty-seventh time I have been arrested and I ain't going to jail no more! The only way we gonna stop them white men stop whuppin' us is to take over. What we gonna start sayin' is* **Black Power!**" He then proclaimed, "What we need is **Black Power**." Typical of the African 'Call and Response' routine [2] that was to echo in many settings, where the speaker asked the crowd, "What do we want?" and the crowd responded "**Black Power**." Call: "What do we need?" Response: "Black Power!" Call: "When do we want it?" Response: "Now!" Here the concept **Black Power** emerged to *represent a new **assertiveness** as well as a new racial **consciousness** about* *injustice and the violence meted out to them in their non-violent struggles for civil rights.*

Carmichael had become 'seasoned' by his experiences of struggle and organising in the segregated South during which time he witnessed non-violent and peaceful black protesters being beaten, shocked with cattle prods and sometimes killed for seeking what white people in America took for granted: civil rights. As a result of his peaceful freedom activities he was arrested and jailed at least 32 times; abandoning the passive, non-violent approach he took the message of **Black Power as** self-determination and black self-defence to the ghettos of northern cities.

It proved to be an awakening and galvanising force among socially disenfranchised urban youth, while those black people seeking *integration* with white Americans saw it as anti-white, as a reverse racism that would lead only to black separatism. This was the view of especially 'mainstream' black organisations such as *Congress of Racial Equality (CORE)* and the *National Association for the Advancement of Coloured People (NAACP)*. Dr Martin Luther King, diplomatically, called the **Black Power** phrase "an unfortunate choice of words" because it came across as non-compromising, threatening and even violent. Between 1966 and 1967 Carmichael toured American cities lecturing on University campuses to black and white students, but the **Black Power** philosophy was aimed particularly at young black people. He travelled abroad to North Vietnam, China, Cuba and Britain. Inspired by the Cuban revolution and hero, Ernesto Che Guevara, Carmichael said in Havana: "*We are preparing groups of urban guerrillas for our defence in the cities. It is going to be a fight to the death.*" He denounced American aggression in Vietnam and, on his return to the USA after visiting to Britain, had his passport confiscated.

Black Power and the Black Panthers

On his return to America in late 1967, SNCC cut ties with Carmichael and soon he after was invited to join the Black Panther Party as its spokesman, with the title of Honourary Prime Minister, to speak to the 'Free Huey Newton' campaign (Carmichael, 1971:111-130). The **Black Power** Movement and the *Black Panther Party* had common origins in the organising of black people in the southern states for civil rights, and Stokely was instrumental in choosing and raising the **Black Panther as a political sign for Black Power** for the

Lowndes County Freedom Organisation (LCFO). The icon of black men with guns as popularised by the Black Panther Party also symbolised a maxim espoused by Mao Tse Tung in the 1960s: that *'political power comes out the barrel of a gun'* and was an expression of another 1960s revolutionary maxim: *'war is politics with violence and politics is war without violence.'* [A 1970 Fasimba song saw the AK47 as one antidote to black powerlessness].

The Black Panther Party established a number of programmes in northern cities such as Chicago, Los Angeles, Philadelphia and Oakland, California, where they initiated a free breakfast programme for school children. They helped to establish a Free Medical Centre and started a door to door programme of health service to test for sickle cell anaemia, encouraged blood donors from black communities and began to reach out to local gangs.

However, despite these common roots in services to and for black communities in southern and northern cities of America, he departed after just a year as important ideological and organisational differences became apparent between the **Black Power** Movement and the *Black Panther Party* (Carmichael, 186-187). While Carmichael did not criticise the Panthers' growing Marxist approach to black problems (Ibid: 186-187), he did disagree in principle with black organisations forming links with white groups, citing the black radical position of Malcolm X three years previously. In Britain this same ideological 'fault line' came to exist between **Black Power** and other Black organisations of a Marxist orientation. In Carmichael's view, moving on from CLR James' position:

> Black Power is **more than a slogan**; *it is a way of looking at our problems and the beginning of a solution to them.* It attacks racism *and* exploitation (capitalism), the horns of the bull that seek to gore us ...Because our color has been used as a weapon to oppress us, we must use color as a weapon of liberation, just as other people use their nationality as a weapon for their liberation ... But even if we destroy racism, we would not necessarily destroy exploitation; and if we destroyed exploitation, we would not necessarily end racism. They must both be destroyed; we must constantly launch a two-pronged attack; we must constantly keep our eyes on *both* of the bull's horns (Carmichael, 1971: 106; 107: *my emphasis*).

Black Power and the 'Dialectics of Liberation'

Stokely Carmichael (aka Kwame Toure) was therefore an important figure in helping us in the Fasimba fashion our **vision** of **Black Power,** our cultural practice and our political outlook in an *urban, national and international context.* It was during the autumn of 1970 that I first heard a recording of the talk he gave on **Black Power** at the *Dialectics of Liberation Conference,* July 1967in London. I listened also to recordings of Malcolm X's speeches: 'The Ballot or the Bullet' and 'Message to the Grassroots' as all were played at Sunday and Thursday meetings, with Carmichael's **Dialectic** becoming the topic of Friday night discussions at a location in Peckham. Such discussions involved a group of us trying to understand the relevance of Marxism to the black struggle in Britain and across the world with brothers from the Youth Forces for National Liberation (YFNL) and other Jamaican Marxists like Bros. Len and Palmer, and Owen, to whom I am grateful for the insights they provided to expand my understanding of the *national* and *international* dimensions of this debate. Below I offer my thoughts and recollections on my Fasimba experience of **Black Power** organizing.

Carmichael was banned from re-entering Britain soon after that 1967 Conference appearance for giving a speech likely damage 'race relations' and was unable to address the **Black Power** generation of the 1970s, the 'young bloods' as he would refer to their counter-parts in the US. However by 1970 he had changed his name to Kwame Toure, expanded **Black Power's** ideology of Black Internationalism into Pan-Africanism, and left America for Conakry, Guinea, West Africa. His banning by the Security Services had put the *likely effects* of his speech in Britain on par with the racial violence that was permeating US cities, examples of black protest the Labour Home Secretary, James Callaghan, did not want happening in Britain. Carmichael's *fiery* speech at the Round House in London was set against a background of newspaper headlines as: "Riots Blaze across US' (*Daily Mirror,* 24/7/67), reporting that *"Racial Violence"* was sweeping across America, *"from New York to the Deep South."*

A different kind of heat was being felt in London that July as temperatures soared to a "sweltering" 70^f. It was in such an atmosphere that Obi Egbuna appeared on stage alongside Stokely Carmichael during his Black Power speech and was, after that event, asked to lead a *moderate* Universal Coloured Peoples Association (UCPA) and invest it with a *militant* **Black Power** ideology of the type espoused by Carmichael. One year later, on 25th July, 1968, Egbuna was himself arrested and charged, along with two members of UCPA, with "conspiring to murder police officers" (Cashmore, 1979), for which, after months in custody on remand, was found guilty at the Old Bailey and given a 3 year suspended sentence. It was during his time in jail that he set out plans for a British version of the American *Black Panthers*—the *Black Panther Movement*. By 1970, south London had a number of organisations representing the interests of black people: the *Black Panther Movement* with branches in Brixton and west London, with the *Black Unity and Freedom Party (BUFP)* and the Fasimba operating in the Lewisham area. Allies of the Fasimba were the *Black Liberation Front (BLF)* with branches in west and north London.

Studying Carmichael's speech a bit more closely members of that study group believed there might have been other reasons behind him being banned from speaking further in Britain, and it was more likely to be the *implications* of the less publicised contents of his speech. In a section of his speech on **Black Power** Internationalism Carmichael presented what amounted to be an assessment of the tactical strength of black people in terms of their location in the cities of former colonial and imperialist nations. It was our belief that the British state may well have paid more attention to what he said in this context and its implications for likely *oppositional activity* by 'black militants' of a covert nature in England than anything he said that could be likened to be 'inflammatory' to 'race relations' itself.

In fact invoking the Race Relations Act, 1965, may well have served a dual purpose. On the one hand as a test of the new Act and, on the other, as a smokescreen behind which to cover or to conceal another *reason* why Carmichael was banned from re-entering Britain: the likelihood that he might address '*secret cells*' of Black militant organizations and radical Black personalities to focus their attention on a particular vision of Black international solidarity. This was not to say, however, that the British state was not concerned with the kinds of urban disorders that were happening in cities across the Atlantic might happen in English cities but were more concerned, I suggest, that such 'public disorders' might lead to *covert action* of a type practiced by the *Irish Republican Army (IRA)* and the as yet unrecognised *Angry Brigade*.

Some indications of this thinking was apparent in the *Guardian* report (12/8/70) on Home Office and Special Branch interests in **Black Power** organising and activism. The report mentioned in the Introduction that was being studied by Home Secretary, Reginald Maudling, called for more staff to be detailed for work with the '*special squads*' keeping an eye on Black organisations to provide "*details of*

Black Power *leaders and a breakdown of membership.*" Also sought was information on the *organisational behaviour* of Black Power groups such as *"the formation of underground cells"* in areas like Notting Hill and the *"steady growth"* of "militant anti-police attitudes."

Once seen as imitative of American Black Power, the emergence of Black Power in Britain, certainly London, would be regarded as a *home grown 'threat'* and worthy of *"extremely tight surveillance."* The "extremely tight surveillance" of Black groups sought by the Special Branch for operations in Notting Hill in 1970 would lead to the arrest of Tony Soares of the *Black Liberation Front* in March 1972 on 'terrorism' offences, which suggested that such a vision was already in the minds of those keeping **Black Power** activists under surveillance and were, presumably, acting in anticipation of any potential 'threats' they imagined.

Black internationalism and the Octopus analogy

In a section of Carmichael's talk he likened Western imperialism to an **Octopus** with the *Eye* representing the imperialist nation/state and its *tentacles* stretched across the globe in an economic, cultural and political *stranglehold* on *former colonial* territories, such as those in Africa, Asia, Latin-America and the Caribbean— *'The Third World.'* The descendants of former *slaves/colonial* subjects who now occupy the 'ghettos' or 'internal colonies' in those imperialist nations are posed as in a position to play a **key** role in the process of revolutionary change. The situation he witnessed in the industrialised cities in the North was quite different from that seen in the rural southern states and presented activists with a different *format* for struggle. In recognition of changing tactics he posited that:

> In a highly industrialized nation the struggle is different. The heart of production and the heart of commercial trade is in the cities. *We* are in the cities. We can become, and are becoming, a disruptive force in the flow of good, services and capital. Whilst we disrupt internally and aim at the eye of the octopus, we are hoping that our brothers are disrupting externally to sever the tentacles of the US.
> (*Black Power' in Dialectic of Liberation*, 1968: 160-161, **original emphasis**)

'Black Internationalism' or a blue-print for 'urban Guerrilla warfare?'

Carmichael's analogy of British imperialism as an **Octopus** with its tentacles stretched across the globe in the territories of the former 'British Empire' was used regularly by George Campbell at Sunday meetings to highlight the political and economic importance of black people's position in the West. With the post-war migration of Caribbean peoples to the 'Mother' country he suggested, like Malcolm X had done in 1964 following the assassination of President JF Kennedy in 1963, that the *'chickens had come home to roost.'*

Malcolm X's remarks were a comment on the racist violence used by the US government at home and overseas, and took the assassination of JF Kennedy as indicative that the violence was now 'coming back home to roost' and directed to the heart of government. For those remarks Malcolm X was suspended and eventually expelled from the Nation of Islam as many African Americans saw JF Kennedy as representing a 'white hope' for Black civil rights. What George meant by his reference to Malcolm's "chickens coming home to roost" phrase was the question posed by Jean-Paul Sartre to the white West, that Carmichael repeated at the Conference: "*What then did you expect when you unbound the gag that had muted those black mouths? That they would chant your praises? Did you think those black heads that their fathers had forcefully bowed to the ground, when raised again that you would find adoration in their eyes?*" (Carmichael, 1968: 167).

Our question was: could Carmichael's *political analogy* double as a framework or 'blue-print' for an *international struggle* against Western imperialism and its global interests? Emerging from those Friday night discussions was the notion that beneath the *political analogy* might lay a *formula for urban guerrilla* action for use as a *disruptive tactic* in support of the undermining and destabilising Western capitalism and imperialism from within. His talk seemed to suggest what role Black liberation groups could or perhaps should play located, as they were, in the eye of the Imperialist Octopus. Such a role might include organizing and directing the spontaneous rebellions of the 'young bloods' into coherent guerrilla urban actions in cities designed to oppose US or UK support for repressive measures against legitimate protests of 'brothers and sisters' in colonised countries, like South Africa or Rhodesia (Carmichael, 1968: 152; 166; 172).

Both forms of action were considered two (*regional*) aspects of the same global struggle, necessary and integral to the successful outcome of the struggle against 'international capitalism' and 'international white supremacy—the two horns of the bull (Carmichael, 1968:150). Black internationalism was presented as a *political counter* if not an *ideological antidote* to the *minority group mentality* issuing from the acceptance by black people that they constituted a *minority* in the nation states of the West. This *minority status* was posed, however, by Black Power as either a *tactical* issue or one of *perspective* because black people, as part of the African Diaspora and integral to the *peoples of colour, the 'Third World,'* constituted a *majority in a global context.*

From colonialism (direct rule) to neo-colonialism (indirect rule)

The Octopus analogy is pertinent because European imperialism immediately after the 2nd Imperialist War was faced with the *anti-colonial struggles* of Nationalist organisations in the former colonies of Britain (Kenya, Ghana) and France (Algeria) for political independence which led, eventually, to the granting of *formal* independence to these territories. However, in the process of *decolonisation* the 'Mother' country kept in place economic arrangements which would keep these newly 'independent' states tied to the economies of European nations in a 'neo-colonial' relationship—a 'new' colonialism (Nkrumah, 1965; Woddis, 1975). Lenin (1970) rightly described *imperialism as the* '*the **highest** stage of capitalism*' and Nkrumah (1965: ix) pointed out that '*neo-colonialism was the **last** stage of imperialism,'* defining *neo-colonialism* as *indirect rule,* a situation whereby the former colonies were granted *formal independence, with* "*all the outward trappings of international sovereignty*" but "*in reality its economic system and thus its political policy is directed from the outside... through economic or monetary means.*"

Under imperialism the "*export of capital as distinguished from the export of commodities*" from the West acquired an "*exceptional importance*" (Lenin, 1970: 86), characteristic of the subservient relationship of neo-colonial states and their rulers had within the 'Octopus-like' global network. "*The result of neo-colonialism*" writes Nkrumah (1965: x), "*is that foreign capital is used for the exploitation rather than for the development of the less developed parts of the world. Investment under neo-colonialism increases rather than decreases the gap between the rich and the poor countries in the world.*" Walter Rodney, in '*How Europe Underdeveloped Africa*' (1984), made much the same point, that Western imperialism had begun the 'underdevelopment of Africa' through the slave trade and colonialism that continued with 'Overseas Aid' and 'Foreign Investment' following the demise of colonialism. It was on the basis of this analysis that it became possible for Carmichael to say that: *"The American (and European) working class enjoys the fruits of the labours of Third World workers. The proletariat has become the Third World, and the bourgeoisie is white Western society"* (Carmichael, 1968, 165), shifting political allegiances in the Black struggle for revolutionary change from the *national* to the *international* arena, just as *racial capitalism* in the post-war period had internationalised to become *racial imperialism*:

> We have to extend our fight internationally because such a consciousness will destroy within black communities the minority complex so carefully calculated by the American press, but also because when the black man realizes that the counter-insurgency efforts of the US are directed against his brothers, he will not fight in any of their wars ...Then it will become crystal clear that the imperialist wars of the US are nothing less than **racist wars** (ibid, 169, **emphasis added**).

Black consciousness had evolved to include not only a *historical* consciousness but also an *international* one, captured in the notion of a *Black or African Diaspora*. But this Black consciousness though African in origin was internationalist in its scope, because by linking-up with the 'Third World' the advocates of Black Power embraced the *'majority of mankind'* (James (1967:7). Black Power's global focus was therefore not only on the Emancipation of peoples of African decent or on saving the *majority of mankind, the peoples of colour* who happen to live in the Third World; its ultimate aim was the saving of all humanity. Strategically, "hooking up" with *peoples of colour* in the **Third World** was the "only salvation" because the Black struggle at that stage in its development was fighting to save not just the humanity of black people but the humanity of all peoples. On this Carmichael said: *"We are indeed fighting to save the humanity of the world, which the West has failed miserably in being able to preserve"* (Carmichael, 1968; 168).

The term **'Third World'** was coined in 1952 by French economist/demographer Alfred Sauvy (1898-1990) to refer to countries that are now called 'developing' or 'underdeveloped,' especially those in the Southern hemisphere that were not aligned to either the Soviet nor

American blocs during the 'Cold War.' The *First World* referred to the Capitalist West, the *Second World* to the Communist or Eastern European Bloc; and *the Third World,* to the 'overexploited' and former colonial territories, that included Africa, Asia, Latin-America and the Caribbean. During the late 1960s and 1970s it was used by Carmichael and others as an *umbrella term* for countries still economically exploited and culturally and politically dominated in the 'Octopus-like stranglehold' of the neo-imperialist Western nations, including Britain and France, against which Third World countries were involved in a liberation struggle. Carmichael's reference to **Black Power** struggles in America and Britain linking up with the Third World to forge a *new humanity* is drawn from the conclusion of Frantz Fanon's *Wretched of the Earth* (1963), based on his experiences as a psychiatrist in the war of National liberation in Algeria against French colonialism. It was a text quoted regularly at Sunday meetings, as what Fanon had to say then was poetically beautiful as it was politically inspiring to those who heard or read the words.

For activists in the Fasimba it became a statement of commitment, an allegiance to a *Cause that loomed larger than your own vision* of what work needed to be done and as a part the *revolution of ideas* it offered a *global vision of change* to counter the global domination of Western imperialism's vision of humanity. The Black struggle was not to just establish a new African or Black history or a new Black humanity it was also to inaugurate a new history of humanity. Importantly, it provided an *ethical rationale, framework and vision* for resisting, rejecting and countering the cultural domination of the *white* West in the establishment of their conception of humanity. The *ethical issues* it raised and addressed are as pertinent now as they were in 1963, when they were first published, raising the revolutionary question: *on what basis should the struggle for human emancipation be waged?* In Chapter 7, I try to answer this question when I discuss further the *ethical issues* with which I was confronted and attempted to resolve to my own satisfaction, but all the time seeking a resolution within the context of the particular Black tradition from which I emerged.

Black Power organising and its 'particular application' in Britain

Following James' framework on the relationship between *historical periods* and the *specificity of political manifestations*, it becomes possible to argue that while there are similarities in application of *the general principle* of **Black Power** in both the USA and the UK as a rallying and organizing banner and a vision of change, there are different histories and political dynamics responsible for its emergence and application in Britain, as opposed to the history of its emergence in America. While, as I have suggested, there are some continuities between 1960s and 1970s **Black Power** in Britain, the latter was essentially Caribbean, post-colonial, urban and *youthful—differences of a cultural, political and historical character.* Both British and the US experiences provide therefore *comparative examples* of the *particular application* of Black Power as a ***rallying*** banner, ***organising*** principle and **vision** of change in terms of their respective political histories (see Boggs, 1970, on those issues in the USA).

The Fasimba and the 'particular application' of Black Power

As an organization the Fasimba envisioned their ***particular application*** of the ***general principles*** of **Black Power** as one of engaging the hearts, souls and minds of black people by speaking **to them** directly through the organisational programmes, especially the young people, and not necessarily speaking to the agencies and institutions of the local or national state. The *Cause* as we saw it was to *raise Black Consciousness* and not necessarily to tell the government what we were planning to do or were doing. The work of the Fasimba was to build a strong Black organisation and to establish links with the local community and with other organisations with a similar political outlook and policy programme, hence the close collaboration between the Fasimba, the *Black Arts Workshop*, and the *Black Liberation Front* and *Youth Forces for National Liberation* from Jamaica based in London. Most of the plays, posters and the limited amount of propaganda produced by the Fasimba therefore spoke to black people directly through the mediums particular to black culture. At the same time, these mediums were transformed upon handling by the Fasimba.

As a youth-based organisation we envisaged the struggle for Black Emancipation as having both cultural and ideological dimensions, and effected through the organisation and re-education of black people, particularly the youth. Central to the **Black Power** struggles of the 1970s were issues of *re-education* and *organization,* as expressed in 1970 a Fasimba poster which announced: *"There can be no individuals in the Black Revolutionary Struggle.* ***Organise!*** *Alone you are nothing.*

BLACK FOR A CAUSE ...

We considered Black Art as a necessary instrument in the struggle for Black emancipation, and Art aimed to not just motivate and inspire, but to represent and re-constitute the meanings of past and contemporary struggles of black people. In this light Keith Piper's 1984 'Black Revolutionary' parody of the 1971 FBI 'wanted' poster for Angela Davis fulfils this function. In four separate screens the original image of Angela Davis is replaced by four Black Icons called 'The Black Assassin Saints' who were not there to 'stand-in' for the 'crimes' for which she was being sought, but point to the tradition of organised Black resistance, for which she stood as a living symbol. This time round 'The four Black Assassin Saints' were:

> "Wanted: for **undermining colonialism** through the *re-education* of black people."

> "Wanted: for **undermining racism** through the *organization* of black people."

> "Wanted: for **undermining neo-imperialism** through the **radicalisation** of black people."

> "Wanted: for **destabilizing capitalism** through the **revolutionary mobilisation** of black people."

Black (Power) artist, Keith Piper, had put on an exhibition at the Black Art Gallery, Finsbury Park, north London, in 1984, called 'Past *Imperfect, Future Tense'* and in the booklet accompanying the exhibition he wrote: "... the work of the Black artist involves the task of definition the task of analysing and defining our Blackness, **past, present and future**, and understanding the social and economic forces which have shaped us. It is also the task of sharing our findings with each other, the raising of consciousness necessary for collective activity and coherent struggle." He continues:

> This 'Revolution' is as much a revolution of ideas, as it is the inevitable clash between vested economic interests, and those whom those interests exploit worldwide. *It is the task of the Black-artist to involve him or herself in this revolution of ideas, seizing upon issues from within that revolution, and returning them to that revolution; giving dry theoretical concepts rich material and visual form. The forms should be taken out of our own traditions.*

Fasimba plays were therefore an expression of Black Art, a creative expression of the 'revolution of ideas' we saw as integral to the cultural and ideological struggle. Of the plays produced by the Fasimba under the direction of Brother Dudley the one called *'Black Versions'* was performed at the 'Dark and Light Theatre' in Camberwell, south-east London in 1970. Consistent with our practice of speaking to black people directly, in this play we focused on the dynamics between Caribbean young people and their parents over *their new* Black consciousness, as discussed in this Chapter 5. Another section of *Black Versions* aimed at a youthful black audience featured a monologue in which a Fasimba member, Bro. Chamberlain, recited a mystical poem written by Sister Andrea from the *propaganda committee*. Again, consistent with the Fasimba method of using material from past or contemporary black culture, the poem was recited over an equally mystical Lee Perry produced tune called *'Hot and Cold*,' the harmonica version to the DJ side, *'Lik a Pipe Peter'* by *Jah T*.

The poem has since become untraceable in written form.[3] As a *mystical monologue it* had the youthful and *Ras Tafari* members of the audience crying out, "*Yes! Yes!*" and "*Chat it god,*" "*Express yourself brother,*" hailing the speaker as if in a *Revival Church* sermon or at a *Nyabingi* gathering, where audience participation is expected. However, the major play produced by the Fasimba was called '*The Black Experience'* and was performed at *Lewisham Church Hall* in late 1970, and at the '*Dark and Light'* theatre in 1971 and was well attended by members of the black communities from near and far, which was 'sold out' on a number of occasions. In this play we traced the journey from Africa via the Slave Trade and Slavery to Europe; the play was divided into three parts: *part 1 Africa; part 2, 'Capture and Slavery' and; part 3, 'The trial of the West.' In the final part the 'White Man'* was put on trial for crimes against humanity. These themes may seem dull and worn in 21st Century terms but in terms of the 1970s these were revolutionary ideas.

In 1971 the Fasimba took part in the play, *'Malcolm X,'* with the *Black Arts Workshop (BAW)* at the *Dark and Light Theatre* in Camberwell. Ansel Wong, Creative Director of the *BAW* and the play, was assisted by Dudley Arthurs, responsible for Art and Culture in the Fasimba. The production was part of our ongoing collaboration with Black groups of a 'like mind' and part of our propagandising about the Black Cause, to which Malcolm X was an important figure in the ancestry of black struggles as he 'stood on the shoulders of his ancestors' to complete his Revolutionary work.

Even as Malcolm X was standing on the shoulders of Marcus Garvey, we in the Fasimba were standing on both their shoulders. Malcolm X was therefore an important and *iconic* figure for the Fasimba. Not only did we wear Malcolm X T-Shirts and Badges and sell the books with his speeches on our bookstalls, the group followed closely his teachings either by listening to his speeches on recordings such as the *'Ballot or the Bullet'* and *'Message to the Grassroots'* or reading his speeches as put into writing by George Breitman. His Autobiography by Alex Haley was on our booklist as a 'must read' as well as other books, such as Archie Epps' *'Malcolm X and the American Negro Revolution.'*

Many of us could identify with aspects of Malcolm's early and adult life experiences. Moreover, in his speeches he had directness in the words he chose and used that appealed to us as young people. Like Malcolm X, we in the Fasimba also inherited the spirit of Marcus Garvey's teachings and were proud to take part in a Black Movement that identified with and participated in the life of *this* 'X Man.' It was only natural that when we heard that his cousin, Hakim Jamal, was to visit the Fasimba and give a talk, we were excited and looked forward to listening to what he had to say.

But before Hakim Jamal is introduced, I want readers to get a taste of the drama, poetry and politics of the Play 'Malcolm X' performed by the Fasimba with the *'Black Arts Workshop.'* The play opened to packed and excited audiences, many of whom travelled miles to partake in the *visual and cultural spectacle and intellectual feast it provided.* The events described below are part of the first scene dealing with the circumstances of Malcolm's birth, the murder of his father leading to the eventual nervous breakdown, the institutionalisation of his mother and the intervention of social workers. This small extract, taken directly from the script, takes us up to where an actor, in a monologue, describes his father's brutal slaying for spreading the teachings of Marcus Garvey. The scenes, settings and text speak for themselves.

Opening to Scene 1

Seen from the perspective of the audience, the stage is dark, blacked-out, at the rise of curtain. In the first seconds of darkness we begin to hear the chant of Artie Shepp's *"Malcolm, Malcolm, Semper Malcolm."* After the poem [4] has begun, the dim lights brighten slightly, enough for us to make out the dark shape of the ACTORS arranged on the levels of the stage. Throughout the rest of the poem, projections are flashed on a retractable screen. The slides are of the distorted faces and bodies, expressing the anguish suffered by African-Americans since they were first bought to America as slaves: slides of slave trading, of slave dwellings, of people working, dancing, and crying and, finally, several slides of lynching scenes flash startlingly before the faces in the audience. After the poem is completed, Artie Shepp's haunting Jazz music is slowly faded.

As the ACTORS begin their opening chants, the lighting brightens slowly until it reaches a full glaring light, revealing the stage and the actors.

ACTOR THREE
(Cries out)
Maaaaaaaaaaal-colm!

ALL ACTORS
(Chanting)
Mal-colm
Mal-colm
Mal-colm

ACTOR ONE

(Through the chanting which dims)
Mal-colm man
Mr X man
Reach out and touch this land

ALL ACTORS
(Chants rise)
Mal-colm
Mal-colm
Mal-colm

ACTOR TEN

(Through dimmed chant)
Mr X man
We touch your hand
And filter out like bitter sand

ACTOR TWO

(Through dimmed chant)
Preach it man
And preach it Grand

227

And scourge it with your burning hand
Touch us with your finger fan
And tell us where to make our stand

ALL ACTORS

(Chant rises very loudly)
Mal-colm
Mal-colm
Mal-colm

ACTOR SIX

Out of Michigan running fire and green-hot trees

ACTOR SEVEN

And with them the glory blaze of life

ACTOR EIGHT

Burst from that North-western womb
Be born to the hoof beats riding out to the South

ACTOR NINE

And across the nation

ACTOR TEN

And watch with infant eyes the light racing deep into the forests

ACTOR ONE

Watch the incendiary venom of the masked aurora

ACTOR SIX

Watch the flaming Jesus burning the leaves

ACTOR FIVE

And his army cleansing the hooded night of you

ACTOR FOUR

Watch black baby from the shadows of your skin

ACTOR NINE

(The persona of Malcolm X takes stage)
My earliest memories are of the clan and the violence done to us

My earliest memories are of the threats and shouts and angry curses spat
upon my frightened mother

My infant memories are of the righteous Klan
Sailing like white-hot ghosts in the night settling on our house flaming
it and sending it into a thousand sparks and shuddering ash
My prenatal dreams fled naked and vulnerable from that flaming house

In my mother's belly I was the hunted

(In the next sequence the ACTORS speak urgently in hushed tones and half-
whispers, like Halloween spooks.... to create a night of terror).

ACTOR EIGHT

Hide your husband and your sons

ACTOR TEN

Hide your husband and your sons

ACTOR EIGHT

There's an awful wind out tonight

ACTOR FIVE

Ooooooo, lady, awful men's ridin' out tonight

ACTOR NINE

Hide your husband and your sons

ACTOR EIGHT

Keep 'em outta sight

ACTOR SEVEN

Put your daughters underneath the bed

ACTOR EIGHT

Quiet! Here they come

ACTOR FIVE

Ooooooo, look at the whip

ACTOR NINE

Ooooooo, look at the gun
Ooooooo, look at the horses breathin' fire

ACTOR EIGHT

And see the blood, oooooooohh, the blood

ACTOR SEVEN

Ooooooohh, lady, hide your husband and your sons

ACTOR TEN

Put your daughters underneath the bed, ooooooo

ACTOR SEVEN

Oooooooohh, that awful wind, ooooooo, them awful men's

ACTOR EIGHT

They out killin' tonight, lady
They killin' everything in sight

ACTOR NINE

They killin' everything black in sight
It's terrible, lady, it's terrible

ACTOR SEVEN

Keep 'em out of sight
Keep 'em living through the night

ACTOR FIVE

If they can't find the one they want

ACTOR NINE

Oooooooo, they kill the first black man they see they leave
him hanging from a tree

ACTOR EIGHT

'Cause when that man done met his end
they let him blow in the midnight wind

ACTORS EIGHT AND NINE are talking about the terrorism waged against black men by lynch mobs and was what Billie Holiday sang about in the acclaimed song, 'Strange Fruit':

> *"Southern trees bear strange fruit*
> *Blood on the leaves, blood at the root*
> *Black bodies singing in the southern breeze*
> *Strange fruit hanging from poplar trees"*

ACTOR SEVEN

Oooooooo, lady, oooooo

ACTOR FIVE

KEEP 'EM OUTTA SIGHT

ACTOR EIGHT

Keep 'em livin' though the night

ACTOR NINE

Say your prayers, bow your head

ACTOR FIVE

Keep your men from being dead

ACTOR SEVEN

Cry and pray, cry and pray

ACTOR EIGHT

Cry your tears and pray for day

ACTOR NINE

For the killin' night to go away

ACTOR THREE

(The persona of Malcolm X, takes stage)
My father was a Baptist minister and disciple of

Marcus Garvey, Black Nationalist and dangerous man of 1925
my father preached that cause and they got him for it

They fired his house those good Christian people and sent his family
wailing and frightened into the night

But my father was not afraid
He continued to spread the word of Marcus Garvey
He dared to persist and they killed him for it
When I was six they killed my father

ACTOR TWO

Quiet! Here he comes!

ACTOR NINE

Hey boy, boy! Hey, come here!

ACTOR EIGHT

Come here, nigger!

ACTOR NINE

Come here! Come over here!

ACTOR EIGHT

Come here, nigger!

ACTOR TWO

He's backing away

ACTOR FOUR

Don't be afraid, boy. Don't we know you?

ACTOR EIGHT

You scared him. He's trying to get away!

ACTOR NINE

Get him! Get him!

ACTOR FOUR

Screams!

ACTOR EIGHT

He's down! Get him!

ACTOR TEN

Still breathing...

ACTOR TWO

He ain't dead yet

ACTOR NINE

Look at his eyes! Hit him! Hit Him!

ACTOR FOUR

His head! His head!
(Sound of train approaching)

ACTOR NINE

Drag him over here. Lay him there!

ACTOR FOUR

Scatter! (And makes a loud scream that becomes a moan ...)

ACTOR TWO

The wind. The midnight murder wind
Like a rake dragging dried leaves across the concrete
And too much blood in the wind, too much on the fallen leaves

ACTOR THREE

(The persona of Malcolm X, takes stage)
My father went out one day when I was six and didn't come back

He went out one day and they attacked him
They smashed in one side of his head
then they laid him on some tracks
and ran a streetcar over him
Cut his body almost in two

Cut him with those big scissor wheels
and in that condition he lived

For nearly two and a half hours more
my father was a tough and angry man

ACTOR ONE

But with him dead his family struggled to stay alive
We struggled to keep together our pride and dignity
That's when the social workers came.

-END-

That was just a small section of the dramatisation of the play, Malcolm X, and it was against the background of having participated in it that we received Hakim Jamal.

The Hakim Jamal Episode

In the winter of 1971 the guest speaker lined up for a Sunday meeting was Hakim Jamal, famed to be the cousin of our slain hero Malcolm X, and as we had all seen the play, 'Malcolm X,' we all hoped that his visit and talk would provide us with insights into Malcolm X, examples of Hakim's own organising, his working philosophy and, generally, what was going on in black communities in America. His visit and reception, like the visit of Penny Jackson, sister of recently slain George Jackson to Collingham Gardens earlier in the September, was an ongoing part our Internationalism and we were looking forward to hearing from him. He'd already arrived for the 3pm meeting and was chatting to members of the central committee on what he would be talking about. During this introductory chat he shocked committee members by revealing that he had a white woman in the van outside and he would like her to come into the meeting; she, he said, was a rich and important person,

235

an MP's daughter, no less, called Gale Benson. He was told that it was organisational policy not to allow white people into our meetings as these were for black people only so he arranged for her to remain in the van outside with the driver and the other person accompanying them. We reminded him that it had been his cousin's position that black people needed to meet by themselves, first and foremost, to sort out their own problems and divisions; that there had to be black unity **before** there could be any unity between black and white people. He nodded in recognition of our position—or so we thought.

Bro. Dudley introduced the speaker and his claim to fame: that he was a cousin of Malcolm X, at which he was cheered and clapped, at which he smiled, but he hadn't got far into his talk when he began swearing: "motherfuckin' pigs" and "motherfuckin' honkies." An uncomfortable silence fell on the congregation as we were not used to guest speakers using that kind of language. He then revealed that he had bought a white woman along with him, but she had to remain in the van outside as we did not allow white people into our meetings. To our shock he then told the audience that he was **only** using her to teach him French: "*While I'm fucking her,*" he said "*she speaks to me in French. Even better,*" he chuckled "the *lessons are free. In fact, I'm paying her.*" There was even more of an uncomfortable silence.

Well, that kind of remark, with its explicit sexual innuendos, might have raised some laughs during street-corner 'raps' in the USA or even among some groups in London, but not amongst the people congregated in New Cross that Sunday afternoon. When he finished the first part of his talk, he was called to one side and had it explained that that sort of language was not ordinarily used in our Sunday meetings, as there were elders and young people present. During the break Fasimba members gathered around talking to him and some refreshments were taken to the occupants of the van outside. When the second part of his talk—the 'questions and answers' session—was over we thanked him, he shook hands with many people, and then left the basement followed by some of the Fasimba and other visitors to the van. That was the last we saw of him.

At the Thursday and Saturday meetings, we reviewed his visit and the content of his talk and learned that a number of Fasimba members had followed him back to his flat where they spent a lot of time talking to him. When we asked one person, Bro. J., what he and Hakim had talked about he became quite evasive and was not willing to say much. We found his behaviour strange and, over the coming weeks, came to realise that others had been in contact with Hakim and were also behaving strangely. They were also quite secretive about their visits to him and what he and they had been discussing. A female member of the Fasimba who was among those who visited him seemed to go 'mad' soon after, and we began to suspect that she and the others who had been acting strangely may well have unknowingly imbibed some *LSD* or some other 'mind blowing' substance. As suspicions grew there was wild speculation that Hakim Jamal may be some sort of 'spy' from the CIA or, we queried, might even be working for Britain's own Intelligence Service and sent to collect any information he could on the Fasimba, as part of their work to *disrupt and sabotage* Black Power in the UK, similar to what the FBI were doing in the USA with regards to the Black Panthers.

We queried also whether he had really expected us to admit his female companion into the meeting, given that our position was similar to Malcolm X's, as we had explained to him. We then had to ask ourselves if he really *knew* Malcolm X and was *personally familiar* with his politics and philosophy. Even stranger, we asked, why were the people who had close contact with him acting so weird? Within a matter of a few months we would to learn that our suspicions were not too far-fetched as worse was to emerge about Hakim, his links to Michael X, and both their links to white philanthropists. Soon after visiting the Fasimba in the winter of 1971, Hakim Jamal and Gale Benson, who had changed her name to Hale Kimga (an acronym of Gale and Hakim), left Britain for Trinidad to join Michael X and his group of 'revolutionaries' at his *commune* at Christina Gardens, not too far from Port of Spain. That was January 1972.

Michael had left Britain the previous year, in February 1971, after he and four others were accused of extortion. Known as 'the slave collar affair' a white businessman was supposed to have been paraded around the Black House with a spiked slave collar around his neck. But having returned to Trinidad just after a coup attempt against Trinidad's Prime Minister, Eric Williams, rumours were spread that he was behind the Black Power revolt against Eric Williams' corrupt regime. Williams ended up asking Britain for help to put down the revolt. Near the end of January 1972, his 'commune' at Christina Gardens burnt down and the police came to investigate; but given his pronouncements, they also took the opportunity to search the grounds for firearms. Instead they found the bodies of Gale Benson and Joseph Skerritt (said to be Michael's cousin) buried in shallow graves in the grounds. Warrants were issued for the arrest of Michael De Freitas, aka, Michael Abdul Malik, aka Michael X, who was eventually arrested, tried and sentenced to death. Hakim Jamal, Gale's partner, left Trinidad for the USA where, just over 1 year later, on 1st May 1973, he was shot dead in a bar in Boston, allegedly by the Mau

Mau Brothers. Michael X was hung in Trinidad in 1975, despite appeals from literary figures and pop stars, like John Lennon who had given him a piano to sell to raise money for the Black House in Holloway Road. He had taken it back to Trinidad with him.

Michael X and Hakim Jamal

The one link between Michael X and Hakim Jamal was, of course, Malcolm X. Michael De Freitas first met Malcolm X on his second visit to Britain in 1965 in London at the *Congress of African Unity* held at *Nkrumah House,* Collingham Gardens, Earls Court. When Malcolm returned to America, he was assassinated. In London Michael De Freitas changed his name to Michael Abdul Malik and took on the persona of Michael X, a radical Black Muslim, and launched a semi-religious organisation based on *the Nation of Islam* called the *Racial Action Adjustment Society,* whose acronym spelt *RAAS,* a Jamaican swearword. Many people, black and white, saw his conversion to Islam as a sign that Michael was beginning to follow a similar path and pattern to that taken by Malcolm X—his inspiration and mentor. But was Michael's conversion to righteousness only 'skin deep?'

When he founded and named the new 'religious' organisation in 1965, did he consider it proper to present to the 'Black World' an organisation whose acronym spelt out a Jamaican 'badword?' To whom would the acronym, *RAAS,* appeal? To the white liberals from whom he sought and got funding or to the hippies among whom he moved? If this was meant to be a joke, who would the joke be on and who would have the last laugh? We found the Hakim Jamal episode most bizarre— from his behaviour that Sunday afternoon at Musgrove Road, to his influence on members of the Fasimba, his flight to Trinidad and friendship with Michael X, the slaying of his girlfriend, Gale Benson, to his flight from Trinidad to Boston, USA, and his death by shooting in 1973. That event concluded the Hakim Jamal episode. However, in her book, *'Make Believe'* (1993; 2004), Diane Athill, editor with Andre Deutch during the 1970s, tells how she and Hakim were lovers when he stayed with her at her flat in London while she edited his book, *'The Dead Level: Malcolm X and Me'* (1971). Also revealed was that they 'dropped acid' together, providing a possible explanation for the bizarre behaviour of Fasimba members who visited and befriended him.

The David Oluwale episode and the Fasimba

The story of David Oluwale is worth recounting for many reasons. One, soon after the Court case of the two policemen who 'hounded him to death', there was an incident in Peckham one Saturday night between the police and *Chris* that resulted in being given the nickname, 'Oluwale. Two, the story gives an *indication of the reasoning* behind our social and political consciousness and actions, as well as providing *an insight into the basis* of the *tactics of resistance* used by us as Fasimba members and as the 'Oval 4' a year later.

An understanding of David Oluwale's treatment by the police, the manner of his death and the trials of the two policemen for his 'manslaughter' are important elements in the transformation of our evolving *conception* of 'Blackness' and our political *practice*. Of importance was the fact that *Chris* lost two cultural artefacts of Blackness, as was symbolised in the 1970s, in his confrontation with the police in Peckham. This is how the story of David Oluwale comes to fit into our 'politics of Blackness' and our transformation of 'blackness' to 'Blackness': the moving from object to subject; from just a **'B' Cause** to **'A' Cause.'** This argument is developed further down.

On the morning of 18th April, 1969, the body of David Oluwale was recovered from the River Aire in Leeds. The death certificate prepared after the inquest on 14th May recorded he was "Found Drowned". He was 38. An understanding of David's case is important to a mapping of the contours of Black experience in Britain for a number of reasons.

One, it helps to establish a framework for determining the nature of police/black community relations, especially the interpersonal racial antagonisms and conflicts between white police-men and black-men. **Two**, it helps to demonstrate that these relations as essentially 'relations of domination' and 'resistance to domination.' **Three**, though David Oluwale died in 1969, his death was predated by 20 years of appalling violence by the police and the judicial system: harassment, physical and psychological brutality, kidnapping, arbitrary arrest and incarceration in a seemingly endless cycle of terror only to be interrupted by his death by drowning. In his article, 'The Death of One Lame Darkie', Ron Philips observed that *"by his anguished life and humiliating death (he) was to demonstrate the extent to which racism dominates all the important institutions of social control in Britain"*(Phillips, 1975), David Oluwale has the dubious 'honour' of being the first black person to die in modern Britain as a result of his repeated encounters with the police, the first in a line of over 1000 black men and women who have met untimely deaths whilst in their custody, either on the streets, during arrest, in police cells, prison or mental institutions, since 1969 (*One in 1000 deaths in police custody*, David Leider, Blaqfaire). **Finally**, his biography fits the *symbolic narrative* of the so-called 'Windrush' migrants, with whom he shared dreams and ambitions that could only be fulfilled by 'risk' of transportation to the 'Mother Country.'

David was born on 8th September, 1930, in Lagos, Nigeria. In 1949, aged 19, he stowed away on the cargo ship, 'Temple Star' bound for the port of Hull, Britain. Having been discovered during the voyage he was 'welcomed' to the 'Mother Country' with a 28-day stay in Armley jail, the "price of a one way ticket from Lagos." The symbolism of him stowing away on a *cargo ship* cannot be lost on students of the transatlantic slave trade, where David's future lies in his *commodification,* in him blending in with and lying amongst other African produce—'goods'— being transported from Nigeria to Britain. The Caribbean novelist, George Lamming, described this transportation as one of *"commercial deportation,"* (cited by Baker, Jnr.,1984: 240) a journey similar to the *Triangular Trade* that originally bought Africa and Africans in touch with European economies and cultures, in the Caribbean and the Americas. Like other black 'human cargo' before him, David 'pays' for his transportation with penal labour, and over the next twenty years various social institutions are called upon to 'season him'—to break his will, to prepare him for *menial labour*. But he resists and he 'pays' for that resistance with his life. Philips quotes another Nigerian, 'Widey' Williams, who lived in Leeds at the time and knew David. He remembers Leeds in the 1950s as "a very hostile place" for black exiles:

> We had three enemies: the labour exchange, the landlord and the police. A lot of us gave up—just bothering about clothes, dancing and girls. Not this David Oluwale, he was always trying. The police were the biggest problem; whatever we did we couldn't avoid them. Sometimes they would stop us two or three times between the city centre and Chapeltown—especially late at night. If we argued they would run us in for obstruction or something—anything. Then they would charge us with something bigger, either drugs or assault—and that was it.

In November 1971 Geoffrey Ellerker and Mark Kitching were put on trial for manslaughter and for perjury. What emerges in the trial at Leeds Assizes over the weeks is a horrifying catalogue of violence and abuse of

David, including being kidnapped and dumped miles outside Leeds in the night, being urinated upon, beaten with truncheons and kicked in his genitals so hard that he screamed, and being framed for 'assaulting the police.' The combination of systematic police terror, detention in prisons and psychiatric hospitals, and judicial collusion finally helped to seal a seemingly inevitable fate.

Three hours before David ended up in the River Aire, he was attacked by Ellerker and Kitching after they found him sleeping in a doorway. David runs off screaming, holding his head. On the news of David's death the following day, Kitching is said to have remarked: *"lot of them would be better off if they went for a swim, like David."* The logic of this view was shared by the Chief Constable of Durham, Alec Muir, who was quoted in the *Guardian* (27/2/69) as saying that *'criminals should be quietly eliminated, rather than locked away.'* Despite overwhelming evidence of their terrorism and complicity in his death, the trial Judge directed the jury to clear these officers of his manslaughter and perjury charges, but the jury convicted Ellerker of 5 charges of assault and Kitching of 4 charges of assault on the Nigerian. They were sentenced to 3 and 2 years in prison respectively.

The above is by no means a detailed description or analysis of the horror David Oluwale's life and death but to echo Ron Phillip's observation that *by his life and death he demonstrated the extent to which institutional racism intersects with the lives of Black people in Britain.* His story is a *dramatisation* of the routine nature of police terror when unleashed upon black people who are considered as having no economic value, *just objects* upon which to practice acts of appalling inhumanity. A group of us spoke at length about what happened to David Oluwale at one of our Thursday meetings. Some of us cursed the police for their brutality on and 'murder' of David Oluwale and as we absorbed the horrifying details of his ordeal in the papers, some of us 'took oaths' and vowed that there could be no circumstance in which we could be treated like that—that was 1971.

But not even two weeks later, on a Saturday night, *Chris* was coming home from a meeting in Peckham Rye and found himself being followed by two plain-clothes policemen near Holly Grove on Rye Lane. Knowing they wanted to 'question' him he decided to elude them, crossing Rye Lane, headed for Consort Road and sped off. They gave chase and would have held him had he not left them holding onto one of his shoes and his new coat as he clambered over a wall and along the back streets to New Cross. By the Sunday morning, news had spread amongst the Fasimba that *Chris* had to run from the police to escape a possible beating and a night at Peckham police station.

At the Sunday meeting his tale was told by his brother Ossie to those gathered. At the time of his escape *Chris* had on him a 7' copy of Syl Johnson's Soul hit, '*Is it because I'm Black?*'—which he had to leave behind with the pursuing policemen, as well as his new black Crombie-style, calf-length coat, similar to the leather one worn by Richard Rowntree in the 1971 Black movie, '*Shaft*'. On hearing of him losing his new coat, we started a collection to raise enough money to give to him to buy a new one. Legal advice to him was that he should not attempt to retrieve the coat from the police, least of all the 7' single. He would be arrested and charged. We joked about what the police would make of the fact that he had on him a record with *that* title.

The following Thursday, *Chris* walked into the meeting and everyone cheered and clapped. He had on a coat given to him a by family member and as he entered the meeting, "*Yes, Oluwale,*" was what someone said triumphantly. And those of us who had that discussion about David Oluwale just two weeks earlier hailed him and agreed: "*Yes, Oluwale,*" while saluting with our clenched fists. And from that day *Chris* was nicknamed 'Oluwale.' The naming of *Chris* as 'Oluwale' was instant, and yet the result of quite a complex process of reasoning and symbolism that was shared by many in the Fasimba. By his nicknaming we were neither dishonouring *Chris* nor the memory of David Oluwale, but honouring the name and the type of resistance it had come to stand for, as through *Chris*' renaming, David Oluwale became a Fasimba. How and why was this done?

The Fasimba and the 'Blackness of Blackness'

Firstly, as already told, some of us were quite familiar with the *symbolism* of David Oluwale's case, and of his experience in British institutions, from the time he arrived in the country until his suspicious death some twenty years later; **second**, *Chris* had with him a copy of the popular 1971 Soul hit that asked '*Is it Because I'm Black*?' which he had to leave behind with the police so as to escape; **third**, we considered then and still do now that running or fleeing from potential captivity and/ or violence as an act of *agency*, of self definition, of self preservation. This act was an integral part of our humanity, *the impulse to be free*, and; **fourth,** we came to understand that David, like the subject in Syl Johnson's song, was persecuted *because he was black*. His blackness mediated his 'vagrant' status and exposed him to lethal racial violence from the police. In us rejecting his positioning as an 'object', the outcome of someone else's 'looking', 'seeing' and 'framing'—the result of the 'white man's gaze'—we as Fasimba were "Black for a Cause" and our *Blackness* was an *act of agency*, of *self-definition*, not one of external categorisation or imposition.

We were Black not *'just because'* we were considered black and should somehow regard the treatment meted out to us and other black people as consequent to that 'external' definition of blackness. To us the symbolism was obvious. As Fasimba, we were *'Black for a Cause,'* the *Black Cause*, one based on a *self-fashioned* and therefore *elevated* definition of Blackness. It was a **Cause** that began with providing an answer to Syl Johnson's question *'Is it because I'm black?'* with *'Yes, I am black ....but not just because I am black. I am Black for A Cause not just Because."* We therefore transformed a **B**-cause into **A**-Cause— t*urning the **object** of economic exploitation, discrimination and racial violence into the **subject.** *The transformation from object to subject is a political act, an act of self definition and, at the same time, is also an act of subversion* (Gates, Jnr, 1984 in Walker, HE, 1984: iv). Thus the 'written about' and 'written on'— the 'semantically marked'—becomes the 'writer' and 'author' of his or her own story, and shaper of their own destiny; S/he becomes someone who charts for himself or herself a self-defined, self-chosen journey.

Though David tried to move from *object* to *subject status, to begin to define his own destiny, on his own terms by his efforts to study and train as an engineer, his efforts were thwarted as he was held back by a society that sought to deny his efforts and, by that, deny his humanity.* It succeeded in keeping him objectified as a non-person, as an Object; in a 'non-human' designation. Our or nicknaming or (re)naming of *Chris* as 'Oluwale' was one way we could begin to subvert and destabilise David's former status and re-inscribe his *blackness* with a Black humanity so that it would no longer stand as a 'negative' of that Universalised category, *whiteness*; that his *blackness* would not be the *darkness* against which *whiteness* becomes *luminous.*

During the trial *the police posed David as virtually sub-human,* described as "a physical menace" to the policeman whose job it was to "move him on." On this the trial Judge, Mr Justice Hinchcliffe concurred, agreeing that David was 'a menace to society, a nuisance to the police, *a frightening apparition to come across at night'* (Philips, 1975:18). For a group of us in the Fasimba, he not only becomes humanised by our *renaming ritual* but also by being *relocated* in the *Black Cause.* It was our understanding of this *Cause* that enabled us to *transform* how David Oluwale had been handed down to us, and how he had previously been framed by British history and society, dislocating him from a *white* perception of blackness to a relocation in a *Black* conception of blackness.

NOTES

1   The two quotes are from the 'Autobiography of Malcolm X' is found on the Spartacus website , Accessed 28/8/2005, http://www.spartucus.schoolnet.co.uk/USAmalcolmX.htm p.3.

2   'Call and Response' is described as a form of spontaneous verbal and non-verbal interaction between speakers and listeners in which all the statements ('calls') are punctuated by expressions ('responses') from the listener. In African cultures, 'call and response' is a pervasive pattern of democratic participation—in public gatherings, in the discussion of civic affairs, in religious rituals, as well as in vocal or instrumental expression. It is this tradition that African bondmen and women have transmitted over the years in various forms of expression—in religious observance; public gatherings; even in children's rhymes; and, most notably, in black music and its multiple forms: gospel, blues, rhythm and blues; jazz and jazz extensions, hip-hop, mento, rock steady, reggae, dance-hall, and Jamaican DJ music.

3   The 'remembered' extract of this mystical poem is as follows:

I who is he who walks in the shadows of death
My weary soul can no rest get
The cows in the fields say moo
As they eat grass that grew
I hear them say
Where is the RSPCA
I walk the street
No slanders on my feet...

4   Artie Schepp's ode 'Malcolm, Malcolm—Semper Malcolm' is on his 'Fire Music' Album released in 1965. The track opens with this poem:

A song is not what it seems
A tune perhaps

Bird whistled while leaving America
Listened
We play
But we aren't always dumb
We are murdered
In Amphitheatres
On the Podium of the Audubon
The Earl
Philadelphia 1945
Malcolm
My people
Dear God
Malcolm

CHAPTER 7

The 'Oval 4' Episode and
The Ethics of Black Resistance

For we wrestle not against flesh and blood, but
against principalities, against powers, against the
rulers of darkness of this world, against spiritual
wickedness in high places.
(Ephesians: Ch.6:12)

I an' I no come to fight flesh and blood,
But spiritual wickedness in high and low places,
so while they fight you down,
Stand firm and give Jah thanks and praises.
I an' I no expect be justified by the laws of men
(by the laws of men)
O, the jury found me guilty, Jah prove my innocence.
Cos when the rain fall, it don't fall on
one man's housetop (remember that),
I say, when the rain fall, it don't fall
on one man's housetop.
They got so much things to say, right now, so
much things to say.
('So Much Things to Say,' Bob Marley, from the
album 'Exodus', 1977)

Conclusions

This final Chapter brings together my experiences and thinking as
one of the 'Oval 4' and how that relates to my experience as a Black
Power activist and a member of the Fasimba. The Fasimba experience
of Black Power activism gave me *an angle of vision* not just on the
development of my identity, my personal and cultural history and my
chosen destiny, but also *an angle of vision* on the attempts by the police
to deny this development by a 'grand deception.' *It is my argument that
this deception attempted to subvert if not deny the basis of my own sense*

246

of 'Beingness,' as a part of wider Historical attempts to undermine the total 'Beingness' of black people in Britain and in the modern world, a displacement set in motion by the transatlantic slave trade.

By 'Beingness' I refer to the *fact* and *quality* of being and *existence of black people following the European attempt to dehumanise them globally*. To conclude the story of the 'Oval 4,' its connection to the Black Power story of the 1970s, Black resistance and its link to contemporary debates about the abolition of the transatlantic slave trade in 1807, I offer a *radical* reading of the 'confession' as a *tactic of resistance*. This tactic, this small act, was a component in a wider *strategy of counter-deception and subversion* in which I engaged in an attempt to disrupt their 'grand deception.' My attempt to counter their *grand deception* with a *strategy of counter-deception* was designed to undermine their 'truth claims' and the basis upon which these were constructed.

The Grand Deception of the Transport police

I call the Transport police 'truth claims' a 'grand deception' because it was large, huge and encompassing; it recruited and involved a range of legal and media institutions and personnel to play their part in carrying out the deception. The deception was 'grand' also because it thoroughly deceived the 'eminent Judges' at the Old Bailey and the Court of Appeal; in fact, Ridgewell and his 'gang' even fooled the Press, the British Transport Police, the Home Office, the Director of Public Prosecutions, the Metropolitan police, even Parliament and other 'official definers' of the State, and did so for several years. Their *deception* was possible and seen as a 'truth' because it chimed with political attitudes and institutional (policing and immigration) practices towards black settlement even as it opposed and criminalised black dissent to these discriminatory and oppressive practices (*Police Against Black People, 'Race & Class*, 1979). *Deception* is defined as the *"practice of misleading someone."* It also means *"deliberately making someone believe things that are not true"* and is *"an act, a trick or device intended to mislead or deceive someone"* (Encarta online Dictionary: English, U.K; Thesaurus on line: English, U.K). While *deception* involves misleading or deceiving someone else were Ridgewell and his 'gang' ultimately deceiving themselves?

I have called *my* response to their 'grand deception' a *counter-deception*. To 'counter' has two levels of meaning. First, it is *"to do something in opposition to what someone else is doing,"* like launching *counter-argument to establish an alternative or an opposing argument.*

Second, a 'counter' is a *"response made in retaliation to something that has been said"* or *done*, and 'deception' is defined as the practice of *"deliberately making someone believe things that are not true"* (*Encarta Dictionary*: English, UK; Thesaurus: English, U.K).

My *counter-deception* was therefore a response to their *grand deception*, and was designed to move beyond their initial deception and get them to the point of *deceiving themselves even further by believing what I was telling them was what they wanted to hear: things they thought were true but were not true.* The point I wish to emphasise is that a 'confession' is normally based on the *idea of the person* 'confessing' telling the listener *what they expect to hear: an admission of guilt. But the making of a 'confession' may also be regarded as an act of deception or a tactic of concealment in that the listener, while being told what they expect to hear are, at the same time, being misled or having other things hidden or concealed from them.* My admission of guilt was not just an act of deception, it was a counter-deception. It was my intention to get the police to the point of believing and accepting what I was saying was a 'truth' they needed to hear; misleading them by getting them to deceive themselves even further and then in Court expose the *false basis* of their 'truth claims.'

Set in a broader political context and at a particular historical moment, the 'Oval 4' case may be imagined as symbolic of the contours of modern Black struggles and of the State's attempts to contain or eradicate those struggles, especially resistance to aggressive policing methods and the working practices of the police, such as the notorious 'stop and search' tactic. As young black men the case was illustrative of the antagonistic dynamics that existed, and still exist, between young black men and the police, antagonisms that had been fostered by a history of false arrests, deliberate violence and the fabrication and planting of 'evidence.'

Because we were black (or 'coloured' as we were described then) we were 'suspected persons.' Ridgewell said in evidence at the trial of two Zimbabweans in April 1973 that he was on the look-out particularly for "coloured youths travelling on the Northern Line" whom he suspected of "interfering with citizens using the underground," as the trial Judge had once phrased it.

Importantly the case opens up an *angle of vision* on the story of Black resistance against overwhelming odds and, at the same time, makes a statement about the ingenuity and fortitude of Black activists against police violence and perjury, and judicial and press complicity in the imprisonment of many innocent black people. *Police violence and corruption as practiced by Ridgewell and its resistance by black people lie at the heart of these issues.*

British abolition of slave trading or the struggle continues?

March 2007 marked the 200th Anniversary of the Abolition of the Atlantic Slave Trade Act by the British Parliament in 1807, said to have abolished British participation in Slave Trading across the Atlantic. *This closing Chapter attempts to link the struggles of our ancestors against captivity, transportation and bondage with the traditions underpinning the Black Power struggles of the 1970s. The Black Movement and struggles of that era , I suggest, were bound up in different ways to the struggle for a new sense of 'Beingness' and new humanity, a struggle that began in earnest with the capture and transportation of our ancestors to become 'unfree beings' in the so-called 'New World'. To begin this 'closure' we must return to the final stages of the trial at the Old Bailey in November 1972 when, during his summing up the trial Judge, Edward Cussens, QC, told the jury that the trial was characterised by a "**clash of evidence**" between the four accused and the Crown. He told the jury it could be but one way or the other: "either the accused are lying or it is the police" and directed them "to consider carefully whether the statements are really fiction made up by Detective Sergeant Ridgewell" (Hall and others, 1978:40).*

During the Appeal hearing in July 1973, Lord Justice James made a similar observation on evidence given at the trial. His view was that there had been a **"head-on collision"** between the testimony of the Crown and that of the Appellants and went even further, suggesting that "*some of the defendants deliberately misled the police in their statements.*" Well, that was his way of looking at it. I would say that the 'Oval 4' case was characterised by a **"head-on collision"** between two diametrically opposed traditions: the tradition of colonialist and imperialist domination, to which the police and Courts belonged, versus the cultural practices and political aspirations of a *radical* tradition of resistance, to which 1970s Black Power was integral.

Tradition versus tradition

To anticipate a point to be made concerning our connections to the radical tradition of Black resistance, when the policemen in disguise 'rushed' us at the top of the escalator at the Oval, they didn't just 'drape-up' four ordinary black young men. *The moment they pounced on us, shouted, grabbed and tried to force us against the wall and began to 'push-up' themselves in our faces, all that we knew as black men and Black activists came into operation. We took our past with us into the confrontation with them and into the police station.* We were certainly not the kind of passive black people they took us to be; we were four Black activists who belonged to the Fasimba and were part of a Black Cause underscored by a *tradition* of *resistance* to and *subversion* of the forms of bondage, exploitation, violence and terror inaugurated by the transatlantic slave trade and plantation system (Robinson, 1983). This *tradition* was the foundation of the *Black Consciousness* into which we were born, a tradition we inherited and had been fashioning 'in our own image' in the 1970s Black Movement. Peter Fryer in his book '*Staying Power*' (1984:386) makes the following point about this Black consciousness:

> Throughout the 1970s, as the settlers' children—the second generation—strove to make sense of the situation they found themselves born into, it was precisely this *consciousness,* with its rich tradition of militancy, resistance, and struggle, to which they would increasingly turn for guidance. And it was there they would find their strength.

CLR James said in a speech in London in 1967 that modern Black Power activists stood "on the shoulders of their ancestors" and were thus the inheritors of all the struggles for Black emancipation that had gone before (James, 1967). I found not only *strength* by placing myself within this "rich tradition" but also the *inspiration* and *determination* to overcome my present adversity. From this perspective part of me already understood that in Court none of us could rely on countering the police lies and deception with claims to a 'truth' expressed in terms of their own language and legal concepts as, for example, those enshrined in the 'rules of evidence.' Within these 'rules' our defence tactics and evidence were ruled 'inadmissible' by the trial Judge as he monitored and interpreted these 'rules' in favour of the Crown.

Nor was there a 'higher truth' to which we could have referred or drawn upon that was not framed by these concepts, language and traditions. Our 'truths' meant nothing.

The Counter-deception

To overcome these hurdles I resorted to a strategy of *counter-deception,* to a 'subversion' of their 'truth claims' that was cut from a *language of resistance and subversion* informed by this *radical tradition of resistance.* By the 'confession' statement I had unleashed and set in motion 'forces' that would come to be manifest in the near-destruction of their 'truth claims,' the abandonment of the Transport police's so-called 'anti-mugging' squad, and the demise and destruction of the police officer in charge that night: Detective Sergeant Derek Ridgewell. My *'confession-as-deception'* tactic served to deepen the 'war of position' I was locked into with my captors but was not a struggle in which I sought the *moral high ground* in the terms of the society's traditions or standards. It was a struggle in which I sought to move to a 'higher ground,' beyond their definitions, to a place from where I could counter their deception with a *counter-deception* that drew on other 'truths.' These 'truths' were not so much the *opposite* to their 'lies' but were 'truths' beyond their codes of 'true/false' oppositions which are fundamental to the English language and, thus, beyond their 'rules.' However, there was one 'truth' this *counter-deception* did rely on, and it was the fact that *I knew* something they did not know, *and I knew they didn't know it.* My strategy was launched, therefore, from a position as knowing something that they could not possibly know. That was the only way I thought it could work.

The 'totality' of our entrapment by the police, as I perceived it, required a change in what I will call the 'rules of engagement;' that is, a change in the *basis* of our *confrontation* and thus in the *assumed power relations* between 'captor' and 'captive' and a change in how this *confrontation* would be played out, tactically. I decided I was not going to act-out the role of a 'victim' even as they acted out the role of 'aggressor:' nor was I going to remain in a defensive position where they could continue to apply violence nor as a blank sheet of paper upon which they could write their story, their 'truth claims.' I would go on the offensive. I would move from *object* to subject *status* (Walker, 1984: li, Introduction) and within the confines of the interrogation try to 'turn the tables' on them in some way. In them setting us up I made it so happen that they were also setting themselves up.

My *act of compliance* was really an *act of defiance, a manoeuvre, a tactic of 'resistance,' a counter-deception* that was designed to undermine their 'truth claims,' to sabotage and subvert the case against us. I can now reveal that *my mind was the 'concealed weapon' that I took with me into the police station, and was a 'weapon' sharpened by the fact that I knew something they did not know, could not possibly know, and I knew they didn't know it. My intention was to use this 'weapon' to not only destroy the police case against us but to also damage and wound some of them in the process, particularly their leader, Ridgewell. And much of this 'wounding' would to be caused by the 'naming and blaming' of Ridgewell as author of the 'false confessions.'*

Black activists under scrutiny

At the time of our conviction and imprisonment some people in the black community and in black organisations may have been entitled have seen the 'confession-statement' as an act of *complicity* in our journey to prison and felt, perhaps, that we should have taken the beatings and still gone to prison but as 'heroes'—presumably *without* the police-induced 'confessions' of guilt hanging over us. We presume also these same people felt or imagined that we should not have 'succumbed' to *police terrorism*, but instead should have restarted the fight with the police while *in* the police station—with no means of escape and risked even more serious injuries, as was their intention that night. Or should we have claimed our right to silence? We went further than that and claimed our right to our one telephone call each in the police station, but Ridgewell told us, "*You got no bloody rights!*" None the above were therefore options open to us. The 'rights' that arrested persons now have did not exist in 1972, as the Police and Criminal Evidence Act (PACE) and code of practice did not become law until 1984. *Therefore all the mutterings from those who said they 'would' or 'wouldn't have done this' or 'that' say so from the privileged position of being in the relative safety of the present looking back on the interpreted past.* Indeed this looking back is based on a particular reading of the past and was one that privileged physical resistance at any cost. Such a view ignores or omits any attempts by us to *manage the consequences* of present actions on future outcomes.

What has remained controversial since then and is raised now were our reactions to the threats and beatings that were applied by the police to gain our submission. On the surface, the popular version of our captivity *reads*, correctly, as the violence of the police (the aggressors) on four black male activists (the victims of aggression), but in that narrative we are posed principally as 'victims' of police violence and terror, to which we 'succumbed.' That is an important part of the telling of the story of 'Oval 4' but is nonetheless a partial and one-sided view of our captivity and reactions to it. In that narrative we are posed as 'victims' but this view omits another very important dimension; that of black resistance to oppression and of black people as principally *agents, self-conscious actors* in opposing the adverse *conditions of existence* and not just 'victims' of their circumstance. This is a crucial point to get across as it not only privileges modern Black resistance, it relates also to an argument I will develop further on concerning black resistance to the slave trade and plantation slavery as a source **for** contemporary black resistance.

Malcolm X, a powerful example of Black political agency, said in a speech in Detroit in 1965: *"Don't lay down a life all by itself. No, preserve your life, as it's the best thing you've got. And if you've got to give it up, let it be even steven"* (Eppes, 1968:69). In other words, "laying down a life"—making a sacrifice—should or *must count for something.* The 'half that's never been told' now shows that the 'confessions' were produced in an attempt to make it "even-steven," to make our wrongful arrest *count for something.* So what did the 'confessions' count for? What was evened-up by them? The Jamaican poet, Claude MacKay, in his poem, 'If We Must Die,' suggests one way that the "even-steven" might be imagined:

> O kinsmen! we must meet the common foe!
> Though far outnumbered, let us show brave
> And for their thousand blows, deal one death-blow!
> What though before us lays the open grave?
> Like men we'll face the murderous, cowardly pack,
> Pressed to the wall, dying but fighting back!

Claude McKay wrote this poem whilst in London to express his sentiments about the racial injustices that led to the 1919 'race riots' in Harlem (Fryer, 1984: 318)[1] and, at the same time, it provides a rallying point for *heroic resistance* against overwhelming odds. It was a favourite of ours in the Fasimba. The false 'confession' may therefore be read as part of my 'fight-back' against overwhelming odds; my "one deathblow" for their "thousand blows." These sentiments by Claude McKay stand alongside those of Malcolm X and Henry Highland Garnett on issues of 'Black Beingness' and its preservation.

An analysis of the Court case shows that the 'confession' that was *forced out of me* did NOT contribute to my conviction as I was found Not Guilty by the jury's unanimous verdict on those charges arising from the 'confessions.' What prevailed was what I was trying to prevent from happening in the first place: the *establishment* of what the police said they saw us doing on the night as a 'truth claim,' a claim that I had hoped that the 'impossibility' of the 'confession' would unseat or, at least, show them to be 'unclothed'—naked.

Re-reading the Verdicts

By a 10-2 majority verdict two members of the jury DID NOT believe the police version of what went on at the Oval station that night. Perhaps the other ten jury members who did assent to the guilty verdict were intimidated by the weight of 'responsibility' the trial Judge's analysis had placed in their minds: that their verdicts would establish "either the defendants are lying or it is the police." The jury 'erred' therefore on the side of caution and found us guilty—no matter how absurd the police 'truth' claims were, as for example, that *Chris* assaulted the woman detective and stole her handbag as he ran from the Oval station. According to evidence from two new witnesses he was "running for his life" with his shirt hanging off him and no bag was seen in his hand. We learned later that it was North and Ridgewell's idea to 'do' *Chris* for Wood's lost handbag (*Time Out*, 27th October-2nd November, 1972.) Although I did not know it when I fabricated the 'false confession' to undermine the police, the use of threats and violence to force his 'victims' to make statements admitting the police version of events and to other 'crimes' *was the modus operandi* of Ridgewell and his 'gang' in the two cases before ours. But with the 'Oval 4' case this *modus operandi* came apart as it was subverted by *unshakable* alibi evidence that *countered directly* the admissions of guilt in the 'confession-statements' so much so that Lord Justice James expressed his belief that *"some of the defendants deliberately misled the police in their statements"* and could not understand why.

John Rodgers, in defence of Ridgewell's 'truth claims,' told the jury that we must have lied about events at the Oval underground *and* lied in the police station when making the 'confessions.' According to the 'logic' of his bizarre summing-up, we had *lied when we denied* attempting to steal from passengers and *lied when we admitted* stealing from shoppers. In other words, because we were liars *only the police evidence could be believed*; or so he told the jury at the time. Chapter 4 told a different story.

In his 4th and last case, Ridgewell didn't get as far as forcing 'confessions' from the 'Tottenham Court Road 2.' The 'false victory' given him by appearing to triumph over the 'Oval 4' meant that he was so inflated with 'over confidence' that he and his accomplices overzealously and clumsily pounced on two black students from Rhodesia. This irony would have been lost on him. From claiming to disdain the brutal treatment he was being trained to inflict on Africans in Rhodesia, he was prepared to do just that in London. After losing that case so dramatically in April, three months later in July at our Appeal hearing Ridgewell was still being defended and protected by the Courts.

Lord Justice James' explanation and defence of the jury's decision to acquit us on the charges we 'admitted' but convict us on the charges we *denied* were on the basis of the Courts accepting the *false* 'truth claims' made by Ridgewell and his accomplices in their evidence. Justice James' reading of the meaning of jury's verdicts was certainly at odds with the defence submission given at the Appeal, and confirms that these different readings were derived from opposing traditions, hence both Judges admitting there was either a *"clash"* or a *"head on collision"* between the evidence of the 'Oval 4' and the police. The *"false confessions"* emerged to be the basis and terms of this *"head on collision"* between traditions.

The tradition of Black resistance

I intend to now demonstrate the 'false confessions' were *beyond* what could be considered as just a *'clash of evidence'* between the 'Oval 4' and the police as this would confine it's understanding to a quasi-legal framework and its legitimising discourse on black criminality. I spoke earlier of how in the police station I had moved beyond the *true/false* binary constraints of the English language to a **place** where I could counter their deception. From this perspective, the 'false confession' is more properly understood as a *tactic of resistance, itself part of a* wider *strategy of counter-deception and subversion and was a tactic* derived from the cultural and political practices of a *tradition* of radical black resistance, a *tradition* into which Fasimba members were born and had been fashioning in their own image during the 1970s.

It is my argument that this periodic refashioning is indicative that the tradition of resistance inherited by the Fasimba was and is an unfinished project, having no final form or shape because it is continually being refashioned, reshaped and moulded according to the needs, expectations and vision of those for whom it has become utilised. This tradition of resistance is therefore not 'closed.'

Another consideration is that this tradition has in the main employed tactics that have fallen outside of the framework of *the normalising and legitimising discourses* of the society against which it was being used. In line with this tradition of resistance, the Fasimba held an angle of vision on the demise of the slave trade and plantation slavery that privileged the struggles and acts of self-sacrifice and self-emancipation by Black ancestors that made British parliamentary 'abolition' not just a possibility but a necessity. The **place** to which I moved to counter the ethics of domination-as-deception was one of both self-sacrifice and self-emancipation, a place of Action not inaction.

During the 2007 bicentenary celebrations the Wedgwood 'anti-slavery' logo appeared to present a counter-image to the image of black ancestors' struggles against transportation and chattel slavery. It was a subservient posture that presented not just a distorted view of black experience but sought to foreground the intervention of British abolitionism as the *right, proper and only solution* to black bondage and freedom. A foregrounding of Black resistance is the *angle of vision* framing this *counter-narrative* to British abolitionism, as symbolised by the Wedgwood logo, and it is within that *counter-narrative* that I intend to locate my own act of resistance, *outside of and beyond* what was seen as just a 'clash of evidence.' As I had mentioned earlier the 'clash of evidence' was also a 'clash of traditions;' between the tradition of *self-conscious struggle* and a tradition of *imposed subservience*.

This counter-narrative is to be based therefore on two propositions: the **first is** that insurrections and revolts by black ancestors against captivity not only originated *in struggles prior* to their arrival on plantations in the Americas, but also that these *struggles were integral* to the fight against the slave trade. This poses the enslaved as *originators* of the fight against the transatlantic slave trade and as *authors* of their liberation, pushing the point of origin of those acts of emancipation further back in history, certainly beyond what we understood in the 1970s as *the scope of black resistance*. According to Eric Taylor (2006), in 'Shipboard Insurrections in the Era of the Atlantic Slave Trade,' the almost 500 incidents of shipboard resistance to enslavement revealed in his study of slave trading between the seventeenth and nineteenth centuries forces a redefinition of the **scope** of *African resistance* and suggests some continuity between those geographically distant acts of emancipation.

Taylor (2006: 6) further argues that the omission of shipboard rebellions "imply that the tactics utilised by slaves spontaneously emerged once Africans set foot in a plantation environment, ignoring the tradition of resistance that began on the other side of the Atlantic, which were first tried and tested, attempted and occasionally perfected, on the ships of the transatlantic trade." A genealogy of black resistance and black revolt then "cannot ignore the tradition of revolt that developed prior to the arrival of Africans in the Americas." **Second,** it was on the basis of these *inaugural acts of shipboard revolt and insurrection* that the *impetus and framework* were set for subsequent plantation-based acts of resistance and insurrection against slavery. These provided also the framework for conceptualising *continuities* between these apparently geographically distant acts, transported not only across the *space* of the Atlantic but also across the *time* of history; a transported *historical consciousness* passed on to members of the African Diaspora in the post-emancipation world to be inherited by their descendents in post-war Britain.

It is by this *inherited, active and directed historical consciousness* that some *continuity* has come to be established between the 'confession-as-deception-as-resistance' tactic used in the police station with those tactics of 'deception-as-resistance' used by black ancestors during a period of intense economic bondage and institutionalised cultural negation. Resurrecting that history of resistance is to connect an act in the twentieth century as having a *similar intent* as those acts "first tried and tested, attempted and occasionally perfected" by black ancestors in the nineteenth century. I refer specifically to the *acts of deception* undertaken by Denmark Vesey in his *thwarted fight against slaveholders* in Charleston, Virginia, 1822, and the *deception successfully* undertaken by Harriett Jacobs in *her flight from slavery* in Edmonton, Virginia, in the wake of the violent insurrection led by Nat Turner in Southampton County, Virginia, 1831, when over 55 whites were slain. In acts of revenge, red-eyed slaveholders went on a *killing-spree of* over 200 black people not involved in the insurrection.

To emphasise a point made earlier under *tradition versus tradition;* it is that when the policemen in disguise rushed us at the top of the escalator in 1972, they hadn't just 'draped-up' four ordinary black men; we were four politically conscious black men, Fasimba activists and, instantly, all that we knew as Black activist came into operation; we took our past into the confrontation with them at the Oval underground and into the police station. What we summoned was the *repertoire of resistance* handed down to us and stored within social and cultural memory, text, secular, religious and spiritual song, music and dance, and in black folktales, told and retold by communities of slave descendents throughout and beyond bondage in the Caribbean and on migration to Britain.

Located as we were in the 'Eye of the Octopus,' membership of the Fasimba *reshaped* this history and tradition of resistance. *Consciousness-raising* was for us, therefore, more than just becoming *aware* of our *past and its impacts on the present* but were also *acts of personal, social, cultural and political empowerment* by which we took our destinies in our hands; re-defined and directed the *future* according to our terms and for our benefit; shifted the relationships we had to particular local and global issues; rejected those we no longer *identified with* and embraced what was to become a *Black Consciousness throughout and beyond the 1970s. Black Consciousness therefore amounted to a historical, cultural and political connection to and identification with this past and its tradition* of resistance, a tradition that had been *shaped further* by the circumstances surrounding the confrontation of the 'Oval 4' with the police and interrogation in the police station. *It was in the shaping of this tradition and in applying it to needs as they were current in 1972 that as modern Black activists we became connected to the tradition of resistance fostered by our ancestor's fight against the slave trade.* At the same time, we became connected to a tradition *wherein black ancestors figured as actors in* their liberation rather than as passive recipients of abolitionist benevolence.

It is by this reading that I locate my specific act of resistance within this *tradition of radical resistance.* The *confession-as-deception-as-resistance* tactic was what I would call *radical* action for two reasons: first, it tampered with the power relations between *captive* and *captor* and, second, it operated outside the framework of police/state expectations by our rejection of the *ethics of subservience* forced on us by our police-captors. *An acceptance of the ethics of subservience would have meant us behaving in such a way as to validate the police 'truth claims' by making a 'confession' that would work to their benefit. Our rejection of the ethics of subservience by way of the confession-as-deception tactic worked to the disbenefit of our captors, echoing a tradition of struggle used successfully and unsuccessfully by black ancestors. The emergence of this tradition of rejecting the ethics of subservience is set out below.*

Black resistance versus the British abolitionists' narrative: reclaiming the past

It is my belief that any commemorations of 1807 in 2007 by the descendants of 'emancipated' slaves should have focused more on that year as marking a *stage* in the history of these acts of resistance to the transatlantic slave trade and chattel slavery waged by black ancestors, and less on viewing this history through the lens of sentiments underpinning British abolitionism. Such sentiments have their roots in eighteenth and nineteenth century 'Christian humanism' that was built into Josiah Wedgwood's *anti-slavery logo* depicting the figure of a *pitiful male slave* on one knee, clad in rags, with hands clasped in obvious supplication, made intelligible by the caption asking: "*Am I not a man and a brother?*"[2] The figure appears to be pleading to be seen as human and be included in the European 'human family'—albeit at its base. In this pose of *supplication* the figure presents as a "humble petitioner addressing a heartfelt appeal to someone who has the power to grant his request" (Online Encarta English Dictionary).

Richard Juang (2005), the reviewer of *Blind Memory: Visual Representations of Slavery in England and America,* explains this representation as follows:

> (T)he mainstream of abolitionist thought during the late eighteenth and nineteenth centuries relied on images of black passivity and suffering, while recoiling from the idea of black men and women taking their fate in their own hands, as in the Haitian revolution. In their woodcuts, etchings, and portraits of slave ships, abolitionist attempted to show the squalor and violence inherent in slave ships. *However, they quickly reached the limits of representational possibilities by relying upon a vision of slaves defined by their captivity and who possessed agency insofar as they pleaded for succor (my emphasis).*

It is within this framework of sentiment that the publication of the Narratives of former slaves were used and, in so doing, painted a horrific picture of the slave trade, chattel slavery and black captivity to eighteenth and nineteenth century Britain. Ouladah Equiano's (aka Gustavus Vassa) *Narrative* was published in 1789; the *Letters* of Ignatius Sancho in 1782; and the '*Thoughts and Sentiments on the Evil Slavery and Commerce of the Human Species*' by Ottabah Cuggano in 1787. Such *personal* stories represented the brutalised journey of a slave to the ignorant British audience: kidnapped from their homes and families, sold into slavery, and transported on slave ships to be sold onto new owners in the Americas (Ignatius Sancho was actually born on a slave ship in mid-Atlantic) and; finally, by different routes, ended up in Britain. All had been baptised as Christians at various points in their journeys. How these personal stories were *originally* represented to eighteenth and nineteenth Britain was to, therefore, **justify** the abolition of the transatlantic slave trade "*as their value lay in their full and vivid presentation of the abuses inherent to the system*"

(Juang, 2005). In an analysis of the *'rhetoric of suffering and cruelty'* that featured so prominently in abolitionist writing, Elizabeth Clarke (1995: 467) shows that graphic accounts of slaver's cruelty were *"riveting ... and proved to be among the most effective and dramatic weapons in the reform arsenal."*

The vision of abolitionist's intervention to which Clarke refers may be illustrated by reference to the infamous case of the slave ship, 'Zong,' and the story of the 132 Africans who perished in the Caribbean Sea after being thrown overboard by slave traders in an act of cruel deception. The case of the slave ship 'Amistad,' on the other hand, illustrates another strand of abolitionism, what Taylor (2006) describes as its "distorting influence" on black agency and revolt. Both, in my opinion, may be seen to represent two strands of abolitionist thinking and action.

The Slave Ship, Zong

On 6th September, **1781**, the slave ship 'Zong' set sail from the coast of West Africa bound for Jamaica with 442 black captives and at least 14 white crew members. As was the tradition among slavers the ship was "grossly overcrowded" and carried insufficient provisions for the transatlantic journey to Jamaica. During the Atlantic crossing slaves began to die of disease and malnourishment and if many more perished the captain, Luke Colingwood, knew those who survived would not fetch a good price on arrival to Jamaica; so he claimed there was a shortage of fresh water and upon this basis ordered the crew to jettison 'cargo' (Lang, 1969:215-217). On 29th and 30th November he ordered that a total of 97 to be thrown overboard. There was a heavy rainfall on 1st December providing plenty of fresh water yet he ordered 26 more Africans to be thrown alive into the Caribbean Sea. A further ten, seeing the fate of others, attacked the crew and jumped over board of their own accord (Lang, 1969: 217).

When the ship arrived in Jamaica on 22nd December, they had over 400 gallons of water to spare. Colingwood's efforts were to cover an insurance claim for the slave-trading Underwriters at Lloyds and that he lost the claim is perhaps as important as what it revealed; that the economist attitude underpinning his claim was widespread in Britain at the time, and rested on the equation of *profit over humanity*: that enslaved Africans were chattel, equal to cargo and therefore not human. Such attitudes did not just underpin slave trading across the Atlantic but plantation slavery also. It was actually Ouladah Equiano who reported the dumping at sea of his enslaved 'brethren' to Granville Sharpe, who took up the case and used it to illustrate the atrocities of the Middle Passage, the ill-treatment of slaves, and the self-seeking greed of slave traders (see Shyllon, 1974: Chapter 12).

This and other horror-stories, publications, visual representations and personal presentations allowed British spectators to contrast the cruelty and ignoble past of these men and women *overseas*, with their noble and free status *in* Britain. At the same time, the images of *distance, difference* and, ultimately, *feelings of superiority* were reinforced, "eliciting *sympathy* from white spectators within the context in which alleviating pain and preventing cruelty were good things, while racial equality was nearly unthinkable" (Juang, 2005, *emphasis added*).

However, as terrifying as this abolitionist portrayal of their journey was, the fate of the black captives on board the slave ship, 'Zong,' is but a one-sided view of black experience of and responses to captivity during the transatlantic crossing. An example of an attempt by white abolitionists to colonise black agency and experience is illustrated below in the case of the slave ship, 'Amistad.'

The slave ship, Amistad

The case of the Amistad, a Spanish owned slave ship, is held as an example of a 'successful' shipboard resistance by rebellious slaves in 1839 off Cuba's north coast. But the insurrection on board this ship serves more as evidence of the 'internal slave trade' around the Americas and less as an example of shipboard resistance by African captives. Eric Taylor (2006: 8-9) points out the ways in which the Amistad case misrepresents the wider picture of shipboard resistance. **First,** the case so prominently involved white abolitionists that it makes a misleading example of shipboard insurrections and the *overemphasis* on the role of whites as pivotal to the slaves' freedom, albeit subsequent to their insurrection, distorts the historical record because the wider examples of shipboard rebellions show Africans as the authors of their liberation. **Second,** the case of the Amistad becomes particularly significant for the events that occurred "off the ship" and this, according to Taylor, is precisely why it is such a misleading representation of ship-board resistance. In the wider picture of shipboard resistance it is what occurs "on board the ships" that is important and regards the tendency to emphasise the case of the Amistad above all other revolts as likely to have a *"distorting influence for those attempting to see it as part of a wider tradition."* And, he argues, when the wider tradition of shipboard rebellions are considered along with the later traditions of plantation-based rebellions, there is a strong argument for a *redefinition* of how slave insurrections are conceptualised and to thus "acknowledge a level of success" in these revolts (Taylor, 2006:4). It is because the Amistad stands as *misrepresenting* acts of shipboard resistance that it appears as a further attempt to superimpose a 'white abolitionist authority' on black revolt and, as a consequence, an understanding of self-liberating agency among African captives therefore becomes sidelined, diverted or even distorted.

Karen Beardslee (1999) in her critical essay, *'Through Slave Culture's Lens Comes the Abundant Source: Harriet A Jacobs's Incidents in the Life of a Slave Girl,'* [3] states that it is now more common for slave Narratives to be used to study not only the institution of slavery and the cultural practices of the slaves in resisting dehumanisation but, in particular, as evidence of slaves' "ability to define him/herself in a world resistant to such an endeavour" (Beardslee, 1999:1). The ability to define oneself resistant and in opposition to the dehumanising 'white gaze' of slavers (Diawara, 1990) has been one of the triumphs of black self consciousness and black resistance, and it is the angle of vision characterising these triumphs which is the concern of this Chapter.

Shipboard resistance: a counter-narrative to the Wedgwood logo

From the onset of the transatlantic slave trade few of the transported Africans accepted their status as slaves. At the same time, most slave traders and slave owners were quite aware of the 'will to be free' that existed among those whom they kept captive, and lived in fear and dread anticipation of violent uprisings (Bennett, 1969; Apetheker, 1969; Genovese, 1981).

Not only did land-based slavers expect escape attempts from those whom they kept forcibly in bondage, the expectation of fierce resistance was also built into the planning and execution of slave trading and transportation from Africa across the Atlantic to the Americas. On 26th July 1753 the consortium of Liverpool merchants, owners a Gambia-bound ship, warned its captain to *"keep a watchful Eye over you(r) Slaves to prevent any insurrections, which have all too often been the* case, especially among those from Gambia" (Richardson, 2003:205, in Diouf, 2003).

This warning to the ship's captain suggests that "shipboard rebellions" were a well known and frequent occurrence. According to Eric Taylor (2006) in *'Shipboard Insurrections in the Era of the Atlantic Slave Trade'* the struggles of slaves before and during the Middle Passage not only confirms the importance and frequency of these revolts, it also suggests that such activities must have been part of a 'West African strategy' to fight against the Slave Trade (Diouf, 2003). The inclusion of shipboard resistance in the genealogy of black revolt means that is it possible to extend the contours of Black resistance as originating prior to arrival in the Americas and prior to plantation-based revolts. Once a month, on average, a European slave ship carrying enslaved Africans was "violently and aggressively and sometimes successfully taken" by the enslaved. The 'risk' for the slavers was always present as, John Newton, "slave ship captain turned Abolitionist hymn-writer," describes below:

> One unguarded hour, one minute, is sufficient to give the slaves the opportunity they are always waiting for. An attempt to rise upon the ship's company brings an instantaneous and horrid war: for when they are once in motion they are desperate; and when they do not conquer they are seldom quelled without much mischief and bloodshed on both sides (Quoted by John McAleer (2007) in a review of Taylor's Shipboard Resistance (2006)

For the slavers these insurrections occurred at every stage: along the African coast, during the middle passage, and off the coast of the Americas and the Caribbean islands, and at each of these stages of insurrection their profits from the slave trade decreased and was a threat to further 'investment' as it deterred other would-be slave-trading 'investors.' The following figures are revealing:

- 10% of voyages had some form of organised, collective resistance to the balance of power on board slave ships
- one third of all crew on board slave ships were there to manage and control the enslaved
- 120 out of the 500 insurrections unearthed led to the freedom of at least one of the Africans on board the ships
- 3 out of every 4 rebellions took place within sight of the African coast
- Once at sea, assaults, attacks and attempted take-overs frequently occurred at night or at scheduled moments, such as mealtimes when crewmen were less alert, using whatever implements or means at their disposal.

- The role of women and children were often pivotal, as women were usually unshackled and had access to parts of the ship and to information men did not; and children were almost 'invisible' to crewmen (cited by McAleer's, 2007, review of 'Shipboard Resistance, by Taylor, 2006).

Below is a sample of incidents of shipboard insurrections, some of which were successful and others not, and are taken from Joseph Holloway's (2007) *'Insurrection on Board Ships,'* with the original source cited below each entry:

In 1721, eight enslaved Africans on board the slave ship *Henry* of London managed to free themselves of their irons and attempted to subdue the ship and its 50-man crew. After being driven back by cut lances and firearms, they jumped overboard
[**Source: William Snelgrave, A New Account of Some Parts of Guinea and the Slave Trade, 164**]

In **1730,** Captain George Scott of the sloop, *Little George,* sailed from the Guinea Coast en route to Rhode Island with a cargo of some 96 enslaved Africans. Several days into the voyage, several Africans slipped out of their irons and killed three watchmen who were on deck. The Captain and his crew were forced into their cabins, where the Africans imprisoned them. For several days, the Africans controlled the ship and managed to sail it back to the Sierra Leone River. Finally, the Captain and the enslaved Africans made a deal and agreed to grant each other their freedom. After making it to shore the Africans left the ship.
[**Source: Elizabeth Donnan, Documents Illustrative of the History of the Slave Trade to in America, vol. III, 118-121, 207.**]

In **1731** Captain Jump of the Massachusetts schooner, *William,* was surprised by Africans on board his ship in an uprising off the coast of Africa. According to English newspapers, all his crew except three were killed in the uprising.
[**Source: Reads Weekly Journal and British Gazetteer, January 28, 1731.**]

In **1732** Captain John Major, of Portsmouth, New Hampshire, while on the coast of Guinea lost his life along with all of his crew. It was reported that he "was treacherously Murdered, and his Vessel and cargoes seized upon by the Negroes."
[**Source: News letter, Swept. 7, 1732; South Carolina Gazette, Nov. 18, 1732.**]

In **1742**, while taking on slaves in the Sierra Leone River, a vessel named *Jolly Batchelor* was attacked and captured by the enslaved captives on board and Africans on shore. In the fighting the Ship's captain and two of his men were killed. The Africans stripped the vessel of its rigging and sails, freed the other Africans in the hold, and then abandoned the ship.
[**Elizabeth Donnan, ibid**]

In **1747** Africans on board a Rhodes island ship rose up and killed the Captain and its crew just after the ship set off from Cape Coast Castle, Ghana. The incident is told in a letter, that "Captain Bear in a Vessel belonging to Rhode island, [set] off ... with a Number of Negro Slaves, and a considerable Quantity of Gold Dust on board; the said slaves found an opportunity to rise up against the Master and Men, and kill'd the said Master and all the crew except the two Masters [Mates], who by jumping over board and swimming ashore sav'd their lives." The Africans took flight and most probably destroyed the vessel.
[**Source News Letter, May 7, 1747.**]

In **1764** the sloop, *Adventure*, based in Rhode Island or New London, was overthrown by Africans while trading for slaves at Sierra Leone on the West Coast of Africa. The news report reads: "Capt. Joseph Millar, in a Sloop from New London, died on the Coast of Africa, and all his Hands, except two, and that the Negroes soon after availing themselves of that Opportunity, came off from the shore and killed the two surviving Men, and then took Possession of, and pillaged the Vessel.
[**Source: Gazette Jan. 5, 1764, Feb. 5, 1764;
News letter, Sept, 20, and Oct. 25, 1764.**]

It is suggested therefore that the wider *resistance* and *resilience* shown by members of the African Diaspora in America and the Caribbean against plantation-based enslavement derived directly from the *formative experiences of black ancestors in rebelling against transportation itself and not just against the conditions of that transportation.* These tactics were passed down to future generations as a *source of continuity* for their own uprisings. The *seeds* of the *counter-narrative defining self in resistance* to the 'white gaze' of enslavement were first *sown* along the coasts of west Africa in the fight against European slave traders and their local allies, continued on boards slave ships moored off the African coast, and during the Atlantic crossing prior to arrival in the Americas. As Taylor (2006: 4) explains:

> Bonds were established within the holds of slave ships that helped infuse Africans with the confidence and determination they needed to mount effective rebellions. *Each side waged a war of manipulation, deception, and observation throughout a vessel's voyage" (my emphasis).*

The slave ships are envisaged as a 'womb' nurturing the seeds a *black self-consciousness* and *black solidarity* as the basis for collective resistance to the dehumanising 'white gaze' of domination. Sterling Stuckey (1983: 3) explains further that:

> During the process of their becoming a single people, Yoruba's, Akins, Ibos, Angolans, and others, were present on slave ships to [the] America[s] and experienced a common horror—unearthly moans and piercing shrieks, the smell of filth and the stench of death, all during the violent rhythms and quiet coursing of ships at sea. *As such, slave ships were the first real incubators of slave unity across cultural lines, cruelly revealing irreducible links from one ethnic group to the other, fostering resistance thousands of miles before the shores of the new land appeared on the horizon... (Emphasis added).*

Robinson (1983:173) posits, therefore, that the slave ships didn't just carry passive female and male bodies to be sold and trained as servile labour; the cargoes also contained:

...African cultures, critical mixtures and admixtures of language and thought, of cosmology and metaphysics, of habits, beliefs and morality. These were the actual terms of their humanity. These cargoes, then, did not just consist of intellectual isolates or deculturated blanks—men, women and children separated from their previous universe. African labour bought its past with it and settled on it the first elements of consciousness and comprehension.

In other words:

> The transportation of African labour to the mines and plantations of the Caribbean and ...the Americas meant also the transfer of African ontological and cosmological systems, African presumptions of the organisation and significance of social structure, African codes embodying historical consciousness and social experience, and African ideological and behavioural systems for the resolution of the inevitable conflict between the actual and the normative (ibid, 174).

For those who survived enforced migration, their *transportation* to enslavement in the Americas was a *personal and collective* relation of domination (Patterson, 1979), and it is necessary to perceive and indeed understand this domination from the standpoint of the dominated. In this the maxim 'oppression breeds resistance' was fully understood by the Mozambique liberator, Amilcar Cabral who, in Return to the Source (1973: 42-43), explained this dialectical process as follows:

> [I]t is understood that imperialist domination, by denying the historical development of the dominated people, necessarily also denies their cultural development. It is understood why imperialist domination ... for its own security, requires the cultural oppression and the direct or indirect liquidation of the essential elements of culture of the dominated people... it is generally within culture that we find the seed of opposition ...

Intergenerational bondage: the limits of abolitionist benevolence

What enabled black ancestors to resist, survive and even transcend the "existential constancy" of slavery **was** what Amilcar Cabral called "the seed of opposition" and that *seed* contained within it a *dynamic element* far beyond abolitionists' vision and vocabulary of benevolence. It would take a black preacher-come-abolitionist, himself a fugitive from slavery, to make explicit the arrangements driving the continuing dehumanisation and spiritual negation of the enslaved. His name was Henry Highland Garnett (1815-1882), an abolitionist contemporary of Frederick Douglass who, in 1843, gave a speech to the delegates at the National Negro Convention in Buffalo, New York. There he called for the utter destruction of slavers and slavery, directing his concerns to the prospect of *spiritual negation: the erasure of the existential and ontological being of black captives through a process called 'intergenerational bondage.'* Garnett's reflections on how the suffering wrought by slavery had produced in him what he hoped for in the enslaved: "a consciousness of their plight so acute that the need for revolt sprang logically to their minds "(Stuckey, 1987: 154-155). His consciousness of the consequences of the failure to revolt led him in his Address to the slaves of the United States to make what was described as one of the "most original formulations of his time, one that established the need for revolt by calling attention to the continuum of black suffering, from the living to the unborn, in seemingly endless cycles of birth and death":

> Years have rolled on, and tens of thousands have been borne on stream of blood and tears, to the shores of eternity... Nor did the evil of their bondage end at their emancipation by death. Succeeding generations inherited their chains, and millions have come from eternity into time, and have returned again to the world of spirits, cursed and ruined by American slavery ... TO SUCH DEGRADATION IT IS SINFUL IN THE EXTREME FOR YOU TO MAKE VOLUNTARY SUBMISSION ... NEITHER GOD, NOR ANGELS, OR JUST MEN, COMMAND YOU TO SUFFER FOR A SINGLE MOMENT. THEREFORE IT IS YOUR SOLEMN AND IMPERATIVE DUTY TO USE EVERY MEANS ...MORAL, INTELLECTUAL AND PHYSICAL THAT PROMISES SUCCESS ... Brethren, it is as wrong

for your lordly oppressors to keep you in slavery as it was for the man thief to steal our ancestors from the coast of Africa. *You should therefore use the same manner of resistance, as would have been just in our ancestors* when the bloody foot-prints of the first remorseless *soul-thief* was placed upon the shores of our fatherland" (ORIGINAL EMPHASIS; *my emphasis*). [5]

Garnett makes a connection between the acts of resistance by black ancestors on the shores of West Africa against transportation and the methods of the land-based revolt he advocates; for them to *"use the same manner of resistance, as would have been just in our ancestors...,"* something Malcolm X would over a century later phrase as *"by any means necessary."* But his "inspirational speech" shocked and stunned the 'conservative' delegates at the Convention, including the 'radical' Frederick Douglass, as it was interpreted by the gathering as a 'Call to Rebellion'—for slaves to rise up and slay their masters in a similar fashion to Nat Turner's insurrection of 1831. The 'conservative' delegates to the Conference saw only apocalyptic chaos and violent retribution from the slavers resulting from these actions—as was the case after Nat Turner's insurrection. They and Douglass preferred ordered and non-violent methods (an approach Douglass was to later reject, Takiki, 1999: 23).

Yet when Garnett's motion (the "Call to Rebellion") was put to the vote the 'conservative majority' defeated the 'militant opposition' by only a single vote. However in my opinion Garnett's address to his suffering kinsfolk spoke both in the 'spiritual' and the 'temporal,' picturing their 'worldly' enslavement as an 'evil' and failure to wage a moral and physical rebellion against their captivity also as a 'sin.' Crucially, his address to the enslaved masses was underscored by the widespread belief in *ancestral authority:* that the ancestors found their enslavement 'deeply immoral' and, in that context, understood that their forebears would approve of the violent destruction of slavery and with it the destruction of the basis of their *intergenerational bondage* and *its spiritual* effects (Stuckey, 1987: 156). Garnett's advocacy of violent revolt by the oppressed was anchored firmly in a concept derived directly from values and ethics in the African cosmology, common among the slave community.

The future in the past

Stucky (1987:187) makes a number of points on the historical, political, and spiritual relevance of Garnett's awareness of the consequences of slavery for succeeding generations. **First**, it is relevant to the historical Black Movement as it is an "original contribution" to Black Nationalist thought in *particular* but also that it "illuminates revolutionary thought in *general;*" **second**, his consideration of "generational oppression provides a sense of the necessity to revolt on *spiritual* and *psychological* grounds" as well as on cultural and socio-economic grounds and; **third,** the failure to overthrow slavery would condemn black offspring, *the future generation*, to *bondage in perpetuity* and put, what Robinson (1987) described as, the *ontological totality* under threat, leaving the future of 'black existence' in the hands of slave traders and 'soul thieves.' His focus was, therefore, on the 'cultural' and the 'political' as well as on the 'inner' or 'spiritual world' of the enslaved; their individual and collective being and their spiritual, moral, and ethical existence. In short, he had an *angle of vision* on the *inherited consciousness* of slaves and an in-road into their *individual subjectivities and collective spirituality*.

As a black preacher, Garnett's concerns were not just about the nature of life in the world of the living but on the nature of death, the afterlife and of rebirth, and these concerns raised not merely abstract questions. The apparent 'totality' of the slave system meant that questions about slavery in the *here and now* raised questions about its impact on future existence. For black communities under slavery the relationship to the *future* was determined by the relationship to their children and the relationship to the *past* was determined by the relationship with parents. For the enslaved the concepts of *past, present and future* were therefore clearly linked. Beardslee (1999:11) reminds us that from wherever black people originated in Africa, a concern for *past, present and future* was a fundamental and common outlook in slave communities.

It was also a common belief that *"if the deceased lived a good life, death, a mere crossing over the threshold into another world, was a precondition to being carried back into the mainstream of the living, in the name and body of grandchildren"* (Bearsdslee, 1999:3). The nature of life was clearly linked to the nature of death. The *radical* nature of this 'sermon' is revealed in Garnett's suggestion that 'white power' sought power not just over *life and death* on the material plane, on earth and in the *here and now*; but sought power over the 'future' and therefore over 'time' by enslaving the lives of the unborn. To prevent *"succeeding generations"* from *"inheriting their ancestor's chains"*—physically or psychologically (as 'mental slavery')—it becomes necessary to break the cycle of incarnation into slavery, where black souls *"come from eternity into time and have returned again to the world of spirits,"* having left the world of the embodied unable to have prevented the incarnation of future generations into slavery.

'White power' had effectively colonised the gateway to earth for black souls by the 'totality' of the system of slavery. Not only had the presence of black slaves in the present been enslaved, their futures had also been bonded and their past distorted. In his 1843 address he revealingly posed the archetypal European slave trader as both a "man thief" and a "soul thief;" that in capturing black bodies black souls were also captured. Slavery, he conceived, must be destroyed. In her narrative Harriett Jacobs expressed an awareness of the *generational effect* of her own bondage, declaring: *"Whatever slavery might do to me, it should not shackle my children"* (Beardslee, 1999:2). His *radical vision of intergenerational bondage* indicated that the spiritual needs of *the enslaved could not* be met *within the terms* orthodox Christianity as those *traditional religious convictions, in support of the system of slavery,* took suffering and death on earth as a prerequisite to ever-lasting life in heaven. Such an attitude in Garnett's view could result only in a future characterised by *intergenerational bondage and spiritual negation.* In this context Stuckey (1987:43) observes that: "Being on good terms with the ancestral spirits was overarching conceptual concern for Africans everywhere in slavery." Slaves' adherence to the ancestor ethic was in direct opposition to the morality, values and ethics of slavery.

Moral and ethical dilemmas

As Edwards (1984:92) has pointed out, moral and ethical dilemmas cropped up constantly in the lives of a people forcibly prevented from developing socially *cooperative* contracts for their long-term physical, cultural and spiritual well-being. The main reason for *their recurring moral and ethical dilemmas* was that the **system** of slavery amounted to an *inversion the morals* of *right and wrong,* producing a situation wherein *virtues* such as kindness, loyalty, honesty and mercy had all been perverted into *vices,* while greed, deceit, betrayal, cruelty and violence become *virtues* (Forbes, 2000: 2). In other words, the regime of slavery generated changes in the paradigm of moral values and ethical behaviour, producing a *topsy-turvy* world wherein right was wrong and wrong was right; and because slavery itself was a perversion of human values, whatever values, morals and ethical behaviour slaveholder's held dear were themselves perversions, permeating the upside down world created by slave traders and slaveholders.

In their attempts to resist and counter the perversity of slavery Africans had to rely on their own traditions (e.g. the ancestor ethic) as a 'moral compass' to gauge *rightness and wrongness, truth and falsehood, vice and virtue.* Frederick Douglass tells of an incident that to him illustrated the up-side-down world that was slavery quite well. In his Narrative (Douglass, 1973: 19) he recounts that a slave was asked by a 'stranger' (his master in disguise) about any maltreatment or overwork experienced by him whereupon the slave replied that he was not treated well by his master. His penalty for "telling the plain and simple truth" about his captivity was to be handcuffed, chained and sold to a slave trader (Douglass, 1973:20). Under slavery, it was the duty of the slave to lie when asked about his/her conditions or the character of his/her master: that they are *contented* and their master *good.* So frequent was this deception required that there grew a maxim amongst the enslaved, that: *a still tongue makes a wise head* (Douglass, 1973:20). As their lives depended on suppressing the[ir] truth rather than telling it, they soon learnt as a consequence that there was only one truth and it was the slavemaster's 'truth,' which they knew to be a lie. And because their truth did not exist they wore the "mask of obedience" (Forbes, 2000: 2) when telling this 'truth.'

Slaves knew therefore what lie to tell and when, to either sustain or subvert any circumstance or activity in which they were engaged, be it for their own benefit or the slavemaster. But slaves knew also, as a Jamaican saying explains, that "*the knife that stick the sheep a-go stick the goat,*" carrying a meaning that whatever 'truth'—that is, *tool of deception*—was of use to the slavemaster-oppressor is of use also to the enslaved-oppressed, but in an entirely different framework. For the enslaved it meant that: "*Whatever the slave owner considered right, was wrong. Whatever he considered wrong, was right. For the slave, it was only considered stealing if you took something from a fellow slave. To take from the slave owner was merely to appropriate that which was, in actuality, yours. It was only through your labor that the slave owner acquired what he had*" (Lester, 1973: 100) - providing examples of ethical and unethical behaviour amongst slaves in their communities.

In her Narrative, Harriett Jacobs provide further examples of *how* and *when* this 'truth'—the slavemaster's *tool of deception*—was applied to her benefit, making her acts of deception *righteous and honourable acts. In contradistinction,* those acts by the slavemaster class become known to the enslaved as acts of *dishonourable deception; deceptions applied in pursuit of dishonourable goals.*

It was therefore in *dishonourable acts* that slavemasters demonstrated and realised their individual and collective power: the will and ability to use another human being for their own needs and ends while denying they ever had humanity. In the context of slaves' powerlessness, acts of *deception* by the enslaved are transformed into acts of individual or collective empowerment and honour (Patterson, 1973: 33-37). In their transformation from victim-status to that of an actor, they begin to experience themselves as changing from the status of an object into that of a *subject*. These points will be discussed further down when looking at the ethics of enslavement and the ethics of the slaves' struggle against it.

Deception: an Art of Resistance

James Scott's (1999) arguments are relevant to these *acts of deception* by the enslaved. *In his book, 'Domination and the Arts of Resistance: Hidden Transcripts' (1999), deception is* regarded by him as both a *strategy* of domination used by the ruling group or dominant culture in their 'management' the oppressed and, is in turn, used by the oppressed as a *tactic of resistance, as a weapon of counter-deception* in a 'war of position' with the oppressor. Taylor (2006: 4) has told that *deception* was one of the many tactics used by slave traders to maintain control of the ship **and** a was tactic used by the enslaved to alter the balance of power, take control of the vessel and enable their escape.

Two examples of *deception-as-resistance* are illustrated and explored below: the first by **Denmark Vesey**, the second by **Harriett Jacobs**, and both highlight the different contexts in which this tactic was used and to what end. Scott (1999) refers also to what he calls the *Hidden Transcript,* a counter-narrative produced by the powerless in opposition to their powerlessness aimed at *subverting* the *Public Transcript* of the powerful. He uses the term *Public Transcript* to describe the 'interactions' between the dominating and the dominated groups that occur in the public sphere, and the term *Hidden Transcript* for the *critique of power* that goes on outside of and beneath the awareness of the powerful. In the public sphere those who are oppressed *appear* to accept their subordination and wear a "mask of obedience" but are in constant opposition, either challenging, subverting or, in the final analysis, waging a rebellion against their circumstance—making *explicit or public* that which they had kept *hidden.*

It is in the 'war of position' between the dominator and the dominated that the *Hidden Transcript is* generated and in this struggle *deception* is both an *'art of domination* and *an art of resistance.'*

Vesey's Deception: Slavery's 'hidden transcript' of resistance

Higginson (1861) and Forbes (2000), writing on the 'Vesey Design' and its betrayal, both agree that the *'game of deception'* was played out on both sides, by slaveholders and the enslaved, for entirely different reasons. Just before we look at Vesey's acts of *righteous deception*, I want to make two further Caribbean connections. The first to be mentioned is of the routine traffic in slaves around the Americas, especially between North and South Carolina from the Caribbean islands of Jamaica and Barbados between the eighteenth and nineteenth centuries (James, 1998). Second, Denmark Vesey (1767-1822) was an example of this traffic. Originally named Telemanque, he was bought as a teenage slave from the Dutch island of St Thomas in 1781 by the Bermudian slave trader, Joseph Vesey, and sold to a plantation owner in Haiti. In Haiti, Telemanque tricked his way out of Haiti's brutal plantation regime by feigning 'epileptic fits' and was returned to slaver Vesey as 'damaged goods' when he returned with more slaves. Now owned by Joseph Vesey and his name 'corrupted' to Denmark, he travelled around with the slave trader as he applied himself to further slave trading across the Caribbean and the transatlantic route (Forbes, 2002; Young, 2001). By the time he was taken to Charleston with Joseph Vesey in 1783, Denmark was a well-travelled, well-read, linguistically competent and articulate teenager who had witnessed the *slavemaster's 'truth' in operation*. In Charleston Joseph Vesey continued his work as a slave trader, involving Denmark in his people trafficking across the city as he grew more and more resentful of what he was being made to do.

In 1800, aged 33 years, he bought his freedom and, thereafter over the years, set about organising a sophisticated plan for violent revolt. However, once Denmark Vesey's 1822 plan for violent revolt had been betrayed by Christianised house servants (Higginson, 1861) the authorities in Charleston sought to find out who was involved. In the weeks that followed the first betrayal a 'war of wits' took place between Vesey and the white authorities as they strove to find out more about the planned revolt and Vesey strove to further conceal the remnants of the plan by acts of *deception and counter-deception*.

In the first instance two of those named, Denmark Vesey himself and Peter Poyas, *daringly* and *boldly* presented themselves to the authorities, denying knowledge of any plot or that they were involved. Both were questioned then released while the two informers were held in custody for weeks and interrogated (threatened/tortured) but could not supply the jailers with further information. Forbes (2000), citing Pearson's application of Scott's framework to the power dynamics between master and slave, posits that the Vesey plan to revolt against slaveholders and slavery as well as the testimony from the *Vesey Trials* "shattered the paternalistic presumptions" of Charleston's slaveholders and "*laid bare the reality asserted long before by John Locke: that slavery is a state of war continued between captor and captive.*" (Second Treatise of Government; of Slavery: s24, 1609). He writes:

> Nowhere is the "mask of obedience" more starkly thrown off than in the indelible encounter between the planter Elias Horry and his coachman, John. Incredulous at his slave's involvement in the plot—"he would as soon suspect himself," Horry had said— the master plaintively asked his coachman what his intention had been. *"To kill you, rip open your belly and throw your guts in your face,"* the man exploded (Forbes, 2000: 1).

This stark revelation of slaves' hatred of their *condition* and for their *master*s proved so "disturbing" to the Magistrates, slaveholding interests and the higher echelons of Charleston society that they refused to believe this to be the case. Intoxicated by the *inversion of morals and ethics* that was slavery—*that slaves had accepted their captivity*—the court that stood in judgement over the captured 'plotters' actually censored the most "inflammatory details to conceal the horrifying extent of the danger" from an anxious public. For example, in the testimony of Harry Haig, a would-be insurrectionist, several lines in the typed transcript had been deleted "with a string of asterisks." The line the court attempted to delete [later discovered in the handwritten notes] was that Harry Haig had testified that one of Vesey's lieutenants, 'Gullah Jack' "was going to give me a bottle with poison to put into my master's pump & into as many pumps as ... (I) ...could about town & he said he would give other bottles to those he could trust" (Forbes, 2000:2).

On this, Forbes (2000:2) notes: "Poisoning, unlike armed rebellion, is an individual act that could be undertaken by anyone and which could not be effectively prevented. At no other time in Southern history had the assumptions of the slaveholding paternalism collided more violently with the reality of slavery as a deferred state of war." Forbes (2000) quotes Pearson (1999:120) to say that the Vesey Trials represented "one of those rare moments of political electricity when the hidden transcript [was] spoken directly in the teeth of power."

Returning to the *inverted morality* of slaveholders, when Thomas Bennett, Governor of Charleston, heard that his 'trusted slave,' Rolla, was part of the insurrection plan, his mind refused to believe it, accepting instead his slave's denial of any knowledge of or involvement in planned insurrection. The basis of Bennett's denial of this was that he was drunk on the *inversion of morality and ethics that was slavery* and, therefore, had a "difficult time" grasping the idea that the enslaved actually *wanted to be free.* Young's (2001:5) review of Egerton's (2000) text on Denmark Vesey explains that:

> The slaveowners' response to the Vesey conspiracy... conveyed the conflicted psychology of the planter elite. On the one hand, while planters needed to take seriously the threat of insurrection, lest they lose control of their slaves. On the other hand, to maintain their collective sanity in the face of the low country's black majority, white planter planters invested in the proslavery fiction of the obedient and happy work-force.

The *deceptions* undertaken by Harriett Jacobs below seem to chimemore with my act of subversion rather than Denmark Vesey's as mine involved, at most, just four people while Vesey's involved a large religious organisation, albeit broken down into a revolutionary cell structure, as was the organisation of the Fasimba. Our cells of two to three people tended to foster cohesiveness and prevented information leakage or betrayal - as was the case with the Vesey plan to overthrow slavery following the successful Haitian revolution.

Chapter 6 has revealed that the *decentralised* and cell structure of the Fasimba had within it a *cell within a cell,* the *inner one* hidden from other members of that particular area and even from the wider organisation. This is what I described as the *Fasimba within the Fasimba.*

Towards an Ethic of 'Honourable Deception'

I now make reference to *deception* as a tactic of resistance utilised during slavery to illuminate my own tactic of resistance as a 'righteous' or 'honourable' *act of deception* in the order of the trickster strategy in African folklore. In African folklore trickster strategies raise and attempt resolve moral and ethical issues that arise within a slave community

(Beardslee, 1999) or issues which arise between that community and slaveholders (Edwards, 1984). It is these latter acts of deception which are to be explored through this strategy, to either facilitate their *flight from* or *fight against* slavery.

A variation of a trickster strategy was adopted by Harriett Jacobs in her narrative, *Life of a Slave Girl* where through 'Linda,' her protagonist, she relates how she engaged in a series of manoeuvres and deceptions to outwit her owner and the slave catchers on patrol after Nat Turner's insurrection in her *flight from slavery*. Her moves are cast as acts of **"honourable deception"** as they were designed to facilitate her escape from captivity and from the lascivious designs of 'Dr Flint' (Beardslee, 1999:8). Jacobs's deceptions were possible as they were based on what she knew that she knew her adversary did not and could not know. She told them things that were untrue as if they were true, things she knew that they could not check for truthfulness or accuracy.

In a series complex manoeuvres, she sets out to match "cunning against cunning" to outwit **her** adversary, 'Dr Flint,' and **his** "cunning nature."

> The trickster ethic Linda embodies here is one of the many trickster ethics presented in the folktales of slaves. And although... she manifests this ethic again— an ethic of honourable deceit—she also shows us in the portrayal of Dr Flint's conduct, another popular trickster code of behavior—dishonourable deceit. The folktales in which the trickster follows this model were often used to illustrate the kind of behaviour slaves found *unacceptable* from members within their own community. But such a trickster was understood as representing the deceitful nature of the white master. In either case, however, the trickster is bound to fail, (as) s/he is not the type of person one should strive to emulate or associate with (Beardslee, 1999:9, *my emphasis*).

The following illustration of my *subversion* draws on the behaviour of the trickster figure and its characterisation in the Caribbean, specifically Jamaican folklore. As tactic of resistance by the oppressed it has already been referred to as an 'art of deception' as in the Vesey episode. Set out below is the origin and applications of the trickster strategy, showing how it may be applied in explaining how I sought to out-manoeuvre my captors.

The 'trickster' model and the Ethic of 'Honourable Deception'

The trickster figure embodies a variety of animal and human characterisations in black folklore, and in Jamaican folklore is known popularly as Anansi-Spider, a descendant of the Spider God of West Africa, especially among the Ashanti people of Ghana. The Hare is the chief character in Yoruba folktales as is the Tortoise in stories among the Ibo people of Nigeria.

These animal characters were brought from the west coast of Africa by black captives held as slaves and have become part of the cultures of their descendants ever since, often taking on the guise of an oral historian interpreting the past, setting out a moral framework for everyday life, and divining the ethics of present or future action. Anthropologist, Paul Radin, (1955: xxiii) makes the following *general statement* about the trickster figure in folklore (although Edwards (1984:91) questions whether such a generalisation is possible):

> Trickster is one and the same time creator and destroyer, giver and negator, he who dupes others and is always getting duped himself. He wills nothing consciously. At all times he is constrained to behave from impulses over which he has no control. He knows neither good nor evil yet he is responsible for both. He possesses no values, morals or social, is at the mercy of his passions and appetites, yet through his actions, *all value comes into being (my emphasis).*

The essence of trickster tales, such as *Brer Rabbit* in the southern United State and *Anansi-Spider* in Jamaica, is that the figure plays the role of 'hero,' often using cunning, guile and resourcefulness to overcome strength, despite their size and lack of strength—itself a metaphor for the power imbalance effected by slavery. In the Caribbean such animal tales, like their African and European models, often depicted a smaller animal, such as the Hare, Spider or Tortoise, as capable of outwitting or triumphing over larger or stronger animals because they were more intelligent, cunning or better equipped when it comes to relying on their own devices. *In Caribbean social history, Anansi-Spider, like the people to whom he spoke, emerged as a survivor of the Middle Passage and was transformed to become "representative of the principle of cunning, subtlety and intelligence as **techniques of survival**"* (Rohlehr, 1981:184-

185) employed by slaves in the so-called New World. Anansi-Spider is said also to have spoken to their **empowerment** while they underwent immense subjugation and, in this sense, may be considered a 'liberator' or 'hero' to the subjugated and downtrodden.

Edwards (1984) identifies a *structure type* to the trickster folktales in which the 'hero' alternates between two roles, playing either the "Power Broker" or the "Dupe." As Edwards explains (1984: 61-62) ordinarily the dominant character of the trickster roles (especially in the USA) is one in which he is the "Power Broker" as "*it is he who has the power to deceive for his own benefit or for the benefit of others.*" In what is described as a 'role reversal' the trickster can also assume the role of the "Dupe." Anansi-Spider in Jamaica is an example of this *type*, where his 'duality of character' is built into the role of trickster and into the structure and morality of folktale cycles, where he either 'loses' or 'wins.'

The two character roles of Anansi-Spider are as trickster, the 'Hero' or 'Power Broker,' and his opposite role as the 'Dupe' or 'Fool,' and the two following tales illustrate the contrasting trickster roles quite well. The first tale is called 'My Fada's Best Riding Horse' in which Anansi tricks Tiger to gain his trust, and having gained his trust uses Tiger as a 'riding horse,' thereby presenting Tiger as a *Fool*. In this story, Anansi is the *Power Broker* and wins against Tiger, 'deceiving him for his own benefit' but not for the benefit of others. In the second called 'Cherry Tree Island, Anansi, having gained the trust of the birds to grant him flight to Cherry Tree Island, but once there, he becomes *greedy and ungrateful*. The birds take back their feathers and Anansi is left stranded on Cherry Tree Island with all the fruit to himself. In this tale Anansi's trick backfires on him, loses the power of flight and ends up as the *Fool*, while the birds, the object of Anansi's deception, emerged as the *Power Broker*. This may be regarded as an example of *dishonourable deceit*, where *greed* and *ungratefulness* are values frowned upon by members of the black community. One rendering of the moral of this story is the saying, "Craven Choke Puppy" which, incidentally, is also the name of an early reggae single by the Wailers and a DJ version by Big Youth called 'Craven Version: Do Good.'

Resolving moral dilemmas

For Edwards (1984: 92) the significance of this *type* of folktale lay in the special role it played in the daily live of slaves and their descendants in the USA and the Caribbean:

It provided a cultural cognitive model which enabled them to reflect on the moral dilemmas imposed on them under conditions of servitude and economic bondage. Though neither trickery nor trust is clearly favored in the folktale cycles (the trickster loses as well as wins) the problem of which strategy to adopt was one which constantly cropped up in the lives of people forcible prevented from developing cooperative social contracts for their long range self improvement. The favoring of a specific structural type can be accounted for only by the clarifying ethical vision it provided in the context of recurring moral and philosophical problems.

In other words, ethical and moral dilemmas and their possible resolutions were built into the cycle of trickster tales because, according to Edwards (1984:92): *"Trickster strategies involve the maximisation of short-term (economic) gain at the expense of long-term social cohesion,"* providing instructions and guidance on **what not to do** when motivated by greed or base self interest, or taking inappropriate advantage over others. Thus, as each Anansi story is completed, the hearers, usually children, are required to declare their rejection of the choices and their moral implications with the words: *"Jack Mandora, me no choose none." Jack Mandora* is reputed to be the *Celestial Gateman, the Guardian at Heaven's door* where it is necessary for souls to declare their rejection of the Anansi-choices (trickery/trust) before gaining entry.

This *negative* declaration is similar in type to the '147 Negative Confessions' in the 'Egyptian Book of the Dead' which are declared by the soul in the Underworld before Osiris, the Black god, prior to the transition to the *afterlife* (Wallis Budge,1895/1967). In Jamaican folktale cycles, *the Trickster in his Divine character role, is both "fooler and fool, maker and unmade, wily and stupid, subtle and gross, the High God's accomplice and his rival"* (Davidson, 2003). The Anansi stories that emerged from the Jamaican experience of slavery were seen as symbolic of the routine strivings and disappointments of slaves, while the other larger and differently gifted animals, whom Anansi often uses as 'Dupes' or 'Fools,' such as Tiger, Monkey, and Snake, represented the white slave master's power, his moral or ethics, hence Anansi's routine triumphs and failures against them.

'Honourable Deception:' the act of 'creating an illusion'

In line with the *ethic* (of 'honourable deception') that guided Harriett Jacobs' use of a *trickster strategy* to facilitate her escape from captivity, I characterise my own act in making that *false* 'confession' as a *variation* of that *trickster strategy,* a tool I now utilise in an attempt to explain how I sought to resolve the ethical dilemma imposed on me and by which I felt trapped.

In all, the situation presented options that were quite unsatisfactory, and over the past three decades I have revisited this experience again and again, and from many different standpoints, including those mentioned in Chapter 1 of Section 1. In this final Chapter of Section 2, I present *another reading* of that situation and will try to show how my actions and choices chimed with my historical circumstance, my political values, moral principles and ethical obligations, and drew on aspects of the subversive culture and tradition inherited from the *Jamaican experience* of slavery and its resistance.

Whose ethics?

An observation I made at the end of Chapter 1, **"Is it because I'm Black?"** was that the police, like slaveholders, could not have held any thoughts whatsoever of black people as moral and *ethical beings;* as people who would have been *outraged* by the accusation that they were involved in "nicking handbags." *Our behaviour following that accusation was based on a rejection of the premise of those accusations and a rejection of the ethics guiding their actions: that we were black and because of that were 'suspect persons' and liable to a 'stop and search.'* This initial verbal encounter set the framework for all the decisions I made thereafter to resolve the situation into which I had been thrust. The following is therefore an attempt to understand this experience from an ethical perspective and, in so doing, attempts to link this problem-solving behaviour to the values and ethics that were *available* to our ancestors in their resistance to the institution of slavery. As Edwards (1984: 92) observed above, the favouring of a specific trickster figure and structural type, such as Anansi-Spider in Jamaica, *"can only be accounted for in the clarifying ethical vision it provided in the context of recurring moral and philosophical problems"*

It was noted that trickster strategies ordinarily involve the maximisation of short-term economic gain at the expense of long-term social and cultural cohesion (Edwards, 1984: 92) and, in so doing, identifies what not to do within the slave community. A trickster strategy also identifies and clarifies what would be wrong not to do as a way of regulating behaviour between the slavemaster class and the slave community. In this context, the wrong thing to do would be to not oppose the designs of your captors or oppressors.

Ethical dilemmas and their resolution

I now try to set out below the basis of the received ethical frame-work by which I sought to resolve the ethical dilemma that had been thrust onto me, and how this was done—*what I took into consideration and what I rejected, and the criterion by which I valued what I was going to do as the right and proper thing to do: indeed, what I saw as a* **righteous** *and* **honourable** *thing to do.*

Up to this point it was my understanding that not all dilemmas in life are *ethical* in nature. A *dilemma* is ordinarily a situation in which someone must choose between two or more *unsatisfactory* choices. An *ethical dilemma* arises when those choices coincide with moral claims, or when choices amount to moral claims that *conflict* with one another and give rise to questions such as: *What ought I to do?" What is the right thing to do?" What harm or benefit result from this decision or action, and harm/benefit for whom?"* Moreover, in a situation in which moral claims *conflict,* as we have seen, what one considers *good* may not necessarily be *right* and this consideration varies from person to person, from context to context and from culture to culture. This *tension* reveals a *conflict* between two moral claims in Western philosophy: *virtue* and *duty* and between claims to 'truth' and 'reality.'

A *virtue* is seen as a *good feature* or *desirable quality* in a person, such as *goodness* or *generosity*, while a *duty* is something someone is *obliged to do* for moral, legal or religious reasons. *Truthfulness* might be considered a *virtue* in some people while for others it is a *duty*, an obligation; something they must do *irrespective* of circumstance. Duties refer, in the main, to *professional obligations* which apply to doctors, nurses, teachers, priests, solicitors and, importantly, to *policemen like, for example, being under a professional duty to tell the truth.* A question which arises for both professional and non-professional subjects is whether there are circumstances that are exceptions to the rule, like revealing information or the whereabouts of someone which might result in them or others being harmed in some way or placed in danger? In such circumstances telling the 'truth' might be the 'right' thing to do but not a 'good' thing to do, as harm could result from that decision to be 'truthful' *irrespective* of circumstances.

However, as I have been trying to show, the *rightness* or *wrongness* of a particular moral stance or behavioural ethic is, in reality, a site of power and a site for contesting power, such as the relations of domination and resistance to domination that underpins the story told in this book.

Ethics and morals

While ethics are concerned with moral standards it emphasises how these standards affect or determine behaviour and assist in deciding what is the right or wrong thing to do. Ethical behaviour is concerned, therefore, with matters of consequence: *who benefits for your acts? Morals,* on the other hand, is concerned with issues of *right* and *wrong* and with how individuals *ought to* behave in a situation and, is concerned therefore with issues of intentionality: the *rightness* or *wrongness* of what an individual *intends* to do. A person is said to be acting *morally* if s/he is able to *distinguish between the values of right and wrong* (in the culture and society) and *make decisions* based on that *distinction. Ethical* issues arise because decisions based on those distinctions have implications for the *rightness* or *wrongness* of the *criterion* by which *action* is taken; that is, *it's harmful or beneficial consequences for all those involved in or affected by the decision.*

A recurring problem is that *right* and *wrong* are not 'either/or' *absolutes* and do not necessarily exist at *opposite* ends of a spectrum; definitions of *right* and *wrong* are intimately and ultimately bound up with prevailing socio-economic and political *conditions* and with the existing and dominant moral *authority,* as with the conflicting bases of the views taken on Denmark Vesey's intended uprising (see Michael Johnson, 2001, who says the 'conspiracy' was a result of "white orthodoxies" and "black heresies"). With the 'Oval 4' case 'race' and colour were defining features in determining our access to claims to *right* and *wrong,* as they were during the period of black enslavement. But, questions of 'morality' do not revolve solely around questions of definition; 'morality' is ultimately a *site of power* and a site for *contesting power. And with the notion of power the concept of justice and its uneven distribution therefore enters the equation.*

But despite the complexity of this situation, it was reduced to me having to deal with two basic and conflicting alternatives to resolve the dilemma imposed on me by my circumstance of captivity: **to give in or to resist**. The first amounted to *self-condemnation*: to make a statement admitting to crimes I knew nothing about but to which the police were anxious for me to admit to complete their deception or, second, offer *physical and psychological resistance* to these suggestions: not admitting to any of these 'crimes' and take the inevitable beating that would surely continue, beyond the revenge-violence I had already received for fighting with them.

Self-condemnation

A continuation of the fight from the Oval underground *was not an option* open to me nor was a resolution reliant on either of the conflicting choices and their consequences. *Telling the 'truth' was not an option also as we understood quite clearly that the police were not interested in our truth, only their truth, which was a lie.* Of this Frederick Douglass has already provided examples, which I have already referred to as the *inversion* of the values of 'right' and 'wrong' and 'truth' and 'falsehood' that permeated slave society and which, I now suggest, permeated the thinking and practices of the policemen upholding the values of a society that once benefited and still benefits from the transatlantic slave trade and black slavery.

The first option involved conscious self-condemnation; the unwelcome, immoral and *unethical choice* of self-deprecation and self-negation, of admitting to the police version of events that night and to other 'crimes' to escape the inevitable violence and pain and would ensue if I did not. With this option came the added *immorality* of including my brethren in this condemnation and, by those admissions, confirm that similar tactics could be used successfully on other black captives. *The main problem with this option was that conscious self-*condemnation and self-negation were not options as it was not possible for me to give moral assent to the conditions of mine and my brethren's ultimate negation. Only harm for myself and the Black Cause and benefit for the 'deceivers' would result from this course of action.

Physical resistance

The other option was to remain silent, say nothing and refuse to accede to the police vision and version of events (which I had attempted to do); and to offer active or passive physical and psychological resistance to the intimidation and beatings. *The choice was a stark one: to continue to fight or to take a further beating.* The main problem with this *choice* is that I had no control over the amount or outcome of the physical violence that would be applied which could result in serious physical injury and hospitalisation—against my will to *self-preservation*. It might also result in a painful 'involuntary' admission and to the self-condemnation that the physical resistance was designed to have prevented.

Moreover, I was not willing to see how much punishment I could take before I reached the limits of my physical and psychological endurance. Only personal harm and injury to me seemed a likely outcome to this latter option, with an additional 'unknown outcome' that I did not want to risk finding out about. I perceived no benefits in this course of action, only harm against all my instincts *for self-preservation*. Both options presented a lose/lose situation for me and a 'win/ win' situation for the 'deceivers,' and would be a decision that carried with it unwelcome, immoral, and unethical outcomes. There were no "lesser of two evils" between which to choose.

A third way came to me which involved neither of those choices, but was what Beardslee (1999:8) described as *"creating an illusion of doing what is expected by the dominant culture when one is really doing what is wanted or needed by oneself or by one's own culture."* In adopting a trickster strategy, the subversive application of this required a response to the situation of 'choicelessness' by creating a 'choice.' My intention was to *disrupt the power relations* between my captors and myself and turn their deception against them by, first, gaining their trust so I could mislead them and get them to believe what they were being told by me was a 'truth' *they needed to hear* to complete their deception: a 'confession' of my guilt. But this was not to be a 'true confession' but was a deception intended to *tamper with the power relations* in such a way that they were no longer acting as the 'Power Broker' but as the 'Dupe'—the object of a deception which they had designed to entrap us. *It was a moment of 'role reversal.' It was a counter-deception.*

To gain their 'trust' I decided to feign compliance ('wear the mask of obedience') while really subverting that *act of compliance* by including in the admissions 'crimes' that were impossible for me to have committed, and for which I had concrete alibis. To complete the illusion of 'trust' I became what the police described as a "great talker" during their interrogation (*South London Press*, 27/1/73). I had chosen to make a 'confession-statement' under conditions chosen by myself in which the act of making a 'confession' was an act of deception. As Edwards (1984:92) would have it, their trust (in me telling them what they wanted to hear) was their loss (because it was not true). *What they lost for a brief moment was the initiative as they became bound by what I said and did inasmuch as I had been bound by what they said and did.* It was at that moment, that brief moment, when power was contested and, as a consequence, sidetracked the designs of our captors. It was what I have described above as a brief *role reversal*.

My adoption of the trickster strategy was a political act: that of "creating an illusion" of doing what is expected of me by the dominant culture, but where I was really doing something for myself, for my brethren and for my Cause. *My act of compliance was therefore an act of defiance.* This retaliatory move was itself also an act of self-definition, an act of political *renunciation* where *I repudiated their ethics* that lay behind the attempt at my negation and, at the same time, *affirmed* my agency, the self-generative impulse and *will to be free*, the basis of reconstructing my identity as a human being.

Final Thoughts: the ethics of Black resistance

In this final Chapter I have attempted to show how the meeting of two *mutually conflicting forces*, *Black resistance* and *police malpractice*, *were played* out through the case of the 'Oval 4' as a struggle between our 'freedom' and our 'captivity.' The interpersonal and institutional contexts of its *playing out*, as a matter of necessity, revealed the moral and ethical dimensions of black resistance: that there **were** values of *right* and *wrong* and principles of ethical behaviour to be drawn upon from **within** the history of Black resistance. These principles provide instructions on **what is the right and proper thing to do and what not to do** when faced with an ethical dilemma of the type forced upon us by our illegitimate arrest.

My attention was drawn to the 'ethics of *Black* resistance' rather than just to the 'ethics of resistance' for one principal reason. *The ethics or principles of Black resistance*, as I have tried to show, needed to be perceived from the particular *angle of vision* on resistance consistent with that experienced by the oppressed in the Black Diaspora. It is an *angle of vision* that first emerged with the onset of the transatlantic slave trade whereby black ancestors fought against the *physical and social death* that lay beyond the horizon of the Atlantic. Their dilemma, as presented to them by slave traders, was between a rejection of the slaver's *certainty* by violent rebellion, or to face an *uncertain future* by not rebelling. It was a dilemma Margaret Garner and her family faced and resolved when trapped by slave catchers, and that faced by black ancestors as slaves ship were about to cast off from the west African coast. In Margaret Garner's case what she rejected was the *certainty* of that which was lying in store for her and her daughter as female slaves. Any discussion therefore of the *ethics of Black resistance* must first take into consideration this history as a point of reference for its emergence.

As I neared the end of writing the book it was becoming clear that literature on Black Power activism and independent Black community struggles in Britain were sparse (barring the Journal *Race & Class*) and even less, if any, existed on the *ethics of Black resistance. By 'ethics' I refer to the principles by which we value what we do as Black activists in Black organisations and how we act in accordance with those principles in the interests of the communities we serve.* It was left for me to try and theorise from the concrete and lived experiences characterising of the 'Oval 4' episode.

The ethics closest to the type of resistance I wanted to focus on were found in Frantz Fanon's '*The Wretched of the Earth*' (1963) in which he spoke of the *values and ethics* of Third Work liberation in the context of refusing Western values as they denied the human worth and deprecated the political legitimacy of the colonised (1963:33). In the Chapter called 'Concerning Violence' he writes about the use and legitimacy of violence in fighting against European colonialism/imperialism, a configuration in which the violence underpinning racial slavery was a core value. Speaking primarily of the relations of domination the *coloniser* imposes on the *colonised*, Fanon regards a *rejection of the* coloniser's *values* as a pre-requisite to the 'mental liberation' of the colonised from adherence to those values. His view was that the *colonised* have no choice but to reject the values of the *colonist* and operate outside the framework of those values.

Operating outside the framework of Western values is Edwards' (1984) text on the ethics underpinning the trickster strategy. This work has been helpful in identifying what would be the *right, proper and honourable thing to do* and, equally, clarifying *what not to do when faced with an ethical dilemma.* He has shown how in the slave/master relationship, the enslaved Africans had to rely on their own values of right and wrong and on their principles of ethical behaviour so as not to be totally consumed by slavemaster ethics. The *angle of vision* framing the ethics of resistance are, quite rightfully, those coming from the standpoint of the oppressed, as the ethics of the oppressor required self-deception on the part the enslaved. Frederick Douglass has revealed that in bondage it was the *duty* of a slave to lie about their conditions of captivity and servitude. Failure to adhere to this code resulted in being sold and transported, if not flogged.

Violence and terror were not the only weapons of domination. From James Scott (1990) we learnt that *deception* was and is an *art of domination* used routinely by regimes of domination throughout history. On the other hand, *deception* has been an *art of resistance* or *a counter-deception* when used by the subordinate or oppressed groups. Looking again at the *art of deception* as operationalised by the enslaved in the *trickster strategy,* I have shown how it was used successfully by Harriett Jacobs in her flight from bondage and by me in the police station against police violence and malpractice. Of course the trickster strategy would not, could not, work if the police had not raised their expectations by insisting on a 'confession-statement' as a confirmation of my guilt. In short, the police were deceived by their own expectations of being successful in their deception.

Edwards (1984: 91) points out also that a trickster strategy is employed not only for personal benefit but for the benefit of others. My adoption of the trickster strategy was, therefore, not just for my benefit but for the benefit of my brethren and my Cause. Politically, the use of trickster strategy was a rejection of the *ethics of subservience,* and while the benefits of its rejection took into consideration my personal empowerment it was, in reality, beyond the scope of my individual benefit. It was an act or series of acts integral to wider acts of resistance in the *tradition of resistance* to which I have laid claim. Their aims were to act as examples of strategies of personal and social empowerment to wider black communities in their struggles for political legitimacy and, at the same time, act to discredit the ethics behind police actions, as supported by the judicial system against the 'Oval 4. As a trickster strategy, it was a righteous deception *against* the police and *for* the benefit of others in Black communities.

To conclude, I have tried to reveal moral and ethical dimensions to acts of resistance and struggles for emancipation by black captives, struggles which challenge the ethics of their domination, while seeking to set out a *new angle of vision* on resistance to domination. I have argued that the values which support regimes of domination leave the oppressed no choice but to use *extra-institutional* means and *styles* to advance their Cause. The *style of resistance* I have tried to highlight in my case is that of that of the 'art of deception' as a tactic in resistance to the regime of domination. To illustrate this *style of resistance* I have drawn on a *trickster strategy to* show how in the 'Oval 4' case the police *engaged* in what I have called a 'grand deception' to send us to prison, and how I tried to *meet deception with deception* by engaging in the art of 'counter-deception,' using the *false confession* as a tactic in this *strategy of resistance.* A Fanonian reading of Nat Turner's actions will show that he *met the violence of domination with the violence of emancipation* and was, as he put it, "using their own weapons against them." It was an act of *counter-violence* (Zahar, 1974: 77; Bulhan, 1985). Following Nat Turner's intention to 'slay his enemies with their own weapons,' my *counter-deception* used the 'weapon of deception' the police had fielded against us against them.

It is to be emphasised that if the designs and actions undertaken in the police station in 1972 can be likened to a *trickster strategy* at all, then it must be posed as an act of honourable deception against dishonourable people and a dishonourable situation. As an act of honourable deception it was intended and purposeful cultural action. And if those acts are to be valued as "creating an illusion" then that illusion involved "wearing the mask of obedience" in order to reject the 'ethics of subservience.' *The ethics of subservience I rejected demanded me foregrounding values and actions which would act to my personal disbenefit and as a disbenefit to the Cause for which I stood.* And if this behaviour amounts to rejecting the 'ethics of subservience' then its scope would include being of benefit to the living and the unborn and of benefit to what Frantz Fanon (1963: 251-255) envisaged, quite correctly, as the *unfinished struggle* for a new humanity.

NOTES

[1]   The poem 'If We Must Die' by Claude McKay. He penned the poem (a sonnet) for the Liberator, a socialist magazine in London. The poem is found in 'America Negro Poetry: An Edited Anthology,' (Ed) Arna Bontemps, New York, Hill and Yang, 1974:31.

[2]   The Josiah Wedgwood anti-slavery 'cameo' was produced in 1787 in his pottery factory. It was commented that the passive attitude of the kneeling figure gave the misleading impression that slaves were helpless when, in fact, they actively opposed their conditions of captive servitude.

[3]   Harriet Jacobs was born into slavery in Edenton, North Carolina, Virginia, in 1813. In 1835 Harriet became a 'runaway slave' eluding slave catchers on the road and paths, living for 7 years in an attic. In 1861 she wrote a Narrative about her ordeal in slavery. In Chapter 12 of 'Incidents in the Life of a Slave Girl, Written by Herself,' she describes the harassment, framing and killing of slaves in Edenton, North Carolina, following Turner's rebellion.

[4]   Garnett's Call to Rebellion found at http://www.pbs.org/wgbh/aia/part4/4h2937t.html; accessed 14/7/2006

BIBLIOGRAPHICAL NOTES

Primary sources:

I have drawn on a range of primary sources for the text of this book: my recollections were a primary source, newspaper cuttings and documents from the trial which together helped form the basis of Chapters 1, 2 and 3. A primary source, particularly for Chapter 4, was information obtained under the Freedom of Information Act, 2000. These, along with information from the newspaper archives at the British Library, Colindale, formed the substance of the final chapter of Section 1.

Section 2 is based also on a range of sources on Fasimba activism, including cultural artefacts from the 1970s: books, records, posters and publicity and propaganda from the Fasimba as well as interviews, meetings and discussions with former Fasimba members. Over the decades Chris and I had a number of deep discussions about the 'Oval 4' episode and its links with Fasimba activism. Even though some of the organisational documents and records were lost as a result of moving, and by their dispersal following our arrest, this was more than compensated for by discussions with Fasimba members as well as by the way the book eventually developed. Other primary sources used for Section 2 were publications with the words of Kwame Toure (aka Stokely Carmichael), Malcolm X, Marcus Garvey, CLR James, George Jackson and Angela Davis.

Other primary sources of information were:

- Transcript of the Judgment in the Appeal hearing at the Court of Appeal, 30/7/73
- Transcript of the Nationwide, *Cause for Concern*, transmission on 30/7/73
- Recording of Nationwide, *Cause for Concern*, transmission, 30/7/73
- Transcript of Radio 4 programme on *Black Power*, 18/9/70
- Social Science Section, British Library, St. Pancras, London
- Newspaper Archives, British Library, Colindale, London
- The Huntley Collection, Metropolitan Archives, London

Information requested under the Freedom of Information Act, 2000, from:

- British Transport Police headquarters, Camden
- National Offender Management Service (NOMS), Home Office
- Her Majesty's Court Service (Central Criminal Court; Court of Appeal, Criminal Division; Tower Bridge Magistrates Court; Camberwell Magistrates Court)
- Department of Constitutional Affairs

Other sources contacted for relevant information:

- The Parole Board for England and Wales
- The Law Society
- National Archives, Kew Gardens
- Institute of Race Relations, London

Secondary sources:

Secondary sources included a collection of books and documents on Black Power and Black consciousness in my collection since the 1970s. These include Black community newspapers such as *Grassroots* and *Black Voice* and journals such as the *Black Liberator, Race Today, Race & Class*, and the popular weekly, the *West Indian World*, all carried reports on aspects of the 'Oval 4' case. *Time Out* magazine not only reported on the 'Oval 4' case from trial and imprisonment to Appeal and release from prison, but set the episode withina wider context. Following *Time Out's* coverage of the case, journalist Duncan Campbell I became friends after my release from Prison, and over the years made a number of contributions to *Time Out* magazine, moving with other journalists to *City Limits* magazine when it was formed in the 1980s. Still a journalist, he and Julie Christie married recently and are now resident in California, USA. *'Staying Power'* by Peter Fryer made reference to the 'Oval 4' case, and *'Policing the Crisis: Mugging, the State and Law and Order'* carried a worthy analysis of the 'Oval 4' case in relation to the 1972 'mugging hysteria' promoted by the media and the police, and sections of this book rely heavily on that publication.

REFERENCES

Anim-Addo, J   1995   *The Longest Journey: A Black History of Lewisham,* London: Deptford Forum Publishing

Apetheker, H   1969   *American Negro Slave Revolts*, New York: New York International Publishers

Athill, Diane   2004   *Make Believe—A True Story*, London: Granta Publications

Baker, Jnr., HA   1984   'To Move without Moving: creativity and commerce In Ralph Ellison's Trueblood Episode.' *Black Literature and Literary Culture,* Ed., Gates, HL, Jnr., New York: Methuen Books

Beardslee, K   1999   'Through Slave Culture's Lens Comes the Abundant Source: Harriot Jacobs's Incidents in the Life of a Slave Girl—Critical Essay', in *Melus,* Spring 1999

Bennett, L, Jr.,   1969   *Before the Mayflower: A history of the Negro in America 1619-1964* (revised Edition). Middlesex, Penguin.

Benston, K   1984   'I (y)am what I am: the topos of (un)naming in Afro-American literature' in *Black Literature and Literary Theory*, ed., Gates, Jnr, HL, London; Methuen

Benyon, J   2002   *Masculinities and Culture: Issues in Culture and Media Studies*, Buckingham: Open University Press

Boggs, J   1970   *Racism and the Class Struggle: Further Pages from the Black Worker's Notebook,* New York: Monthly Review Press.

Brake, M   1980   *The Sociology of Youth Culture and Sub-Cultures,* London: Routledge, Kegan Paul

Brown, R M   2005   *Strain of Violence: Historical Studies of American Violence and Vigilantism*, Oregan: Oxford University Press

Bulhan, HA   1979   'Black Psyches in captivity and crises.' *Race & Class.* Vol. XX, no. 3, Winter 1979, London, Institute of Race Relations

Bulhan, H A   1985   *Frantz Fanon and the Psychology of Oppression*,
                              New York: Plenum Press.

Bunyan, T   1976   *History and Practice of the Political Police in
                              Britain*, London: Julian Friedmann

Cabral, A   1973   *Return to the Source: Selected Speeches of
                              Amilcar Cabral*, New York: Monthly Review
                              Press

Carmichael, S   1967   *'Black Power' in Dialectics of Liberation*, ed.
                              David Cooper, London: Pelican

Carmichael, S   1971   *Stokely Speaks: Black Power to Pan Africanism*,
                              New York: Vintage Books

Cashmore, E   1979   *Rastaman: the Rastafarian movement in
                              England.* London: Macmillan.

Clarke, S   1980   *Jah Music: The Evolution of Jamaican Popular
                              Song*, London: Heinemann Educational Books

Clarke, E B   1995   'The Sacred Rights of the Weak: Pain,
                              Sympathy, and the Culture of Individual Rights
                              in Antebellum America.' *Journal of American
                              History*, Vol. 82, 463-473.

Coard, B   1971   *How the West Child is Made Educationally Sub-
                              Normal in the British School System: the Scandal
                              of Black Children in Schools in Britain*, London:
                              New Beacon Books

Coard, B   2004   'Why I Wrote the ESN Book.' *Guardian
                              Unlimited. Education Guardian*.co.uk/ Special
                              Reports, Feb, 2005 http://education.guardian.
                              co.uk/racism/story/o,,1406216,oo.html.
                              Accessed 27/3/2006

Cullen, C   1974   *'Heritage' (1925). American Negro Poetry*,
                              Revised Edition, ed Bontempts, A, New York:

Davis, A   1972   *If They Come in the Morning: Voices of
                              Resistance*, London, Obach and Chambers

Davidson, M   2003   Anancy Introduction: http://www.jamaicans.
                              com/culture/anansi/anancy intro.shtml,
                              Accessed 22/7/08

Diawara, M	1990	'Englishness and Blackness': Cricket as Discourse in on Colonialism. *Callaloo*, Vol. 13,N4/Fall, 1990
Diouf, S A (ed)	2003	*Fighting the African Trade: West African Strategies,* Ohio University Press and James Currey Publishers
Douglass, F	1973	*The Narrative of the Life of Frederick Douglass,* Written by himself (1845), New York, Anchor/ Doubleday
Edwards, J	1984	'Structural Analysis of the Afro-American trickster Tale.' *Black Literature and Literary* Theory. Edited Gates, LH, Jnr., London: Methuen
Egerton, D	2000	*He Shall Go Free: The Lives of Denmark Vesey.* *Wisconsin: Madison House.*
Epps, A	1969	*Malcolm X and the American Negro Revolution,* London: Peter Owen
Esedebe, P,O	1980	'The Growth of the Pan-African Movement' in *Pan-Africanism.* Tarikh, Vol 6, No 3, 18-34.
Fanon, F	1971	*The Wretched of the Earth*, London, Penguin Books
Fanon, F	1970	*Black Skin, White Masks,* London: Pelican Books
Forbes, R P	2000	'Vesey Reviews,' *North Star,* Vol. 3 Number 2, Spring, 2000
Fryer, P	1984	*Staying Power: The History of Black People in Britain*, London: Pluto Press
Garvey, A J	1970	*Garvey & Garveyism,* London: Collier/ Macmillan
Gates, Jnr, HL	1984	'Criticism in the Jungle,' in *Black Literature and Literary Theory*; ed., Gates Jnr, HL, London: Methuen
Genovese, E	1979	*From Rebellion to Revolution: Afro-American Slave Revolts in the Making of the Modern World*, New York: Vintage Books.

| Gillian, A | 2005 | Garvey's Legacy in Context: Colourism, Black Movements, and African Nationalism. Race and History. Amenhotep.com |

| Gutzmore, C | 1983 | 'Capital, 'black youth' and crime.' Race & Class, Vol. XXV, No.2, Autumn 1983, London: Institute of Race Relations |

| Hall, S; Jefferson, T; Roberts, J; Chritcher, C; | 1978 | *Policing the Crisis: Mugging, the State and Law and Order*, London: Macmillan |

| Hall, S and and Jefferson, T. (eds) | 1975 | Resistance through Rituals: Youth subcultures In post-war Britain, London: Hutchinson in association with Centre for Contemporary Cultural Studies |

| Hansard | 1963 | 7 February Vol. 671, cc656-657 |

| Hansard | 1963 | 7 February, Vol. 671, c 657 |

| Hebdige, D | 1975 | Reggae, Rasta's & Rudies,' *Resistance Through Rituals: Youth Subcultures in post-war Britain,* Eds Hall, S & Jefferson, T, London: Hutchinson |

| Higman, BW | 1976 | *Slave Population and Economy in Jamaica, 1807-1834,* Cambridge: Cambridge University Press |

| Hiro, D | 1973 | *Black British, White British*, London: Pelican |

| Holloway, J | 2003 | 'Shipboard Revolts, African Authority, and the Atlantic Slave Trade,' Chapter 12, in *Strategies for fighting the Atlantic Slave Trade,* Edited Diouf, SA,Ohio University Press and James Currey Publishers |

| Humphrey, D | 1972 | *Police Power and Black People*, London: Panther Books |

| Institute of Race Relations | 1979 | 'Police against Black People:' Evidence Submitted to the Royal Commission on Criminal Procedure, *Race & Class*, Pamphlet, No 6, London, Institute of Race Relations. |

| Jackson, S | 1972/3 | *The Illegal Child-Minders: A report on the growth of unregistered child-minding in the West Indian community.* Priority Area Children Report: Cambridge Educational Development Trust |

| James, W | 1998 | The History of Caribbean Migration to the United States, Columbia University. The Schomberg Center, ed., http://www.inmotionaame.org/text.ocr_print.cfm?id=100T&page=&an ho, Accessed 24/4/2008 |

| Johnson, M | 2001 | 'Denmark Vesey and His Co-Conspirators.' *The William and Mary Quarterly.* Vol.54, No. 4, October 2001 |

| Juang, R | 2005 | 'Blind Memory: Visual Representations of Slavery in England and America, 1750 – 1865.' *Symbiosis*, Vol. 9 No. 1, April, 2005 |

| Kleinig, | 1999 | Quoted by Newburn (1999) |

| Klockars, CB | 1977 | Quoted by Newburn (1999) |

| Kushnik,, L | 1981/82 | 'Parameters of British and North American Racism,' *Race & Class*, Volume XXlll, Autumn/Winter. Nos. 2/3. |

| Lang, J | 1969 | *Land of the Golden Trade,* New York, Negro Universities Press |

| Lee, TE | 1977 | 'Race and residence: the concentration and Dispersal of immigrants in London,' *Oxford Research Studies in Geography*. Oxford: Clarendon Press |

| Lenin, IV | 1970 | Imperialism: The Highest Stage of Capitalism. *Scientific Socialism Series,* Moscow: Progress Publishers |

| Lester, J | 1973 | *To be a Slave.* Middlesex: Puffin Books |

| McKay, C | 1974 | 'Outcast' in American Negro Poetry, Revised Edition; Ed, Bontempts, A. New York: Hill and Wang. |

Mackie, L	1987	*The Great Marcus Garvey*, London: Hansib Educational Book
Manley, M	1982	*Jamaica: Struggle in the Periphery*. London: Third World Media/Readers and Writers Cooperative
Marsh, H	1974	*Slavery and Race*, London: David & Charles
Mc Mullen,	1961	Quoted by Newburn, (1999)
Naughton, M	2006	'Wrongful Convictions and Innocence Projects in the UK,' *Web Journal of Current Legal Issues* 3, http://webjcli.ncl.ac.uk/2006/issue3/naughton3.html, Accessed 4/9/2006
Newburn, T	1999	'Understanding Police Corruption: Lessons from the Literature.,' *Police Research Series*, Paper 110, London: Policing and Reducing Crime Unit
Nkrumah, K	1965	*Neo-Colonialism: the last Stage of Imperialism* African Writers Series. London: Heinemann Educational Books
Patterson, O	1973	*The Sociology of Slavery*, Kingston, Sangster Books
Patterson, O	1979	'Slavery in Modern History' in *New Left Review*, 117; September-October, 1979, London
Peach, C	1968	*Black Migration to Britain: A Social Geography*, London: Oxford University Press
Peach, C	1984	'The Force of West Indian Island identity in Britain,' in Clarke, C., Ley, D. and Peach, C. *Geography and Ethnic Pluralism*, London: Allen & Unwin
Pearson, D	1999	*Designs Against Charleston: The Trial Record of the Denmark Slave Conspiracy of 1822.* Chapel Hill: University of North Carolina Press.
Philips, M & Philips, T	1983	*Windrush: the Irresistible Rise of Multi-Racial Britain*, London, Harper & Collins
Philips, R	1975	'The Death of one Lame Darkie.' Unsourced

Piper, K	1984	*Past Imperfect, Future Tense. Exhibition at Black Art Gallery, Finsbury Park, London*
Proyect, L	1999	CLR James and Malcolm X, Black Radical Congress. http://www.hartford.hwp.com. archives/45a/139.html accessed
Punch, M	1985	*Conduct Unbecoming: The Social Construction of Police Deviance and Con*trol: Tavistock
Race Today	1973	Dock Brief, Volume 5, number 4, April, 1973, London.
Radin, P	1956	*The Trickster: A Study in North America Mythology*, New York: Schoken Books
Robinson, C	1983	*Black Marxism: the Making of the Radical Black Tradition*, London: Zed Press
Rodney, W	1972	*The Groundings with my Brothers*, London: Bogle L'Overture Publications
Rodney, W	1984	*How Europe Underdeveloped Africa*, London: Bogle L'Overture
Rohlehr, G	1981	*Akan-Ashanti folktales*. Oxford: Clarendon Press.
Royal Society of Health Journal	1970	'Oil Heater Fires' in *Perspectives in Public Health*,' Health Journal 90: 1-2
Runnymede Trust	1980	*Britain's Black Population*, London: Heinemann Educational Books
Scott, J	1999	*Domination and the Arts of Resistance: Hidden Transcripts*. New Haven/London. Yale University Press
Shyllon, F	1974	*Black Slaves in Britain*, London: Oxford
Sivanandan, A	1976	'Race, Class & the State: the Black Experience in Britain,' *Race & Class*, Vol. XV11, No.4, 1976, *London: Institute of Race Relations*
Stuckey, S	1987	*Slave Culture: Nationalist Theory and the Foundations of Black America*. London: Oxford University Press

Takaki, RT	1993	*Violence in the Black Imagination: Essays and Documents [Expanded Edition]*, Oxford: Oxford University Press
Taylor, E R	2007	*If We Must Die: Shipboard Rebellions in the Era of the Atlantic Slave Trade*, Louisiana: Louisiana State University Press
Wilson, H,E	1984	*'Our Nig' or Sketches from the Life of a Free Black: A Novel* by Harriet E Wilson, London: Allen & Busby
Woddis, J	1967	*Introduction to Neo-Colonialism*, London: Lawrence and Wishart
Young, R	2001	'Review of Douglass R Egerton, He Shall Go Free: The Lives of Denmark Vesey. H-South, H-Net Reviews, February, 2001. http://www.h.net.msu.edu/reviews/showrev.cgi?path=25142982863664. Accessed 20/02/08
Zaher, R	1974	*Frantz Fanon: Colonialism and Alienation*, New York: Modern Reader

ELECTRONIC SOURCES

On This Day   1970   '*1970: Shock Election Win for Heath,*' BBC News http://news.bbc.co.uk/onthisday/hi/dates/stories/june/19/newsid_3829000/3829819.stm, Downloaded, 31/12/2005

On This Day   1971   '*1971: UK restricts Commonwealth migrants,*' BBC News, http://news.bbc.co.uk/onthisday/hi/dates/stories/ february/24/newsid_251, Downloaded, 5/12/2005

On This Day   1970   *1970: State of Emergency called over dock strike,*' BBC News: http://newqs.bbc.co.uk/onthisday/low/dates/stories/july/16/newsid_2504000/2504223.s. Downloaded, 21/7/2006

Spunk Library   2001   '*Angry Brigade Chronology,*' Spunk Library, agb Catalogue Angry Brigade UK : http://www.spunk.org/texts/groups/agb/ sp000540.txt, Downloaded, 27/7/2003

AUTHOR BIOGRAPHY

Winston Trew

Winston Trew was born in Jamaica, the son of a policeman in the colonial police force. In 1954 his father left for England followed by his mother in 1955. In 1956, he and his two younger brothers left Jamaica with an older sister to join their parents in England. He regards his early life in London as mirroring the pattern of black migration and settlement he speaks of in his book.

In 1970 he joined a local Black Power organisation, the Fasimba (Young Lions) and as he tells in the book it proved to be a *life-changing event* in more ways than he could have imagined. Black Power was his political awakening and led eventually to a violent encounter with undercover police, to the 'Oval 4' episode, to his imprisonment and release from prison, and to his aptly named book, *Black for a Cause.*

To him the *'Oval 4' episode* was also an *eye-opening event* because it not only illustrated the character and contours of Black Power activism in Britain in the 1970s, it also debunks the myth that the 1960s was the only period of Black Power in Britain. Black Power politics as practiced by the Fasimba is symbolised in the book as confronting the 'ethics of subservience' the police tried to engender in the 'Oval 4' in the police station.

The 'ethics of subservience' he sees as encoded in the Wedgwood 'anti-slavery' logo, a pose unwittingly 'celebrated' by the descendents of emancipated slaves in 2007. *Black for a Cause* is offered as a counter-narrative to the 'pose of subservience' represented by that logo and, instead, directs our attention to an unexplored dimension of Black resistance: the ethics of self-emancipation. He considers Black self-emancipation to be an unfinished project, one that began with the enforced migration of black ancestors from Africa. The 1970s represents a stage of development in that unfinished project.

Microsoft® Access 2000 MOUS Cheat Sheet

by Joe Habraken and Doug Klippert

A Division of Macmillan Computer Publishing
201 W. 103rd Street, Indianapolis, Indiana 46290 USA

Microsoft® Access 2000 MOUS Cheat Sheet
Copyright© 2000 Que® Corporation

International Standard Book Number: 0-7897-2117-1

Library of Congress Catalog Card Number: 99-63519

First Printing: December 1999

01 00 99   4 3 2 1

Trademarks, Warning and Disclaimer

Publisher *Jim Minatel*

Managing Editor *Lisa Wilson*

Executive Editor *Angie Wethington*

Acquisitions Editor *Tracy M. Williams*

Series Editor *Jill Hayden*

Development Editors *Jill Hayden and Beverly Scherf*

Technical Editors *Mark Hall and Connie Myers*

Team Coordinator *Vicki Harding*

Media Developer *Andrea Duvall*

Project Editor *Natalie Harris*

Copy Editor *Kelly Talbot*

Cover Designer *Nathan Clements*

Interior Designer *Anne Jones*

Indexer *Tina Trettin*

Proofreader *Benjamin Berg*

Production *Cheryl Lynch*

Dedication

To all the people around the world who have written communicating their hopes and expectations concerning these exams.

Acknowledgments

Access is a complicated program. It would be easy to lapse into technical jargon and obscure the basic elements of the application. Thanks go to Jill Hayden, Beverly Scherf, and Tracy Williams for keeping the goal in focus. Connie Myers and Mark Hall examined the minutiac and, at the same time, were still able to see the whole picture.

One of the biggest acknowledgements has to go to the computer users around the world who are using the Microsoft Office User Specialist exams as one tool in the pursuit of a goal. Whether it's just to certify their knowledge of these applications or to use the tests to seek a new career and fulfill a dream, there are a lot of you out there. Good luck in all your endeavors.

Introduction

At the present time, the only version of the Access 2000 exam is at the core level. There are 48 skills that you are required to know to pass the exam.

Some of the activities covered by the Access 2000 exam are common to other programs such as Excel or Word. You will need to know how to open a file from the File menu, for instance. By reading the chapters and completing the practice exercises in this book, you can make sure that you understand these basic skills. Knowing how to perform basic skills quickly might give you extra time to use with more time-consuming procedures.

There are some new features in Access 2000, such as sub-datasheets. However, if you are familiar with previous versions, this exam should not present any major difficulty. Make sure you understand each of the activities in the Objectives list. Practice using the new features until they become second nature.

How This Book Is Different

Unlike most Access books on the market, this book is strictly exam-focused. You will find that there are no tasks on the test that will require you to use modules. Therefore, modules are not covered in this book.

Examine the Cheat Sheet to see whether there are any skills that you have not used before or have used only infrequently. Go through the Practice Lab until you can quickly do what's asked of you without relying on the book or the Help file. You will have little time to look up information during the test.

How to Use This Book

Each chapter in this book covers a number of related activities such as operations that focus on controls. There is an Objectives Index in the back of the book that lists the official Objectives determined by the test distributor and the page number in this book where you will find the discussion of each objective.

At the end of each chapter, there is a Cheat Sheet with a list of different ways to perform the action. Use this Cheat Sheet to review each chapter as you are progressing through the book. The Cheat Sheet can also be used as a recap in the last few hours before the exam.

There is a Practice Lab at the end of each chapter, in which you can practice the objectives learned. The tasks are in the same form as the real exam. To begin each Practice Lab, download the designated practice file from the CD-ROM. Then complete the tasks listed. When you have finished the last task of the Practice Lab, download and open the designated solution file to check your work. You'll know immediately if you need to review the objectives in that chapter.

Books, papers, laptops, and so on are not allowed in the examination room itself.

Appendix A contains some thoughts about Exam Preparation. This exam is a little different from others you might have taken, in that it is a hands-on test of your application savvy. Read what others have learned about successfully passing the tests.

What's New in Office 2000

Office 2000 has some characteristics that differ from previous versions. You will need to be familiar with them so you are not thrown for a loss when under pressure.

Personalized Menus

The menus and toolbars in Office 2000 will show the most recently used items. They will, in effect, customize themselves as you work. When Access 2000 is first opened, you will see only the basic menu items and buttons. As you continue to work with the program, the commands you use most often will start to appear, and others might go away.

This can be disconcerting. At the bottom of the short version of the built-in menu there is a downward pointing arrow that will expand the menu to show all the commands. You can also double-click the menu or wait for a few seconds for it to expand. Toolbars also have an arrow at the far right that will display more buttons.

Contents

Chapter 3 Building Tables

Chapter 4   Building Tables II: Entering Data   49

Chapter 5   Modifying Tables: Data Modification   61

Chapter 6 Modifying Tables II—Table Structure Modification   71

Planning Databases

Following is a list of MOUS Objectives:

- Understand relational databases
- Determine appropriate data inputs for your database
- Determine appropriate data outputs for your database
- Plan a new database
- Use the Office Assistant

Understand Access Relational Databases

For a database to be of any value, you must have the ability to access, retrieve, and use the information kept in that database. Computerized database management systems provide the greatest flexibility for working with data in a database.

Microsoft Access 2000 is a special kind of database management system. It enables you to create relational databases. A relational database divides information into discrete groups—tables—which can then be related to each other. For instance, one table might contain customers, another table might show products, a third table might consist of suppliers, and a fourth table might contain orders. A relational database enables you to set up relationships between these different tables and then create queries, reports, and forms that tie together and display the information in the different tables.

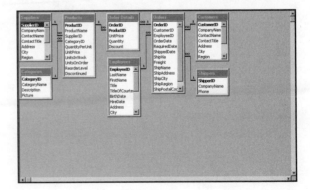

Relational databases, such as those built in Access, do two important things for the end-user: First, they enable you to avoid entering repeated or redundant data, and second, their basic design (a group of related tables) makes it very easy for you to manipulate and then view the data in a number of different ways. You will build a relational database in Chapter 8, "Viewing and Organizing Information II—Finding and Filtering Records," by relating several tables together.

Access provides you with different ways of entering, viewing, and manipulating your data. These data manipulations are accomplished by using Access objects. You can think of your Access database as a container that will hold a collection of various database objects such as tables, forms, queries, and reports.

Two basic classes of objects exist in Access: objects that enable you to input data and objects that enable you to view your data after you input it. Tables and forms provide input vehicles, whereas queries and reports output the information in the database. A form is a graphical data input screen that assists in the process of entering information. The next two sections discuss data input and output and cover two objectives that you will be responsible for on the Access 2000 Core Exam.

2

Determine Appropriate Data Inputs for Your Database

To determine the appropriate inputs for your database, you simply organize your information in a logical fashion and make sure it ends up in the database. For example, a small business might have customer information placed in a customer table, sales information in a sales table, and so on.

To help determine the appropriate data inputs for a new database, you first should ask yourself these questions:

- What information will I want to get out of the database when it is operational? This will drive how the data is stored and organized and will dictate the number of tables you will need.

- How do I want to input the data, and how would I like to view this data as I input it? This question should prompt you to consider how you would use forms to make your data entry easier and more reliable.

Data input is then handled by either an Access table or by an Access form that you create based on a table. Both of these objects are discussed in the next two sections.

The most important Access object and the basic building block of your databases is the table. Each table holds a category of information. Access tables look like spreadsheets, displaying the data that they hold in rows and columns. Each row holds all the information for a particular person, place, or thing; table rows are called *records*. Each column contains a different piece of information pertaining to that person, place, or thing; the columns are referred to as *fields*.

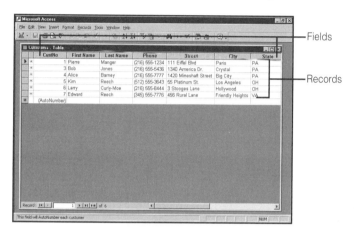

Fields

Records

Most Access databases consist of a number of tables, and you do most of your data entry in the table. Chapter 3, "Building Tables," covers the creation of Access tables.

Even though your tables hold the data that you enter into your database, there is another Access object that provides an alternative way for entering and viewing the information—*forms*. The form provides you with the capability to view and enter data one record at a time. Custom forms can also be designed that enable you to enter information into more than one table.

Forms can also be used to view special data types such as linked objects (an employee photo for example). You will learn how to create forms in Chapter 10, "Building and Modifying Forms." You will work with advanced form design in Chapter 11, "Building and Modifying Forms II."

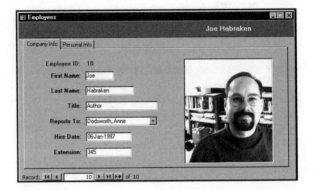

Determine Appropriate Data Outputs for Your Database

As mentioned earlier in this chapter, when you have entered the data in your various database tables by either using a form for data entry or entering the data directly into the appropriate table, you can view the data—ouput the data—in a variety of ways. For example, you might want to sort the data in a particular table such as a customer table by the total amount of purchases each customer has made. You can use a query to accomplish this type of data output (which combines information from more than one table).

In another situation, you might want to actually print out a hard copy of information in your database that has been summarized or even charted. You can use reports to create print-ready output that enables you to summarize, combine, and even chart data from the database.

To determine the types of data output you want to create from your database, ask yourself the following questions:

- How will I want to manipulate the data when it has been entered in my tables? This question should help you begin to consider the type of queries you might want to run.

- What types of printouts will I need from the database and how should the data be arranged on the printed page? This question should start you thinking about what kind of reports you will want to design for your database.

The next two sections briefly describe how queries and reports are used for data output.

Use Queries The query is the Access object that enables you to manipulate the data in your table. You can use queries to sort and select data from your Access tables; you can also design queries that summarize and do calculations on the information found in a table or tables. Queries can be used to delete records that match certain criteria, or they can be used to update information in a particular field of a table. The next figure shows the Query Design view.

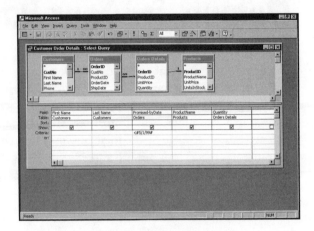

When you run a query, the results appear in a table format, providing you with the familiar geography of an Access table. You will learn to design simple queries in Chapter 12, "Designing Queries."

Use Reports A report is the database object that enables you to take the data in your table and place it in a format that is suitable for printing. Reports provide you with a number of format and layout options for presenting your data.

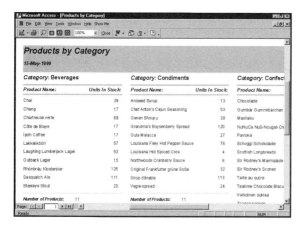

Access reports also have the capability to pull information from more than one table or to provide you with a printable review of information in a query. Reports also can do calculations and summarize data. You will learn to create reports in Chapter 13, "Producing Reports," and work with advanced report design in Chapter 14, "Producing Reports II—Modifying Report Design."

Plan a New Database

The truly hands-on nature of Microsoft Access and its capability to get a new database up and running quickly might seduce the typical end user into creating a new database without any preplanning. However, a little planning up front can help you circumvent the painful trial-and-error process that many users experience when they first work with Access.

Too much or too little information can make a database less efficient or even unsuitable for its intended purpose. You can be called on in the exam to identify data that should be excluded or included.

The most important aspect of creating a new database is determining the tables that you will have in your database and what type of information you will include in each of them. A properly designed database should avoid unnecessarily redundant data. As you create your tables for your database, you will want to use a technique called normalizing. Normalizing a database simply means that you need to structure your tables so that you are not constantly re-entering the same information. Take a look at a poorly designed table: a table that holds the customer data for a small business.

Customer Name	Customer Address	Customer Phone	Order Date	Order Total
ABC Plumbing	201 W. 44th St.	(317) 555-2394	2/5/98	$155.90
ABC Plumbing	201 W. 44th St.	(317) 555-2394	2/12/98	$90.25
ABC Plumbing	201 W. 44th St.	(317) 555-2394	3/17/98	$225.00
Jack's Place	15 Conway	(317) 555-1234	4/1/98	$1500.00
Kim's Pizza	11 Fair Rd.	(317) 555-2222	4/4/98	$990.00
Jack's Place	15 Conway	(317) 555-1234	4/12/98	$40.00

Notice that the table contains a lot of redundant information. Each time a transaction is recorded, all the customer's information (such as the company name, address, and phone number) must be entered into the table. This means that the same information is entered over and over again for repeat customers.

The best way to avoid the repetition of data (as shown in the preceding table) is to assign each of the customers a customer number. The data could be broken down into the two following tables: a customer table and an orders table.

Customer ID	Customer Name	Customer Address	Customer Phone
1	ABC Plumbing	201 W. 44th St.	(317) 555-2394
2	Jack's Place	15 Conway	(317) 555-1234
3	Kim's Pizza	11 Fair Rd.	(317) 555-2222

Order ID	Customer ID	Order Date	Order Total
1	1	2/5/98	$155.90
2	1	2/12/98	$90.25
3	1	3/17/98	$225.00
4	2	4/1/98	$1500.00
5	3	4/4/98	$990.00
6	2	4/12/98	$40.00

The customer ID is used to tie the two tables together. Breaking large tables with redundant data down into smaller tables that are linked by a common field (in this case customer ID) is the essence of normalizing a database. Establishing relationships between related tables is covered in Chapter 9, "Defining Relationships—Building a Relational Database."

You will also learn in Chapter 3, "Building Tables," that each table needs to have a field that uniquely identifies the records. Keep this in mind when planning new database tables (notice that both the preceding tables have an ID number that uniquely identifies each of the records).

Use the Office Assistant

As you work with Access, you will certainly find times when you need help with a particular feature or need to get more information related to creating and using databases in Access. You've probably already noticed Clippit, the default Office Assistant that appears when you open the Access application window. The Office Assistant provides the most straightforward method of getting help as you work in Access.

When you click the Office Assistant, a balloon appears above its box asking What Would You Like to Do? You can do any of the following:

- Type a question in the balloon and then click the **Search** button to get help.

- Select one of the Office Assistant's guesses about what you need help with.

- Click the **Options** button to customize the way the Office Assistant works.

- Click outside the balloon to close it (but leave the Office Assistant onscreen).

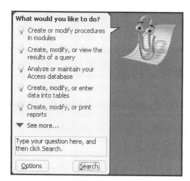

If you need help on a particular topic, you can type a question into the text box that appears in the Assistant Balloon. Follow these steps to see how it works:

1. Click the Assistant to open the balloon.

2. Type a question in the text box. For instance, you might type **How do I create a table?**

3. Click the **Search** button. The Office Assistant provides some topics that might match what you're looking for.

4. Click the option that best describes what you're trying to do. A Help window appears, providing you with help related to the topic that you chose.

If none of the options describes what you want, click See More to view more options, or type a different question into the text box.

The Help window that appears (containing the task instructions) is the same window that will open when you ask for help with the Office Assistant turned off.

13

When a light bulb appears above the Office Assistant, click the Assistant to get help on the task you're currently performing.

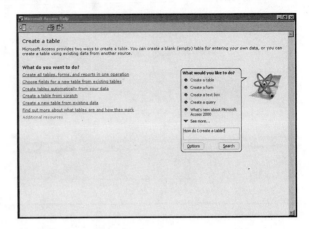

Turning the Office Assistant On and Off

By default, the Office Assistant is activated, and it sits in your application window. You can hide the Assistant by right-clicking the Assistant and then selecting Hide, and the Assistant will be removed from the application window.

To return the Office Assistant to the application window, click 🔃 Help on the Standard toolbar or click the <u>H</u>elp menu and then select Microsoft Access <u>H</u>elp. You can also bring up help with the F1 key.

TAKE THE TEST

In this practice exercise, you will work with features related to Objective 2, "Determine appropriate data inputs for your database." This is a conceptual task, and you should write your answers on paper.

Task 1

1. List on paper the types of database input objects you would want to create for a mail-order shoe business. Keep in mind that tables will hold the data and that forms are used for viewing and entering data.

2. Use the information in the table shown as the data for a new database. Determine the number of tables you want to create to hold the data. Remember to avoid designing tables that will lead to redundant data entries and to include at least one identical field in each table so you can link the new tables together.

Employee Name	Address	Ext.	Training Date	Class Taken	Credits
Phil Sharp	211 W. 16th	234	02/17/98	Access Database	6
Becky Rowan	40 West St.	543	03/19/98	Customer Service	3
Phil Sharp	211 W. 16th	234	03/19/98	Customer Service	3
Nick Gianti	59 Point St.	122	03/20/98	Leadership 101	9
Martha Donat	72 Warren Blvd.	333	3/23/98	Customer Service	3
Becky Rowan	40 West St.	543	03/24/98	Access Database	6

15

Answers to Task 1 exercises:

1. A mail order shoe business would require several tables to properly manage the information in a database. These tables would include the following:

   • Customers Table (lists customer information such as name and address)

   • Product Table (provides stock numbers and other information related to the shoes sold by your business)

   • Supplier Table (lists information on the shoe suppliers that you use)

   • Invoice Table (provides information on items purchased by your customers)

   Forms for the database would probably include at least two types: a Customer form for the entering of customer information and an invoice form.

2. The following tables were created after normalizing the table shown in Task 1, Exercise 1. Note that an identifier field has been included in each of the tables to uniquely identify the records and that common fields are used to tie the tables together. The first table and the third table have the Employee ID field in common. The second and third are linked by the Class ID.

Employee ID	Employee Name	Address	Ext.
1	Becky Rowan	40 West St.	543
2	Phil Sharp	211 W. 16th	234
3	Nick Gianti	59 Point St.	122
4	Martha Donat	72 Warren Blvd.	333

Class ID	Class	Credits
C1	Customer Service	3
C2	Leadership 101	9
C3	Access Database	6

Class ID	Employee ID	Training Date
C3	2	02/17/98
C1	1	03/19/98
C1	2	03/19/98
C2	3	03/20/98
C1	4	3/23/98
C3	1	03/24/98

Task 2

In this practice exercise, you will work with features related to Objective 3 "Determine appropriate data outputs for your database." This is a conceptual task, and you should write your answers on paper.

1. Review the tables and forms that you created in Task 1 for the mail order shoe database. Now determine (write on paper) the type of queries and reports you would want to create for this database.

Answers for Task 2, Exercise 1:

Queries for the database would include a query that sorts your products by number sold and a query that would give you the total value of all the merchandise you have in stock.

Reports for this database would include printed invoices, shoe types ordered by supplier, and total sales detailing the sales on each shoe type.

Task 3

In this practice exercise, you will work with features related to Objective 5, "Use the Office Assistant." Start Access to perform this task and make sure the Office Assistant is available in the Access window.

1. Use the Office Assistant's balloon to enter a question regarding the creation of a report.

2. After you've asked the appropriate question, click the option that takes you to the Create a Report Help screen. Follow any of the links provided to get more information on creating a report.

Cheat Sheet

Determine Appropriate Data Inputs for Your Database

What details will be required?

Is the information stored in one location or many?

Is there a unique way to identify the data?

How often does the information need to be updated?

Terms

Table   A grouping of related data; made up of fields and records, columns and rows.

Field   A general name given a type of data, for example, FirstName, Date, City, and so on. A field is a column in a table.

Record   A set of data items that are related, such as the details of a sale: Date, Item, Salesman. A record is a row in a table.

Form   A graphical box that enables the user to input or view records one at a time. The data entered in a form is collected in a table.

Query   A question that can filter records so that only information that matches certain criteria is seen. A query can also create new tables and perform updates and computations.

Find the Office Assistant

If the Assistant is hidden, select Help, Microsoft Access Help.

Press the F1 key

To Use the Assistant

Click the Assistant and type a question in the Assistant query box.

Designing Databases

This chapter covers three of the required objectives for the Access 2000 Core Exam:

- Create a database
- Select an object using the Objects Bar
- Print database objects

6

Create a Database

Before you can create any Access objects, such as a table, or enter data into a database, you must create a database file. The database file is basically a container that will hold all the Access objects (tables, forms, queries, and reports) that help you manage your database information.

You have two options for creating a new database file: You can create a blank database and then build all the objects that will be used in the database, or you can create a ready-made database using the Access Database Wizard. The Wizard-created database is ready-made in the sense that a collection of tables, forms, queries, and reports will be built for you automatically.

Before you can use either method to create your new database file, you must start the Access software. Click the Start button, select Programs, and click the Access icon on the Programs menu. The Access Window opens.

When you start Microsoft Access, the Microsoft Access dialog box appears. This dialog box prompts you to create a new database using a blank database or by using the Database Wizard. This dialog box also gives you the option of opening an already existing database.

When you use the wizard to create a new database, you need to select a database template. These templates are blueprints for a particular type of database, such as a Contact Management database, Event Management database, or Inventory Control database, and contain ready-made database objects that you would use when building this type of database from scratch. How closely your database needs fit one of the Access templates will determine how many new objects you will need to create for the database or how much restructuring you will need to do to the built-in tables, queries, forms, and reports.

To create a new database using the Database Wizard, complete the following steps:

Create a Database Using a Wizard

1. From the Access dialog box, click the Access Database Wizards, Pages and Projects option button, and then click OK.

   In the Access application window, if you've already closed the dialog box, select the File menu, and then New. In either case, the New dialog box appears.

2. Click the Databases tab to display a list of the available database templates.

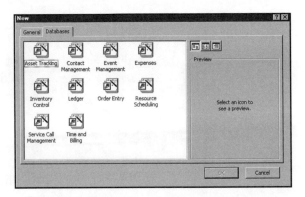

3. Choose one of the database templates and double-click it. (For example, if you are asked to create a contacts database, choose the Contact Management template.) The File New Database dialog box appears.

4. In the File New Database dialog box, type a name for the new database and select an appropriate drive and folder for the new file. Click Create to continue.

   The Database Wizard starts and indicates what type of information the new database will store. (Contact Management database stores contact information and information related to the calls you make.)

5. Click the Next button to see a list of ready-made tables for the new database and the fields specific to each table.

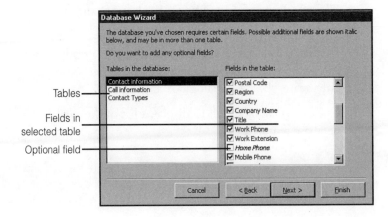

6. Click a selection in the Tables in the database box to view the fields for that table. The fields in the table appear in the scroll box to the right. Required fields for the new table already have a check mark in their selection box.

7. Select optional fields (in italics) for inclusion by clicking them. Click the Next button to continue.

8. The next screen asks you to select a screen display style for the new database. This style will determine the "look" of the forms that the wizard builds automatically. Click a style in the list box, and a sample will be displayed in the sample window. After making your style selection, click the Next button.

9. The next screen is where you select a report style for the new database. Click a style to preview it. After making your report style selection, click the Next button.

10. The next screen asks you to provide a title for the new database. You are also given the option of selecting a picture that will be included on the forms and reports in the database (for example, a company log). If you want to include a picture, click the Yes, I'd Like to Include a Picture checkbox. Select the picture by clicking the Picture button. Use the dialog box that opens to move to the appropriate drive or folder and select the picture. Clicking OK will return you to the Database Wizard. Click the Next button to continue.

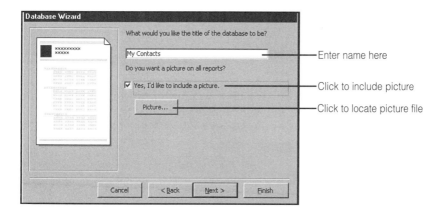

23

11. The Finish screen asks you if you want to start the new
database. To start the new database, click the Yes, Start
the Database check box and then click Finish.

The wizard creates the new database, and a Main Switchboard
window then appears. A switchboard is a form that provides
easy access to the various tasks that you will perform on the
database such as entering new data or running predesigned
reports. It provides a good interface for new users, but it pre-
vents you from directly viewing the objects that are present in
the new database. You can remove the Switchboard window by
clicking its Close button in the upper-right corner.

The title bar for your new database appears (minimized) in the
lower left corner of the Access window. Restore the Database
window by clicking the restore icon on the right side of the
database title bar to open the Database window for your new
database. You can also use the F11 key on the keyboard or the
Database Window icon 📠 on the Form View toolbar.

When you have the Database window open, you can then select
and open any of the objects in the database. Selecting objects
will be discussed in the "Select Objects Using the Objects Bar"
section later in this chapter.

Creating a blank database enables you to create an empty database "container" that you can then fill with your own custom objects such as tables, forms, and reports. You can create a blank database from the Access dialog box (when you first start Access) or from inside the Access application window.

Create a Blank Database

Follow these steps to create a blank Access database:

1. With the Microsoft Access dialog box on the screen, click the Blank Access Database option button, and then click OK.

    Alternatively, in the Access application window, click 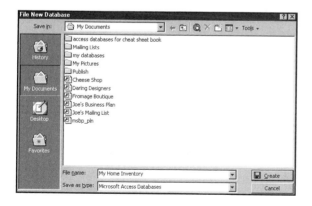 New on the Database toolbar. Then select the General tab on the New dialog box and double-click the Database icon.

2. Enter a name for your file in the File Name text box in the File New Database dialog box.

3. Click the Save In drop down button and select the drive you want to save the file on.

4. After you've selected the drive, a list of the folders on that drive will appear in the folder box. Double-click the folder you want to use, and click Create. A new Database window will appear in the Access application window.

25

Select Objects Using the Objects Bar

After you have created a new database (such as tables, forms, queries and reports), Access gives you the ability to quickly select and open objects in the database using the Objects bar. The Objects bar appears on the left side of the Database window.

Each Database window is divided into two panes: the Objects bar and the Objects pane, which contains a list of the objects in a particular object category. For example, click Tables in the Objects bar to list the tables in the database in the Objects pane.

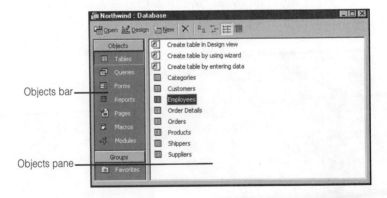

When an object is selected in the Objects pane, you can open the object, view the object in its design view, or delete the object. To select an object, follow these steps:

1. Open a database that contains several database objects. (If you haven't created your own database with objects yet, open the Northwind database that is provided as a sample database with the Access software.)

2. To open an object, such as a form, table, or report in the database, click the name of the object—Form in this example—on the Objects bar.

3. Select a particular form in the Objects pane (such as Customers).

4. To open the form, double-click Forms or click ▦ Open at the top-left of the Database window.

5. When you finish viewing a particular object, click its close box in the upper-right corner of its window.

Deleting an Access object is very straightforward. However, be advised that when you delete an object, there is no way to undo the deletion. Be particularly careful about deleting tables. You will lose any data that you entered into the tables.

To delete an object, follow these steps:

1. Click the appropriate object type using the Objects bar (such as Reports).

2. Click the object that you want to delete in the Objects pane (such as a particular report).

3. Press Delete. You will be asked if you want to permanently delete the object. Click Yes if you are certain you no longer want that object. Objects can also be deleted by using the Delete icon ✕ or by clicking Edit on the menu bar and choosing Delete.

Database toolbar buttons provide you with different views of the objects on a Database window tab.

27

Print Database Objects

The fastest way to print a database object is to select the object in the Database window and then click 🖨 Print on the Database toolbar.

Click the mouse pointer to zoom in and out on your object in the Print Preview window.

You can also preview the printout of any of your database objects by clicking 🔍 Print Preview on the Database or object-specific toolbar (such as the Table toolbar).

When you are ready to print the object, click 🖨 Print on the Print Preview toolbar.

If you want more control over the print job, such as which printer you will print to or what paper size you want to use, you must access the Print Dialog box:

1. In the Database window, select the object that you want to print.

2. Select the File menu, and then select Print. The Print dialog appears.

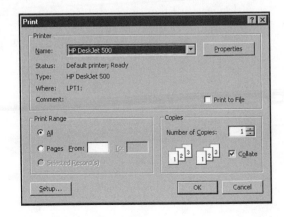

3. Use the Name drop-down list to select the printer you want to print to.

4. If you've selected certain records in a table for printing, click the Selected Record(s) option button.

5. For objects that contain multiple pages (particularly a report), click the Pages option button and set a page print range when you only want to print selected pages found in the object.

6. When you have completed making your choices in the Print dialog, click OK to send the print job to the printer.

Objects such as forms, tables, queries and reports can also be printed when you have that object open. Click 🖨 Print on the particular object's toolbar (such as the Form toolbar or the Table toolbar) to print it.

TAKE THE TEST

Task 1

In this practice exercise, you will work with features related to Objective 6, "Create a Database (using a Wizard or in Design View)." Because you will build both of these databases from scratch, there is not an accompanying database file on the book CD.

1. Create a new database using the Access Database Wizard. Base the new database on the Contact Management template.

2. Save the file as `Mica Steel Contacts.mdb`.

3. Create a blank database using the blank Database template that Access provides.

4. Name the database `My Home Inventory.mdb`.

Task 2

In this practice exercise, you will work with features related to Objective 7, "Select an object using the Objects Bar". Copy the `Practice2.mdb` database from the CD to a folder on your computer. Open the `Practice2.mdb` database in Access.

1. Open the Customer Orders report.

2. Close the report and return to the Database window.

3. Open the Products table.

4. Close the table.

5. Open the Suppliers form.

6. Delete the form.

Open the database `practice2fin.mdb` on the CD to view the results of the exercises in this task.

Task 3

In this practice exercise, you will work with features related to Objective 8, "Print database objects (tables, forms, reports, queries)". Copy the `Practice2.mdb` database from the CD to a folder on your computer. Open the `Practice 2.mdb` database in Access to complete the following exercises:

1. Select the Customers form in the database. Print Preview the form.

2. Open the Customers table in the database and print the table.

3. Open the Customer Orders Report in Print Preview. Print the Report.

Because this task only produces printouts, your hard copies will serve as the solution to the exercises.

Cheat Sheet

Create a New Database

Using a Wizard:

1. File, New (Ctrl+N).

2. Select the databases tab, and double-click a selected template.

3. Provide a name and location for the new database; click Create. Then follow the prompts.

Using the Blank database template:

1.

2. Select the general tab, and double-click the Database icon.

3. Provide a name and location for the new database, and then click Create.

Select an Object Using the Objects Bar

In the Database window, click the Object type icon on the Objects bar, and then click the object in the Objects pane.

Open, view, or delete a selected Object.

Print an Object

In the Database window, select the object and Print.

Print Preview.

File, Print opens the Print Dialog.

Building Tables

This chapter covers four of the required objectives for the Access 2000 Exam:

- Create table structure
- Use multiple data types
- Set primary keys
- Create tables by using the Table Wizard

Create Table Structure

Access tables, the basic building block of your databases, are arranged in a column and row format that looks very much like a spreadsheet. This *spreadsheet* view of a table is called a *datasheet*. Each row in the table is called a record. A particular record holds information that relates to a particular person or thing. For instance, a customer table holds records (rows) for each of your customers.

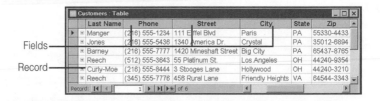

Records consist of more discrete pieces of information called fields. The columns in the table serve as the fields and hold information such as a customer name or address. Each column in the table has a field heading. The field (column) heading, known as the *field selector* (when you click it to select the field), has a name that describes the field's content.

You can choose any of three methods to create a table in Access: using the Design view, using the wizard, or entering data (entering data means you create a new blank datasheet and then immediately begin to do data entry). The most flexible way to create the structure for a new table is in the table Design view. The Design view enables you to select the names you want to use for the fields in the table and all the parameters related to the fields such as data type and field size.

To create a table in Design view, complete the following steps:

1. Create a new database or open an existing database. Select the Tables icon on the Objects bar in the Database window.

2. Double-click the Create Table in Design view shortcut in the Objects pane to open a new blank table.

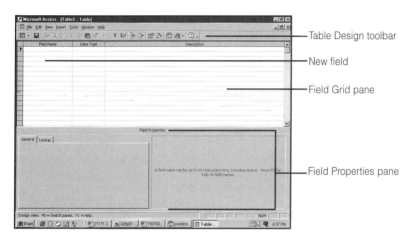

The Table Design view provides you with all the tools you need to design a new table. The Design view is divided into two panes: the Field Grid pane and the Field Properties pane.

The Field Grid pane is where you specify the fields that will be in the table. Each field must have a unique *Field Name* and a *Data Type*. The Field Name provides a label for the field. For instance, name a field "state" to specify where the state data would be entered in each record. Your Field Names can be a maximum of 64 characters and can include spaces.

Access suggests that spaces be avoided in Field Names if you are going to use them in formulas, expressions, or Modules. The caption or display name can have spaces with no problems.

You can set field-related items such as field size, caption, and format in the Field Properties portion of the Table window.

To set up a new field in the Table Design view, make sure that the insertion point is in the first row of the Table Design area. Type the field name and press Tab or Enter to advance to the Data Type column. Tab again to the Description field.

Map out your table fields on a piece of paper before creating the table to make sure that you have all the fields you will need.

Use Multiple Data Types

After naming a field, you progress to the Data Type column where a drop-down box arrow appears. To select the field type for the field, click the Data Type drop-down box arrow to select the appropriate data type from the list. The Data Type column displays your selection.

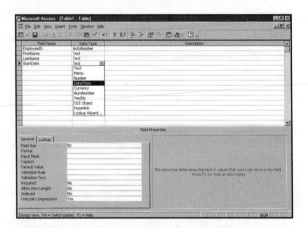

The data type for a field should be related to the kind of information that you want to enter in that field. Access provides ten different data types, described in the following table. Sample Fields are also provided for each Data Type.

Data Type	Description Is Limited To	Sample Fields
Text	Alphanumeric (text) or numeric entries, a text field can contain up to 255 characters.	Name Address
Memo	Lengthy text entries, the field size can be as great as 64,000 characters.	Comments Notes
Number	Numeric information, this data type will not accept non-numerical entries such as text.	Number in Stock Field Number Ordered Field
Date/Time	Date and Time values, will display date and time information in a particular format.	Date Hired Field Order Date Field
Currency	Monetary values, formats number as currency.	Available Credit Field Item Price Field
AutoNumber	Unique sequential number automatically assigned by Access when a record is added.	Customer Number Field Order Number Field
Yes/No	Answers a question with one of two values such as True/False, Yes/No, or On/Off, field can be toggled between yes and no.	Order Filled Field Customer Contacted Field
OLE Object	Object Linking and Embedding field, enables you to link or embed an object from another software program such as a picture, spreadsheet, or other file type.	Employee Photo (embedded picture) Current Sales Chart Field (linked Excel Chart)
Hyperlink	Enables you to jump from the current field to another file or location on the Internet.	Suppliers Web Page Field Part Specifications Field (hyperlink to spreadsheet file)
LookUp Wizard	Provides a list of values for the field, this field type enables you to select the field values from a list based on another field column in a table or query, or a list that you create. The LookUp Wizard is not really a field type but a tool that helps provide you with a list of values for the field.	SuppliersID Field ProductSKU# Field

It is important that you select the appropriate data type for the fields in your table; for instance, fields holding text would have the Text data type. A field that will hold numerical values (values that have mathematical significance such as number of items) would be set up as a Number data type. Dollar or Euro figures can be designated as Currency. Press Enter or Tab to advance to the Description column.

The information that you place in the Description column will appear on the status bar of the Table window when you are in the Datasheet view and enter the field.

After you finish entering the fields for your new table, you might be asked to change the properties associated with a particular field, such as the field's size. The modification of field parameters will be covered in Chapter 6, "Modifying Tables II—Table Structure Modification."

Set Primary Keys

As you set up the fields for your new table, you must make sure to create a field that uniquely identifies each of the records that will eventually appear in the table. This field is called the *Primary Key*. The primary key must contain a unique entry for each and every record in the table.

In an Employee table, you might think that a last name field would suffice as a key field. However, remember that last names can be repeated in a table. Having more than one Smith or Jones in the table makes the last name field inappropriate for the primary key. Fields such as Employee ID, customer number, product code—fields that assign a unique number or identity code to each record—make excellent primary keys.

To designate a field as the primary key, complete the following steps:

1. Place the insertion point in the field row that you want to designate as the primary key. This will be an existing field.

2. Click ⚷ Primary Key on the Table Design toolbar.

A key icon appears next to the field you've designated as the key field. If you inadvertently assign the primary key status, click ⚷ Primary Key again (toggle) to remove and then reset the key icon to the appropriate field.

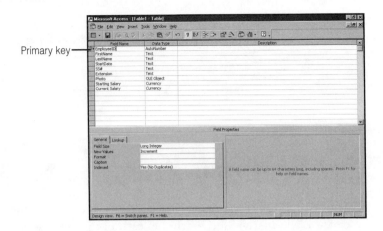

Primary key

To ensure that primary key fields have a unique value entered during the data entry process, use the AutoNumber data type. Access then creates a new incremented number when a new record is created.

It's very important to save the table structure for the new table as soon as you begin to enter the field names and data types. You don't want to lose any of your work if the machine locks up or your electricity goes off. (Access requires you to save the table before you exit the Design view, regardless). To save the new table, follow these steps:

1. Click ⊞ Save on the Table Design toolbar. The Save As box will appear.

2. Enter an appropriate name for the new table in Save As, and then click OK to save the table.

If the test asks you to create a table, pay close attention to the name requested. Until the table is saved, the exam won't be able to find your answer. Pay close attention to whether the test wants the table in Design or Table view.

Create Tables by Using the Table Wizard

The Table Wizard enables you to create a new table using a list of sample tables and the fields that you would typically find in them. You select a particular sample table type and then determine which of the sample fields you want to include in your new table.

Open the database you want to create the new table in. The exam will ask you to use the wizard to create a specific type of table. Familiarize yourself with the samples under the both the Business and Personal options. To create the table using the Table Wizard, complete the following steps:

Select Tables and Fields

1. Click the Table icon on the Objects bar in the Database window, and double-click the Create Table By Using Wizard shortcut to begin using the wizard.

2. Click one of the tables in the Sample Tables drop-down box. The fields available in the sample table appear in the Sample Fields box.

3. Select a field in the Sample Fields box and then click the Add button to add the field to the Fields in My New Table box. Click the Add All button to add all the fields to your table.

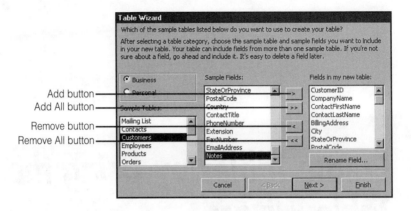

4. If you want to rename any of the fields you place in the Fields in My New Table box, select the field and then click the Rename Field button.

5. A Rename Field box will appear. Type the new name in the text box and click OK to continue.

   The fields can, of course, be renamed later in Design view.

6. Click the Next button when you complete the selection of all your fields for your new table.

Name Table and Set Primary Key

On the next screen you are asked to provide a name for your table. This screen also asks whether you want Access to select the Primary Key for you or you want to select it yourself. Follow these steps:

1. Type a new name to replace the default that Access has placed in the Name text box.

2. Select either the Yes, Set a Primary Key for Me option button, or the No, I'll Set the Primary Key option button. If you select Yes, the primary key is set for you, and you are taken to the final Wizard screen when you click the Next button.

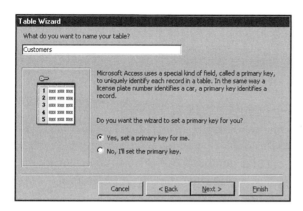

3. If you select No, you will be taken to a screen where you must set the primary key. Use the field drop-down box to select the primary key field.

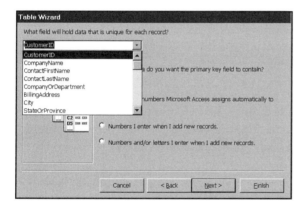

4. Click the Next button after making your choice.

If you selected the Yes, Set a Primary Key for Me option button, the next screen asks you if any relationships exist between the new table and tables already in the database; click Next to continue with the table creation process. Table relationships and how to create them will be covered in Chapter 9, "Defining Relationships: Building a Relationship Database."

If you selected the No, I'll Set the Primary Key option button, the next screen asks you to select a field to serve as the primary key and choose a data type for the key field. You choose the primary key in the drop-down list box provided.

Three data types are provided for your primary key:

- Consecutive numbers Microsoft Access assigns automatically to new records. Choose this if your primary key field is a simple record number that can be assigned consecutively by Access as you enter the data in the records.

- Numbers I enter when I add new records. Choose this if you want to enter your own numbers for the records. This choice precludes you from entering any alphanumeric characters (letters of the alphabet) in this field. This data type works well for license numbers or product numbers such as numerical bar codes.

- Number and/or letter I enter when I add new records. Choose this data type if you want to enter your own identification numbers that are a combination of text and numbers.

After selecting the primary key and the data type, click the Next button to continue. You will be asked about table relationships in the database as previously discussed. Click Next to continue.

The Finish screen provides you with three options:

- Modify the table design. This takes you into the Table Design view so that you can modify the new table's structure.

- Enter data directly into the table. This takes you to the Table Datasheet view, where you can begin to enter records into the table.

- Enter data into the table using a form the wizard creates for me. This choice will create a form that enables you to enter data as you view only one record at a time. Forms and how to create them will be covered in Chapter 11, "Building and Modifying Forms II."

After making your choice, click the Finish button to end the table creation process and jump to the option that you selected.

TAKE THE TEST

In this practice exercise, you will work with features related to Objectives 9, "Create Table Structure," 10, "Use Multiple Data types," and 11, "Set Primary Keys." Copy the `practice3.mdb` database from the CD-ROM that accompanies this book to a folder on your computer using the Windows Explorer. Open the database.

1. Create a new table in the Design view using the information in the table that follows.

Field Name	Data Type	Description
EmployeeID	AutoNumber	Automatically assigns a number to each employee
First Name	Text	
Last Name	Text	
Department Code	Text	
Phone Extension	Text	Enter three-character extension
Home Address	Text	
City	Text	
State	Text	Enter two-digit abbreviation
Zip	Text	
Home Phone	Text	
Salary	Currency	

2. Set the EmployeeID field as the Primary Key.

3. Name the table **Employees**.

To view the solutions to this task, open the database
practice3fin.mdb on the CD-ROM. Look at Employees table.

Task 2

In this practice exercise, you will work with features related to
Objective 12, "Create Tables by Using the Table Wizard."
Open the Practice3.mdb database.

1. Create a second table using the Table Wizard.

2. Use the Suppliers table in the Wizard's Sample Table box
   to provide your list of sample fields.

3. Include the following fields in your table: **SupplierID**,
   SupplierName, **ContactName**, **Address**, **City**,
   PostalCode, **StateOrProvince**, **PhoneNumber**, and
   FaxNumber.

4. Rename the StateOrProvince field **State**.

5. Name the table **Current Suppliers**.

6. Have the Table Wizard open the new table in the Design
   view when you click the Finish button.

To view the solutions to this task, open the database
practice3fin.mdb on the CD-ROM and look at Current
Suppliers table.

Cheat Sheet

Create Table Structure

Open or create a new database. Double-click **Create Table in Design View** in the Database window. Supply field names as needed.

Use Multiple Data Types

In the Table Design view, click the Data Type column and select a data type from the drop-down list.

Set Primary Keys

In the Design view, click the field that will serve as the key field. Click ⚷.

Create Tables by Using the Table Wizard

In the Database window, double-click Create Table by Using Wizard. Select a sample table and add fields to the new table. Follow the wizard prompts.

Building Tables II: Entering Data

- Enter records using a datasheet
- Navigate through records in a table, query, or form
- Enter records using a form

13

Enter Records Using a Datasheet

Open the Database

After you create a table in the Design view or by using the Table Wizard, you are ready to begin the data entry process. Open the database that contains the table that will hold the new data and select the Table icon in the Database window. Double-click the table that you will enter the data into.

You might want to maximize the table by clicking its Windows Maximize button.

Enter the Data

To enter data in the table, complete the following steps:

1. Click the first empty field for the record you want to enter data for.

2. Type the data for the field. If you make a data entry error in a field, press the Backspace key to delete the character to the left of the insertion point. Press the Tab or the Enter key to advance to the next field.

3. Enter the appropriate data in the field. Continue to advance through the fields using the Tab key. Complete the records that you have data for.

4. If you need to move back a field and reenter data, press Shift+Tab.

One thing to keep in mind as you enter your data is any AutoNumber fields you've placed in the table. If you've set up an AutoNumber field (such as customer number or employee ID) to automatically enter sequential numbers for the records, you don't need to type a value in those cells.

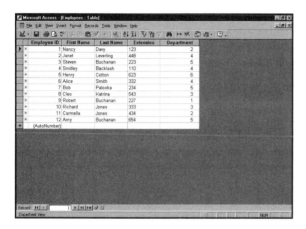

Entering data is really nothing more or less than taking the time to get all the information into your database tables. It is certainly the least glamorous and most time-intensive aspect of building databases. There are, however, some data entry tricks that can be used to lighten the typing that takes place. You might be asked to enter data during the exam, and every minute you can save gives you more time to do the more difficult tasks.

Data Entry Tricks

- If you need to enter the current date into a field, press Ctrl+; (semicolon).

- If a certain value already exists in your table, you can copy and paste it into another field. Use the Tab to move to the field information you want to copy (it will be automatically selected), and then press Ctrl+C to copy the data. Move to the field you want to paste the information into, and press Ctrl+V to paste the data. More about moving and copying data will be covered in Chapter 5, "Modifying Tables: Data Modification."

- If you have entered data in a field in a record (such as the State field) and want to place the same data in the field in the next record, press Ctrl+' (apostrophe). The data will be repeated automatically.

- Use field masks to enter repeating values. When you create your fields during the table design process, you can create a field mask for a field; the mask will enter repeating display characters. An example would be the parentheses around a phone number's area code: (216)555-1212. You will learn how to create field masks in Chapter 6, "Modifying Tables II: Table Structure Modification."

Save Changes

When you enter data into a table, your natural inclination is to click 🖫 Save on the Table Datasheet toolbar to save the information. This is not necessary, however. As soon as you enter information into a field and then advance to the next field, the data is saved to the database table.

Obviously, if you use other applications, such as Word or Excel, you have gotten into the habit of saving your valuable work. The fact that Access is automatically saving your data entry takes some getting used to. You will, however, have to save any changes that you make to a table's structure. This includes things such as widening a field column or moving a field. Always click the 🖫 Save button after making structural changes to a table.

Navigate Through Records in a Table, Query, or Form

After you've entered data into the table, you will want to move about the datasheet to view its contents. Be sure to follow the directions given in the exam. If you are asked to navigate to a location in the database, it is usually necessary to leave the table so that the final results can be seen. In other words, don't go to a location and then go back to the first record unless asked to do so.

Use the Keyboard

The Tab and Shift+Tab will move you one field at a time through the table either forward or backward respectively. Table 4.1 is a summary of other keyboard shortcuts for moving around in a table.

Keystrokes	Results
Tab	One field forward
Shift+Tab	One field back
Up Arrow	One field up
Down Arrow	One field down
Ctrl+Down Arrow	Same field in the last record
Ctrl+Up Arrow	Same field in the first record
Home	First field in a record
End	Last field in a record

continues

53

Continued

Keystrokes	Results
Page Up	Up one screen of records
Page Down	Down one screen of records
Ctrl+Home	First field in the first record
Ctrl+End	Last field in the last record

Use the Mouse

You can also navigate through a table using the mouse. A set of navigation buttons are provided at the bottom left corner of the table window.

These naviga-tion buttons are particu-larly useful when you have a table that holds a large number of records.

First Record button
Previous Record

New Record
Last Record
Next Record

Enter Records Using a Form

As you enter data in the datasheet view, you might find that as the number of records increases, the more difficult it becomes to concentrate on the information that must be placed in each field. Forms are actually a better venue for entering data than attempting to navigate through a large database.

An AutoForm feature is available that you can use to help you focus on one record at a time during the data entry process. AutoForm creates a form that includes all the fields in the current table. The form also only shows you one record at a time, enabling you to focus on the data for that particular record.

Use Autoform

To create an AutoForm for data entry, complete the following steps:

1. Click the ▦ New Object drop-down arrow on the Table toolbar. A list of possible new objects is displayed.

2. Click on AutoForm on the menu list. Immediately, a generic form appears in the Access window. The form incorporates all the fields from the table.

Each record in the table appears separately on the form. The new form has the same set of navigation buttons in the form window's lower left corner that was found in the Table window. You can use these buttons to navigate through the records that are contained in your database table. You can also use the keyboard shortcuts to navigate through the forms. (see Objective 14, "Navigate Through Records in a Table, Query, or Form".)

Enter a New Record

If you want to enter a new record using the form, click the New Record button. (It's the navigation button with the asterisk on it.) A blank form appears. Enter the data in the new record as you would enter data in a table. Use the Tab key to move to the next field or the Shift+Tab to move to the previous field.

When you have completed entering your data using the AutoForm, you can close it and return to the table. Click the form's × (Close) button in the upper-right corner of the form box.

Close and Save

When you close the form, a message box appears, and Access gives you the option of saving the AutoForm or closing it without saving.

If you select Yes, a Save As dialog box appears and prompts you to enter a name for the form. After entering the name, click OK. The form is saved and appears on the Forms tab of the Database Window. If you select No, the form is closed without saving.

Update the Table

When you close the data entry form, you will notice that records that were added using the form do not appear in the table. You must update the table.

Click anywhere in the table. Press Shift+F9 (function key). Records entered using the AutoForm will now appear in the table.

TAKE THE TEST

In this practice task, you will work with features related to Objective 13, "Enter Records Using a Datasheet," and Objective 15, "Enter Records Using a Form." Because it is a basic skill, Objective 14, "Navigate Through Records in a Table, Query, or Form," will also be covered in this task.

Copy the practice4.mdb database from the CD that accompanies this book (you will find the file in the Chapter 4 folder) to a folder on your computer. Then open the database.

1. Open the table Customers and enter the data shown in the table.

Cust No	FName	LName	Address	City	State	Postal Code
1	Pierre	Manger	111 Eiffel Blvd.	Paris	MN	55330-4433
2	Janet	Dugong	12 Coastal Way	Waterford	NC	44240-5567
3	Bob	Jones	1340 America Dr.	Crystal	NV	35012-6894
4	Alice	Barney	4443 Maine Ave.	Spokane	WA	65437-1234
5	Kim	Reech	55 Platinum St.	Los Angeles	CA	85434-9354

2. In the practice4 database, open the Suppliers table. Use the keyboard shortcuts outlined in this chapter and the navigation buttons to move through the records and fields in the table.

3. Open the Customers table and use the AutoForm feature to create a data entry form for the Customers table. Enter the following data using this form.

Cust No	FName	LName	Address	City	State	Postal Code
6	Larry	Smith	1314 Mockingbird Lane	St. Paul	MN	55110-4563

4. Save the AutoForm as **Customers Form**.

5. Update the table. Print the table.

Open the database `practice4fin.mdb` on the CD-ROM accompanying this book to see a completed version of the Customers table you worked with in this practice.

Cheat Sheet

Enter Records Using a Datasheet

1. Open the appropriate table in the datasheet view.

2. Click the first field of the empty record that appears in the table.

3. Enter the first field's data.

4. Press Tab to move to the next field.

Navigate Through Records in a Table, Query, or Form

- **Tab** to move forward.

- **Shift+Tab** to move backwards.

- Click the navigation buttons at the bottom left of the table, query, or form.

Create an AutoForm

New Object.

Enter Records Using the Form

Click the New Record button on the record navigation bar, and then enter the appropriate data in each field.

Modifying Tables: Data Modification

This chapter covers two of the required objectives for the Access 2000 Exam. It also covers some basic Access skills that are closely associated with these exam objectives.

- Delete Records from a Table

- Insert New Records

- Delete a Field

- Use the Office Clipboard

Deleting records and using the Clipboard are listed as test objectives. Inserting records and deleting fields in a table are skills that everyone should know so they can perform maintenance chores.

16

Delete Records from a Table

After you enter data into a table, you will find that the data remains fairly dynamic, especially in cases where you are maintaining a business related database. New customers and new products are added to your database, and information within each record changes and needs to be edited. You might also have situations where an entire record is no longer valid (such as the record for a customer who no longer uses your services). Access gives you the capability to delete entire records from a table. To delete a record, complete the following steps:

1. Click the record's selection button, or with the insertion point in a record, click the Edit menu, and then select Record. All the fields in the record are selected.

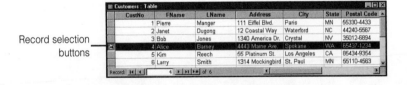

Record selection buttons

2. Click ✖ Delete Record on the Table Datasheet toolbar or press Delete on the keyboard.

3. A message box appears, telling you that the selected record will be deleted if you continue. Click OK. The record is removed from the table.

You can also delete a record without selecting it. Click any field of the record, then select the Edit menu, and then select Delete Record. This will not work for tables that are in a relationship with another table where referential integrity has been enforced; see Chapter 9, "Defining Relationships: Building a Relational Database," for more information.

Be aware that after you delete a record from the table, you cannot use the Undo feature to get it back. Deleting a record from a table is permanent.

To delete several records (the records must be contiguous), click the first record and then press Shift and click the last record in the series. All the records in between will also be selected. Then press Delete. A message box will appear, telling you that the selected records will be deleted if you continue. Click OK. The records will all be removed from the table.

AutoNumber does not reuse numbers that have been deleted from the table.

63

Insert New Records

New records are added automatically in the last row of a table. You can't insert new records between existing ones. However, you can sort records in any order you want, which you will learn in Chapter 7, "Viewing and Organizing Information: Sorting Records." Complete the following steps to insert a new record:

1. Click the New Record button (it's the table navigation button with the asterisk on it). Then click the first field of the new record and enter the appropriate field data. (If the first field is an AutoNumber, you cannot add a new number yourself. You must start entering data in some other field.)

2. Complete the data entry in the new record (fill in the last field or tab or use the Enter key). This will place another new record in the table. Alternatively, you can also repeat Step 1 if you want to add additional records.

3. (Optional) You can also select the Records menu and then select Data Entry. This will hide the current records in the table and place you in a blank record row. Enter the date into the fields of the record.

4. To return all the records to the Datasheet view (including the new records), click the Records menu, and then select Remove Filter/Sort.

Delete a Field

You can delete a field from a table in the Datasheet view. This will delete all the data in this field in all the records in the table. Deleting an entire field obviously has a dramatic effect on the table (and you cannot undo the deletion of a field in the datasheet view). To delete a field column from the table, complete the following steps:

Deleting a field column from a table removes a field from the table's structure.

1. Click any field in the column you want to remove.

2. Click the Edit menu, select Delete Column. Click Yes to delete the column at the prompt if you are sure you want to remove all the data in that column.

To remove contiguous fields from a table, follow these steps:

1. Click the first field heading and then press Shift and click the last field column heading. Use the Edit menu to remove a group of fields as you did a single field.

2. Access warns you that the field and all the data that it holds will be deleted, which means all the data in this field in each record. If you want to delete the field column, click Yes in the dialog box. The column is removed from the table.

When columns are deleted in Datasheet View, Access automatically saves the new layout. When fields are deleted in Design view, the table must be saved.

65

Use the Office Clipboard

An excellent way to ensure that data you enter in a table is accurate is to copy information from another record or field. This saves you time and gets the data into the appropriate field quickly. The easiest way to select an entire field is to place the mouse pointer on the left side of the field until the pointer becomes a large plus symbol. Click once to select all the text in the field. Follow these steps:

1. Select the field or content you want to move or copy. Click the Edit menu, and select Cut or Copy.

2. Click the field you want to paste the information into (select the field's data if the paste is to replace the entire entry), then click the Edit menu, and select Paste.

You can also cut, copy, and paste using the Table toolbar buttons. Keyboard shortcuts are also available for cut, copy, and paste.

Command	Keyboard	Toolbar Button
Copy	Ctrl+C	
Cut	Ctrl+X	
Paste	Ctrl+V	

When you select data and then cut or copy it, the data is placed on the Office Clipboard. The Office 2000 Clipboard actually enables you to keep several items on the Clipboard at a time (up to 12 items), which enables you to actually compile a list of items that you want to paste into your table or tables, and then paste the appropriate item as needed. This is a huge improvement over the way the Clipboard worked in past versions of Office, where you could only keep one item on the Clipboard at a time.

To use the Clipboard as a docking place for several copied or cut items, follow these steps:

1. Right-click any of the Access toolbars (such as the Table toolbar or the Form toolbar), and then select Clipboard from the shortcut menu. The Clipboard toolbar appears in the Access application window as an undocked toolbar.

2. Copy or Cut any item in a table (after selecting an item, you can click 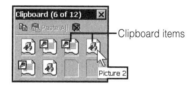 Copy on the Clipboard). The copied or cut item (such as a field) appears as an icon on the Clipboard.

3. Copy or cut other items as needed. Each item appears as an icon on the Clipboard.

Clipboard items

4. When you are ready to paste a particular item from the Clipboard, place the insertion point into the field using the I-beam.

   To identify the contents of an icon in the Clipboard, hold the pointer over the icon to read its screentip preview information (up to 50 characters). When you locate the appropriate icon, click it. The item is pasted into the appropriate field at the insertion point.

Because the Office Clipboard functions in each of the Office applications (Access, Word, Excel, and so on), you can actually cut or copy items from more than one application to the Clipboard. This enables you to paste items from Excel or Word into your Access tables.

TAKE THE TEST

Task 1

In this practice task, you will work with features related to Objective 16, "Delete Records from a Table." Copy the Practice5.mdb database from the CD-ROM that accompanies this book (you will find the file in the Chapter 5 folder) to a folder on your computer. Then open the database.

1. Open the table Customers and delete record 2.

2. In the same table, delete record 5.

To view the solutions to this task, open the database practice5fin.mdb on the CD-ROM and then open the Customers table.

Task 2

In this practice task, you will work with features related to Objective 17, "Insert New Records." Open the Practice5.mdb database.

1. Open the Customers table and insert a new record.

2. Enter the appropriate data into the appropriate field using the following information (the remainder of the information will be pasted into the record in Task 4).

Company Name	First Name	Last Name	Address	City	Phone Number	Email Address
Ace Cleaners	Joe	Barnes	111 2nd Ave	St. Cloud	(612) 555-4444	barnes@ ace.com

To view the solution to this task, open the database practice5fin.mdb on the CD-ROM and then open the Customers table.

In this practice task, you will work with features related to Objective 18, "Delete a Field." Open the Practice5.mdb database.

1. Open the customer table and delete the Fax Number field column.

2. If you deleted the field in Design view, save changes that you have made to the table's structure.

To view the solutions to this task, open the database practice5fin.mdb on the CD-ROM and then open the Customers table.

In this practice task, you will work with features related to Objective 19, "Use the Office Clipboard." Open the Practice5.mdb database.

1. Open the Customers table.

2. Copy the field information **MN** and the postal code **55101-8954** to the Office Clipboard from record 3.

3. From the Office Clipboard, paste **MN** into the State field and **55101-8954** into the postal code field of the Joe Barnes record (the record you added in Task 2).

To view the solutions to this task, open the database practice5fin.mdb on the CD-ROM and then open the Customers table.

Cheat Sheet

Delete Records from a Table

1. Place the insertion point in record.
2. Click ⚔ or press **Delete** (Ctrl+X).
3. Click Yes.

Insert a New Record

Click the **New Record** button (*).

Alternatively, click the first field and enter data.

Delete a Field

Select the field, select **Edit**, **Delete Column**, and then click **Yes**.

Use the Office Clipboard

1. Right-click any toolbar to open the Clipboard toolbar.
2. Copy (Ctrl+C) or Cut (Ctrl+X) items to the Clipboard.
3. Place an insertion point in the table for a paste destination, and then click the item icon on the Clipboard toolbar or press (Ctrl+V) to paste the last copied or cut item.

Modifying Tables II— Table Structure Modification

Following is a list of MOUS Objectives:

- Modify Tables Using Design View
- Modify Field Properties
- Use the Lookup Wizard
- Use the Input Mask Wizard
- Change Field Column Widths
- Change the Font for a Table

20

Modify Tables Using Design View

In Chapter 5, "Modifying Tables: Data Modification," you primarily worked with an Access table in the Datasheet view, which provides the basic workspace that you use to enter, edit, and view your database data. Although structural modifications can be made to the table in the Datasheet view (such as moving a field in the table, changing the column widths of the table, or changing the row height of a particular record—which are discussed later in this chapter), the best place to make major modifications to table and field parameters is the Design view.

Switch to Design View

To switch to the Design view, click 🖼 View on the Table toolbar. In the Design view, the fields are arranged in rows in the Field Grid box. Each field has a field selection button (the gray box) just to the left of the field's name. You can use the field selection box to select a field for deletion, to insert a new field at that position (the selected field will move down one row in the table hierarchy), or to select a field and then move it to a different position in the table hierarchy.

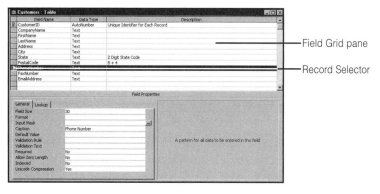

Field Grid pane

Record Selector

You can also modify any basic parameters related to the fields in the table, such as the field name, the data type, or the description of the field.

Move a Field

Rearranging the fields in a table enables you to optimize the table for data entry. For example, you will want to have a table structure where the sequence of information is arranged in a logical fashion as you read it from left to right in the Datasheet view. Name, followed by company information, followed by address information is the typical sequence for a customer or client's table. However, if you find that you use the customer's phone information a great deal, you might want to move that particular field closer to the name information, making it easy for you to quickly view a customer's name and phone number as you prepare to phone him. This is a basic skill and as such it is fair game to be included in the exam.

To move a field in the Design view, complete the following steps:

1. Click the row selector button for the field. The entire field row is selected.

2. Drag the field to the new location. Place it on top of the field that currently holds the position you want it to occupy. The field currently in the position will move down one row.

3. Click 💾 **Save** on the toolbar to save this layout change.

Add a Field
Fields can also be easily added or deleted in the Design view. This enables you not only to add the field but also to select parameters related to the field such as data type, field size, and whether the field uses an input mask. To add a field in the Design view, follow these steps:

1. Select a row in the Field Grid box. The new field is entered above the selected row.

2. Select the **Insert** menu and then **Rows**, or click the **Insert Rows** button on the Design toolbar. A blank field appears and the selected row moves down.

3. Enter a Field Name, Data Type, and Description for the field.

New field —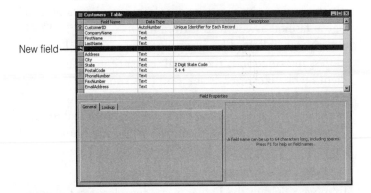

Delete a Field
Deleting a field is as straightforward as adding a field. Follow these steps:

1. Select a field in the Field Grid box.

2. Press the **Delete** key, or select the **Edit** menu and then **Delete**.

3. You will be asked if you want to permanently delete the selected field or fields. Any data residing in the table in that field will also be deleted. Click **Yes** to delete the field.

Modify Field Properties

Regardless of whether you create a table from scratch or use the Table Wizard, the test might ask you to edit the field properties for some of the fields in the table. Field properties are changed in the Table Design view.

Field Properties can affect the way the data entered in the field looks or limit the number of characters that can be placed in a field. For instance, the Field Size determines the maximum number of characters that can be placed in a text or number field during data entry.

The Field Properties that you can set in the Field Properties pane go way beyond simple items such as field size and format. You can set default values for a field and even set validation rules that only allow a certain range of values to be entered in the cell.

The default field size for text fields is 50 characters; the maximum field size for a text field is 255 characters.

Field size cannot be changed for Time/Date fields or Currency fields. Their field size is handled by their format (see the section "Change Field Format" in this chapter).

Setting the field size for number fields can be important depending on the size of the number you want to enter in the field. There are seven field sizes for numbers; their selection depends on the range of numeric values you want to store in the field. The default field size for a number field is Long Integer. The field sizes are as follows:

- **Byte**—Stores numbers from 0 to 255 (no fractions).

- **Integer**—Stores numbers from –32,768 to 32,767 (no fractions).

Change Field Size

Limiting the field size assists you in getting the appropriate kind of data into the field during data entry.

75

- **Long Integer**—Stores numbers from –2,147,483,648 to 2,147,483,647 (it does not handle fractions).

- **Single**—Stores numbers from –3.402823E38 to –1.401298E-45 for negative values and from 1.401298E-45 to 3.402823E38 for positive values.

- **Double**—Stores numbers from –1.79769313486231E308 to ∠4.94065645841247E–324 for negative values and from 1.79769313486231E308 to 4.94065645841247E–324 for positive values.

- **Replication ID**—This field size is only used when you have several copies of the database in different locations and the databases are synchronized periodically. Replication IDs play an important part in the synchronization. You will rarely, if ever, use this field size for a table, even in databases that are shared on a network.

- **Decimal**—Stores numbers from –10^38-1 through 10^38-1(.adp). Stores numbers from –10^28-1 through 10^28-1(.mdb)

To change the Field Size for a text field, make sure the field is currently active (the insertion point is in the field's row), and complete the following steps:

1. Double-click the Field Size box in the Field Properties pane to select the current field size.

2. Type the new field size.

For number and AutoNumber fields, click the drop-down arrow in the Field Size box and select the appropriate field size. After you have changed a field property, make sure you save the table. Click 🖫 **Save** on the Table Design toolbar.

Change Field Format

The Format property enables you to customize the way dates, times, numbers, and text are displayed in the table Datasheet view (or in forms or queries based on the table). For example, if you have a field that holds a date (such as the starting date for an employee), you can determine the format for how the date will be displayed in the table (and how the date will appear when you print the table).

Specifying a format for a particular field simply means that you predetermine the number of characters or how the data should appear when entered into the field. For instance, you might want characters entered into the State field to always appear in uppercase letters. By placing the greater than (>) sign in the Format box, you ensure that entries in the field always appear in uppercase.

Several special symbols can be used to format the text entered in text fields, as shown in the following table.

Symbol	Description	Example
@	Text character (either a character or a space) is required.	@@@-@@-@@@@ enter 555443333 appears as: 555-44-3333
&	Text character is optional.	ISBN 0-&&&&&&&&&-0 Both of the following are valid. ISBN 1-222333-444-9 and ISBN 1-874659237-6
<	Force all characters to lowercase.	< Enter cat or DOG appears as: cat, dog
>	Force all characters to uppercase.	> Enter mn or oH Appears as: MN, OH

To enter a format for a text field, type the format in the Field Properties pane Format box.

The Date, Number, and Currency data types have ready-made formats that can be selected in the Format box itself. To change the format for the date, number, or currency fields, follow these steps:

1. In the Field Grid box, click the field row for the field for which you want to modify the format.

2. Click the Format box in the Field Properties pane, and then click the drop-down arrow that appears. A list of formats for the field (based on the field type such as Date/Time) appears.

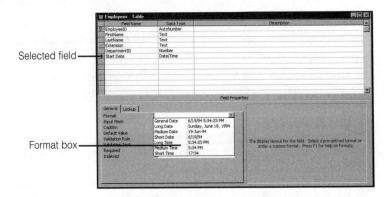

Selected field

Format box

3. Click the format that you want to use on the drop-down list.

4. Click 🖫 **Save** on the Design toolbar to save changes that you make to the field's properties.

Use a Caption

A caption is used to provide a name for a field when the table field is included on a form. You already know that by default the field's name will appear on the form. However, if you want to replace the field name with a different (more descriptive) name for use on a form, you use a caption. The caption replaces the default name of the field on the form.

For example, if you have a field called *custno* (which you used as an abbreviation for customer number) and you would like *customer number* to appear as the title of the field on a form (rather than the abbreviation) you enter **customer number** in the caption box in the Field properties pane. Using captions makes it easier for someone who did not create the database to do data entry because the type of value expected in the field is made obvious by the caption used.

To create a caption for a field, follow these steps:

1. In the Field Grid box, click the field row for the field for which you want to set the caption.

2. Click in the Caption box in the Field Properties pane.

3. Type a caption for the field.

4. Click 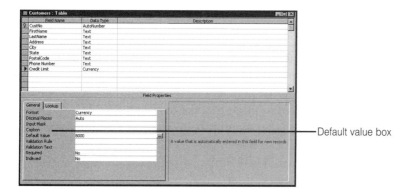 **Save** on the Design toolbar to save changes that you make to the field's properties.

Specifying a default value in a field property speeds data entry and specifies a value that is automatically entered into a particular field for new records. Setting a default value in a field does not preclude you from entering other values when you enter data in the table. It provides a possible value and should be set as the most likely entry to appear in that field.

Specify a Default Value in a Field

For example, if you have a credit limit field for your customers that is usually $8,000 (except in unusual circumstances); it makes sense to set 8,000 as the default value.

Follow these steps to assign a default value to a field:

1. In the Field Grid box, click the field row for the field for which you want to set the default value.

2. Click the Default Value box in the Field Properties pane.

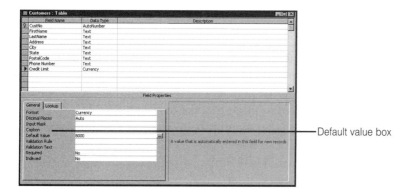

Default value box

3. Enter the default value for the field. You can enter text and/or numbers in the Default Value box. For instance, if most of your customers reside in Minnesota, you might want to put MN as the default value for the State field, or if the typical credit limit is $15,000, you would place 15,000 in the Default Value box for the Credit Limit Field.

4. Click the **Save** button on the Design toolbar to save changes that you make to the table structure.

When you return to the Datasheet view and enter new records, the default value appears in the field. To override the default value, select the default value and type a new value or text entry.

The following table gives examples of fields, their data types, and what the default value that you would set for them might look like (this is how the default value would be typed in the Default Value box).

Field	Data Type	Default Value
Items On Order	Number	50
Credit Limit	Currency	10000 The Currency data type will supply the dollar sign and decimal places for you.
Region	Text	Midwest
Title	Text	"Secretary, Department of the Interior" If a default value has punctuation in it, you must enclose the default value in quotation marks.
Order Date	Date	Date( ) This enters the current date.

Set Required Fields

You can also mark fields in a database table as required. This means that the field in the data must have data entered into it before you can proceed to another field. Although setting fields as required does not mean that the data in the field is correct, it does mean that an entry must be made in the field; it cannot be left blank. This is particularly useful in cases where you definitely require the data in a particular field, such as the social security field in an employee table.

To specify a required field, complete the following steps:

1. Open the table in the Design view; click the row of the field you want to make a required field.

2. In the Properties pane, click the Required box. A drop-down arrow appears. Click the arrow, and select Yes. The field is now required.

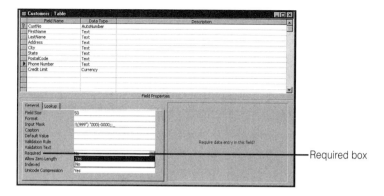
Required box

3. Save changes that you make to the table's structure. The Data integrity message box opens, notifying you that Data Integrity Rules have been changed; existing data might not be valid for new rules. You are given the option of having the fields currently in the table tested for data in the required field. If you want to check the fields, click Yes; if not, click No.

4. As you enter new records in the table, if you try to skip a required field, you will receive an error message stating that the required field cannot contain a null value. Access will not let you leave the record until you place a value in the required field.

Use the Lookup Wizard

An excellent way to ensure that the correct data is being entered into a field is the use of LookUp fields. A LookUp field provides you with a list of the legal data values during the data entry process. This list of legal values can be derived from information in another table—called a *LookUp list*—or from a list that you create during the creation of the LookUp field—called a *value list*.

If you want to use a LookUp list for your new Lookup field, there must be another table that shares the field that you plan to work with. For instance, an Orders table would contain a CustomerID field to identify what customer placed a particular order. You could use the CustomerID field in the Customers table as the LookUp list for your look-up field (CustomerID in the Orders table). Tables you have created relationships between supply you with the shared field you need to create look up fields.

If you want to create a Lookup field using a field that is not shared between tables, you will have to create a value list, which provides the legal values for the field.

When you create a new field or plan to edit an existing field to take advantage of the LookUp feature, you select LookUp Wizard from the Data Type drop-down box. The LookUp Wizard walks you through the LookUp creation process.

To create a LookUp field, follow these steps:

1. In the Table Design window, create a new field or select the field that you want to make a LookUp field.

2. Click the Data Type drop-down arrow and select LookUp Wizard from the list. The LookUp Wizard opens. In the first screen, you must determine whether the values will come from an existing field in another table or from a list you create. Click either I Want the Lookup Column to Lookup the Values in a Table or Query or I Will Type in the Values I Want. Click <u>N</u>ext to continue.

3. A list of the tables in your database appears (you can also select an option button to show the queries in the database or both the tables and queries). Select the table that contains the field (the primary key) that you will use for the Lookup list. After you select the appropriate option, click <u>N</u>ext to continue.

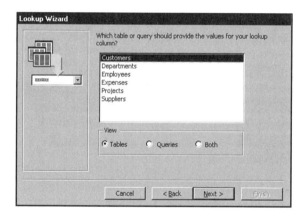

4. The next LookUp Wizard screen asks you to select the fields that you want to appear in the LookUp list. The list can contain more than one column. For instance, in the case of the Orders table, you want to place the CustomerID in the field that you are creating the LookUp list for. However, it will be easier to select the customer by their first and last name from the LookUp list. You can include the CustomerID as a column in the LookUp list as well as the Last Name and First Name for the customer.

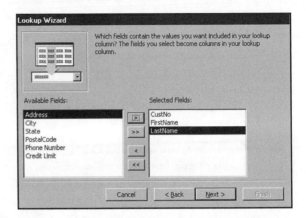

5. After selecting the field columns, click the Next button. The next screen enables you to adjust the widths of the field columns that you have selected for the LookUp list. This enables you to make sure that all the data in a particular column will show in the list. A check box is also provided that will hide the key column in the Lookup List when checked. This is selected by default. If you hide the key column, the first column in the LookUp list is the data that appears in the field when you enter your data. However, the key field value is actually what is stored in the field. Click Next to continue.

6. You are asked to supply a label for the LookUp column. The default name consists of the field name that you gave the field when you created it in the table Design window. After you type a name, click Finish to complete the process.

7. Make sure that you save the changes that you have made to the table structures.

When you return to the Datasheet view of the table to enter data, a drop-down button appears when you enter the field that you created the LookUp list for. Select the appropriate value from the list. The data from the first column in the LookUp field is placed in the table. The table actually stores the primary key information in the field, even though it displays the first column information from the LookUp list.

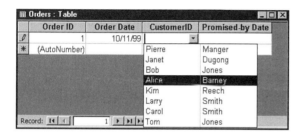

Use the Input Mask Wizard

An input mask can do many of the same things that a format can (see the "Change Field Format" section in Objective 17 "Modify Field Properties"), and it is actually easier to create because an Input Mask Wizard walks you through the steps.

For instance, social security numbers have a dash (-) between each sequence of numbers. An input mask can ensure that you enter the right number of characters for a social security number, and it will automatically enter the dashes for you.

To create an input mask for a field, complete the following steps:

1. Select the field in the Field Grid box for which you want to create the input mask.

2. In the Field Properties pane, click the Input Mask box. A Build button (the gray button with the ellipsis) appears on the right side of the Input Mask box.

3. Click the Build button to start the Input Mask Wizard. The Input Mask Wizard window opens. The first screen provides you with a selection of input masks. There are pre-existing formats for social security numbers, phone numbers, zip codes, and dates, among others.

4. To select a pre-existing mask, click an Input Mask in the scroll box. To try the mask, press the Tab key. The insertion point moves to the Try It box. Type some sample data into the box to see how the mask works.

5. After you select your mask, click the <u>N</u>ext button. The next screen provides you with the option of editing the mask. For example, the standard zip code mask to set up is 5 plus 4 (xxxxx-xxxx). If you want to remove the last four digits for the zip code masks, do so in the Input Mask box. A Try It box is also provided for you to test your changes to the mask. You are given the option of changing the placeholder character for the mask. In most cases, you will want to leave it at the default value. When you are satisfied with the edited version of the mask, click **Next**.

6. The next screen asks you how you would like to store the data in the table, with the symbols in the mask or without the symbols in the mask (the hyphen (-) in the zip code or social security masks is a symbol). A few stored symbols will not really affect the size of your database file. (In the case of very complex masks that enter a large number of symbols, you might decide not to store them with the data). Select the appropriate radio button, and click **Next** to continue.

7. Click the <u>F</u>inish button to end the input mask creation process.

Now when you enter data into the field in the Datasheet view, the input mask will limit the number of characters that can be entered in the field and will supply special symbols such as parentheses and hyphens.

24

Change Field Column Widths

The default column width for the Datasheet view of your tables is approximately one inch, or 14.75 characters. You might find that you will enter data in a particular field that is not accommodated by the default column width; the data will appear truncated. There are two ways to alter the field column width: using the mouse and using menus. The following sections will cover both ways.

Drag to Resize

Changing column width in the Datasheet view is extremely simple. Complete the following steps:

1. Place your mouse pointer on the dividing line between two fields that is to the right of the field column that you want to adjust. The mouse pointer becomes a column-sizing tool.

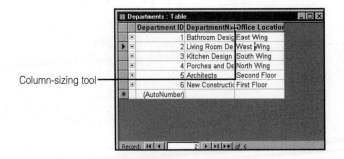

Column-sizing tool

2. Click and hold the left mouse button. Using the column-sizing tool, drag the column border to the right until the widest entry in the field column is accommodated by the new width.

You can also change a column width to *best fit.* Best fit changes the column width so that the widest entry in the field column is accommodated. To set the width to best fit, place the mouse pointer on the column border to the right of the field you want to widen. When the sizing tool appears, double-click. The column width adjusts to the widest entry. You can also select several contiguous columns and then double-click one of the fields' borders to apply the same best fit width to all the selected columns.

Click to Best Fit

To adjust the column width using the menu, select column, then click the Format menu, and choose Column Width. The dialog box displays the number of field characters. Type the number of characters you want to display, or click the Best Fit button.

Use the Format Menu

Change the Font For a Table

You can change the font for the data in the table. Any change in font affects the entire table, including the field column headings.

Font changes are made in the Datasheet view and will not affect any of the other objects (forms and reports) in the database that work with the data in the table.

To change the font for the table, complete the following steps:

1. Click the Format menu, and then select Font. The Font dialog box appears.

2. Choose a new font from the Font list box.

3. Choose a style from the Font style list box.

4. Choose a size from the Size list box.

5. Choose a color from the Color drop-down list.

A sample of your changes appears in the Sample area. When you have selected the font changes you want to make, click **OK**.

TAKE THE TEST

In this practice exercise, you will work with features related to Objective 20, "Modify Tables Using Design View." Copy the practice6.mdb database from the CD-ROM that accompanies this book to a folder on your computer using the Windows Explorer. Open the database. Open the Customers table and modify the table as follows:

Task 1

1. In the Design view, insert a new field below the Address field and name the new field **Available Credit**. Set the data type for the field as **Currency**.

2. Move the Available Credit field below the email address field.

3. Change the name of the Email Address field to **Email**.

Open the database practice6fin.mdb and open the Customers table in Design view to examine the solution to this practice exercise.

In this practice exercise, you will work with features related to Objective 21, "Modify Field Properties." Open the Practice6.mdb database. Open the table Customers in Design view and modify the table as follows:

Task 2

1. Change the Field Size of the City field to 35.

2. Change the Field Size of the State field to 2.

3. Change the Format property of the State field so that characters entered in the field are automatically placed in uppercase.

4. Set the Phone Number field as a Required field.

5. Create a caption for the custno field called Customer Number.

6. Specify MN as the default value for the State field.

7. Save the changes that you have made to the field properties.

Open the database `practice6fin.mdb` and open the Customers table in Design view. Compare the City, State, Phone Number, and Customer Number field properties you modified in `practice6.mdb` with the solution to this practice exercise.

Task 3

In this practice exercise, you will work with features related to Objective 22, "Use the Lookup Wizard." Open the `Practice6.mdb` database. Open the table Orders in Design view and modify the table as follows:

1. Change the data type of the CustomerID field to **Lookup Wizard**.

2. Use the Lookup Wizard to create a Lookup column that provides the customer's First and Last Name as values in the column and that enters the customer's number into the Orders table (use the Customers table as the source for the Lookup list).

3. In the Datasheet view of the Orders table click in the CustomerID field of an empty record to view the Lookup list box.

Open the database `practice6fin.mdb` and open the Orders table in Datasheet view to see the solution to this practice exercise.

Task 4

In this practice exercise, you will work with features related to Objective 23, "Use the Input Mask Wizard." Open the `Practice6.mdb` database. Open the table Suppliers table in Design view and modify the table as follows:

1. Create an input mask for the Postal Code field in the Suppliers table. Use the Zip Code input mask and store the data with the symbols in the mask.

2. Save the changes you make to the Suppliers table structure.

3. View the input mask results for the field in the Datasheet view of the table.

Open the database practice6fin.mdb and open the Suppliers table to view the solution to this practice exercise.

Cheat Sheet

Move a Field

In Design view, select field and drag to a new location.

Insert a Field

1. Select the existing field row below where you want to add.

2. Select Insert, Rows.

Change Field Size

1. In Design view, click in Field Size box.

2. Type new size for text fields.

3. Select new size for numerical fields.

Change Field Format

1. Click in field, and then click in Format box.

2. Enter formatting code for text fields.

3. Select formatting option from drop-down list for numerical or Date/Time fields.

Use a Caption

Click in field, and then enter caption text in Caption box.

Specify a Default Value in a Field

Click in field, and then enter value in Default Value box.

Set Required Fields

1. Click in field, and then click drop-down list in Required box.

2. Select Yes.

Use the Lookup Wizard

Change field's data type to Lookup Wizard. Use Wizard to select source for Lookup list.

Use the Input Mask Wizard

1. Click in field, and then click in Input Mask box.

2. Click Input Mask Wizard button and use Wizard to select and test mask.

Change Field Column Widths

1. In Datasheet view, drag column divider to size column.

2. Double-click to use best fit.

Change the Font for a Table

1. In Datasheet view, select Format, Font.

2. Select a new font in the Font dialog box.

3. Click OK.

Viewing and Organizing Information: Sorting Records

Following is a list of MOUS Objectives:

- Sort Records
- Create Advanced Sorts
- Freeze Columns

26

Sort Records

The records in a table are initially ordered as you enter them; the first record entered appears before the second record entered (unless you are using AutoNumber for the primary key field, in which case the records are ordered by the key field, such as customer number). Access provides a sort feature that enables you to reorder the records in a table by the information in a particular field. You might need to sort an employee table by the employees' start dates or alphabetically by last name and then first name. Access provides you with the capability to do both simple and complex sorts.

The sort feature can sort the records in an ascending or descending order. You can also create a sort that will sort the table records by more than one field. Sorting is done in the Datasheet view of the table.

Sort By a Field

To sort by a single field, click anywhere in the field column you want to sort by. The Table Datasheet toolbar provides two buttons for sorting: ⬆ Sort Ascending and ⬇ Sort Descending. If you choose, you can also access the Sort commands by clicking the Records menu and selecting Sort.

Right-click on a field; then choose Sort Ascending or Sort Descending from the shortcut menu to quickly sort by one field.

An example of a single-field sort would be a Products table sorted by the units (of product) that are currently in stock. To sort in ascending order, complete the following steps:

1. Click the field column you want to sort by (in this case Units in Stock).

2. Click 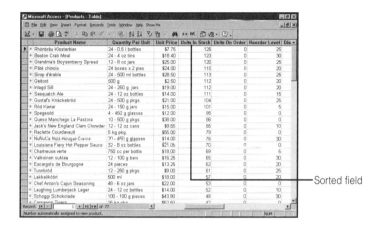 Sort Descending on the Table Datasheet toolbar. All the records in the table are sorted by the field that you choose in the sort order (ascending or descending) that you choose.

Sorted field

Sort By Multiple Fields

To sort by multiple fields using the Sort Ascending and Sort Descending commands, the fields must be adjacent to each other in the table. For instance, you might want to sort a customer table by Last Name and then First Name. Access determines the order of the sort by reading the field columns selected for the sort from left to right. So, to sort a table by last name and then first name, the Last Name field column must be to the left of and adjacent to the First Name field column.

You can move a field column to a new position, so that it is positioned appropriately for a multiple field sort. Click the field name to select the field and drag to a new position. Moving a column does not affect the underlying data.

To sort by more than one field, complete the following steps:

1. Click the field name to select the first field column for the sort and then press Shift and click to select other fields for the sort (they must be directly to the right of the field that will be the primary sort parameter). You can also click and drag across the two field column selectors to select the fields.

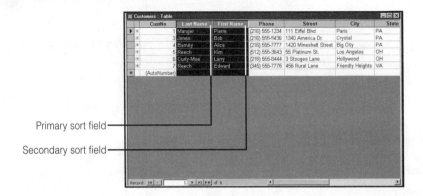

Primary sort field

Secondary sort field

2. Click [⬆️] Sort Ascending or [⬇️] Sort Descending on the Table Datasheet toolbar to do the sort.

The table will be sorted by the primary sort field first (the first selected field) and then by any subsequent fields to the right. When you have completed a sort and would like to return the records in the table to their previous order, click Records on the menu bar and then select Remove Filter/Sort.

Create Advanced Sorts

With an advanced sort, you can sort by as many as 15 fields. Click the Records menu and select Filter to access Advanced Filter/Sort.

A filter is a list of certain criteria (such as customers in Germany) that will give you a subset of the records in your table. Filters will be covered in Chapter 8.

An example of an advanced sort would be a situation where you have clients all over the world. You want to sort them by country, city, and the name of the company. When you sort by more than one field, you need to assign a primary sort field (in this example, Country) and at least a secondary sort field (in this case, the City field) and determine which direction (ascending or descending) you want the sort to follow. When you give Access all these instructions for your advanced sort, you're setting up the sort parameters.

To conduct an advanced sort, complete the following steps:

1. Open the table you want to sort.

2. Click the Records menu and then point at Filter; select Advanced Filter/Sort to open the Filter window.

The Filter window is where you select the fields you want to sort by. You also select the direction of the sorts, such as ascending or descending.

The Filter window has two parts: the upper half of the window shows the field list (the current table and the fields that it contains). The design grid, located in the lower half of the window, is divided into several rows and columns. For designing a sort, the first two rows of the design grid are used; the first one is marked Field, and the one below it is marked Sort.

When you sort by more than one field, you should place the field names in the design grid in the order that you want the sort to take place. Follow these steps:

1. To enter the primary sort field, click the first field column next to Field; a drop-down arrow appears. Click the drop-down arrow, and a list of the fields in the table appears. Select the field you want to sort by.

2. Click the Sort box and choose the sort direction (either Ascending or Descending) from the drop-down list.

   To quickly add a new field to the design grid, click the field column you want to place the field in and then double-click the field name in the Field List box to quickly place it in the field column. Every time a field name is double-clicked, it will appear in the next available column.

3. To add a secondary sort field, click the second field column. Select a field name via the drop-down list and click the Sort box to select the order of the sort.

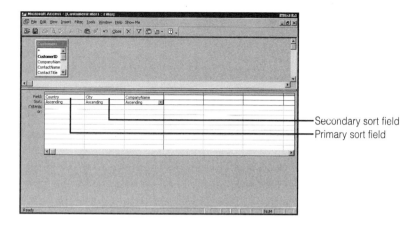

Secondary sort field
Primary sort field

4. When you complete your selection of fields for the sort, click ▽ **Apply Filter** on the Filter/Sort toolbar. You are returned to the Table window.

The records in the table are sorted first (in the appropriate order) by the primary sort field and then sorted as needed by any subsequent sort fields.

103

Freeze Columns

A sort only orders the records by a particular field or fields, it does not guarantee that field columns will appear in an order that makes it easy for you to cross-reference information.

Freezing a field column means that when you scroll to the right and the left in the table, the frozen fields will remain onscreen. This enables you to place two field columns side by side that are normally on opposite ends of the table.

To freeze a field column, complete the following steps:

1. Click the field selector to select the field column you want to freeze.

2. Click the Format menu and then click Freeze Columns.

3. Click anywhere in the table to deselect the field column. A solid line appears on the right border of the field column, letting you know that the particular field is frozen.

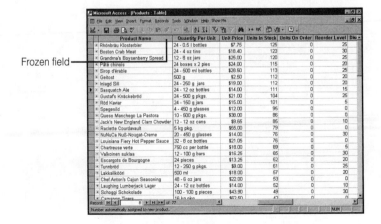

Frozen field

4. Scroll to the right, and the frozen column remains on the screen.

To freeze multiple field columns, the fields must be adjacent to each other in the table. Select the first field selector for the column you want to freeze and then press Shift and click any additional adjacent field columns you want to also freeze. To unfreeze columns in the table, click the Format menu, and then click Unfreeze All Columns. The datasheet will now scroll normally, with columns moving off the screen to the left as you scroll to the right.

TAKE THE TEST

Task 1

In this practice exercise, you will work with features related to Objective 26, "Sort Records". Copy the practice7.mdb database from the CD-ROM that accompanies this book to a folder on your computer using the Windows Explorer. Open the database and follow these steps:

1. Open the Suppliers table and sort the records by the Supply Type field in ascending order.

2. Open the Expenses table and sort the records by the Amount Spent field in descending order.

3. Open the Customers table and in the Datasheet view, sort by the LastName and FirstName fields in ascending order. (You might have to move one of the field columns.)

Open the database practice7fin.mdb file and open the Suppliers, Expenses, and Customers tables to view the solutions to this practice exercise.

Task 2

In this practice exercise, you will work with features related to Objective 27, "Create Advanced Sorts." Open the Practice7.mdb database and follow these steps:

1. Open the Employees table and use the Advanced Filter/Sort feature to sort the table by Start Date, Last Name, and then First Name.

2. Sort each field in ascending order.

Open the database `practice7fin.mdb` and open the Employees table. View the Datasheet to see the results of the sort. To see how the sort is set up, Select the Records menu and then point to Filter and select Advanced Filter/Sort.

In this practice exercise, you will work with features related to Objective 28, "Freeze Columns". Open the `Practice7.mdb` database. Open the Projects table and follow these steps:

Task 3

1. Freeze the Project Name column and then scroll to the right until you can see the Project Begincolumn.

Open the database `practice7fin.mdb` and open the Projects table to view the solution to this practice exercise.

Cheat Sheet

Sort by a Field

In Datasheet view, click the field and then do one of the following:

- Click either ▲▼ Sort Ascending or ▼▲ Sort Descending.
- Right-click and select Sort Ascending or Sort Descending from the shortcut menu.

Sort by Multiple Fields

Drag to select multiple field columns.

Then click either ▲▼ Sort Ascending or ▼▲ Sort Descending.

Advanced Sort

1. In the Datasheet view, Select Records, Filter, Advanced Filter/Sort.

2. In the Filter window, insert fields for sort.

3. Select sort order in the Sortcell.

4. Click the ▼ Apply Filter button to run sort.

Freeze Columns

Select the column and then do one of the following:

- Click Format, Freeze Columns.
- Right-click and select Freeze Columns.

Unfreeze Columns

Click Format, Unfreeze All Columns.

Viewing and Organizing Information II: Finding and Filtering Records

- Find a Record
- Apply and Remove Filters (Filter by Form and Filter by Selection)

29

Find a Record

The Find feature is useful for locating a particular record in a database table. For instance, in a table of customers, you might want to quickly find the record for a customer who has called you with a question about a recent purchase.

Find is only really useful if you are looking for one particular record. A tool for finding groups of records based on the information they hold is the filter (covered later in this chapter).

Enter the Find Data

To find a particular record in a table, complete the following steps:

1. In the Datasheet view, click the field that contains the data you want to search for. For instance, if you want to find a customer by his last name, click the Last Name field. If you're not sure which field might hold the data you are searching for, click any field.

2. Click 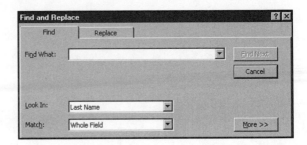 Find on the Table Datasheet toolbar; or select the Edit menu and select Find; or press Ctrl+F. The Find and Replace dialog box appears.

110

3. Type the text or characters that you want to find into the Find What text box.

After you enter the data that you want to search for using the Find command, you have several options that you can set that will control how the search is conducted. You have options concerning how the search matches potential items to be found with the text or character you provide in the Find dialog box. You also have control over the direction that the search progresses in. To set the search parameters in the Find dialog box, complete the following steps.

Open the Match drop-down list and select one of the following:

- **Any Part of Field**—Finds fields that contain the specified text in any way. "Smith" would find "Smith", "Smithsonian", and "Joe Smith".

- **Whole Field**—Finds fields where the specified text is the only thing in that field. For instance, "Smith" would not find "Smithsonian".

- **Start of Field**—Finds fields that begin with the specified text. For instance, "Smith" would find "Smith" and "Smithsonian", but not "Joe Smith".

If you want to search only forward from the current record, click the More button on the Find box and select Down from the drop-down list. If you want to search backward, select Up. The default is All, which searches all the records from the currently selected field.

To limit the match to only entries that are the same case as the information you type in the text box (upper or lower), select the Match Case checkbox. After doing this, "Smith" would not find "SMITH", or "smith".

To only find the fields with the same formatting as the text you type, select Search Fields as Formatted. With this option selected, "3/3/98" would not find "3-3-98" because even though they are the same date, they are formatted differently.

Run the Search

After you enter the data you want to search for and set the various options in the Find box, you are ready to actually run the search.

Follow these steps to begin the search process:

1. In the Find dialog box, click the <u>F</u>ind Next button to find the first match for the search. You might have to move the search dialog box out of the way if you cannot see the found field. Access will highlight the first field that it finds that holds the data you are searching for.

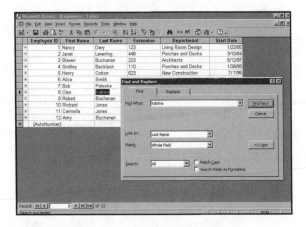

2. To locate the next match, click the <u>F</u>ind Next button. If Access cannot find any more matches, it tells you the search item was not found. Click OK to clear the message.

3. When you have completed the search, click the Close button to close the Find dialog box.

Use Wildcards with Find

There might be times when you want Access to search for parts of words or a particular pattern of alphanumeric or numeric characters; you can do this using *wildcard characters* as placeholders. Wildcards can represent one character, several characters, a list of characters, or even a number. Some of the most commonly used wildcard characters and their usage follow:

* This character can take the place of any number of characters. You can use it at the beginning, middle, or end of a character string. An example would be **C*a**. A search for this text string in a field column of countries would return countries that begin with a capital *C* and end with *a*, such as Canada and Cambodia. The number of characters represented by the asterisk can vary.

? The question mark can be used anywhere in your search string to represent a single alphanumeric character. Say that you use the Find feature to search for the text string f?ll. Some of the possible matches you could get in a search such as this would be words that differ by just one character such as fill, fall, full, and fell.

[] The brackets are used to specify a list of possible matches for a single character found in the items you are searching for. For instance you could set up the Find feature to look for the text string Jo[ah]n. Matches to this text string would be limited to Joan and John.

\# The number sign is used to represent a single numeric character in a search string. It works very much like the question mark wildcard. Say that you have a Product number field that contains data in the form of three-digit codes (such as 142 or 333). Your supplier calls and tells you all the products ending in 22 are going to be discontinued. No problem—you can do a search using #22 to find them.

Wildcards can be quite useful when you are using the Find feature and know only part of the field data that you are searching for. Wildcards can also help you make a search much more precise when you want to find matches for only a portion of a text or numerical entry or to match a pattern.

The exam could ask you to locate records that begin "Smi". An entry of "Smi*" might bring up "Smith", "Smithson", and "Smithy".

Use Replace

Replace is a tab on the Find dialog box. Using Replace not only enables you to find certain data entries, but it also enables you to replace them with different data. For instance, if you misspelled a certain brand name in your inventory table (something that the Spell Checker will not help you with), you can use the Replace feature to find the misspelled entry and replace it with the correctly spelled data.

To find and replace data, complete the following steps:

1. Select the Edit menu and then select Replace, or press Ctrl+H. The Replace dialog box appears.

2. Type the text you want to find in the Find What text box. Type the text you want to replace it with in the Replace With text box.

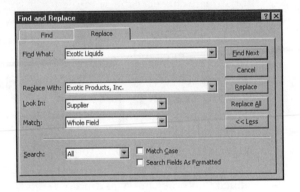

3. Select any of the search options you want to set (see "Setting Search Parameters" earlier in this chapter for help).

4. Click Find Next. Access finds the first occurrence of the Find What data and selects it. To replace the data, click the Replace button.

5. Click the Find Next button to continue, and replace the data found as desired.

To replace every occurrence of the data that you are searching for, click the Replace Al button in the Replace dialog box. You do have recourse if you find that you inadvertently replaced an item that should not have been replaced. Close the Replace dialog box and immediately click ↶ Undo on the Table toolbar or press Ctrl+Z on the keyboard. This will undo your last replacement action.

Knowing how to undo a mistake can be important under the pressure of the clock in the exam.

Apply and Remove Filters (Filter by Form and Filter by Selection)

You've already seen that the Find feature can be used to move through a table and locate records that meet your search criteria. However, all the records, even those that don't match your criteria, still appear on the screen and make it more difficult to concentrate on the records that do match the search criteria.

Filters also use criteria to operate. However, filters are superior to the Find feature in that they only show you the records that match the filter criteria. The other records in the table are hidden. This makes working with the records easier.

Filter by Selection

An incredibly straightforward way to filter records is filtering by selection. All you have to do is show Access an example of the field data you want to filter the table by, and it will show you only the records that match. For example, a Products table will contain a field for suppliers. By selecting a specific supplier in the table and then invoking the Filter command, a subset of the table will appear only showing the products that are supplied by the particular supplier.

To Filter by selection, complete the following steps:

1. Locate the data in a field column that you want to filter the table by.

2. Select the value for the filter as follows:

- To find all records where the field value is identical to the selected value, select the entire field entry.

- To find all records where the field begins with the selected value, select part of the field entry beginning with the first character.

- To find all records where the field contains the selected value at any point, select part of the field entry beginning after the first character.

3. Click the 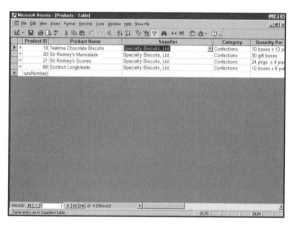 Filter by Selection button on the toolbar, or select the Records menu, point at Filter, and select Filter by Selection. Alternatively, right-click and select Filter by Selection from the shortcut menu. The records that match the criteria appear in the table.

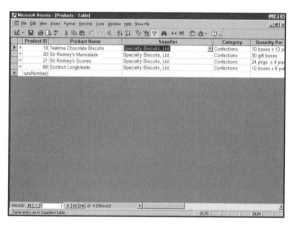

4. To cancel the filter and return all the records in the table to the screen, click [Y] Remove Filter on the Table Datasheet toolbar.

When you Filter by Form, the Filter by Form window opens and a blank Datasheet row appears with all the appropriate Field columns found in your table. Then all you have to do is pick the field or fields you want involved in the filtering. A drop-down arrow appears in each of the field boxes, and all you have to do is click it and select the data that will serve as the filter criteria. All the data that appears in the particular field (data from every record in the table) will be listed as potential criterion.

Filter by Form

The major difference between filtering by form and filtering by selection is the number of criteria that you can set. Filtering by form enables you to set criteria in multiple fields. When you filter by example, you can only select one criterion in one field.

To Filter by Form, complete the following steps:

1. In the Datasheet view, click the 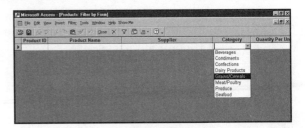 Filter by Form button on the Table Datasheet toolbar. The Filter by Form window opens, and a blank datasheet row appears.

2. Click the field or fields that you want to set criteria for. A drop-down list appears; click it to select the filter information for that field (you can type a value if you want).

3. When you have entered all the criteria for the filter, click Apply Filter button on the Filter/Sort toolbar.

The records that meet your filter criteria appear in the table.

Filtering by form also enables you to set up conditional criteria for a field. For instance, you might want to find which products in your product table have fallen below a certain stocking level in your warehouse (for instance, items that have fallen below six in stock). You could type in the logical expression **<6** in the In Stock Field on the Filter Form. When you apply the filter, only the records for products that are stocked at less than six items would appear in the filter results.

TAKE THE TEST

In this practice exercise, you will work with features related to Objective 29, "Find a Record." Copy the practice8.mdb database from the CD-ROM that accompanies this book to a folder on your computer using the Windows Explorer. Open the database and follow these steps:

Task 1

1. Open the Suppliers table. Use the Find feature to locate the Supplier who has Gordon Mill as the contact person.

2. Open the Customers table. Use the Find feature to locate the record for the customer who lives in California.

3. Open the Employees table and use the Replace feature to replace the last name of Smith with Johnson. (You are looking for Alice Smith's record.)

Because the find feature does not provide a change to a database table, your results for exercises 1 and 2 do not appear in the answer file.

In this practice exercise, you will work with features related to Objective 30 "Apply and Remove Filters (Filter by Form and Filter by Selection)." Open the Practice8.mdb database and follow these steps:

Task 2

1. Open the Employees table, and in the Department field column, select the first entry of Porches and Decks. Use Filter By Selection to filter the table.

2. Click the Remove Filter button.

3. Open the Customers table and use **Filter by Form** to display the records for Minnesota (MN).

4. Open the Employees table and use **Filter by Form** to display records whose Start Date is greater than **8/8/96**. Click the **Apply Filter** button. The results of this filter appear below.

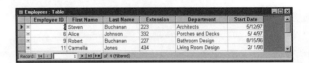

Cheat Sheet

Find a Record

1. In Datasheet view, click the field and then do one of the following:

- Click 🔍 Find
- Edit, Find
- Press Ctrl+F

2. Enter the appropriate search parameters and then click Find Next.

Use Replace

1. Click the field column.

2. Edit, Replace (Ctrl+H).

3. Enter text in the Find What text box and the Replace With text box.

4. Click Find Next to replace the first occurrence.

Filter by Selection

Select the field data for the selection. Then do one of the following:

- Click the 🔽 Filter by Selection button.
- Right-click and select Filter By Selection from the shortcut menu.

Filter by Form

1. 🔽 Filter by Form.

2. Select the filter parameter using the drop-down list in the appropriate field.

3. 🔽 Filter.

Defining Relationships: Building a Relational Database

Following is a list of MOUS Objectives:

- Establish Table Relationships
- Enforce Referential Integrity
- Print Database Relationships
- Display Related Records in a Subdatasheet

Establish Table Relationships

One of the strengths of Access as a relational database is its capability to relate tables together via a common field. For instance, you might have a Customers table that contains all the information on your customers, including a separate customer number for each record (this customer number would be the primary key field for this table).

Another table in your database might be an Orders table that details every order that you've taken. The Orders table would obviously need to reference the customer who made the order. This would be done by entering the customer number in the Orders table. The data in these two sample tables then would be linked (that is, related) by their common field: the customer number.

When you use the Table Wizard, the tables you create with the sample fields will often have shared fields. Access knows that you will want to relate the tables eventually, so the sample fields overlap between the different sample table types. The Table Wizard even offers you the option of relating the table that you are building to any of the current tables in the database during the creation process. It asks you if there is a shared field.

Create Table Relationships

New relationships are created in the Relationships window. Open the database that you want to create the relationship or relationships for and complete the following steps:

1. Click ▣ Relationships on the Database toolbar. The Relationship window appears.

2. In the Relationships window, the Show Table dialog box appears. This provides you with a list of the tables that are in your database. If the tables aren't displayed, click the Show Table button on the Relationship toolbar and double-click the tables you want to add.

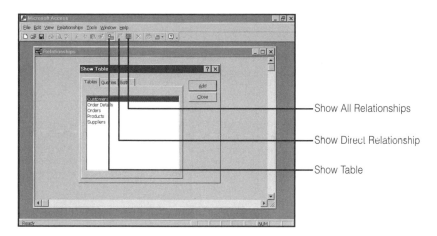

3. Select the tables you want to create relationships for; select a table and then click the Add button. Repeat this step as necessary.

4. When you have added all the tables you need, click the Close button to close the Add Tables dialog box.

When you have the appropriate tables in the Relationship window, you are ready to create the actual relationships between the tables.

As you prepare to create your relationships, you should keep two things in mind: The related fields do not have to have the same names. However, the fields must have the same data type (with two exceptions). When the matching fields are Number fields, they must also have the same FieldSize property setting.

The two exceptions to matching data types are that you can match an AutoNumber field with a Number field whose FieldSize property is set to Long Integer; and you can match an AutoNumber field with a Number field if both fields have their FieldSize property set to Replication ID.

To reopen a closed Add Table box, click the Show Table button on the Relationship toolbar.

To create relationships between two fields in the Relationship window, complete the following steps:

1. Make sure the two tables that you want to create the relationship between appear in the Relationship window.

2. Select the shared field in the table where the field serves as the primary key (or is indexed); the field name will be in bold. Drag the field (a small field box appears) and drop it on the shared field in the other table. The Relationships dialog box appears.

To delete a relationship, select the join line and then press Delete. Select Yes in the caution box that appears.

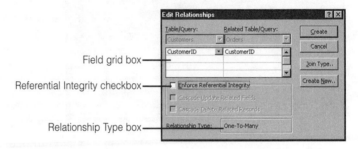

3. To establish the relationship, click the Create button. The relationship line will appear as a link between the two tables.

Set Join Type

The Join Type button in the Relationships dialog box enables you to select the type of join that exists between the two related tables. When you click the Join Type button, the Join Properties dialog box appears. The default join type for table relationships is Only Include Rows Where the Joined Fields for Both Tables Are Equal. This type of join allows Access Queries to display only the records that have matching field data in the related field.

To select a new join type, complete the following steps:

1. Drag a field from one table to a like field in another table to create a new relationship. To change the join type for an existing relationship, double-click the relationship line between the two tables. The Relationships dialog box opens.

2. Click the Join Type button in the Relationships dialog box. The Join Properties dialog box opens.

3. Select the radio button for the join type you want to use.

4. Click OK to close the Join Type dialog box.

5. To close the Join Type dialog box without changing the join type, click the Close button.

To edit a relationship, double-click the join line.

At the bottom of the Relationships dialog box is the Relationship Type box. Each common field link that you create between tables will be categorized by Access as a certain type of relationship:

Understand Relationship Types

> **One-to-many relationship**—This is the type of relationship that you would typically have between a Customers table and an Orders table. A unique customer number identifies each customer. This uniquely identified customer can make a number of orders of your products. So Access can match each of the records in Customers (one) to an infinite number of records (many) in the Orders table. You will find that most the relationships you create for a database will be one-to-many relationships.

> **One-to-one relationship**—In this case, a record in one table would have only one possible matching record in the second table. An example would be a publishing company that only lets its authors write one book. If you had an author table and a book table for the situation described, sharing the common author number field, you would have a one-to-one relationship. Each author record would match one book record. One-to-one relationships can also be used for security purposes. You might have a table just for social security numbers or dates of birth that are linked to the employee table by the person's name or employee ID.

> **Many-to-many relationship**—In this type of relationship, each record in the first table of the relationship can have many matches in the second table, and each record in the second table can have many matches in the first table. An example would be a construction company that hires subcontractors to build houses. The records in the subcontractor table could potentially have many matching records (different house projects) in the house table. The house table could have many matches in the subcontractor table because a number of different subcontractors are used to build an entire house.

127

Enforce Referential Integrity

So far, the relationships that you've created (using the steps discussed) do not take advantage of referential integrity. Referential integrity means that a value entered in a field must be in the same pool of data that is found in its related field.

For example, if the CustomerID field is used to relate a Customers and Orders table, the values entered in the CustomerID field in the Orders table must exist in the CustomerID field in the Customers table. You could not enter CutomerID 100 in the Orders table if a customer with the CustomerID 100 did not exist in the Customers table.

You can't have a sale without a customer.

To enforce Referential Integrity, follow these steps:

1. Drag a shared field from the table where it is the primary key to the table where the field is the foreign key. The Relationships dialog box opens.

2. In the middle of the dialog box is a check box labeled Enforce Referential Integrity. Select the check box.

3. Click Create to create the relationship. The new relationship will appear between the tables in the Relationship window. The join line will be labeled with symbols that depict the type of relationship that exists between the two tables. For instance, in a one-to-many relationship, the join line will be marked with a 1 on the one side of the relationship. An infinity sign (∞) on the join line depicts the many side of the relationship (one-to-many relationship).

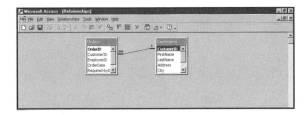

You can also enforce referential integrity on existing relationships. Double-click the relationship join line to open the
Relationships dialog box. Select the Enforce Referential
Integrity check box. Click OK to close the Relationships dialog
box. The join line will be labeled with the relationship.

Print Database Relationships

To print the relationships in the Database window, select the File menu and then select Print Relationships.

A report is created by the Print Relationships Wizard (it handles this task with no further input from you). The report appears in the Print Preview window.

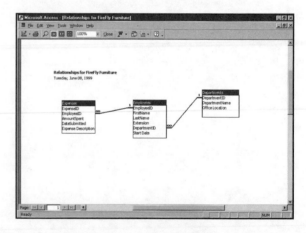

To print the Relationships report from the Preview window, click Print on the Print Preview toolbar. Alternatively, click Ctrl+P.

Display Related Records in a Subdatasheet

After relationships have been established between tables, the related or joined data can be seen and modified in tables, forms, and queries.

In the Cheese Shop database, there are a number of relationships.

A New Feature in Access 2000

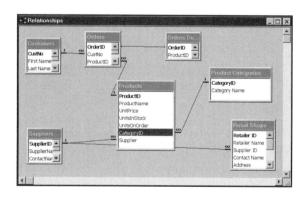

One of the relationships ties the Product Categories table to the Products table by a common field CategoryID. The Orders table is related to Products by the ProductID field. Orders Details is related to Orders by the OrderID field.

When the Product Categories table is opened in Datasheet view, there are plus (+) marks to the right of the first column.

131

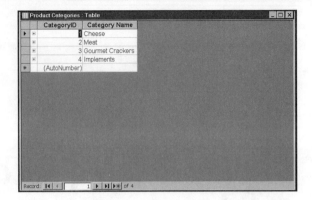

If you click the plus (+) mark, the related table (Products) appears.

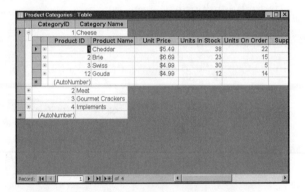

There is also a plus (+) mark in the second sheet. When that mark is clicked, the relationship to the Orders table is displayed. One level below that shows the relationship down to the Orders Detail table.

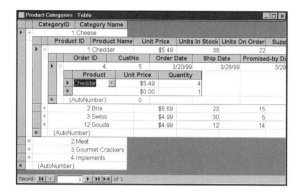

Up to eight levels of relationships can be shown in this manner.

The subdatasheets can be collapsed by clicking the minus (-) sign.

TAKE THE TEST

Task 1

In this practice exercise, you will work with features related to Objective 31, "Establish Table Relationships." Copy the `practice9.mdb` database from the CD-ROM that accompanies this book to a folder on your computer using the Windows Explorer. Open the database and follow these steps:

1. Add the Customers and Orders table to the Relationships window.

2. Identify the shared field that can be used to relate the Customers and Orders table.

3. Create a relationship between the Customers and Orders table. Do not enforce referential integrity.

4. Add the Products table and the Order Details table to the Relationships window.

5. Create a relationship between the Orders Details table and the Products table.

6. Create a relationship between the Orders Details table and the Orders table.

7. Save the changes you have made to the relationships in the database.

Open the database `practice9fin.mdb` and view the relationships for this database, which provides the solution for the preceding exercises.

Task 2

In this practice exercise, you will work with features related to Objective 32, "Enforce Referential Integrity." Open the `Practice9a.mdb` database and follow these steps:

1. Edit the relationship between the Products table and Order Details. Enforce Referential Integrity for the relationship.

2. Edit the relationship between Order Details and Orders tables. Enforce Referential Integrity and add Cascade Update and Cascade Delete.

3. Edit the relationship between the Customers and Orders table. Enforce Referential Integrity, add Cascade Update and Cascade Delete.

4. Save the changes that you have made to the database relationships.

Open the database practice9afin.mdb and view the relationships for this database, which provides the solution for the preceding exercises.

In this practice exercise, you will work with features related to Objective 33, "Print Database Relationships." Open the Practice9.mdb database and do the following:

Task 3

1. Print the relationships found in the Relationship window from the previous exercise.

Your hard copy printout will serve as the solution for this task.

In this practice exercise, you will work with features related to Objective 34, "Display related records in a subdatasheet." Open the Practice9a.mdb database and follow these steps:

Task 4

1. Open the Suppliers table.

2. Display the related subdatasheet for Sausage City.

Your answer should look like the following figure:

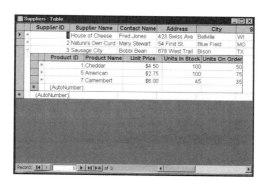

Cheat Sheet

Establish Table Relationships

1. In the Relationship window, use the Add Tables dialog box to add the appropriate tables to the window.

2. Drag one of the shared fields from one table to another to open the Relationships dialog.

3. Click to create the relationship.

Enforce Referential Integrity

1. In the Relationship dialog box, click the Enforce Referential Integrity check box.

2. Click Create to create the relationship.

Print Database Relationships

1. In the Relationship window, select File, Print Relationships.

2. Print to print the relationship report.

Display Related Records in a Subdatasheet

Display table in Datasheet view.

Click plus (+) to display related subdatasheet for any record.

Building and Modifying Forms

- Create a Form with the Form Wizard
- Switch Between Object Views
- Use Form Sections (Headers, Footers, Detail)

Create a Form with the Form Wizard

Although tables serve as the repositories for the information in a database, you are not restricted to entering all your data entry directly into the tables. Forms provide a customizable environment for entering your data. Forms enable you to concentrate on the data that must be entered in a particular record. Forms can be created in the table view using the AutoForm feature; they can be created using the Form Wizard; and they can be created from scratch in the Form Design view.

Select Fields for the New Form

Although AutoForm is the fastest and easiest way to generate a form for a table, the Form Wizard also provides you a great deal of assistance and enables you to select some aspects of the form's design. To use the Form Wizard to create a new form, complete the following steps:

1. In the Database window, click the ⊞ Forms icon on the Objects bar.

2. Double-click Create Form by Using Wizard in the Forms pane of the Database window. The Form Wizard appears.

3. The first screen of the Form Wizard enables you to select the table (or query) you want to base the form on from the Tables/Queries drop-down box. When you select the table, the fields in the table are listed in the Available Fields box.

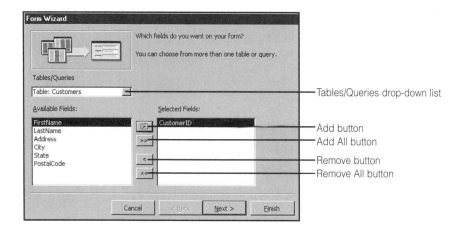

Tables/Queries drop-down list

Add button
Add All button

Remove button
Remove All button

When you create a new form, you can base the form on a table or a query. Also keep in mind that a form can include fields from more than one table or query.

4. To add fields to the form, select a field in the Available Fields box and the click Add (>) to place the field in the Selected Fields box. If you inadvertently add a field, select it in the Selected Fields box and click the Remove (<) button. (Remove all the fields by clicking the Remove All (<<) button.)

5. When you have selected the fields that you want to use from the currently selected table, you can return to the Tables/Queries drop-down list and select another table to use to add fields to the current form.

After you complete your selection of fields for the new form, click the Next button to continue. The next wizard screen asks you to select a format for the new form. You have four layout choices: columnar, tabular, datasheet, or Justified.

- A *columnar* layout places each of the fields on its own line in a vertically oriented form; this type of form only shows one record at a time.

- A *tabular* layout places the field names at the top of the form in separate columns and then lists the data records, each to a line, below the column headings.

- The *datasheet* layout sets up the form to look like a table, using rows and columns.

- The *Justified* layout places the fields in equal rows across the form. These field rows line up or are justified on the right and the left.

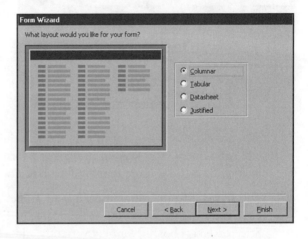

Click each style for a preview.

To see a preview of a particular layout, click its option button; the preview appears in the left half of the wizard screen. When you decide on a particular layout, make sure its radio button is selected and then click Next to continue.

The next screen asks you to select a style. Each style uses different colors and/or design elements to make your forms unique.

After you select the style you want to use for the form, click Next.

If you do not provide a name, the wizard will name the form after the table you based it on.

The last Form Wizard screen asks you to provide a name for the form in the title box.

You are also provided options for what happens after the form is completed. You can open the form to view or enter data or go directly to the Design view of the form to modify its design. To see the form, make sure the Open the Form to View or Enter Information option button is selected; then click Finish.

The new form appears, ready for data entry. Notice that the form has the same kind of navigation buttons that your tables have. You can move forward and backward through the records using these buttons. The New record button (an advance button followed by an asterisk) moves you to a blank record ready for data input.

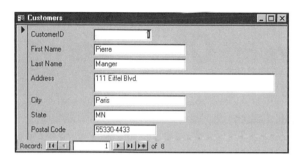

36

Switch Between Object Views

If the form's Header and Footer areas are not showing when you enter the Form Design view, click View, Form Header/Footer.

The Form view is where you enter and view the data that resides in the table (or tables) that the new form was based on. The Design view is where you change the design of the form. To switch to the Form Design view, click the ⬛ View button on the Form View toolbar. The Form Design window opens.

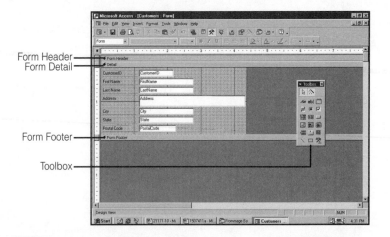

Working in the Form Design view is discussed in the next two sections. If you want to return to the Form view, click ⬛ View on the Form Design toolbar.

Use Form Sections (Headers, Footers, Detail)

The Form Design view is where you can modify a form that is created using AutoForm or the Form Wizard. The Form Design window has three parts: Header, Detail, and Footer.

The Header area is where you display the name of the form and any other information or items that you want repeated on each form as you view the records in the Form view. These items can include special command buttons that you create to open related forms or do special things such as print the form.

The Detail area contains all the fields that appear on the form when you are in Form view or print the form. The Detail area is of special importance because it holds the fields that appear on the form when you are in the Form view and that you use to enter and view data.

In the Design view, the fields are broken down into two boxes: labels and controls. The labels are the field names and were derived from the table fields that you used to create the form. The controls are where the actual data is entered. Controls also can dictate how the data is input into the form. For instance, a control can accept an entry from the keyboard or provide you with a list of data (a list box) that you must select from.

The Footer area is at the bottom of the form window and you can use it for items that you want to appear on each form as the records are viewed or entered. Footer information can include the date, page numbers, or short directions on how to use the form.

Another item that appears in the Form Design window is the Form Toolbox. The toolbox provides you with all the tools that you need to customize your forms. If you want to add a control or other item, such as a text label, to the header or footer area of the form, you must expand that area of the form. To do this, place the mouse pointer on the border between the header or footer area and the Detail area. A sizing tool appears. Drag the border until the header or footer area expands to the size that you will need to add a new item. Adding a text label to the header of a form is discussed in the next section.

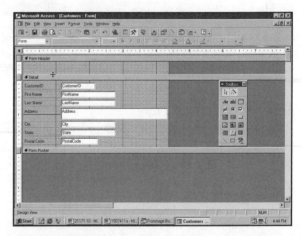

To resize the form, put the window in Normal size. (Use the Restore button to display the form in less than maximum size.) Resize the form by dragging the sides of the window to fit while in Design View. Observe the results in Form View. When the form looks right, save the results.

TAKE THE TEST

In this practice exercise, you will work with features related to Objective 35, "Create a Form With the Form Wizard." Copy the practice10.mdb database from the CD-ROM that accompanies this book to a folder on your computer using the Windows Explorer. Open the database and follow these steps:

1. Use the Form Wizard to create a form for the Suppliers table in this database. Use all the fields in the table for the form. Use the Standard Style. Use the Justified layout for the form. Name the form Dairy Suppliers.

2. Create a new form for the Customers table in the database using the Form Wizard. Include all the fields from the table for the form. Use the Blue Print Style for the form. Save the form as Retail Customers.

Open the database practice10fin.mdb on the CD-ROM, and view the forms that you were to complete for this task.

In this practice exercise, you will work with features related to Objective 36, "Switch Between Object Views," and Objective 37, "Use Form Sections (Headers, Footers, Detail)." Open the Practice10.mdb database that you copied to a folder on your computer and follow these steps:

1. Open the New Suppliers form in the Form View. Switch to the Design view.

2. Expand the Header area of the form to a half-inch.

3. Save the changes you have made to the form.

4. Open the New Customers form in the Form View.

5. Expand the Footer area to a half-inch high. Resize the form so that all the fields are visible in form view.

6. Save the changes you have made to the form.

Open the database practice10fin.mdb and view the modifications that were made to these forms in the Form Design view.

Cheat Sheet

Create a Form with the Form Wizard

In the Database window, do one of the following:

- Click the Form icon.
- Double-click Create form by using wizard.

Switch Between Object Views

In the Form View: 🖾 Design View

In the Design View: 🖼 Form View

Use Form Sections (Headers, Footers, Detail)

In the Form Design view:

Drag to expand the any of the Form sections.

Building and Modifying Forms II

- Use the Control Toolbox to Add Controls
- Modify Format Properties of Controls
- Use a Calculated Control on a Form

38

Use the Control Toolbox to Add Controls

After you have expanded the Header area, you can place a new label in the Header that will serve as the title for the form. This title will appear at the top of the form in the Form view when you are entering or editing data in the form.

To add an item to a form such as a label or control, you use the tools on the toolbox. You can drag the toolbox to any position in the Form Design window by clicking and dragging it by the title bar. This can be important if the toolbox is obscuring a part of the form.

To add a new label to the form, click the Aa Label button on the toolbox. The mouse pointer becomes a cross-shape above a capital A. This pointer is used as a drawing tool to create the rectangle that will contain the label text.

Place the mouse pointer where you want to create the new label (in this case in the Header area of your form). Hold down the mouse button and drag the mouse pointer to draw a rectangle in the Header area. When you let go of the mouse, the rectangle becomes opaque, and an insertion point appears in the upper-left corner.

Type the text that you want to appear in the label. When you have finished typing the label text, click outside of the label box. Your new label appears in the Header.

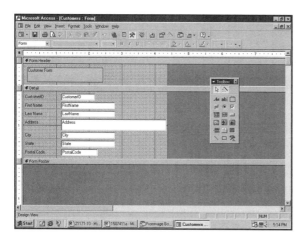

The method used for inserting a new label into the form is also used to insert other items into the form. Select the appropriate button from the toolbox and then place the new item in the appropriate area of the form.

To move a new label or other item that you place in the form, click the item; a frame with sizing handles appears. Place the mouse pointer on the frame. (Do not place the pointer on the sizing handles.) A hand pointer appears; drag the frame to a new position. To size the frame, place the mouse pointer on a sizing handle. A sizing tool appears. Change the size of the frame as appropriate.

You can also use the toolbox to add other controls to your forms.

Bound and Unbound Controls

Controls that you add to your forms fall into two categories: bound controls and unbound controls.

The controls in a form that are associated with a particular field in a table are *bound* controls. Controls not associated with a particular field in a table are called *unbound controls*. Whenever you use a Wizard to create a form, all the controls created will be bound to their respective fields in the table or tables you told the Wizard to use in the form creation process. (You will learn how to quickly add bound controls to a form using the Form Field list later in this chapter.)

Unbound controls contain data that is not associated with a particular field in the table that the form is based on. These unbound controls can take the form of calculated controls.

Calculated controls can do simple things such as place the current date in the control box. Alternatively, they can actually perform math. For example, you might create a calculated control that multiplies the amount of a product that you have in stock (found in an In Stock field) by the item cost of the product (found in a Cost field). This would give you the total value of the item that you have in stock.

Creating calculated controls is a two-step process. First, you add an unbound control to the form in the Design view. Then, you build the math expression for the field using the Expression builder.

First, you will create a simple calculated control that returns the current date in the form footer area. To add an unbound control to footer, follow these steps:

1. In the Form Design view (using a form of your choice), expand the Footer area of the form by dragging it with the mouse.

2. Click the ab Text box on the toolbox. Drag to create a rectangle to hold the new label and control that will be created using the Text tool.

3. Release the mouse button. The new label and control will appear in the Form Footer area.

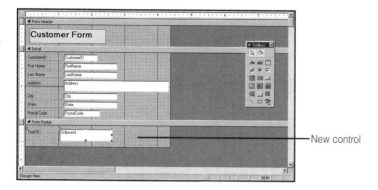

New control

4. The new control actually consists of a label and an unbound control. To edit the text in the label portion of the control (the text box on the left), click and drag to select the text inside the label. (The current text will read "Text", followed by a number.) Type the text that will serve as the label for the new control (in this case Date:).

After you create the control and edit the label text, you can then modify the control. The next section discusses creating the calculated control.

153

Modify Format Properties of Controls

After you add a new label (or control) to a form, you can format the text in the label or control using the buttons on the Formatting toolbar. To change the text format, complete the following steps:

1. Click the label to select it.

2. To increase or decrease the font size, click the Font Size drop-down arrow on the Formatting toolbar and select a new size.

3. To change the font style, click the Font drop-down arrow on the Formatting toolbar and select a new font.

4. To change the font to bold, click **B** Bold on the Formatting toolbar.

5. To change the font color, click the **A** Font/Fore Color drop-down arrow on the Formatting toolbar. Select a new color from the color palette.

6. To color the background of the items box, click the Fill/Back color drop-down arrow and select a new color from the color palette.

7. Use Line/Border Color to change the color of the border.

You can change the alignment of the text in a label using the ▤ Align Left, ▤ Center, or ▤ Align Right buttons on the Formatting toolbar. During the Access exam, you only need to know where the specific buttons are on the toolbar because in most cases, ToolTips will not be available to you.

You can quickly format all the labels and controls on the form using AutoFormat. Select Format and then AutoFormat. Select an AutoFormat from the dialog box and then click OK.

When you make changes to a form in the Design view, you must make sure to save those changes. Click ▤ Save on the Form Design toolbar.

Remember that forms are meant to be used on the screen and that the design of the forms should reflect the fact that they will be used for viewing and entering data. When editing or designing forms, make them easy on the eyes and accommodating for data entry.

Use a Calculated Control on a Form

Creating a Calculated Control

After you add an unbound control to the form, you can then build an expression for the control. Placing the expression in the control makes it a calculated control.

1. Double-click the edge of new control's control box (the control box currently says "Unbound"). Alternatively, click 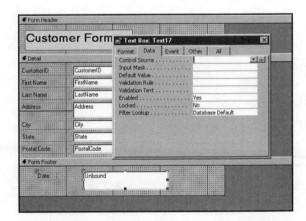 Properties on the Form Design toolbar. The control properties dialog box appears. This box enables you to choose the source of the information that will appear in the control.

2. Click the Data tab in the dialog box. To specify a source for the control, click the Control Source box on the Data tab.

3. The Control Source box contains a drop-down arrow and a button marked with an ellipsis. The drop-down arrow (when you click it) displays a list of the fields contained in the table associated with this form. To make this control a bound control, you would select a field from the list. To create a calculated control, click the button marked with the ellipsis, which opens the Expression Builder.

4. In the Expression folder box, click the Common Expressions folder. In the second column, you now have a list of ready-made expressions; double-click the Current Date expression (in the second column).

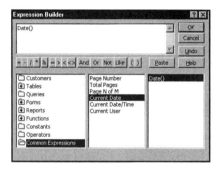

5. The Date( ) expression is placed in the Expression box at the top of the Expression Builder window. Click OK to close the Expression Builder. You are returned to the Properties dialog box, and your expression appears in the Control Source box.

6. Click the Close (×) button on the Control Source box. The expression, in this case Date(), appears in the form control in the Form Footer.

To actually view the results of the calculation in the control (the current date), you must return to the Form view. Click Form View on the Form Design toolbar.

Adding an expression to a control that actually returns a calculated value can also be created using the Expression Builder.

For example, say that you need to keep track of the total value of the products in your warehouse (unit price multiplied by (*) the units in stock). You can use the Expression Builder to create the control that multiplies the data found in other controls (UnitsInStock and UnitPrice) in the form and returns a result.

A control providing a calculated result can be placed in any of the form areas. You will place this control in the Detail area of the form (which puts it right next to the other field data that is seen when the form is in the Form view).

1. Open the form in the Design view that you want to place the calculated control in. Drag the right border of the Detail area if necessary to provide room for the new control (or arrange the current controls in the form to find the ideal spot for your new control).

2. Use the ab Text Box tool on the Control toolbox to create a new control in the Detail area.

3. In the control label, double-click and type a name for the control (in this example, you will use **Total Value**). Double-click on the control box. The Properties dialog box appears.

4. On the Data tab of the control's properties dialog box, click the Control Source box. Click ⊞ Expression Builder to start the Expression Builder.

5. In the first column of the Expression Builder, double-click the Forms folder to open it. Then double-click the All Forms folder to open it. This folder holds all the forms in the current database.

6. Click the folder for your form. (A folder with its name on it will be in the first column.) The controls and control labels in the form appear in the second column box of the Expression Builder. (These are the fields that you placed in the form when you created the form.)

7. Double-click the name of the first control (which will be one of the fields on your form) that you want to include in the new control's expression. The control will appear in the Expression box.

8. Click the appropriate operator, such as the multiplication sign (*), division sign (/), or other operator from the Expression Builder's operator toolbar. After adding the operator, double-click the other controls that you want to include in the expression.

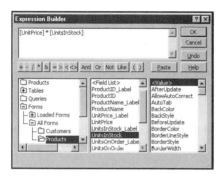

9. When you complete the expression, click OK in the Expression Builder window.

You are returned to the dialog box for the current control. Close the dialog box using its Close button. The expression that you built appears in the new control.

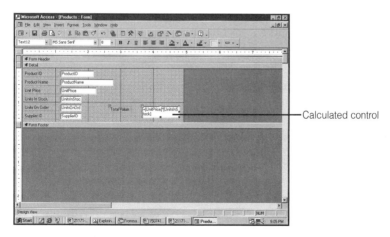

Calculated control

To view the actual results of the calculation, you must return to the Form view. Click the [abl] Form View button on the Form Design toolbar.

TAKE THE TEST

Task 1

In this practice exercise, you will work with features related to Objective 38, "Use the Control Toolbox to Add Controls," Objective 39, "Modify Format Properties of Controls," and Objective 40, "Use a Calculated Control on a Form." Copy the practice11.mdb database from the CD-ROM that accompanies this book to a folder on your computer using the Windows Explorer. Open the database and follow these steps:

1. Create a new form for the Products table using the Form Wizard. Use all the fields in the associated table. Name the form Products. Add a calculated control to the form Footer that displays the current date. Save the form.

2. Create a new control in the Detail area of the form you created in step one (Products). Modify the control with the Expression Builder so it is a calculated control that multiplies the UnitPrice control times the UnitsInStock control.

3. Label the control Total Value and format it as Currency.

4. Save the changes you have made to the form.

Open the database practice11fin.mdb on the CD-ROM and view the form modifications that you made for this task.

Cheat Sheet

Use the Control Toolbox to Add Controls

In the Form Design view, follow these steps:

1. Click the appropriate tool on the toolbox.

2. Drag to create the control on the form.

Modify Format Properties of Controls

In the Form Design view, follow these steps:

1. Click to select the control.

2. Use the Formatting toolbar buttons to modify the control properties.

Use a Calculated Control on a Form

In the Form Design View, follow these steps:

1. Double-click a newly created control. Alternatively, click Properties on the Form Design toolbar.

2. Click the Data tab on the control dialog box.

3. Click Expression Builder (three dots in a square) in the Control Source box.

4. Build the expression in the Expression Builder window.

5. Click OK and click Close (×).

Use Form Sections (Headers, Footers, Detail)

In the Form Design view, drag to expand any of the Form sections.

Use the Control Toolbox to Add Controls

In the Form Design view, follow these steps:

1. Click a tool on the toolbox.

2. Drag to create the control on the Form.

continues

Continued

Modify Format Properties of Controls

In the Form Design view, follow these steps:

1. Select View, Field List.

2. Drag a field from the Field List onto the form.

Designing Queries

- Specify Criteria in a Query
- Create A Calculated Field
- Create and Modify a Multi-Table Select Query

41

Specify Criteria in a Query

A *query* is a question that you pose to your database table or tables; in simplest terms, a query provides you with a more sophisticated way to sort and filter data than the sort and filter features. You might want to know which of your salespeople has reached her sales goal for the year, or you might want to see a list of customers who live in a certain state. Both of these questions can be answered using a query.

The query type that you will most often work with is the select query. A select query finds and lists the records that satisfy the criteria that you set. The Access core test requires that you be able to build select queries.

Building a select query really revolves around choosing the table or tables that the query will be based on and then specifying the criteria that a record must meet to be in the query results. Queries are built in the Query Design window or by using the Query Wizard, and your query results will actually look like a table.

The simplest way to create a single table query is using the Query Design view. First, you specify the table that you will use to create the query, and then you specify the criteria for the query.

When you open the Query Design window to create a new query, the Show Table dialog box opens, listing all the tables in the current database. You use the Show Table dialog box to select the tables that you want to use to build the query.

1. Open the database that you want to create the query in. Click the 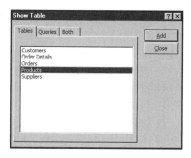 Query icon in the Database window, and then double-click Create Query in Design view in the Query pane. The Query Design window opens, and the Show Table dialog box appears.

2. To select the table (or tables) that you want to include in the query, select the table in the Show Table dialog box and then click Add. After you add all the tables that you want to use for the query (in this case I've added one table to my Query window—Products), click the Close button to close the Show Table dialog box. If you inadvertently close the Show Table dialog box but would like to add additional tables to the query, click View and then Show Table.

When you close the Show Table dialog box, you are placed in the Query Design window. The Query Design window is divided into two panes. The upper pane displays the tables that you selected for inclusion in the query. The bottom pane consists of the Query Design grid, where you will set the criteria for your query.

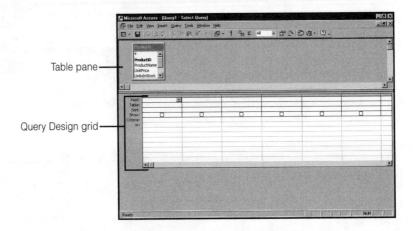

Table pane

Query Design grid

The first row of the Query Design grid is where you designate the field names of the fields you want to include in the query. The order in which the fields are placed in the Query design grid is the order in which they will appear in the datasheet. To select the fields that you want to include in the query, follow these steps:

1. To place the first field in the Design grid, click the first grid column in the Field row.

2. A drop-down arrow appears. Click the drop-down arrow.

3. All the fields in the table or tables selected for the query appear in the list. Select the appropriate field name from the list.

4. Add additional fields to the subsequent columns in the Design Grid until you have selected all the fields that you want to include in the query.

To delete a field from the query, click the grid column that the field occupies, then select the Edit menu, and then Delete Column.

After you select the fields that you want to include in the query, you will want to add criteria that will choose the records that appear in the query results. The criteria are meant to place restrictions on the query. For instance, you might want to restrict the query to show only the customers in your Customer table that live in Minnesota or the products in your Product table that are stocked at a certain level or have a particular per-unit price.

The criteria that you place in your query can be very simple expressions such as "MN", which would select only the customers in Minnesota, or more complex expressions that use operators such as And or Or. For instance, you might want to view only the customer records that have a credit limit "Between 8000 and 15000." Follow these steps:

1. In the Query Design view, click the Criteria row in the desired field's column.

2. Type the criteria you want to use. The sample query that I am building will select only the Units In Stock from the Products table that are less than or equal to 50. So the criteria would read as <=50.

Criteria

If you start to build a query and then decide that you would like to start over, you can clear the QBE Design Grid. Click Edit, Clear Grid.

A number of operators are available to help you define the criteria for your queries. The table that follows lists some of these operators and their uses.

Define the Criteria

Operator	Description	Example
And	Enables you to set compound criteria where both values must be met for a return.	*Not Sales and Not Marketing* Would return records where employees are in neither of the listed departments.
Or	Enables you to set criteria that can be one of two or more values.	*OH Or MN* Would return records that have OH or MN in the State field.
Like	Enables you to use wildcards in criteria.	*Like Sm** Would return records that have Smith or Smythe in the Last Name field.
Between	Enables you to set criteria that selects values that fall into a range.	*Between 01/01/98 and 03/01/98* Would return records where the date in the Date field is after January 1, 1998 and before March 1, 1998.
Not	Enables you to set criteria that selects values that are not the criteria value.	*Not >10* Would return records where number in stock is not more than 10 in a Number in Stock field.

You can combine operators to build more complex criteria. You will also find that you can use operators such as greater than (>), less than (<), and equal to (=) when you set criteria for number and date fields.

After you enter the criteria for a field or fields in the query, you are ready to run the query. Click ⚡ Run on the Query Design toolbar. The Query runs and the results of the query appear in a datasheet format.

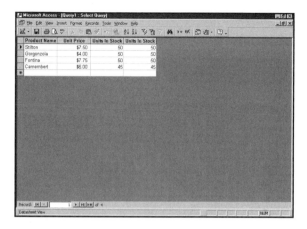

If the query results provide you with the information that you wanted, save the query. Click 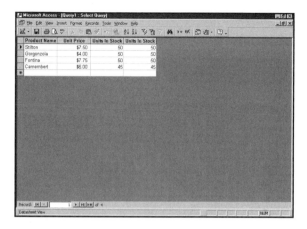 Save on the Query Datasheet toolbar and then supply a name for the query. Click OK to save the query.

Save the Query

If the query does not provide expected results, you can easily edit the query. Click View on the Query Datasheet toolbar to return to the Design view. You can now edit the query as needed and then run it again.

Edit the Query

Create a Calculated Field

Queries also give you the capability to calculate statistical information using field data. This type of query is called a summary query; it has the capability to supply totals, averages, and other statistical calculations for your data fields. In other words, a summary query helps you statistically summarize data from a table or tables.

For example, you can use summary fields to get a total (Sum) of all the products you have in stock or an average (Avg) of the number of support calls that you get at your computer help desk in a month. You can also use a query to find the maximum (Max), minimum (Min), or standard deviation (Stdev) of a certain field or fields.

You can make any select query that you've created a summary query. Create the query as already discussed. Do not, however, place any criteria in the field columns for the fields that will serve as the summary fields.

If you do run into a situation where you want to set criteria for a field or to include the field in the query results and also use that field in a summary calculation, place the field in the Grid box twice. For instance, if you want to calculate the total number of items in your warehouse using the UnitsInStock field, the field must appear in the Grid Area without criteria. If you also want to see the UnitsInStock for each product, you must place the field in the Grid box so that it will supply you this information.

Fields that will supply summary information must have a way of calculating a particular statistical value. To add summary information to your queries, you add another row to the Query Grid box that will hold the formula; to create a summary query, you need to add an additional row to the Query Grid. Click the Σ Totals button on the Query Design toolbar. A Totals row appears in the Query Grid (below the Table row and above the Sort row).

The total row says Group By because a formula has not been chosen for the field. Click any of these Total boxes in the Field columns, and a drop-down arrow appears. Click the drop-down arrow, and you will see a list of statistical formulas.

The formulas (also called *functions*) available to you in the Totals row drop-down box can perform calculations on different kinds of field data types. Nine of the available options in the drop-down box are aggregate functions. The table that follows describes seven of the aggregate functions and their uses. First and Last functions are also aggregate function options.

Formula	Function	Field Types Formula Will Work On
Sum	Totals the values in the field.	Number, Date/Time, Currency, and AutoNumber
Avg	Averages the values in the field.	Number, Date/Time, Currency, and AutoNumber
Min	Gives you the lowest value in a field.	Text, Number, Date/Time, Currency, and AutoNumber
Max	Gives you the highest value in a field.	Text, Number, Date/Time, Currency, and AutoNumber
Count	Actually counts and gives you the number of values in a field.	Text, Memo, Number, Date/Time, Currency, AutoNumber, Yes/No, and OLE Object
StDev	Standard deviation of the values in a field.	Number, Date/Time, Currency, and AutoNumber
Var	Variance of the values in a field.	Number, Date/Time, Currency, and AutoNumber

To actually calculate results in a particular field, you must click the summary formula you want to use. For example, if you have travel expenses for your employees and you want to see the total amount spent by each department, you can use the sum formula. Follow these steps to select a formula in the Totals row for a particular field:

1. Click the drop-down arrow that appears in the Totals row of the field you want to calculate.

2. Select a summary formula from the drop-down list.

3. Repeat steps 1 and 2 as needed for other fields.

After you enter the formulas for your fields, click ! Run on the Query Design toolbar. The Query runs and the results of the query appear in a datasheet format. The field that serves as the summary field will use the formula to summarize the information in that field.

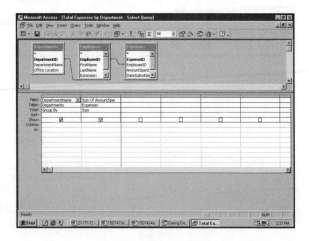

Create and Modify a Multi-Table Select Query

A query is not restricted to just one table. Data from more than one table can be combined to produce a view of related tables:

1. Click the 🖼 Query icon on the Object Bar.

2. Select Create query in Design view, or click the 🔄 New Object icon and choose Query - Design View.

3. Click the 🔲 Show Table icon if the Show Table box is not open.

4. Add the tables required for the query.

   In this case, I have added the Customers, Orders, Orders Details, and Product tables.

5. Double-click or drag the fields needed from each table.

   In this case, I picked the First Name and Last Name from Customers; OrderDate from Orders; ProductName from Products; and Quantity and UnitPrice from Orders Details.

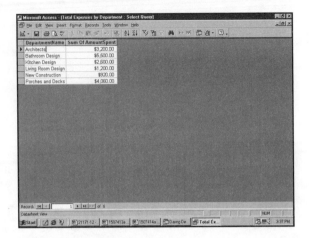

When the Query is run with the ⚠ Run icon, the result shows a multi-table filter of Customers and their orders.

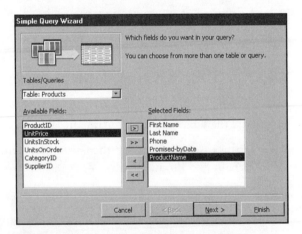

An alternative to creating a query in the Design view is the Simple Query Wizard, which helps you create a query that retrieves data from the fields in one or more tables or existing queries. The wizard does not enable you to limit the information that appears for a particular field by setting criteria as you can do in the Design view. You also cannot set any sort parameters for the fields in the query. The wizard can, however, sum, count, average, and calculate the maximum or minimum value for a field. The Simple Query Wizard is very good at helping you combine field information from several tables.

If you do create a query using the Simple Query Wizard and then determine that you want to limit the information retrieved for a particular field or sort the results of the query by a particular field, you can save the query and then edit it in the Query Design view as follows:

1. Open the database you want to work with and click the Queries icon in the Database window.

2. Double-click Create Query by Using Wizard. The Query Wizard appears.

3. On the first screen of the Simple Query Wizard, you are asked to select the table or query—queries can be based on other queries—that you want to use as the source for the fields that will be used in the query. Select the table in the Tables/Queries drop-down box. The fields in the table appear in the Available Fields box.

4. Select a field in the Available Fields list box; to include the field in the Selected Fields box (and in your query), click Add(>). If you inadvertently add a field and want to remove it, select the field in the Selected Fields box, and click Remove (<). The Add All (>>) button adds all the fields in the Available Field box, and the Remove All (<<) button removes all the fields in the Selected Fields box.

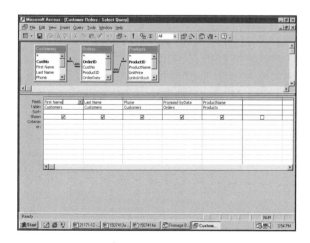

5. To select fields from multiple tables, complete your field selection from the first table and then select a new table in the Tables/Queries drop-down list. Then repeat step 5.

6. After you select all the fields that you want to include in the Query, click Next.

7. The next screen asks you to determine which type of simple query you would like to run: a Detail query or Summary query. A Detail query shows all the data in every field of every record. A Summary query enables you to calculate summary values for numerical or currency data found in the fields you include in the query. Select either the Detail or Summary radio button.

8. If you select the Summary radio button, click Summary Options. The Summary Options dialog box opens. This dialog box displays the numerical and currency fields that you included in the query. You can total (Sum), average (Avg), or determine the minimum (Min) or maximum (Max) for the data in the field or fields. You can choose to have more than one of these values calculated by the query. After selecting the formulas, click OK.

9. After you determine the type of query—Detail or Summary—click the Next button. If you've included a date field in your query and you elected to run a Summary query, the next screen asks you how to group the data in the date field or fields. You can group it by a Unique Date/Time, Day, Month, Quarter, or Year. For instance, if you choose Month, the month and year of the field information will be displayed. If you want the data to appear as it appears in the table field itself, make sure Unique Date/Time is selected. Choose the appropriate radio button and click Next.

The final screen of the Query Wizard prompts you to type a name for your query in the What Title Do You Want for Your Query box. (the wizard will supply a default name based on the table that you used to select the fields for the query.) Type a new name. You are also given the option of opening the query and viewing its results or opening the query in the Design view so that you can modify it. Select either radio button. Click Finish to complete the query creation process. When you use the Simple Query Wizard, the new query is automatically saved for you.

The query appears in the datasheet view. If you want to edit the query and change the formulas or criteria that it used, click the View button on the Query toolbar. You will be placed in the Query Design view, where you can modify the query as needed.

TAKE THE TEST

Task 1

In this practice exercise, you will work with features related to Objective 41, "Specify Criteria in a Query." Copy the practice12.mdb database from the CD-ROM that accompanies this book to a folder on your computer using the Windows Explorer. Open the database and follow these steps:

1. Start a new query in the Design view. Add the Products table to the Design Window. Add all the fields from the table to the Design Grid.

2. Set criteria for the UnitsinStock field so that the query selects the records for items that are stocked at less than 20.

3. Save the query as Low Stock Query.

4. Start a new query in the Design view. Add the Customers and Products tables to Design Window.

5. In the Design Grid, add the First Name, Last Name, and State fields from the Customers table and the Product Name from the Products table.

6. Set criteria for the State field that will select records for customers in PA. For the Product Name field, set criteria that will select for the products Swiss or Brie.

7. Save the query as PA Swiss Brie Query.

Open the database practice12fin.mdb on the CD-ROM to view the queries that you created in this task.

In this practice exercise, you will work with features related to **Task 2**
Obective 42, "Create A Calculated Field." Open the
Practice12.mdb database that you copied to a folder on your
computer and follow these steps:

1. Create a new query using the fields in the Customers and
Order tables to determine the total number of orders
placed by each customer. The query should include the
First Name and Last Name fields from the Customers
table and the OrderDate from the Order table.

2. Save the query as Total Orders by Customer. Run the
query.

3. Open the Total Orders by Customer query in the Design
view.

4. Add the OrdersDetail table to the tables that appear in
the Design window. Add the UnitPrice field to the query.

5. Calculate the total for this field.

6. Use Save As to save this query as Total Owed by
Customer.

7. Run the query.

Open the database practice12fin.mdb and view the query that
you created in this task.

In this practice exercise, you will work with features related to **Task 3**
Objective 43, "Create and Modify a Multi-Table Select Query."
Open the Practice12.mdb database that you copied to a folder
on your computer and follow these steps:

1. Use the Simple Query Wizard to create a query that
includes the following fields from the Supplier, Orders,
and Products tables: SupplierName, OrderDate, and
ProductName. Name the query Orders by Supplier.

2. Open the query in the Design view and add the UnitPrice
field to the query. Save the changes to the query and then
run the query.

Open the database practice12fin.mdb and view the query that
you created in this task.

Cheat Sheet

Specify Criteria in a Query

In the Query Design view:

1. Click in the Criteria box for any field.
2. Enter the criteria text.

Create a Calculated Field

In the Query Design view:

Click the ⌷ Σ Totals button on the Query Design toolbar.

Save a Query

In the Query Design view:

Click the 🖫 Save button on the Query Design toolbar.

Run a Query

In the Query Design view:

Click the ❗ Run button on the Query Design toolbar.

Create and Modify a Multi-Table Select Query

In the Database window:

1. Click the ⊞ Query icon.
2. Double-click Create query by using wizard.
3. Follow prompts on Wizard screens to select fields for the query and name the query.

Or:

1. Double-click Create query in Design view.
2. Click 🔓 Show Table.
3. Add related tables to query.
4. Select fields for query.

To edit the completed query, click 📐 View.

Producing Reports

- Understand Access Reports
- Create a Report with the Report Wizard
- Preview and Print a Report

Understand Access Reports

After gathering data and creating records and tables and after developing forms and queries to gather and present information, the final output of an Access database is, most often, a report.

A report, usually printed, can be handed out to people who need the information. A report gathers data in a layout that is easier to read and understand than a simple printout of a table.

Reports can be a single page, such as a billing for services. They can be multiple pages, such as a catalogue or directory. Reports can include graphics, charts, and notes as well as information extracted from tables and queries.

Components of Reports

Many of the same things that are possible with queries and forms can be included in reports. Calculations can be made directly in a report. Data can be arranged and sorted. Like pieces of information can be grouped for easier understanding.

Reports generally consist of two main components:

- *Header and footer sections* repeat information on each page of a report or the beginning and end of the report.

- The *detail section* groups data and displays calculations, such as subtotals.

Reports can also contain subreports and controls. A control can be a label that identifies the data or a text box that shows numbers or product names. A control can also be a graphic or even a line used to divide groups of data.

There are a number of design choices for Access reports:

A *Columnar report* is a single-column list of the data in each field.

A *Tabular report* attempts to present the fields in each record on one line.

Label reports print each record in a space that can be used with pre-perforated paper to produce labels for mailing or identification tags.

A *Totals or group report* can be designed that shows subtotals, calculated fields, and grand totals.

Subreports can be included that pull information from other sources.

Access can also produce reports that include a chart or graph of the data.

Create a Report with the Report Wizard

The Access 2000 Report Wizard walks the user through the process of creating a report. Most of the time, it is easier to use the wizard to create a report and the make adjustments than it is to try to create the layout from scratch.

Display the Wizard

There are three ways to display the Report Wizard:

- Method 1. Click the Insert menu and select Report.

- Method 2. If you are on the Tables or Queries tab of the Database window, the New Object icon 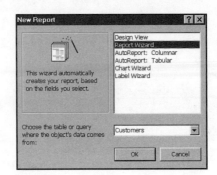 is available on the Database toolbar. Choose Report on the drop-down list.

- Method 3. On the Reports tab, there is a shortcut called Create Report Using Wizard.

If you use method 1 or 2, choose Report Wizard in the New Report dialog box.

If you choose the third method, the Report Wizard opens immediately.

The quickest way to create a report is to use AutoReport. AutoReport is technically a wizard, but you have little control over the output. The exam will probably ask you to use the Report wizard instead of an AutoReport, but rather than chance a surprise, here's a quick look at how an AutoReport is generated:

1. Select a Table or Query on which to base a report.

2. Choose the Insert menu and select AutoReport.

A second way to run an AutoReport is to click the new Object drop-down list 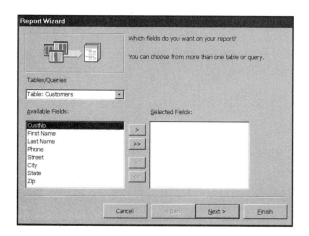 on the Database toolbar and select AutoReport.

These reports do not include report or page headers or footers. If Report is selected, Access presents a choice of the following:

AutoReport: Columnar—Each field appears on a separate line to the right of a label.

AutoReport: Tabular—Each record appears on one line with the filed labels at the top of each page.

A report is based on a table or a query. You can save some time constructing a report if you pick the table or query first and then choose method 1 or 2 (from the "Display the Wizard" section earlier in this chapter). If a table or query is selected, the Report Wizard suggests using that selection as a basis for the report.

As shown in the figure, there is an A̲vailable Fields window that lists all the fields in the selected source. To include any of these fields in the report, use the > (Add) button. To use them all click the >> (Add All) button.

If you use method 3, the shortcut on the Reports tab, or you want to use a different table of query, you can choose a data source from the list box under the label Tables/Queries.

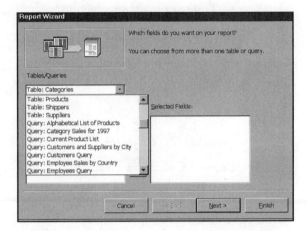

More than one table or query can be chosen. If you are asked to choose more than one, select the source and choose the required fields. Then select the next source and add the necessary fields before moving on.

After the fields are selected, click the N̲ext button.

Group Data in a Report

The next step in creating a report with the wizard is to choose how you want the data grouped. You can group by up to four levels. Normally, if the highest level is chosen first and then subgroups, you will have a clearer report.

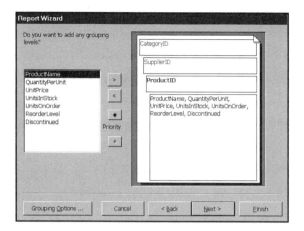

Click Grouping Options to refine the grouping if necessary. Dates, for instance, can be grouped by quarters to simplify the display. Click OK to return to the Report Wizard.

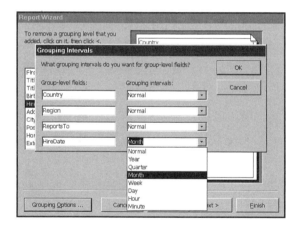

When you are satisfied with the grouping, click Next.

Within the groupings, the detail records can be sorted by up to four fields. Only those fields that were not selected for grouping will be displayed at this stage.

Sort Data in a Report

187

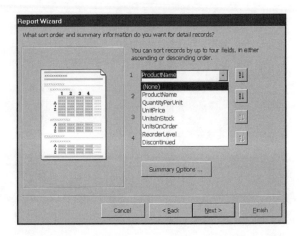

The Sort order 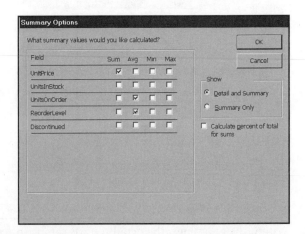 button will toggle between ascending and descending sorts. You can be pretty sure that sorting data will be covered in the exam.

**Set
Calculations**

If the fields contain appropriate data, the Summary Options button appears. Click it to open the Summary Options Dialog box.

This dialog box gives the option of including Sum, Average, Minimum, or Maximum summaries of each grouping. The summaries can also be calculated on a percentage of the total for sums. You have the chance to include the details or just show the summary totals. Click OK to return to the Report Wizard.

When you're ready, click the Next button.

The orientation of the paper and how the data will be laid out is determined on the next page. A preview of the results will be displayed to the left of the Layout list when the radio button is selected.

By default Access checks the box to Adjust the field width so all fields fit on a page.

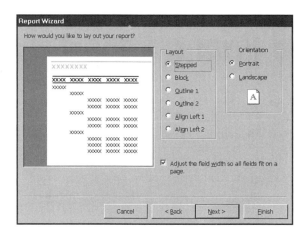

After the Next button is clicked, a style can be selected.

Next, choose a title for the report and choose what will happen when the Finish button is clicked. The choices are to Preview the Report or Modify the Report's Design in design mode. Your choice depends on how the exam's question is worded.

Preview and Print a Report

You will not be connected to an actual printer during the exam. Read the directions to find out how to handle printing. You could be asked to print to a dummy printer or to view the report in Preview mode before moving on to the next question.

Preview a Report

Any report can be examined in Preview mode by clicking the 🔍 Preview button on the Database toolbar or right-clicking the report and choosing Print Preview on the context menu. If those methods are unavailable, the report can be previewed by choosing File on the menu and selecting Print Preview.

The toolbar has a few different command buttons. They are, from left to right, as follows:

📝	View	Change the view from Design to Print Preview or Layout Preview. (In Design view, Layout Preview presents a quick look at the report, but it might not include all the data that the report might contain.)
🖨	Print	Sends the report to the default printer.
🔍	Zoom	Toggles between 100 percent and fitting the size of the page to the window.
▣	One Page	Just one page of the report.
▤▤	Two Pages	Two consecutive pages side by side.
▦	Multiple Pages	Up to 20 pages displayed to fit the screen.
	Zoom Control	Zoom to a set percentage, or type in the amount of zoom and hit the Enter key.
✕	Close	Closes the window and returns to the original view.

	Office Links	Links to Word and Excel.
	Database Window	Brings up the Database window.
	New Object	List of objects such as Tables and Queries that can be created.
	Help	Microsoft Access Help.

The report can be printed by using the 🖨 Print button on the displayed toolbar, but that will send the report to the default printer immediately with out any further refinements.

The printer can be configured to print specific pages by clicking the File menu and selecting Print. The number of copies can be selected as well.

The Print dialog box enables you to choose a printer other than the one selected as default. This is also the place to choose to Print to File and a selection for Setup to adjust the Page Setup.

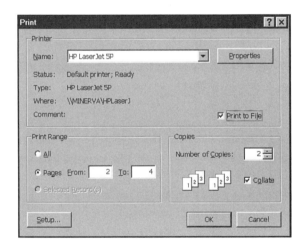

Read the test question very carefully if it asks you to print. You will not be attached to an actual printer, so follow the directions exactly.

Print the Report

The print button is available on the Database, Table Datasheet, Query Datasheet, and Form View toolbars.

When the Setup button is clicked in the Print dialog box, there is a check box on the Margins tab of the Page Setup dialog box that enables you to Print Data Only. This can be useful if you are printing to a preprinted form.

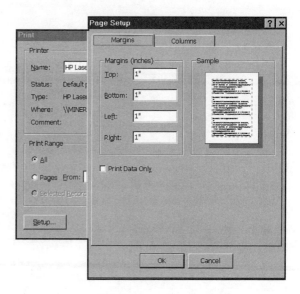

TAKE THE TEST

In this practice task, you will work with features related to Objective 45, "Create a Report with the Report Wizard." Copy the practice13.mdb database from the CD-ROM that accompanies this book (you will find the file in the Chapter 13 folder) to a folder on your computer. Then open the database and follow these steps:

1. Start the Report Wizard.

2. Choose the Query "Total Orders by Customer" for the source data.

3. All the fields will be used in this report.

4. Group the data by SupplierName and then by ProductName.

5. Sort the detail records by OrderDate in Descending order. Next, sort LastName and then FirstName, both in Ascending order.

6. Create a summary of the Sum of TotalPrice. Show both Detail and the Summary.

7. Lay out the report in Landscape, Block style.

8. Use the Compact format.

9. Name the report Orders by Suppliers.

10. Preview the report when you finish with the wizard.

To view the solutions to this task, open the database
practice13fin.mdb on the CD-ROM and then open the
Orders by Suppliers report.

Task 2

In this practice task, you will work with features related to
Objective 46, "Preview and Print a Report." Copy the
practice13.mdb database from the CD-ROM that accompanies
this book (you will find the file in the Chapter 13 folder) to a
folder on your computer. Then open the database and follow
these steps:

1. Open the report named Orders and Products.

2. View the report so that it fits in the window.

3. View the report at 100 percent.

4. Find the Print command on the File menu.

Your screen should look similar to this figure:

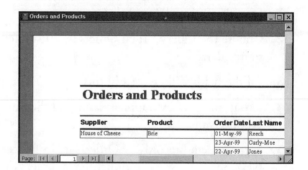

Cheat Sheet

Create a Report with the Report Wizard

- Method 1. Insert, Report.
- Method 2. On the Tables or Queries tab, click 🔲.
- Method 3. Choose Report on the drop-down list.

In the 🔲 Reports window, use the shortcut Create Report Using Wizard.

Preview and Print a Report

🔍 Preview or right-click and choose Print Preview.

🖨 Print to print using default settings.

File, Print to change settings.

Some of the settings are:

    Number of pages to print

    Number of copies

    Print to file

The Setup button on the Print dialog box takes you to the Page Setup box. Print Data Only is a choice in this box.

Producing Reports II: Modifying Report Design

- Working with a Report in Design View
- Modify Format Properties (Font, Style, Font Size, etc.) of Controls
- Move and Resize a Control
- Use the Control Toolbox to Add Controls
- Use Report Sections (headers, footers, detail)
- Use a Calculated Control In a Report

Working with the Report in Design View

The Report Wizard produces a useable document very quickly. In most cases, it is necessary to tweak the results to produce a customized report that presents the information in the clearest, most understandable manner. There might be labels that need to be resized. New fields can be added to the report, or fields can be moved or deleted.

The test will ask you to edit an existing report. You can be asked to work with headers, footers, and detail sections of the report.

To work on a report in Design view, do one of the following:

- Select the report in the objects pane of the Reports window and click ▨ Design on the Database toolbar.

- Right-click the Report and choose Design View from the shortcut menu.

- If the report is open, click ▨ View on the Print Preview toolbar.

As with every question, be sure to read the instructions carefully and leave your answer easy to see. Close all extra toolbars or dialog boxes, unless told to do otherwise. Don't, for instance, leave the Control toolbar floating over the report when you move to the next question.

Modifying Format Properties (Font, Style, Font Size, etc.) of Controls

Controls cover a lot of seemingly unrelated items. The label that displays the title of a report is a control. Check boxes, option buttons, and text boxes are all controls. Controls are objects that perform actions, such as a command button; display data, such as a text box; or just provide design elements, such as a company logo or a line across the page.

Open the Report in Design View.

To make changes to a label, click the label object.

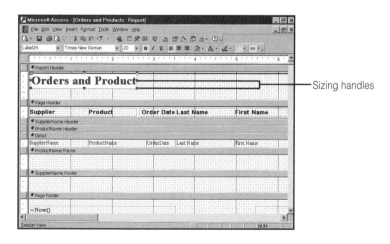

Sizing handles

Sizing handles appear around the label object.

The Formatting toolbar shows the font being used, its size, and other attributes such a color and alignment. Labels are formatted as a whole. Any changes that are applied will affect all the text contained in that label.

To make changes, click the appropriate Formatting toolbar icon.

Font

Font Size

Bold

Italic

Underline

Align Left

Center

Align Right

Fill/Back Color

Font/Fore Color

Line/Border Color

Line/Border Width

Special Effects

The Format Painter on the Report Design toolbar can be used to transfer formatting from one control to another. Choose the source object and then click the format painter. Click a different control, and the formatting will be applied to that object. Double-click the Format Painter to keep it active while formatting is applied to more than one object. When you're done, press the Esc key or click the Format Painter once more to turn it off.

Move and Resize a Control

Controls can be resized and moved just like graphics. Follow these steps:

1. Select the control.

2. Move the pointer over the sizing boxes. It changes to a two-headed arrow.

3. Hold down the Left mouse button and drag the box to the desired size.

When the pointer is in a position to move the control, it changes to a hand.

The control can then be moved anywhere on the page, even across section dividers.

Use the *Control Toolbox to Add Controls*

The Access 2000 Microsoft Office User Specialist exam will ask you to add new controls to a report. Generally, there are two categories of controls, bound and unbound. A bound control is connected to, or uses as its data source, fields in the database. An unbound control can be used to display calculations, pictures, or even objects from other applications such as Excel. You will be expected to be able to add either kind to a report.

Add a Bound Control

A bound control is linked to a specific field on a table. The text box that appears as, say, Quantity on a report in Design view is linked to the same name in a table. (Controls can also be bound to the results of a query.)

To add a Control to a report that is bound to a particular field, follow these steps:

1. Click ▣ Field List on the Report Design toolbar to open a list of all the fields associated with this report.

2. Choose the appropriate field and drag it to the report.

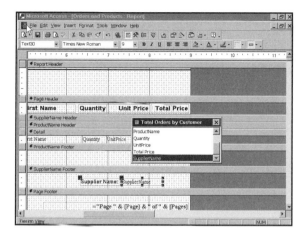

Access supplies the bound text box and the related label.

Another way to add a control is to use the Control toolbox. Unbound controls are added using the Control toolbox. Controls added in this manner can be connected or bound later. Follow these steps:

1. Click 🔧 Toolbox on the Report Design toolbar or click the <u>V</u>iew menu and select T<u>o</u>olbox. Toolbox also appears on the shortcut menu when you right-click a toolbar while in Design mode.

2. To insert a bound control, click **ab** Text Box on the Control toolbox.

3. Click the spot where you want to insert the control.

   The Text Box control inserts an unbound control with a default label with text that merely identifies the object, not the data.

4. Double-click the text box, and the Properties dialog box is displayed. (You can also display the Properties by clicking the 📄 Properties icon on the Report Design toolbar while the text box is selected.)

5. Make sure the Data tab is selected.

6. Click the Control Source box, and a list of associated fields appears.

This is the same toolbox that is used to construct forms.

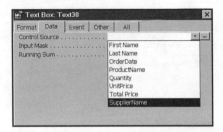

7. To change the text on the label, select the label with the Property box open. The top property on the Format tab is Caption. Enter any name you want in that box.

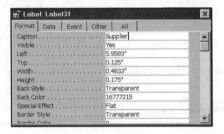

Controls inserted with the Control toolbox have two elements: the text box, which can be bound to a field, and a label. When the pointer is placed over the control, you will see the pointer appear as a two-headed arrow when it is in a position to resize the control. When the pointer is in a position to move the whole control and label, it appears as a five-fingered hand. If it is in a position to move just the label or just the text box, you will see a hand with one pointing finger.

An unbound control is not tied to any particular field. A label control might be considered an unbound control. Later in this chapter, another control, called a calculated control, will be covered. Calculated controls are also called unbound controls because they are not directly linked to a file. They display the result of some form of computation.

Unbound Controls

To insert a label on a report, Click the capital letter Label icon *Aa* on the Control Toolbox. Click the area where you want to place the label or drag out a box on the form.

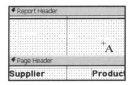

You can start typing immediately and then format the label using the Formatting toolbar.

205

Use Report Sections (Headers, Footers, Detail)

There are three parts to a report:

The Header: A section of the report that is repeated at the top of the page of the report, each page, or each group. Headers are normally made up of labels such as field names, though you can put other items in this section, such as the date or number of pages. This is also a good place to put a company's logo, so that it appears on each page.

The Detail section: An area that usually is composed of Bound or Calculated controls that display data from a table or query.

The Footer: A section that is repeated at the bottom of each group, each page or the end of a report. This is a common place to put the number of pages or filename information. When data is grouped, you might see multiple header and footer sections, one set for each of the groups.

Move Data

A section can be resized by dragging it up or down the page. To make it disappear, drag it so that it has no height.

Fields can be moved from one section to another by dragging. If more than one field is to be moved, hold down the shift key to select and group fields. Then drag the group to the new location.

The order in which sections are grouped can be changed in Design view is as follows:

1. Click 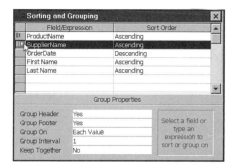 Sorting and Grouping on the Formatting toolbar to display the Sorting and Grouping dialog box.

2. Click the row selector of the field you wish to move and drag the field up or down to a new location in the field list. The Sorting and Grouping dialog box also can be used to change the sort order. Click in the sort order box and choose Ascending or Descending from the Sort Order list.

Use a Calculated Control in a Report

A common use for an unbound control is as a display device for calculations. This can be a box to show the date or page number or to display a computation.

Here's how to do each of these.

Date

The steps to display a date are as follows:

1. Display the Controls toolbox if it is not visible. Click 🛠 Toolbox on the Report Design toolbar, or choose View on the menu and select Toolbox.

2. Click ab Text box and then click the report where you want the date to appear.

3. Select the label and delete it using the delete key on the keyboard.

4. Double-click the Unbound box to bring up the Properties dialog box. You could also click 🗐 Properties on the Report Design toolbar.

5. Make sure the Data tab is selected and type **=Date()** in the Control Source box.

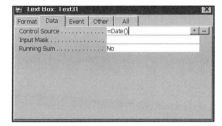

You can also click the Expression Builder button and build the expression.

6. Look at the report in Print Preview to see the date displayed.

The page number is done the same way as Date except the entry is **=[Page]**.

Page number

Add a text box as for Date. In the Control Source box, type the formula or function you need. If, for example, you want the sum of all the products in each group, Total Price is the field you want to total, so the function will be **Sum([Total Price])** (without the quotes).

Calculation

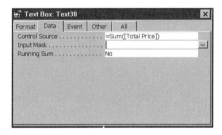

TAKE THE TEST

Task 1

In this practice task, you will work with features related to Objective 48, "Modifying Format Properties (Font, Style, Font Size, etc.) of Controls," Objective 49, "Move and Resize a Control," and also Objective 5, "Use Report Sections (Headers, Footers, Details)." Copy the practice14.mdb database from the CD-ROM that accompanies this book to a folder on your computer. Then open the database and follow these steps:

1. Open the Orders by Suppliers report in Design view.

2. Move the title label in the Report Header so that it starts horizontally at 2.5 inches on the ruler.

3. Change the font to Arial, 20 points, Bold and Red.

4. Resize the title to fit the text. The title control should be 3 inches wide.

5. Resize the Report Header so that it is 3/4 inch high.

6. Save the report.

To view the solutions to this task, open the database practice14fin.mdb on the CD-ROM and then open the Orders by Suppliers report.

Task 2

In this practice task, you will work with features related to Objective 50, "Use the Control Toolbox to Add Control." Copy the practice14.mdb database from the CD-ROM that accompanies this book to a folder on your computer. Then open the database and follow these steps:

1. Open the Orders and Products report in Design view.

2. Add a new label to the Report Header that starts at the 3-inch mark on the ruler. The label should say "Cheese Shop."

3. Use the Format Painter to copy the formatting from the title control to the new label.

4. Save the report.

To view the solutions to this task, open the database practice14fin.mdb on the CD-ROM and then open the Orders and Products report.

In this practice task, you will work with features related to Objective 52, "Use a Calculated Control In a Report." Copy the practice14.mdb database from the CD-ROM that accompanies this book to a folder on your computer. Then open the database and follow these steps:

Task 3

1. Open the Orders and Products report in Design view.

2. Add an Unbound control to the Report header. Make it 1 inch wide starting at the 7-inch mark on the ruler. Delete the attached label.

3. Have the new control display the date.

4. Use the Format Painter to format this control like the other two labels. Resize to fit the Data.

5. Save the report.

To view the solutions to this task, open the database practice14fin.mdb on the CD-ROM and then open the Orders and Products report.

Cheat Sheet

Modify Format Properties

1. Open report in Design view:

- Click ✎ View on the Print Preview toolbar.

- Click Design on the Database toolbar.

- Right-click the Report and choose Design View from the shortcut menu.

2. Select the Control to be formatted and choose the appropriate icon on the Formatting toolbar.

Move and Resize a Control

Select control and drag to correct size.

Select control and after the pointer changes to an open hand, drag to new location.

Use the Control Toolbox to Add Controls

1. ⚒ View, Toolbox.

2. Click the icon for the control and then click the Report to place it.

Modify Report Sections (Headers, Footers, Detail)

Drag controls from one section to another.

Click the Field list icon ▥ on the Report Design toolbar. Drag needed field to report.

Use the Shift key to select more than one object.

Drag Header or Footer dividers to the right height.

Use a Calculated Control in a Report

1. ⚒ or View, Toolbox.

2. Click the Text Box icon on the Control toolbox ab.

3. Click report grid to add text box to report.

4. Double-click Control and choose Control Source.

5. Click ▥ Field List. Drag needed field to report.

Integrating With Other Applications

- Import Data to a New Table
- Save a Table, Query, Form as a Web Page
- Add Hyperlinks

53

Import Data to a New Table

To bring in data from a source outside of an existing database, follow these steps:

1. Click File on the menu and choose Get External Data. The submenu has two options: Import and Link Tables.

> When Access links to an outside table, any changes made in Access or the source application will change the records. When data is imported, Access creates a copy of the original data. Imported data is no longer connected to the original table.

2. When you choose Import, the Import file list appears. If the file you want is not an Access database, change the Files of Type option to the correct format.

3. Highlight the file and click the Import button in the lower right corner of the dialog box.

4. The Spreadsheet Wizard opens. The first action called for in importing an Excel spreadsheet is to select the worksheet or range (if there is more than one) to be brought into Access. Click Next.

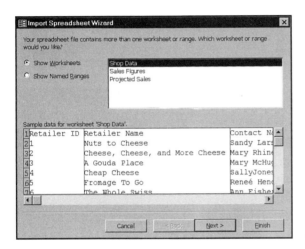

5. The next question the wizard asks is if the First Row Contains Column Headings. Select the check box if the first row contains column headings. Click Next.

6. The third step asks if the data will be included in an existing table or a new data table. If in an existing table, use the drop-down arrow to select the appropriate table. Click Next.

7. Step four gives you the option to look at each field and specify information on the data being imported. You can make changes at this time or later in Design view. Click Next.

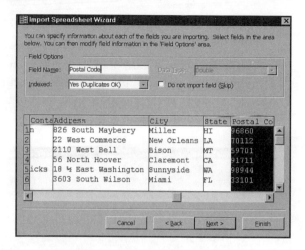

8. You can choose a primary key on the next step, let Access choose on for you, or leave the option for another time. Click <u>N</u>ext.

9. The final step gives you the option to name the new table. Click <u>F</u>inish.

The new table appears in the Objects pane and can be used like any other table. The same process is used to import tables that were created in other formats, such as Lotus, Paradox, dBase or text files.

Save a Table, Query, or Form as a Web Page

Office 2000 and Access 2000 support HTML, the format that is used for Web documents. Any of the objects in a database can be saved, imported, or exported as a Web document.

To save a table in HTML format, see the following sections.

Select the Table or Query that will be the basis for the Web page. Click the down arrow next to 🔲 New Objects and choose <u>P</u>age. Choose Page Wizard. Click OK.

Alternatively, click the Pages Object and choose the Create Data Access Page Using Wizard shortcut in the view pane.

Select the Wizard

This wizard operates very much like the Report or Form wizards.

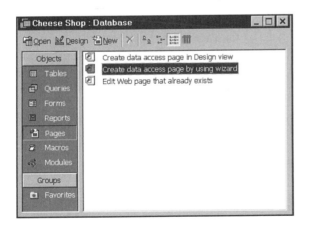

Run the Wizard

Follow these steps:

1. Choose the Table or Query that you would like to save as a Web page and select the fields you want to include. Click <u>N</u>ext.

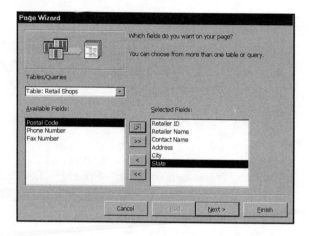

2. The next step lists possible grouping levels and priority levels that can be added. Adding grouping levels will result in a read-only page. Click <u>N</u>ext.

3. The data can be grouped by choosing the fields in the left display and clicking on the > button to move the field to the right. Click <u>N</u>ext.

4. The next panel of the Page Wizard determines the sort order of the records. Up to four level of the data fields can be sorted. Click <u>N</u>ext.

5. The final step in the Page Wizard enables you to name the page and to either open the page directly or go to Design view, depending on which option button is selected.

A theme could also be applied at this point if <u>M</u>odify the Page's Design is selected and the Do You Want to Apply a Theme to Your Page check box is selected. Click <u>F</u>inish.

If Open the Page was selected, a Web style page will be displayed.

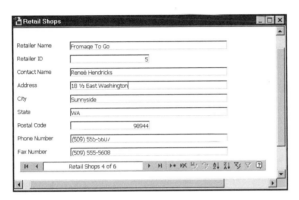

If you look at the page in Design view, the elements that produce the page are exposed.

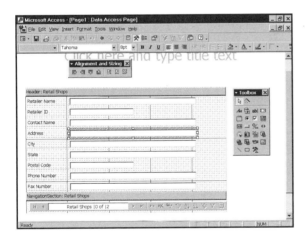

219

When the page is closed, you must supply a name.

These pages are saved outside of the database. You will want to create a special folder to save the file in. You will notice that the file is being saved in HTML format.

The icon that appears on the Pages object pane is a pointer or shortcut to the *.htm file. The file can be opened with your browser, and the source code can be examined by clicking View on the menu and choosing Source.

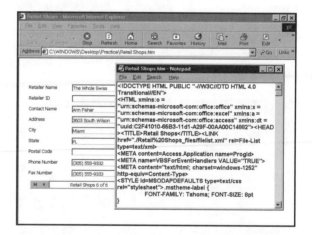

Both Queries and Tables create the same result. The result of the Report wizard is actually a form that can be used to search for records or to filter the underlying data.

Add Hyperlinks

Hyperlinks can be added to forms or reports so that the user can see source documents or find more information. These links can be to documents on your own machine, the local area network, or on the World Wide Web.

There are some quite sophisticated uses for hyperlinks, including a hyperlink data type for fields. The core exam for Access 2000 will probably ask you to add a hyperlink to a report or form. The process is the same for both.

Open the Form or Report in Design view. The three ways to create a hyperlink are as follows:

- Click Insert Hyperlink on the Form Design toolbar.
- Click the Insert menu and select Hyperlink.
- Press Ctrl+K.

Any of these actions opens the Insert Hyperlink dialog box.

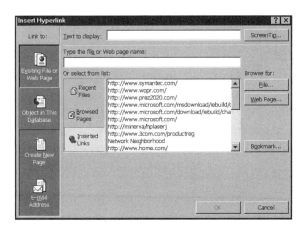

Links can be established to any of the following:

An Existing File or Web Page	A file that is on your machine or the WWW
An Object in This Database	Another form, report, or table
Create New Page	Generates a new document that can be edited later
E-mail Address	A hyperlink that will start up the default email system and put an entry in the To box

Hyperlink to a File or Web Site

Follow these steps to link to a file or Web site:

1. Click 🔛 Insert Hyperlink on the Form Design toolbar.

2. Choose Existing File or Web Page on the Link To bar.

3. The display text can be entered in the top box if you want to show text other than the filename. You can either type the filename into the name box or browse for Files, Web pages, or Bookmark.

Like other controls, the hyperlink can be moved to an appropriate location.

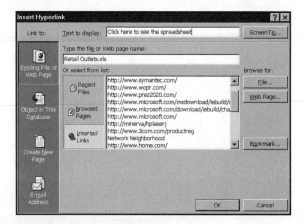

4. Click the OK button. The hyperlink is placed on the form.

When shown in Form view, the hyperlink shows as underlined text and will open the file selected, go to the Web page that was chosen, or move to a bookmark in the open document.

Follow these steps to link to a database object:

1. Click  Insert Hyperlink on the Form Design toolbar.

2. Choose Object in This Database on the Link To bar.

Hyperlink to a Database Object

3. Click the plus sign to open the list of objects.

4. Select an object. Edit the Text to Display box if you want to show text other than the object's formal name.

5. Click the OK button to close the Insert Hyperlink dialog box and place the hyperlink on the form. The hyperlink can then be moved to an open area.

Clicking this hyperlink opens the object (a Table, Form, Report, and so on).

Follow these steps to link to a new document:

1. Click  Insert Hyperlink on the Form Design toolbar.

2. Choose Create New Page on the Link To bar.

Hyperlink to a New Document

223

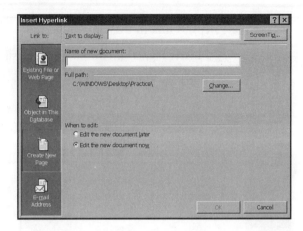

3. Fill in the text you want displayed.

Enter the name of the new document. By default, Access will create an HTML document. If you want to use a different format, add the extension. In this case, .doc is used to produce a Word file.

4. Click the OK button.

Clicking this version of a hyperlink opens a document. After the hyperlink and document are created, content must be added to the blank document.

Hyperlink to an Email Address

Follow these steps to link to an email address:

1. Click Insert Hyperlink on the Form Design toolbar.

2. Choose E-mail Address on the Link To bar to open the Insert Link dialog box.

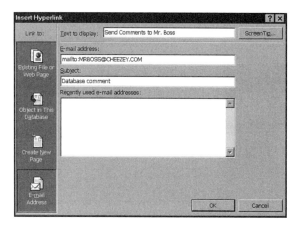

3. You can add text to be displayed as the hyperlink in addition to or instead of the actual email address. The E-mail Address box needs to be filled out. Access automatically adds `mailto:` to the address entered. If you want, the subject for the message can be preset in the Subject box.

4. Click the OK button.

Clicking this hyperlink opens the email program ready to send a comment to the address you have selected.

TAKE THE TEST

Task 1

In this practice task, you will work with features related to Objective 53, "Import Data to a New Table." Copy the practice15.mdb database and the Excel file named Retail Outlets.xls from the CD-ROM that accompanies this book (you will find the file in the Chapter 15 folder) to a folder on your computer. Then open the database and follow these steps:

1. Import the data from the Retail Outlets.xls spreadsheet.

2. Use the information on the Shop Data worksheet.

3. The first row contains the heading names.

4. Choose Retailer ID as your primary key.

5. Name the new table Retail Customers.

To view the solutions to this task, open the database practice15fin.mdb on the CD-ROM, and look at the Retail Customers table.

Task 2

In this practice task, you will work with features related to Objective 54, "Save a Table, Query, Form as a Web Page." Copy the practice15.mdb from the CD-ROM that accompanies this book (in the Chapter 15 folder) to a folder on your computer. Then open the database and follow these steps:

1. Create a new Web page from the Orders by Supplier Query using the Page Wizard.

2. Select all the fields.

3. Don't Group the data, but sort by SupplierName in ascending order.

4. Title the new page Supplier Orders.

5. Open the page for viewing.

6. Close the page and save it in the same folder that the practice files are stored. Name it "Supplier Final Web."

To view the solutions to this task, open the folder where the page was stored, and look at the "Supplier Final Web" page object.

Task 3

In this practice task, you will work with features related to Objective 55, "Add Hyperlinks." Copy the `practice15.mdb` database from the CD-ROM that accompanies this book (you will find the file in the Chapter 15 folder) to a folder on your computer. Then open the database and follow these steps:

1. Open the Retail Shops form in Design view.

2. Add a Hyperlink to the Orders and Products Report.

3. Make the displayed text read Orders and Products Report.

4. Place the Hyperlink on the empty rectangle below the Fax number.

To view the solutions to this task, open the database `practice15fin.mdb` on the CD-ROM, and look at Retail Shops form.

Cheat Sheet

Import Data to a New Table

1. Click File, Get External Data, Import.
2. Locate file.
3. Click Import button.

The wizard walks through the process to import data.

Save a Table, Query, Form as a Web Page

1. Select Table or Query.
2. Click ⊞ New Object drop-down list.
3. Choose Page.

Or

1. Go to the Page view pane.
2. Double-click the Create data access page by using wizard short cut.
3. Select fields to be included.
4. Group and sort if needed.
5. Choose a name and location for the file.

Add Hyperlinks

1. Open form in Design view.
2. ⊞ Insert, Hyperlink (Ctrl+K).
3. Pick the appropriate link on the Link To bar.
4. Fill in information.
5. Click OK.
6. Position hyperlink on layout grid.

Using Access Tools

Access includes what might be considered maintenance tools. These utilities help the user to keep his databases safe and healthy:

- Back Up and Restore a Database
- Compact and Repair a Database

Back Up and Restore a Database

A database is too much work and intellectual effort not to back up the information on a regular basis. In a network situation, the system should be backing up the files as part of its normal routine. However, it does not hurt to take a proactive stand.

Back Up a Database

Access databases cannot be backed up as easily as a Word document or Excel spreadsheet. The entry on the File menu called Save As saves a copy of a Table, Form, or Report, but not the entire database.

When you are experimenting with a table, report, or other database element, it is a good idea to make a copy in case you need to return to the original.

With an element such as a table selected, click the File menu and choose Save As. Access makes a duplicate and places Copy Of in front of the name.

Other ways to make a copy are to click Edit and choose Copy, click 📋 Copy on the Database toolbar, or the old standby keyboard shortcut of Ctrl+C.

After copying, the item can be pasted back to the same location by clicking the Edit menu and choosing Paste. You can do the same thing by clicking 📋 Paste on the Database toolbar. The keyboard shortcut is Ctrl+V. (To remember the shortcut for Paste, think of it as V for Velcro to paste.)

When you attempt to paste the copy, a dialog box appears, asking for a new name.

The simple way to make a backup of a database is to use Windows Explorer or some backup software such as Microsoft Back Up. The file can be copied and renamed. Use some recognizable name such as "Cheese Shop Backup." The safest place to store the backup would be on some other machine than the one normally used or on a tape backup or floppy disk.

There is another way to make a copy of a database that was not intended for the purpose. Follow these steps:

1. With Access open, but with no database open, click the Tools menu and then select Database Utilities.

2. Next choose Compact and Repair Database on the submenu to open the Database to Compact From dialog box.

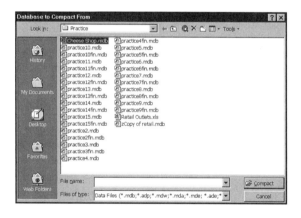

The Database to Compact From dialog box lists the available databases.

3. Select one and click the Compact button in the lower-left corner to open the Compact Database Into dialog box.

4. If you type a new name in the File Name box, Access compacts the database and creates a backup with the new name.

**Restore a
Database**

If for any reason it becomes necessary to return to an earlier version of the database, it can be restored. Be warned that the data in a backed up table or database is not up-to-date.

If you need to restore a table that was copied earlier, rename the active table and also restore the name of the copy. To rename an object, right-click the name and choose Rename from the shortcut menu. You can also rename by selecting the present title and clicking F2 or clicking Edit and choosing Rename.

If the database was backed up by using Windows Explorer to make a copy, it's easy enough to locate the file with Explorer and rename it or open it with the new name.

Compact and Repair a Database

When records are edited or deleted, the space they occupy in an Access database needs to be compacted. Access 2000 does this automatically when the database is closed. There might be times when you will want to manually compact a database.

Databases can also be corrupted if the power should be shut off while Access is attempting to write data.

Compact and repair commands are combined in Access 2000. Follow these steps:

1. Click the Tools menu and then select Database Utilities.

2. Choose Compact and Repair Database on the submenu.

You might see a progress line on the status bar at the bottom of the window, but there won't be any completion statements.

The compacting process can be stopped by pressing Ctrl+Break or Esc.

TAKE THE TEST

Task 1

In this practice task, you will work with features related to Objective 56, "Back Up and Restore a Database," and Objective 57, "Compact and Repair a Database." Copy the practice16.mdb database from the CD-ROM that accompanies this book to a folder on your computer. Then open the database and follow these steps:

1. Make a backup copy of practice16.mdb using the Compact and Repair tool.

2. Leave the backup in the same folder as the rest of the practice files.

3. Name it Backup practice 16.

To view the solutions to this task, open the folder where the practice files are stored. You should find a file named Backup practice 16.mdb.

1. Create a backup using Windows Explorer.

2. Rename it practice 16 backup and store it in the folder where the practice files are stored.

To view the solution, open the folder where the practice files are stored to verify that it exists.

In this practice task, you will work with features related to Objective 56, "Back Up and Restore a Database." Copy the practice16B.mdb database from the CD-ROM that accompanies this book to a folder on your computer. Then open the database and follow these steps:

1. Create a backup of practice16B.

2. Name it Backup of practice16b.

3. Save the file in the same folder as the practice files.

4. Restore practice16B. Name it practice16B again.

To view the solutions to this task, open the folder where the practice files are stored. You should find a file named practice 16.mdb, one called Backup of practice 16.mdb, and a third called practice16B Again.

Cheat Sheet

Back Up and Restore a Database

1. Copy file to a new location with or without a new name.

2. With all databases closed, Choose Tools, Database Utilities, Compact and Repair Database.

3. Give the file a new name and/or location.

4. Choose Tools on the menu bar and select Replication.

Or

Use Windows Explorer to copy or copy and rename the file.

Compact and Repair a Database

Tools, Database Utilities, Compact and Repair Database.

The Student Preparation Guide

Even with the best preparation, a test can be a stressful experience. Be as prepared as you can and try to approach the exam with confidence. This book contains all the objectives over which you will be tested and information about how to do each of them. Glance over the Cheat Sheets in the back of each chapter and review any items that have given you trouble.

Test Specs

There are no multiple choice, Yes/No, or fill in the blank questions on the exam. The test makes use of the actual application.

You will be given about one hour to complete the test. Passing is 75 to 80 percent correct. There is a small leeway given to read the questions, about 20 minutes. As soon as you start to work on the task, the one-hour clock starts. The number of questions varies with each exam, but you should expect about 50.

During the Test

Read each question carefully and don't do any more or less than it asks you. Try to imagine that someone has asked you to do a task and that she will now look at your monitor to see the results.

Unless specifically asked to do otherwise, leave the answer exposed on the screen when you move to the next question. Save the answer only if asked to do so. In many situations with Access, saving is not necessary.

Don't change the view unless asked to do so. Leaving dialog boxes or toolbars floating over the slide should not obscure the view of the answer.

Follow all the instructions given you at the test site. If you have any problems with your machine at the testing center, bring it to the attention of the administrator immediately. Don't try to proceed if the machine itself is presenting problems.

Be Prepared

Do not count on being able to use the Help file to find information. You will have a limited amount of time to complete the test. Try to learn more than one way to do a job. There is usually a keyboard equivalent for items on the menu bar. You will be scored on your results. In the past, some options have been grayed out, forcing the user to find alternative means.

The Office 2000 Cheat Sheet has been designed to help you learn alternative methods of accomplishing tasks. After each Practice element, the Cheat Sheet Short List details in abbreviated form any steps or terms used in the chapter.

The Cheat Sheet Short Lists at the end of each chapter outline the various methods for issuing a command: keyboard shortcuts, toolbar buttons, and menu command strings. Review the shortcuts in the last few minutes before stepping into the exam room.

You will not be allowed to bring any books or papers into the testing area. So, use the Cheat Sheets for review, but do not become dependent on them.

For More Information

The main Web site for information about the exams is `http://www.MOUS.NET`. This site will also give you directions to an Authorized Testing Center (ATC). Call 1-800-933-4493 if you need more details.

The program is international. If you live in Japan, Brazil, or Latin America, there is information concerning test sites and local variations.

There are some news groups that have formed to discuss the tests. Try `msnews.microsoft.com`—either `microsoft.public.cert.exam.mous` or `microsoft.public.certification.office`.

An online "magazine" at `http://OfficeCert.com`. `OfficeCert.com` has a discussion forum and articles relating to the examinations, the applications, and job-hunting techniques.

The standard advice you receive for every potentially nerve-racking situation applies to the MOUS exam.

Take a Break

Try to be well rested before the test. If you don't know it by then, it's probably too late to try to cram it in at the last minute. The Cheat Sheets will give you an opportunity to review the skills to be used, but they are not a substitute for some good practice sessions.

Think of the whole experience as a fun adventure. Enjoy your experience. When the test is over, the administrator will give you a copy of your score.

You can review the test afterwards. The Cheat Sheet books are developed using the Objectives and Activities that make up the examination. Appendix B includes the Objective list and the location in the book for a discussion of that task.

Keep your printout and wait about four to six weeks for your certificate.

Best of luck!

Cheat Sheet Objectives

Standardized Coding

Number	Activity Number	Chapter	Objective	Page
AC2000.1	Planning and designing databases			
AC2000.1.1	Determine appropriate data inputs for your database	Chapter 1	Objective 2	4
AC2000.1.2	Determine appropriate data outputs for your database	Chapter 1	Objective 3	7
AC2000.1.3	Create table structure	Chapter 3	Objective 9	34
AC2000.1.4	Establish table relationships	Chapter 9	Objective 31	124
AC2000.2	Working with Access			
AC2000.2.1	Use the Office Assistant	Chapter 1	Objective 5	12
AC2000.2.2	Select an object using the Objects Bar	Chapter 2	Objective 7	26
AC2000.2.3	Print database objects (tables, forms, reports, queries)	Chapter 2	Objective 8	28
AC2000.2.4	Navigate through records in a table, query, or form	Chapter 4	Objective 14	53
AC2000.2.5	Create a database (using a Wizard or in Design View)	Chapter 2	Objective 6	20
AC2000.3	Building and modifying tables			
AC2000.3.1	Create tables by using the Table Wizard	Chapter 3	Objective 12	41
AC2000.3.2	Set primary keys	Chapter 3	Objective 11	39
AC2000.3.3	Modify field properties	Chapter 6	Objective 21	75
AC2000.3.4	Use multiple data types	Chapter 3	Objective 10	36
AC2000.3.5	Modify tables using Design View	Chapter 6	Objective 20	72

Number	Activity Number	Chapter	Objective	Page
AC2000.3.6	Use the Lookup Wizard	Chapter 6	Objective 22	82
AC2000.3.7	Use the input mask wizard	Chapter 6	Objective 23	86
AC2000.4	Building and modifying forms			
AC2000.4.1	Create a form with the Form Wizard	Chapter 10	Objective 35	138
AC2000.4.2	Use the Control Toolbox to add controls	Chapter 11	Objective 38	150
AC2000.4.3	Modify Format Properties (font,style, font size,color, caption,etc.) of controls	Chapter 11	Objective 39	154
AC2000.4.4	Use form sections (headers, footers, detail)	Chapter 10	Objective 37	143
AC2000.4.5	Use a Calculated Control on a form	Chapter 11	Objective 40	156
AC2000.5	Viewing anorganizing information			
AC2000.5.1	Use the Office Clipboard	Chapter 5	Objective 19	66
AC2000.5.2	Switch between object Views	Chapter10	Objective 36	142
AC2000.5.3	Enter records using a datasheet	Chapter 4	Objective 13	50
AC2000.5.4	Enter records using a form	Chapter 4	Objective 15	55
AC2000.5.5	Delete records from a table	Chapter 5	Objective 16	62
AC2000.5.6	Find a record	Chapter 8	Objective 29	110
AC2000.5.7	Sort records	Chapter 7	Objectives 26, 27	97, 101
AC2000.5.8	Apply and remove filters (filter by form and filter by selection)	Chapter 8	Objective 30	116
AC2000.5.9	Specify criteria in a query	Chapter 12	Objective 41	164
AC2000.5.10	Display related records in a subdatasheet	Chapter 9	Objective 34	131
AC2000.5.11	Create a calculated field	Chapter 12	Objective 42	170
AC2000.5.12	Create and modify a multi-table select query	Chapter 12	Objective 43	173
AC2000.6	Defining relationships			
AC2000.6.1	Establish relationships	Chapter 9	Objective 31	124
AC2000.6.2	Enforce referential integrity	Chapter 9	Objective 32	128
AC2000.7	Producing reports			
AC2000.7.1	Create a report with the Report Wizard	Chapter 13	Objective 45	184
AC2000.7.2	Preview and print a report	Chapter 13	Objective 46	190
AC2000.7.3	Move and resize a control	Chapter 14	Objective 49	201
AC2000.7.4	Modify format properties (font, style, font size,color, caption,etc.)	Chapter 14	Objective 48	199

Number	Activity Number	Chapter	Objective	Page
AC2000.7.5	Use the Control Toolbox to add controls	Chapter 14	Objective 50	202
AC2000.7.6	Use report sections (headers, footers, detail)	Chapter 14	Objective 51	206
AC2000.7.7	Use a Calculated Control in a report	Chapter 14	Objective 52	208
AC2000.8	Integrating with other applications			
AC2000.8.1	Import data to a new table	Chapter 15	Objective 53	214
AC2000.8.2	Save a table, query, form as a Web page	Chapter 15	Objective 54	217
AC2000.8.3	Add Hyperlinks	Chapter 15	Objective 55	221
AC2000.9	Using Access Tools			
AC2000.9.1	Print Database Relationships	Chapter 9	Objective 33	130
AC2000.9.2	Backup and Restore a database	Chapter 16	Objective 56	230
AC2000.9.3	Compact and Repair a database	Chapter 16	Objective 57	234

Index

For an index to specific test objectives, see Appendix B, pp. 241.

Symbols

& (ampersand), 77
* (asterisk), 113
@ (at), 77
[ ] (brackets), 113
[infinity symbol] (infinity), 128
< (less than), 77
- (minus), 133
(number/pound), 113
+ (plus), 131
? (question mark), 113

A

adding
    controls
        Design View, 201, 210–211
        forms, 150, 160–161
        Toolbox, 202, 212
    data, 50–52
    fields, 74, 94, 139
    hyperlinks
        databases, 223, 227
        tables, 228
        documents, 223–224
    email addresses, 224–225
    forms, 221–222
    Web sites, 222
    labels, 150–151
    records
        Autoform feature, 55–57
        datasheets, 59
        tables, 55–56, 58, 64, 68–69
addresses, email, 224–225
alignment of fonts, 200
alphanumeric text, 37
ampersand (&), 77
And operator, 168
ascending sorts, 98–99, 188
asterisk (*), 113
at sign (@), 77
Authorized Testing Centers (ATCs), 238
AutoForm feature, 55–57, 138
AutoNumber data type, 37
AutoReport, 185
averages formula, 170–171

B

backups, databases, 230–231, 234–236
best fit in fields, 89
Between operator, 168
blank database tables, 20, 25, 34

bold fonts, 200
borders for fonts, 200
bound controls
    Control Toolbox, 202–204
    forms, 151–153
brackets ([ ]), 113

C

calculations
    controls, 152, 156–159, 161
    fields, 170–172, 179–180
    reports
        displaying, 209
        summary, 188–189
captions in fields, 78–79, 94
Cheat Sheet Short Lists, 238
closing records in tables, 56
color for fonts, 200
columns
    forms, 139
    freezing, 104–105, 107–108
    reports, 183, 185
    tables, 34
    width, 95
compacting databases, 233
controls
    adding
        Control Toolbox, 202, 212
        Design View, 201, 210–211
        forms, 150, 160–161
        bound, 151–153, 202–204

U–V

W–Z

Other Related Titles

Microsoft Excel 2000 MOUS Cheat Sheet

Rick Winter
0789721163
$19.99 US

Network+ Cheat Sheet

Patrick Grote
0789721775
$24.99 US

LPIC Linux Level 1 Test 1a Cheat Sheet

Marcraft
0789722895
$24.99 US

A+ Certification Cheat Sheet

David Smith
0789723220
$24.99 US

Network+ Exam Guide

Jonathan Feldman
0789721570
$39.99 US

Upcoming Titles

Windows NT 4.0 Server Exam Guide

Emmett Dulaney
078972264x, 12/99
$39.99 US

Windows NT 4.0 Workstation Exam Guide

Emmett Dulaney
0789722623, 12/99
$39.99 US

LPIC Linux Level 1 Test 1a Exam Guide

Theresa Hadden
0789722925, 1/00
$39.99 US

Microsoft Word 2000 MOUS Cheat Sheet

Mary Millhollon
078972114
$19.99 US

Microsoft Powerpoint 2000 MOUS Cheat Sheet

Doug Klippert
0789721181
$19.99 US

CD-ROM Installation

Windows 95/NT Installation Instructions

1. Insert the CD-ROM disc into your CD-ROM drive.

2. From the Windows 95/NT desktop, double-click the My Computer icon.

3. Double-click the icon representing your CD-ROM drive.

4. Double-click the icon titled START.EXE to run the CD-ROM interface.

If Windows 95/NT is installed on your computer and you have the AutoPlay feature enabled, the START.EXE *program starts auto-matically whenever you insert the disc into your CD-ROM drive.*